Apache Chronicle

Books by
John Upton Terrell

APACHE CHRONICLE

AMERICAN INDIAN ALMANAC   BUNKHOUSE PAPERS

THE NAVAJOS   ZEBULON PIKE

THE MAN WHO REDISCOVERED AMERICA

LA SALLE   BLACK ROBE

FURS BY ASTOR   ESTEVANICO THE BLACK

TRADERS OF THE WESTERN MORNING

JOURNEY INTO DARKNESS   PLUME ROUGE

FAINT THE TRUMPET SOUNDS   THE SIX TURNINGS

WAR FOR THE COLORADO RIVER

SUNDAY IS THE DAY YOU REST   ADAM CARGO

THE LITTLE DARK MAN   PUEBLO DE LOS CORAZONES

Apache Chronicle

by John Upton Terrell

WORLD PUBLISHING
TIMES MIRROR
NEW YORK

The author and publisher gratefully acknowledge permission to quote from the following works:

The Social Organization of the Western Apache, published by the University of Arizona Press. Copyright © 1969 by the University of Arizona Press.

General Crook and the Apache Wars by Charles F. Lummis, published by Northland Press. Copyright © 1966 by Turbesé Lummis Fiske.

The Rediscovery of New Mexico by George P. Hammond and Agapito Rey, published by the University of Mexico Press. Copyright © 1966 by the University of New Mexico Press.

Oñate by George P. Hammond and Agapito Rey, published by the University of New Mexico Press. Copyright © 1953 by the University of New Mexico Press.

Federal Control of the Western Apache by Ralph H. Ogle, published by the University of New Mexico Press. Copyright © 1971 by the University of New Mexico Press.

Memorial of Fray Alonso de Benavides, published by Calvin Horn Publisher, Inc. Copyright © 1965 by Horn and Wallace Publishers.

The Indian Wars of the West by Paul I. Wellman, published by Doubleday & Company, Inc. Copyright © 1934, 1935, 1947 by Paul I. Wellman.

Vast Domain of Blood by Don Schellie, published by Westernlore Press. Copyright © 1968 by Don Schellie.

Apache Days and After by Thomas Cruse, published by the Caxton Printers, 1941. Reprinted by permission of the copyright owners, the Caxton Printers.

Life Among the Apaches by John C. Cremony, published by Rio Grande Press. Copyright © 1969 by Rio Grande Press.

PUBLISHED BY THE WORLD PUBLISHING COMPANY

PUBLISHED SIMULTANEOUSLY IN CANADA

BY NELSON, FOSTER & SCOTT LTD.

FIRST PRINTING—1972

ISBN 0-529-04520-6

LIBRARY OF CONGRESS CATALOG CARD NUMBER: 77-173920

PRINTED IN THE UNITED STATES OF AMERICA

PHOTOGRAPHS BY BOB ADELMAN

DESIGNED BY JACQUES CHAZAUD

WORLD PUBLISHING
TIMES MIRROR

CONTENTS

Tales of violence and wrong, of outrage and devilish malignity, committed by Indians, are rife all along our frontiers; but who ever hears the other side? Who chronicles the inciting causes, the long, unbroken series of injuries perpetrated by the semi-civilized white savages. . . ?

CAPTAIN JOHN C. CREMONY
Life Among the Apaches

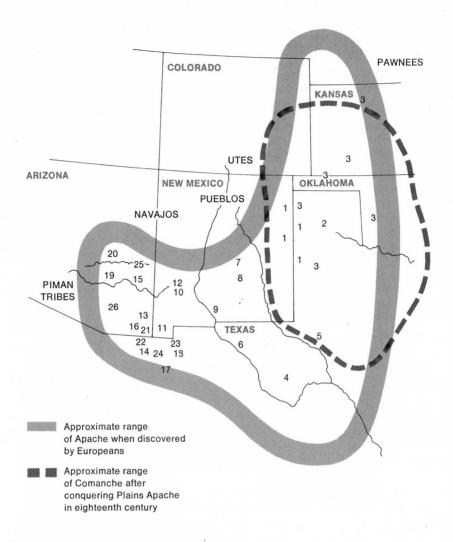

APACHE HISTORY
some important places and events

1 Llano Estacado	10 Santo Rita	19 Gila River
2 Palo Duro Canyon	11 Animas Peak	20 Salt River
3 Great buffalo herds	12 Pinos Altos	21 Skeleton Canyon
4 Davis Mountains	13 Apache Pass	22 Cañon de los Embudos
5 Pecos River	14 Fronteras	23 Janos
6 Rio Grande	15 San Carlos	24 Geronimo agreed
7 Sierra Blanca	16 Chiricahua Mountains	to surrender
8 Sacramento Mountains	17 Sierra Madre,	25 Fort Apache
9 Doña Ana	last Apache stronghold	26 Camp Grant Massacre
	18 Casas Grandes	

AUTHOR'S NOTE

Apache is an American Indian name better known around the world than any other. It has been taken into speech, fiction, and history to indicate fierce and barbaric individuals as well as criminals. There is no comparable word universally applied to white men, who, as the record clearly portrays, frequently excelled the Apache in ruthlessness and savagery.

Every story of an individual American Indian tribe contains an identical record of events, for each tribe suffered similar injustices, ordeals, and tragedies. Moreover, the end for all was the same: physical defeat, social demoralization, and economic destruction.

The story of the Apache, however, presents factors which significantly distinguish it from all the others: (1) The Apache were waiting on the stage as the curtain rose on the era of recorded history in the region of northern Mexico and the southwestern United States. (2) The Apache waged unceasing warfare against white invaders of their homeland longer and with greater success than any other Indian people—for more than three centuries. (3) Neither the Spanish nor the Mexicans ever came close to subduing the Apache. (4) Through four decades of strenuous campaigning against the Apache, strong forces of American troops were not only repeatedly outwitted and outfought by them but sustained embarrassing, costly, and bloody reverses at their hands.

The oft-repeated and widely believed accusation that all Apache were by nature obsessive murderers is as absurd as the postulation that all early white invaders and residents of the Southwest were motivated by laudable ideals. The Apache were no more predatory, no more warlike, than several other western tribes. The reputation as incorrigible malefactors was fastened on them by the circumstance that in defending themselves against white men they demonstrated that they were more cunning, more capable, more determined, and more dangerous as fighters than most Indians.

[xi

It should be understood that almost every Spanish and Mexican *colono* and ordinary American who sought his or her fortune in the Apache Country stood low on the social scale, a great many of them the dregs of their respective societies. There were among them very few persons of education, and even smaller number with any type of professional training, and not very many possessed social amenities acceptable anyplace that ranked above a bawdy-house waiting room. The vast majority—some exceptions shall be noted in their proper perspective—were uncouth, ignorant, bigoted, and looking for something for nothing.

Thus, it could hardly be expected that white persons originating on such low levels would display intelligence in their relations with Indians who, despite their own deficiencies, they considered beneath them and no more worthy of their concern than some coyote yapping in the night. Obviously these white persons could not make use of qualities they did not possess, and they were governed by materialistic, if not animalistic, instincts. The primitive culture of the red people proffered nothing from which they might benefit, and they reacted in all their dealings with Indians with unconcealed contempt and a total lack of compassion.

It is especially true of Americans that their thinking regarding the Apache always has been, and still is, burdened by fallacies. This is not the result of longer and greater exposure to fictitious tales and unfounded reports. It is not because more American settlers than Spanish and Mexican colonists could read. Nor is it because the American emigrants in the Southwest enjoyed freedoms the peons never knew.

The adherence of Americans to fables about the Apache is attributable to their stubborn refusal to rationalize, to seek a just determination of problems involving Indians, and to their deliberately closing their eyes to facts they know are indisputable. The Spaniard and Mexican in the Southwest did what he was told, or allowed, to do by priests and civil and military officials. The American did pretty much as he damn well pleased, handicapped by few legal or social restraints.

The myth persists that every American man or woman who chose to move to the land of the Apache following the Mexican War (and in some cases before that time) was a hero or heroine. It continues today to be propagated by hypocritical southwestern partisans and politicians, by newspapers, cheap fiction, and stupid motion pictures. Paeans of praise continue to ring loudly for the brave souls who set off into the unknown deserts with a burning dream of helping to build a greater America.

They didn't do any such thing. They thought least of all about the future of their country, and this was true of Spaniards and Mexicans as much as it was of Americans. The only dreams any of them had, aside from nightmares caused by fear, were of gold, silver, and free land, of getting rich with a minimum of exertion and little or no expense to themselves.

These people attended mass, listened to sermons, sang hymns on Sunday, and conveniently forgot all biblical admonitions every other day of the week. They turned their religion on and off with an effective mental spigot, and they followed a method of putting the Indian in touch with heaven that was more certain and less complicated than that advocated by the tenets of Christianity. It was: shoot them where you find them.

Religious groups interested in problems involving the Apache held blindly to the theory that every trouble would be eliminated if they could build institutions in the deserts and force the heathens to affiliate with them. These fanatics appeared unable to comprehend—indeed, some still are—that a man whose means of living had been stolen from him, whose wife and children were sick and hungry, whose own belly was empty would not be eager to absorb the gospel and be happy in the belief that the Lord would provide.

The actions of government officials and military leaders may not, however, be explained on such grounds. Few, if any, of them were without some education, many were trained in sciences, and all of them were entrusted with responsibilities much greater than those customarily assigned to field hands, store clerks, sheepherders, and ignorant soldiers of the ranks. In their corruption, their cruelty, their greed, they acted with full knowledge and understanding of what they were doing.

The Apache not only thought of themselves as the rightful owners of the land they inhabited but they also thought of themselves as a part of that land. They saw themselves as being inextricably woven into its scheme, and, actually, into the natural scheme of the entire universe as they conceived it. They were not simply pieces of bone and flesh, not simply possessors of certain faculties. They were those things, but they were also of the sands, the winds, the stars, the plants and grasses, the thunder and lightning and rain, the seasons—everything that was born and lived and died in the eternal cycle of life.

The white man had no such conception or belief. He was interested in a natural resource only to the extent that it could be exploited. He attached no spiritual significance to the land or any of its treasures. His pattern was take, rape, destroy, and look elsewhere for opportunities to repeat the process. Banditry, and its attributable violence, was not an invention of the Indian.

Raiding can be the cornerstone of an economy, but it can with no less feasibility be utilized as a defensive weapon. The Apache did not suffer directly from the first major incursion into the Southwest, that of Coronado (1540–1542), but they were fully apprised of the atrocities committed under his authority. Thereupon was planted the seed of their hatred for white men. From the time of Oñate's arrival in New Mexico as the colony's first governor (1598) until the Mexican Declaration of Independence (1821), Spanish colonial officials and some priests maintained a reign of terror against all Indians, practicing extortion, slavery, peonage, confiscation, and religion by force. Nothing changed when the Mexicans came into power. The same excesses prevailed. Nor did conditions improve with the occupation of the Southwest by the United States (1846).

However, early in the Spanish period the Apache understood, or at least sensed, that they were faced with a greater menace to their security than any they had ever known. In the following decades, as slavers took captives, as treasure hunters, leaving a trail of blood behind them, continued to push in ever-increasing numbers up the southwestern valleys and across the Great Plains, their hatred for the invaders steadily mounted in intensity, until at last it pervaded and dominated them like some narcotic for which there was no control and no cure but death. They struck back with the only means they saw available to them—constant, vicious, and destructive raiding.

The final phase of the long conflict with the Apache was the most costly in human lives and in money of all offensives against an Indian people in American history. It was basically a conquest undertaken and pursued for commercial gain. In the reasoning of those who authorized and waged it, any type of attack on the red vermin—not excluding the slaughter of helpless men, women, and children—was justified, for, as so many contended, "It's our country, ain't it?"

Several times American officials and military officers in the Apache Country succeeded in formulating agreements which, had the Federal Government provided forceful support for their stipulations, would have served as major steps toward a peaceful termination of the terrible war. On each of these occasions, conspiracies of corrupt politicians, swindlers in the Indian service, and grasping commercial interests were able to prevent congressional sanction of the tentative pacts. More than that, these greedy, morally debased persons—especially those in Arizona—instigated violence and committed murders that shattered all hopes of achieving a negotiated peace. They sought only one result: total extermination of the Apache.

More than any other people the Apache were responsible for the creation of a barrier to white settlement and exploitation of the Southwest. The Pueblos, confined and deprived of their resources, capitulated first. The Navajo, starving and demoralized, gave up the struggle in the 1860's. The Apache continued their desperate fight for survival for two more decades.

Through the years, of course, superior American military power gradually drove the Apache closer to the end of their tether, but it never succeeded in completely defeating them. That was accomplished by the perfidy, the treachery, the inhumanity of bestial white civilians, both in Washington and the Southwest, forces which created in them a hopelessness they were unable to combat.

The distorted image of the Apache that is still disseminated through various mediums, that is still accepted by unthinking and uninformed people, was created by white men, not by the Apache.

Apache
Chronicle

THE
SIXTEENTH
CENTURY

1535

DECEMBER

Four strange men, three Spaniards and a Negro Moor, came out of the east into the valley of the Rio Grande.

They were the first Europeans to meet the people who in time would be known to the world as Apache.

During the weeks it had taken them to pass through the rugged country of far western Texas they had encountered the Teya and probably other Apache groups. Now, on the Rio Grande, they were astonished to find Indians living in permanent dwellings constructed of rock and adobe who spoke a tongue almost identical with that of those they had left behind them. These also were Apache—the Jumano, the Cholome, and the Manso.

The three Spaniards, former army officers, had scraggly beards. Long hair bound by deerhide thongs brushed their shoulders. Except for skin breechcloths, they were naked. Their bodies were lean and hard; they were burned and scarred from years of exposure. Crudely made wooden crosses hung from their necks on cords of woven animal hair. Their names: Álvar Núñez Cabeza de Vaca, Andrés Dorantes de Carranca, Alonso del Castillo Maldonado.

In the eyes of the Indians the fourth man was even more startling to behold. He was the color of ebony. His wild, intensely black hair was adorned with feathers. He strode in a regal manner, and muscles moving in his legs, arms, and shoulders attested to his extraordinary physical strength. He was the slave of Dorantes. Cabeza de Vaca recorded his name simply as Estevanico the Black.

More than seven years earlier—during Holy Week of the year 1528 —the expedition of Pánfilo de Narváez, successor to the dead Juan Ponce de León as governor of Florida, had landed near Tampa Bay after a perilous voyage from Santo Domingo by way of Cuba. A few days later, two hundred and sixty men on foot, among them several padres, and forty on horses, all poorly equipped and inadequately

[3

supplied, had set out to find the gold and jewels which their leader was confident awaited discovery in the unexplored jungles of his vast jurisdiction.

In northern Florida a number of soldiers, officers, and priests had been killed in fights with Indians. Others had died of malnutrition, dysentery, and fever. Desperately hoping to save themselves, the remaining men, most of whom were dangerously weakened, wounded, or ill, had constructed five makeshift barges and had sailed westward along the northern coast of the Gulf of Mexico. It had been their erroneous belief that they were closer to the port of Pánuco, in Mexico, than to their starting place at Tampa Bay, where their ships were awaiting them.

All the frail craft had been destroyed in a November storm on the swampy Texas coast a short distance below Galveston.*

Not until September, 1534, almost six years after the disaster, had Cabeza de Vaca, Dorantes, Castillo, and Estevanico—the only members of the company still alive—been able to escape from coastal tribes which had held them captive. It had taken them more than another year to cross Texas.

For three weeks from the vicinity of the mouth of the Rio Conchos, which empties out of Chihuahua, they traveled up the left bank of the great river flowing from the north until they were only a few miles from the site of El Paso. Surrounding them each day and night was an exuberant throng of men, women, and children who thought they had descended from the sky.

In his famous *Relación,* the account he would write of the epic journey into darkness, Cabeza de Vaca would say of the Apache:[1]

"They gave us beans and many squashes to eat, gourds to carry water in, blankets of cowhide [buffalo robes], and other things . . . great festivities were made over us. . . . They have the finest persons of any people we saw, of the greatest activity and strength, who best understood us and intelligently answered our inquiries."

Upon learning of their custom of periodically moving to hunt buffalo on the Great Plains along the Pecos River, he gave them the name Cow Nation.

The Apache men wore little clothing, some of them appearing almost completely naked. The "women are dressed with deerskin, and some few men, mostly the aged, who are incapable of fighting. The country is very populous."

Word of the powerful shamans, or medicine men, sped up the Rio Grande. In some towns the residents awaited their arrival indoors.

---

*Modern place names are inserted throughout this work to aid readers in following the course of events.

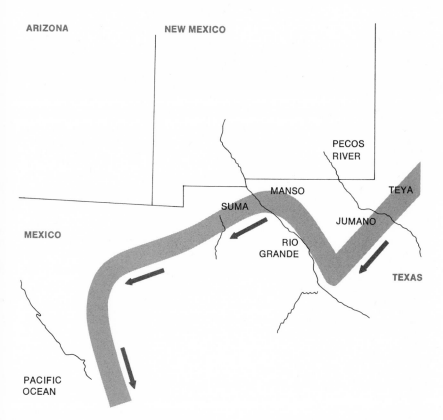

approximate route of

CABEZA DE VACA—1535

Cabeza de Vaca and three companions
are first men of the Old World to meet Indians
who would come to be known as Apache.
They encountered the Teya, Jumano, Manso,
Suma, and possibly other Apache groups.

Men, women, and children sat on the floors of their homes facing the wall, their heads down. Possessions had been gathered and placed in the center of a room. In this way all they owned was offered to the visitors, who, after accepting the gifts with signs of gratefulness, returned them.

Some of the Apache living along the river did not appear to have cultivated fields, yet Cabeza de Vaca noticed that quantities of maize were stored in baskets. Puzzled by this situation, he asked for an explanation and was informed that the corn had been obtained in trade with prosperous farmers who lived far to the north where the river passed through mountains. If the Sun Men traveled that way they would find very large towns with buildings many stories high, and they would be given mantles of cotton and valuable colored stones.

Cabeza de Vaca was being told of the great pueblos which stood along the upper Rio Grande in the beautiful high country of northern New Mexico. It was intelligence that would have a great bearing on the development of events in Apacheria, as well as the entire Southwest, during the next few years.

The Rio Grande Apache who did engage in some type of agriculture apparently depended mainly on natural precipitation—although they must have been familiar with Pueblo methods of irrigation—for they complained to Cabeza de Vaca that for two years a serious drought had prevailed. They beseeched him to tell the sky to rain. He responded with prayers, but the result is not known. He was gone long before the beginning of the next growing season.

One cooking method of these people intrigued him, and he would remember: "How curious and diversified are the contrivances and ingenuity of the human family. Not having discovered the use of pipkins to boil meat they would eat, they fill the half of a large calabash with water, and throw on the fire many stones of such as are most convenient and readily take the heat. When hot, they are taken up with tongs of sticks and dropped into the calabash until the water in it boils with the fervor of the stones. Then whatever is to be cooked is put in, and until it is done they continue taking out cooled stones and throwing in hot ones. Thus they boil their food."

He did not know, of course, that he was seeing a demonstration of how these Apache, even though they now lived in permanent houses, still adhered to a practice of nomadic Plains Indians. Their manner of cooking appeared peculiar to him, but it was common among non-sedentary tribes who could not transport heavy, breakable utensils from place to place. If the Rio Grande Apache did not use pipkins— clay or stone cooking pots—it was not because they did not know of them.

As the year ended the time came when the four men were forced to make a vital decision. Which way should they go?

The Apache told them that to the west was a great *despoblado*, a forbidding desert in which they would find few people and little to sustain them. By continuing up the river, although they would pass through a well-populated country in which they would be assured of shelter and food, they would encounter deep snow and intense cold. In either direction the perils of winter travel were many, and might be insurmountable. They were counseled to remain where they were until spring, when it would be safe to go any way they desired.

* * *

Early Spanish explorations in the vast territory that would become the Southwest of the United States were the fruit of fables.

The fables sired dreams, wild, turbulent dreams that were impervious to any tranquilizing force of reason. Although they were far removed from the scene of the conception—sixteenth-century Mexico City—neither the Apache nor any of the Indian peoples around them were detached from the fetal results, the delusions that swelled in the minds of the dreamers. They were linked to them by the illimitable umbilical cord of Fate.

The oldest legend said that in the eighth century, after the Moors had invaded Spain and Portugal, oppressed Christians led by the Archbishop of Oporto and six other bishops had sailed westward into the mysterious Ocean Sea and had discovered an incredibly beautiful island which they named Antilia. Each of the bishops had built a city, and the whole Island of the Seven Cities became a Utopian commonwealth, unfailingly supplied with rare foods and fabulously rich in gold and jewels. Countless searches had been made for it by voyagers, but it had never been found.

In 1527 Nuño Beltrán de Guzmán was governor of the Mexican province of Pánuco and president of the *Audiencia*, the board that directed the colony's affairs. The posts gave him extreme powers, and he used them with wanton disregard for either New Spain or the subjects over whom he ruled. He looked upon himself as a god to whom all must pay tribute and obeisance. In a foul mood one day, he hanged several natives who failed to sweep the streets before him as he passed through their village. He sold thousands of Indians into slavery in the West Indies. In time, high officers of the Church registered strong protests against his barbarities with the Spanish king, and he was warned to govern his province with justice and in accordance with colonial statutes.

Guzmán had no intention of changing his ways. If he was obliged to curb his brutality somewhat in Pánuco, he was not precluded from looking farther afield for opportunities to gratify his avarice. He let it be known that he was thinking of leading a treasure-hunting and slaving expedition into areas of western New Spain of which little, if anything at all, was known.

At this point one of Guzmán's slaves, an Indian named Tejo, achieved a permanent place in history. Perhaps with the hope of gaining some favor for himself, he told the governor a story, and found him to be a most attentive listener.

Tejo was the son of a trader who had been dead for several years. When he was a youth, he related to Guzmán, his father had taken him on several trading trips into the wilderness. One journey had been longer than the others. On it Tejo and his father had traveled for more than forty days to the north. At last they had reached a fine country in which there were many people and some large cities. In exchange for the plumes of tropical birds which they had carried with them they had received turquoises and stones even more colorful, as well as ornaments of bright metal. Tejo swore he could recall seeing streets filled with silver workers and other craftsmen. The large cities in this bountiful country were *seven in number.*

Guzmán's cold blood grew hot with excitement. Like every other *conquistador,* he was familiar with the story of the long-lost Seven Cities of Antilia. Now he reasoned that with all the geographical darkness existing in the New World there was no justification for concluding that the Magic Kingdom was not to be found. Indeed, an ignorant Indian slave may have come upon it.

The more he considered the idea, the more entrancing it became, and he finally succumbed to its mesmeric power. In 1529 he set out from central Mexico, obsessed with his dream. With him he took an immense expedition of four hundred Spanish soldiers and several thousand Indian servants, burden bearers and livestock herders. Tejo was accorded the rank of guide, but it soon became apparent that he had forgotten most of what he had learned of wilderness trails as a boy. He was certain, however, that it was necessary to cross Mexico to the South Sea (Gulf of California) before turning north. Guzmán did not dispute him.

As he and his great company struggled through some of the highest mountains and roughest terrain in New Spain, Guzmán acted in character. He gave vent to fiendish cruelties, torturing and slaughtering Indians encountered, burning their fields and their settlements. Somewhere along the trail of bloodshed and suffering, the unfortunate, and probably terrorized, Tejo died.

Perhaps it was true that Tejo had gone with his father to trade with Indians in the present states of Arizona and New Mexico. In any case, he knew of their existence, he knew something of their culture and economy, and he knew that they lived in permanent towns. This, of course, was common knowledge among Indians of northern Mexico, for trade between them and the Pueblos of the north had been carried on for centuries before the time of Columbus. Tejo was far from being an ignorant Indian, and, moreover, he knew what Spaniards wanted most of all to hear.

Guzmán's conquest ended in failure. Pedro de Castañeda, who lived in Mexico at the time and who would participate in a later and greater search for the Seven Cities, wrote that after breaking through to the Pacific, Guzmán and his force "found the difficulties very great, because the mountain chains which are near that sea are so rough that it was impossible, after great labor, to find a passageway. His whole army had to stay in the district of Culiacán for so long on this account that some rich men who were with him . . . changed their minds, and every day became more anxious to return."

With his political enemies, one of whom was the famed Cortez, closing in on him, Guzmán abandoned his dream, but he thought it wise to remain on the west coast, and he established himself in Compostela. From that base he continued his trade in human beings, sending slave hunters far north into what would become the state of Sonora. Eventually he would be arrested, stripped of rank, and thrown into prison. He would die in exile, penniless, friendless, and despised.

But the dream of finding the Seven Cities would not die. Even before the avaricious Guzmán had been driven from office, events would take place which would cause it to dominate once more the thoughts of every adventurer in Mexico.

* * *

1536

JANUARY

Cabeza de Vaca and his three companions, accompanied by a group of Apache, were making their way slowly across the tortured country of northern Mexico. They had left the Rio Grande at the site of the village of San Augustin, about thirty miles south of El Paso del Norte.

After seventeen days of wearying travel toward the southwest they reached the Rio Santa Maria, where they learned that not all streams have a common destiny, the sea. The Apache knew that the Santa Maria, a trickle called a river, rose in the desert and flowed some two hundred miles to death in the desert.

They kept on toward the southwest.

FEBRUARY

One evening as the sun went down they saw ahead of them the wall of a great mountain range. They had come in sight of the Sierra

Madre. The Apache turned homeward, for they were nearing the homeland of traditional enemies.

The weather favored the four men. The country grew greener as they climbed, and the little streams became faster and stronger, and there were birds and trees and meadows. At last they started down a long valley, and they came once more to villages of permanent dwellings, and there were storage bins filled with maize. These were the towns of the Opatas, who belonged to the Piman linguistic family.

In every village they were hospitably received. At one banquet the hearts of six hundred deer were placed before them. Cabeza de Vaca named the place Pueblo de los Corazones.* It was there that he was presented with what he thought were five emeralds cut in the shape of arrowheads, and he would write of them: "They appeared to be very precious. I asked whence they got these; and they said the stones were brought from some lofty mountains that stand to the north, where were populous towns and very large houses, and that they were purchased with plumes and the feathers of parrots."

For the second time, and from different Indians, the four men heard of the pueblos of northern New Mexico.

The Opatas gave them fine cotton shawls and turquoises which also had been obtained in trade with the people of the large northern cities. More important in their eyes, however, were the pieces of coral presented to them—coral which came from the South Sea—and they were told that it was not far away!

The Opatas led them over the best trail to the south, avoiding the wastelands, which they said bordered the great water.

M A R C H

On a warm spring day, somewhere along the Rio Sinaloa, a company of Spanish slave-hunters—Guzmán's men—were startled by the sight of a gaunt, bearded white man and a blackamoor dressed in animal skins emerging from a thicket.

Cabeza de Vaca: "They stood staring at me a length of time, so confounded that they neither hailed me nor drew near to make an inquiry."

There were tears in his eyes and his voice faltered as he spoke to them in Spanish.

A P R I L

The four men were guests in the Culiacán headquarters of the lieutenant-governor of the province, Captain Melchior Díaz, a veteran

---

*The present town of Ures, Sonora.

frontiersman, "honest, honorable, and compassionate," who vigorously opposed the brutal policies of Governor Guzmán.

They were not yet able to wear the clothes which had been provided for them. Their skins, so long tortured by the sun and wind and rain, by terrible heat and bitter cold, could not tolerate the gentle touch of linen and silk. No shoes could be found to fit their calloused, misshapen feet—they could not have suffered the best boots in Mexico, anyway—only well-worn Indian moccasins were bearable. The soft beds of Díaz's house were covered by fine cotton sheets and downy woolen blankets, but they could not endure them, and for a time they slept on the bare floor under buffalo robes. Several weeks passed before they were able to adjust to the comforts of civilization.

M A Y

On the fifteenth they left Culiacán for Compostela and the residence of Guzmán. It was not a pleasant visit. By this time Cabeza de Vaca was well apprised of the reign of terror the governor had created throughout western Mexico.

Cabeza de Vaca: "We passed through many territories and found them all vacant; their inhabitants wandered fleeing among the mountains, without daring to have houses or till the earth for fear of Christians.

"The sight was one of infinite pain to us, a land very fertile and beautiful, abounding in springs and streams, the hamlets deserted and burned, the people thin and weak, all fleeing or in concealment. Christians . . . had come through the land, destroying and burning the towns, carrying away half the men, and all the women and the boys. . . .

"Thence it may at once be seen that, to bring all these people to be Christians and to the obedience of the Imperial Majesty, they must be won by kindness, which is a way certain and no other is."

Díaz informed him that under the law only Indians who committed acts of war against the king could be enslaved. Guzmán had circumvented the provision by issuing an official statement in which he charged that virtually every native in the province was a rebel conspiring to overthrow the government, and declared that enslaving and branding them was necessary to preserve order in his jurisdiction.

Cabeza de Vaca obtained a notarized copy of the opinion—probably from Díaz—and, confronting Guzmán with the document, accused him of violating the law, and announced that he would place the matter before the proper officials in Mexico City.

JUNE

As the four men traveled southward with a military escort along the Camino Real, their progress was disrupted in every town by fiestas arranged for them. Thousands of people—Indians, Spaniards, and their bemuddled progeny—crowded the streets to dance, sing, feast, and acclaim them as heroes.

JULY

They entered Mexico City on the twenty-fourth, approximately eight years and three months after they had landed in far-off Florida.

In the capital they were borne along the avenues as the populace cheered wildly and waved flags. They were, said Cabeza de Vaca, "very handsomely treated" by the viceroy, Don Antonio de Mendoza, and the Marquis del Valle, the famous Don Hernán Cortés.

On the twenty-fifth, the day of Saint James the Apostle, a great celebration and a jousting of bulls were held in their honor.

AUGUST

The hoary legend of the Seven Cities was not only restored to youthful vigor but had produced a multivalent band of robust and unruly offspring which created a turmoil throughout Mexico City, from the magnificent *palacio* of the viceroy down to the filthy *barrios bajos.*

Like a fire driven by high wind through dry prairie grass the report spread that Cabeza de Vaca and his three companions had found, no, had actually visited, the Seven Cities of Antilia. The few persons who voiced skepticism were scorned and ridiculed; they were halfwits who would not admit that Christ had died on the Cross because they themselves had not witnessed the crucifixion.

Cabeza de Vaca for weeks had been a guest of Mendoza, hadn't he? The viceroy also had granted numerous long audiences to Dorantes, Castillo, and even to Estevanico, a black slave. Moreover, any number of noblemen and high officials had been present at the conferences, and they had let it get out that they had heard the four men tell of fording streams that flowed in beds of solid gold, of seeing Indian children playing with diamonds, pearls, emeralds, and rubies as large as hen eggs, of meeting people who ate on dishes of pure silver, of passing a mountain which contained so many jewels that one dared not look at it in the sunlight for fear of being blinded. The only reason that the men had not brought back an inconceivable fortune was that they had not possessed any means of transporting it.

The viceroy was planning to send a great expedition to the north to harvest the incomparable treasures and conquer the rich lands, all to the glory of king and country. He would, of course, reserve modest fortunes for himself and for the lucky men who would be permitted to participate in the conquest. Another Peru had been found. Hail to Cabeza de Vaca! To the viceroy! To the greatness of Spain!

The truth was that the Viceroy Mendoza had under consideration a plan that was as conservative as it was vague. He had been sent out to Mexico only a year earlier, and he was still uneasy under the burden of the many complex, strange, and difficult problems weighing upon him. It was pleasant to think about taking possession of new lands—his duty was to increase as well as preserve the value of the royal estate in Spain's New World provinces—but he had no intention of plunging into an expensive conquest without more assurance than had been given to him that it would be successful.

As it was, he could be certain of very little regarding the territory which purportedly extended a vast distance to the north. None of the four men had *claimed* to have factual knowledge of the existence of seven large cities, or, for that matter, of any number of large cities. They had *heard* of them, but they had not *seen* them. Moreover, when repeating stories told to them by Indians, they had more than once reminded him that the tales had been related in native tongues, or in the sign language, which they might easily have misunderstood.

They had, however, seen a few things with their own eyes that were of interest. Among the Apache of the Rio Grande, as well as on the western slope, they found strong permanent habitations. In northern Mexico they had passed through fertile and well-watered valleys in which maize and other wholesome foods were grown, and they had crossed enormous grass ranges on which immense herds of cattle, sheep, and horses could be grazed. Among the Opata they had seen cotton blankets of excellent quality, turquoises, and buffalo robes, which the owners said were obtained in trade from people who dwelt in great pueblos far to the north and who possessed such things in great quantities.

They had seen *signs* which they *believed* indicated that gold, antimony, silver, iron, copper, and other metals *might* be found, but the only evidence of such valuable treasures they actually had acquired had been some scoria of iron, some small quantities of mica, some galena which the Indians used in decorating themselves, some turquoises, and five green arrowheads which *might* have been manufactured from precious stones. Unfortunately, the arrowheads had been lost somewhere along their route.

SEPTEMBER

In accordance with his determination to move with the greatest caution, Mendoza proposed that Cabeza de Vaca lead a small exploring party to determine the locations and sizes of the cities in the north.

Cabeza de Vaca had other ideas. Uppermost in his mind were thoughts of going home, of a reunion with his wife, of sitting in his own Jerez de la Frontera patio in the soft blue light of late afternoon.

Mendoza turned his attention to pressing matters.

OCTOBER

Cabeza de Vaca made arrangements to sail, but a hurricane swept the eastern seaboard of Mexico. The vessel on which he was to have taken passage, as well as most other shipping, was destroyed. He accepted the advice of navigators to avoid a hazardous winter crossing and wait until the spring. He had only to think of his years of captivity to find the patience to endure the delay.

In his comfortable Mexico City quarters, he sat down at a desk, took up a quill, and began the narrative that would give his own name and those of Dorantes, Castillo, and Estevanico the Black high places on the roster of New World pathfinders.

* * *

When the ancestors of the Apache first reached North America, and when the Apache themselves first reached their historical homelands in the American Southwest and northern Mexico, are questions for which there are, as yet, no final answers. While some of the individual findings of anthropologists may be conclusive, they fall far short of providing a complete account of these migrations. Wide chronological gaps exist, and the knowledge that could close them may remain forever locked in the dark vaults of past millennia.

The genesis of the people who would be mistakenly called Indians, but who were Mongoloids, goes far back into the Pleistocene, the latest of the great geological epochs sometimes referred to as the Ice Age. That a land bridge (or bridges) between Siberia and Alaska existed for a great period of time has been indisputably proven by scientists. The same animals lived in both regions. During the Ice Age sea levels were much lower than at present, because a large part of the world's water was locked in great glaciers. The water that made the glaciers came from the sea in the form of fog and clouds. It fell as snow. The glaciated regions were so intensely cold that annual summer melting was less than winter precipitation. The glaciers continued to build up. Over enormous areas the ice cap was a mile high, but in some places it reached a height of nine thousand feet.

The Bering Strait is shallow. If the water level were to fall only one hundred and twenty feet, the Strait would not exist. It would once more be a land bridge between the two continents. Moreover, it is only fifty-six miles in width, and this distance is broken by islands. The widest expanse of open sea is only twenty-five miles. A land bridge would have provided natural fodder for grazing animals.

Never was all of northern North America covered by ice at one time. Through countless millennia, as climatological metamorphoses occurred, glaciers advanced and retreated, reaching deep into the continent and withdrawing. Important as far as the migrants from Asia are concerned is the geological knowledge that for long periods there were ice-free corridors through which both animals and men could have passed. That they had reached the region of the United States long before the end of the Ice Age can no longer be disputed, for evidence of their presence more than forty thousand years ago has been discovered. The center of the last major glacial period of some twenty-five thousand years ago was in the vicinity of Hudson Bay. Far to the west there was considerably less ice, and there were ice-free passages opening the way to the south. However, long before this time, periods called interstadials, during which men and animals would not have been confronted with impassable ice barriers, had occurred in various other northern regions.

Man did not originate in the New World. He evolved from brute ancestry in the Old World, and reached North America as a member of the single modern species called Homo sapiens, wise man. His nearest animal relatives, the anthropoid apes, are all found in the Old World. There is a total absence in the New World of missing links and other intermediate fossil forms in man's family tree. In the Old World, paleontologists have found hundreds of skeletons of persons intermediate in physical type between men and apes.

It is in the shifting of animals that much of the explanation as to why people came to North America is to be found. When northern Europe was glaciated, the animals moved southward and eastward, reaching southern Europe and central Asia, both of which were free of ice. The people depended upon these animals for their existence, and when, in time, it was learned that the northern part of the Asiatic continent was rich in game, they drifted toward it. The animals moved north and east as the glacial ice retreated, and the people followed them in order to maintain a steady supply of fresh meat and furs. They followed them into Siberia, and then they went with them across the Bering land bridge into Alaska.

The qualities, colors, and physiques of the Siberian nomads varied greatly. They had come originally from many places, from many climates, from many types of country. They spoke many tongues. They represented sharply contrasting cultures, had many different customs, held many spiritual beliefs. They had no racial unity, for people of different bloods had moved through the land mass of Asia before any people moved into the land mass of the Western Hemisphere. It cannot be said how large were the influxes into Asia proper from Africa and the eastern Mediterranean, but even small shiftings would have been enough to leave telltale marks of their different bloods. Although they were predominantly Mongoloid, the people who reached Alaska bore some of the telltale marks.

In North America they found two avenues of travel to be the most feasible and the most rewarding. One ran along the Pacific and the other along the eastern slope of the Rocky Mountains. Over these two great natural thoroughfares, through the millennia, the hunters, the scavengers, the carvers, the weavers, the builders, the destroyers, the planters passed, each in their own good time. Over them were disseminated culture after culture, each in turn distributing its own peculiar mores and economic and social systems; and the disasters of the heavens and the earth, pestilence, hunger, and the wars waged were not powerful enough, singly or together, to obliterate completely any one of them. Some vestiges of each were perpetuated by successors.[2]

* * *

1537

MARCH

Dorantes, preparing to go home, committed Estevanico to the service of Mendoza, a gift for which the viceroy was deeply appreciative. He spoke of Estevanico as "very intelligent," and thought his experience would be "valuable" should plans he was contemplating develop.

Cabeza de Vaca and Dorantes boarded a ship in Vera Cruz.

APRIL

Cabeza de Vaca sailed, but Dorantes received an urgent message from Mendoza requesting him to delay his departure and return to Mexico City. One did not ignore a summons from a viceroy, and Dorantes went back.

Mendoza asked Dorantes to lead a small exploring company to the unknown land north of Pueblo de los Corazones. Estevanico would go with him.

After some deliberation, Dorantes agreed to the proposal.

MAY

Mendoza appropriated funds and supplies and organized the expedition.

Dorantes changed his mind. He gave several reasons. He had no stomach for further explorations. He had fallen in love with Mexico.

He was also enamored of a wealthy widow to whom Mendoza had introduced him.

Whether Mendoza made the same proposition to Castillo is uncertain. There are indications that he did not, and that, while he liked Castillo, he considered him too "mild" and unqualified in other respects to command the venture. However, Castillo would have rejected the assignment had it been offered to him. He, too, had decided to settle in Mexico, and had married a widow with considerable income property.

Mendoza to King Charles V: "Andrés Dorantes, one of those comprising the army of Pánfilo de Narváez, has come to me, and I have had frequent conferences with him, thinking he might render a great service to your Majesty if I should send him with forty or forty-five horsemen and all the things necessary to explore that country. I have spent a great amount of silver for the expedition, but for reasons unknown to me the affair has come to naught. From all the preparation I have made there are left to me only a Negro who came with Dorantes, some slaves whom I have purchased, and some Indians, natives of the [north] country, whom I have assembled."

JUNE

A priest known by the name of Marcos de Niza, because he had lived for some years in Nice, was presented to Mendoza. Fray Marcos had been in the capital for several weeks before the viceroy had granted him an audience. For seven years, displaying a craving for adventure and sightseeing which challenged his love for his work as a missionary, Fray Marcos had gallivanted about the New World. He had been in Santo Domingo, Guatemala, and various regions of South America. The cruelty of the conquests of Ecuador and Peru, both of which he had witnessed, had so shocked him that he had taken pen in hand and had written a detailed account of the atrocities to Bishop Zumárraga of Mexico. Zumárraga ordered him to come to the capital.

Mendoza thought Fray Marcos was just the man he had been looking for. The friar's courage had been tested in years of wilderness wanderings. He was physically strong, possessed of an extraordinary imagination, and brimming with ardor and optimism. The bishop agreed, recommending Fray Marcos in the highest terms, and describing him as "reliable, of approved virtue and fine religious zeal." Another high church official added the testimonial that the peripatetic missionary was also "skilled in cosmography and in the arts of the sea, as well as in theology."

In view of future events, one may wonder how well, if at all, Mendoza sensed that inseparably linked with Fray Marcos's imagination, ardor, optimism, and zeal were two other pronounced characteristics: talent as a promoter and the ability to dramatize himself and everything he did. If the viceroy did not suspect that Fray Marcos possessed such gifts —and he probably did not—he would soon become unhappily aware of the fact.

Mendoza got off a letter to the king requesting permission to send Fray Marcos, with Estevanico as guide, on a journey to discover the cities of the north. He stressed the point that it would be a small and inexpensive expedition. No soldiers would be sent. No one would have to be paid. Equipment and supply costs would be negligible. There was, as well, another distinct advantage to his plan. Numerous padres had shown themselves to be fearless explorers and skillful diplomats to the Indians. They went into the wilderness armed only with messages of hope and the word of God, whereas soldiers carried deadly weapons and were not averse to using them.[3]

* * *

More than anything else, language has provided proof of the migrations of the Apache. The Athapascan linguistic family, to which they belong, was more widely distributed than any other in North America. Groups speaking dialects of this tongue occupied areas, separated by hundreds and in some cases by thousands of miles, from the Pacific to the Great Plains and southeastward to the delta of the Rio Grande. Overall this was territory extending for more than forty degrees of latitude and seventy-five of longitude.

The earliest known homelands of a score of Athapascan tribes, some with many subdivisions, were in Alaska and Canada, and their descendants still dwell in parts of this vast region. When the first landings by white men were made on the American Pacific Coast, one Athapascan group lived in Washington, seven in Oregon, and eleven in northern California. Much later, in 1682, La Salle heard from Indians he met on the Mississippi of a fierce people who lived far to the west. The great French explorer called them *Gattackas,* a name by which the Pawnee identified the Plains Apache. Oto Indians of Missouri complained to Father Louis Hennepin, who was with La Salle, of raiders from the west who used spears in attacking them. The priest thought the Otos were talking of Spaniards, but in reality they were telling him of the Apache of the High Plains, who are known to have used long lances in battle. By this time, of course, the Apache were mounted Indians, but it remains that their reputation as warriors had spread among tribes far distant from their homeland, as far east as Illinois. In invading the midwestern prairies the Apache undoubtedly were acting in retaliation for slave raids conducted against them by the Oto, Kansa, and other peoples.

Nearly a century before La Salle's time, however, the Spanish had become well acquainted—to their sorrow—with the Apache of the American Southwest. The region which they sometimes designated as *Gran Apacheria* embraced virtually all of New Mexico, and parts of Texas, Arizona, Colorado, Kansas, Oklahoma, and northern Mexico, reaching from east to west for considerably more than seven hundred miles, approximately from the ninety-eighth to the one hundred eleventh meridian, and from north to south in some parts for nearly six hundred miles between the thirtieth and thirty-eighth parallels.

In this enormous territory dwelt some half a hundred Athapascan groups or bands, but after they came into possession of horses they ranged far beyond its boundaries, not only eastward and northward across the Great Plains but westward through the mountains and deserts and southward deep into Mexico. Distance seldom restrained them in their offensives against enemy tribes or in their violent aggressions against white men who steadily sought to tighten a ring of presidios and settlements about them.

If it is uncertain when Apaches reached the Southwest from the far north, it may be said that they had been there at least for several centuries before the discovery of America. Some scholars maintain that they were the first Athapascans to migrate to the region, but others disagree. In any case, there is nothing to refute the belief that they were there as early as the Navajo, who belong to the same linguistic family; indeed, scientific studies strongly suggest that the Navajo and Apache came south at the same time. Archaeologists have uncovered evidence indicating that the Navajo were in Dinetah—Old Navajo Land—in southwestern Colorado and northern New Mexico, in the eleventh century.

The pace of the southward movement of the Athapascans was extremely slow. There was no mass migration. They traveled in small bands or family groups. People who are totally dependent on game and food gathering are prevented from moving together in large numbers. The bounties of nature guided their individual and group movements. Adverse weather conditions and scarcities forced them to take meandering routes. Their lives were an eternal search for sustenance. In areas where food supplies were stable, bands may have remained through several lifetimes.

They made their clothing and their beds of the furs and hides of animals, their temporary shelters from sticks and brush and leaves, and they carried their small supplies, their few utensils and crude bone and wooden tools in parfleches. They knew nothing of weaving, of metalworking, and very little, if anything, of masonry. They hunted with short sinew-backed bows—a most powerful weapon which may have been of Turkish origin—and with arrows tipped with stone that could be thinned and fashioned in points and sharp edges. They also used pointed sticks, and snares made of vegetal fibers. They did not practice agriculture, except, perhaps, in a few places in which they remained for a considerable period. Usually in times of want they moved on. They were as much a part of the earthly wilderness as the lower creatures they consumed—living on the land.

The Athapascans came southward from the immense Mackenzie River Basin along the western edge of the Great Plains. Navajo origin myths relate that most of their people were "created" in the mountains of southern Colorado, but some emerged into life somewhere beside the western sea, and all the Navajos moved to live together in Dinetah. Considering that some Athapascans did migrate southward along the Pacific, or reached that region from the north by another route farther inland, the myth may not be without some factual substance. The Apache, however, have no such tradition, and archaeological discoveries leave little doubt that the main Athapascan migration route transected the high open plains of Alberta, Saskatchewan, Montana, Wyoming, Nebraska, Colorado, Kansas, New Mexico, and the panhandles of Oklahoma and Texas.

Toward the southern end of the Rocky Mountains, in eastern Colorado or northeastern New Mexico, an important branch in the trail turned toward the southwest. There is no certainty as to where it left the plains and entered the mountains. Some investigators believe it passed through the San Luis Valley of Colorado, crossed the Continental Divide, and descended the San Juan River into New Mexico. Others think it left the plains in northeastern New Mexico, ran through one of several passes in that area, crossed the Rio Grande in the vicinity of Taos, and went on west over the Jemez Range to the valley of the San Juan. Whichever way it went, over it traveled the Navajo. The other fork continued on southward, split into numerous affluents, and over it went the Apache.

If the time of the initial Apache migrations southward must remain in doubt, it can be stated authoritatively that until late in the seventeenth century they were still in control of the High Plains at least as far north as western Nebraska. Shortly after 1700 the Shoshonean Comanche came down from the mountains of Wyoming and Colorado chiefly for the purpose of acquiring horses. They defeated the Plains Apache, and drove them southward and westward into New Mexico, Arizona, and Mexico, all areas that long before had been occupied by other Apache groups.

* * *

1538

AUGUST

Mendoza appointed a young nobleman—only twenty-eight years of age—governor of the west coast province of Nueva Galicia. He was Don Francisco Vásquez de Coronado.

SEPTEMBER

In a royal dispatch Charles V approved Mendoza's proposal to send a small scouting expedition to investigate the reports regarding the Seven Cities.

OCTOBER

As Coronado would soon be leaving for his new post, Mendoza instructed Fray Marcos, Estevanico, and another padre, Fray Onarato, who would accompany them, to travel with the governor to the west coast. There Coronado was to supervise preparations for their mission. It was not an obligation unwelcome to Coronado, for his own dreams of conquest were no less fervid than those of any other *conquistador.*

NOVEMBER

A long procession of soldiers, gentlemen adventurers, Indian servants, and herds of livestock was crawling along the high rocky road that ran out of the valley of Mexico to Guadalajara and on to the distant Pacific. At the rear of the column trudged a group which in appearance contrasted drastically with the splendor and ostentation of Coronado and his mounted escort. They wore no armor that glistened in the sun, no plumes, and carried no banners. Behind the strapping, dark Estevanico paddled the two friars, Marcos and Onarato, clad in robes of dusty Zaragosa cloth. After them came a score of half-naked Indians charged with their personal bundles.

DECEMBER

Compostela, the capital of Nueva Galicia, where Fray Marcos planned to await the coming of spring, was reached shortly before Christmas.

So began one of the greatest adventure stories in the early history of the Apache Country and the Southwest.

* * *

Apache nomenclature has always been confusing and misleading. Old reports and other documents apply different names to tribal subdivisions. The countless shiftings, temporary amalgamations, and

separations, which obviously occurred, have made it extremely difficult
for anthropologists to ascertain the identities, political and social affiliations, and the locations of groups and bands at any given time.
Moreover, Spanish explorers and colonizers frequently included people of other stocks among the Apache. In fact, there is still disagreement among scholars as to whether certain tribes, some of which are
extinct, were or were not Apache.

The Apache call themselves *N'de, Dinë, Tindé,* and *Indé,* the forms
having the same connotation, *people.* The word *apache* itself does not
appear in the Athapascan language. It derives from *apachu,* a name by
which the Zuñi designated the Navajo, and signifies *enemy. Apache* came
into use among the Spanish near the end of the sixteenth century. Don
Juan de Oñate, colonizer of New Mexico, may have been the first
Spaniard to give it official recognition. It appeared in his communications of 1598. After that it began to be widely applied to people of
Athapascan origin throughout the Southwest and northern Mexico.

Ethnologists have separated the Apache into two general divisions,
an eastern and a western, basing their decisions on language, cultural
similarities, and geographical locations. This scientifically significant
structure is utilized—as far as possible—in enumerating the Southern
Athapascan groups and bands, and in designating their historical, but
not necessarily traditional, homelands.

* * *

1539

MARCH *(Seventh)*

Coronado to Viceroy Mendoza: "Fray Marcos, his friend [Fray
Onarato], the Negro, and other slaves and Indians whom I had given
them departed. . . ."

They had traveled only sixty leagues to Petatlán, on the Rio Sinaloa,
when Fray Onarato was stricken with illness. After a wait of three days,
during which he did not improve, Fray Marcos assigned Indians to
carry him on a litter back to Culiacán.*

(Nineteenth)

Vacapan was reached. Here Fray Marcos made a fateful decision. He
announced that he would remain in the Indian village until after
Easter. Because Estevanico, the heathen, would not concern himself
with Christian devotions during the holy period, he decided to send

---

*Fray Onarato recovered and resumed his religious duties in Compostela.

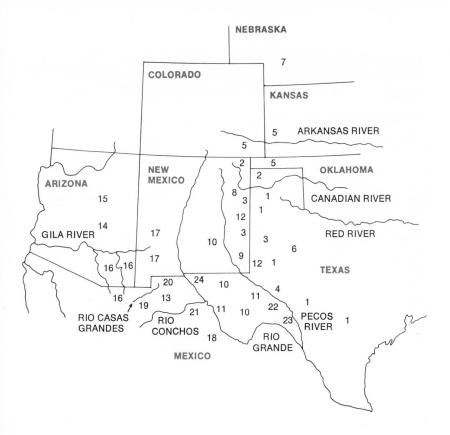

GENERAL LOCATIONS

of Apache groups and bands
in the sixteenth century

1 Lipan
2 Jicarilla
3 Llanero, Natagee,
   Lipiyane, Chipayne,
   Limita, Tremintina
4 Teya
5 El Cuartelejo,
   Calchufine, Fleches de
   Palos, Penxaye, Carlana,
   Coneyeros, Paloma
6 Cantsi
7 Gatakas

8 Rio Colorados and Achos
9 Perillo
10 Mescalero
11 Jumano
12 Faraon
13 Suma
14 Apache Peaks, Arivaipa,
   Pinal, San Carlos, Eastern
   White Mountain, Western
   White Mountain, Canyon
   Creek, Carrizo, Cibicue
15 Eleven Tonto Bands
   and Semi-Bands

16 Chiricahua
17 Mimbreno, Mogollon,
   Warm Spring Groups
18 Toboso
19 Jano
20 Cholome
21 Jocome
22 Sibolo
23 Pelone
24 Manso

Eastern Apache

Lipan—Eastern New Mexico and Texas, at one time as far southeast as the Gulf of Mexico

Jicarilla—Northern New Mexico, Texas Panhandle, and southeastern Colorado

Llanero—Eastern New Mexico and western Texas

Natagee—Eastern New Mexico and western Texas

Lipiyane—Eastern New Mexico and western Texas

Chipayne—Northeastern New Mexico and western Texas

Limita—Northeastern New Mexico and western Texas

Tremintina—Northeastern New Mexico and western Texas

Teya—Western Texas

Paloma Band—Western Kansas and southeastern Colorado

El Cuartelejo Band—Southeastern Colorado

Calchufine Band—Southeastern Colorado

Cantsi Band—Western Texas

Carlana Band—Southeastern Colorado

Fleches De Palos Band—Southeastern Colorado

Gatakas Band—Western Nebraska

Penxaye Band—Southeastern Colorado

Rio Colorados Band—Along Canadian River, northeastern New Mexico

Coneyeros Band—Northeastern New Mexico, western Kansas, and southeastern Colorado

Achos Band—Northeastern New Mexico

Perillo Band—Southeastern New Mexico

(The names **Querecho**, **Vaquero**, and **Llanero** were applied rather generally to the Plains Apache by early Spaniards. Some other Indians called them **Padoucas**, and this designation also was used by French **voyageurs** and missionaries.)

Western Apache

Mescalero—Eastern New Mexico and western Texas

Jumano—Western Texas as far south as the confluence of the Rio Grande and Rio Conchos, and northeastward to the Pecos River

Faraon—Eastern New Mexico and western Texas

Suma—Northern Mexico from the Rio Grande and westward to the Rio Casas Grandes

Apache Peaks Band—Northeast of Globe, Arizona

Arivaipa Band—Arivaipa Creek, Arizona

Pinal Band—Between Salt and Gila Rivers, Arizona

San Carlos Band—San Carlos River, Arizona

Eastern White Mountain Band—Upper Gila and Salt Rivers

Western White Mountain Band—Between eastern White Mountain and San Carlos Bands

Canyon Creek Band—Gila and Navajo Counties, Arizona

Carrizo Band—Gila County, Arizona

Cibicu Band—Between Canyon Creek and Carrizo Bands

Mazatzal Tonto Band—Mazatzal Mountains, Arizona

Six Tonto Semi-Bands—(1) North of Roosevelt Lake; (2) On upper Tonto Creek; (3) Between upper Tonto Creek and East Verde River; (4) Between East Verde and Verde Rivers; (5) North of East Verde River; (6) From Cherry Creek to Clear Creek. (All in Arizona)

Bald Mountain Tonto Band—East of Camp Verde, Arizona

Mormon Lake Tonto Band—Mormon Lake south of Flagstaff

Fossil Creek Tonto Band—On Fossil Creek above junction of Verde and East Verde Rivers

Oak Creek Tonto Band—On Oak Creek, vicinity of Sedona, south of Flagstaff

(**Apache Peaks Band** to **Oak Creek Tonto Band,** inclusive, called **San Carlos Group** by linguists. The name **Coyoteros** has been applied to some bands of this group.)

Chiricahua Band—Southeastern Arizona

Mimbreno Band—Southwestern New Mexico

Mogollon Band—In Catron and Grant Counties, New Mexico

Warm Springs Band—Head of Gila River, New Mexico (Last four bands called **Gilenos Group.**)

Toboso—In northern Mexico, state of Coahuila, from Bolson de Mapini northward to Rio Grande (Some linguists do not consider them Apache, but others so classify them.)

Jano—Northern Mexico and southwestern Texas—related to the **Mimbreno**

Cholome—Northern Mexico along international border west of Rio Grande

Jocome—Northern Mexico and southwestern Texas—related to the **Chiricahua**

Sibolo—Southwestern Texas adjacent to **Jumano**

Pelone—Southwestern Texas

Manso—Mesilla Valley, New Mexico, along border, and into Mexico

(Some of these bands were called by other names by Spaniards. Some names appear once and vanish from the record.)[4]

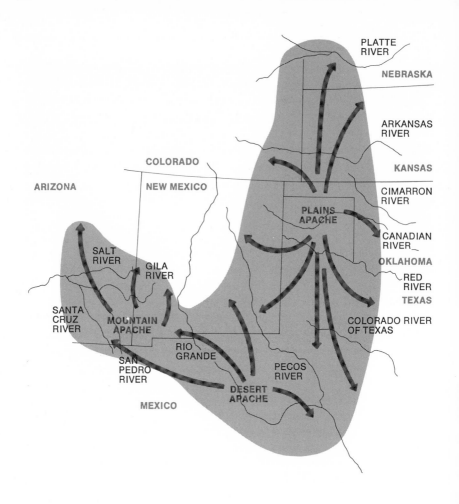

APACHERIA
approximate range of Apache
when discovered by Spanish
in sixteenth century

him ahead a short distance "to see . . . whether information could be obtained of what we were seeking."

Estevanico was to proceed no more than fifty or sixty leagues. If he discovered something of moderate importance he was to send back a cross one palm in length. A cross two palms in length would signify that he had learned something of great importance. If he discovered something "better than anything in New Spain," he was to send an Indian messenger with a large cross.

(Twenty-third)

On Passion Sunday Estevanico, his personal Indian servant, Bartolome, and a group of natives left Vacapan.

Fray Marcos would never see him again.

In his orders for the expedition, Mendoza had commanded that Estevanico was to obey Fray Marcos at all times, and should he fail to carry out the friar's orders, Estevanico "will be at fault and incur the penalties falling on those who disobey the persons empowered by his Majesty to command them." These were strong words for such a commonplace matter. Slaves were not in the habit of being disobedient, and ordinarily a threat in the name of the king was not necessary to hold them in line. However, Mendoza probably realized that Estevanico was not only strong-willed but possessed qualities of leadership, and that, unlike other slaves, would not hesitate to assert himself. If Mendoza did realize this, he was right.

Estevanico had no intention of obeying anyone once he was in the wilderness and beyond the reach of the military. He understood that Fray Marcos would be completely dependent upon him. Undoubtedly his talks with Mendoza had inflated his ego. What other slave ever had been accorded such consideration and called "intelligent" by a viceroy? If he was not in name leader of the expedition, he would be in fact. He had been over the trail as far as Pueblo de los Corazones. He was the one the Indians knew, and their trust would be in him. No longer would he be overshadowed by the great Cabeza de Vaca. Now he would be a god in his own right, a man from the sky, with his own servants to care for him.

He had acquired considerable baggage, clothing and ornaments, a shelter tent, and comfortable sleeping robes, accouterments he felt a man of his high station properly should own. Someone—perhaps Coronado—had given him two greyhounds, and they trotted dutifully beside him. Among his prized personal possessions was a *servicio de mesa* consisting of four large green dinner plates, and on them he was ceremoniously served each meal.

He had adorned himself in a manner he thought suitable for the occasion. His powerful legs and arms were decorated with clusters of bright feathers. A crown of plumes accentuated his height. Little bells tinkled merrily on his ankles. Turquoises and pieces of coral, presented to him by Indians along the way, were strung on thongs and dripped colorfully over his chest. In one of his packs was a medicine rattle obtained when he was with Cabeza de Vaca in western Texas. In their long journey across the continent the four men had come to understand that medicine rattles were among the most highly revered religious paraphernalia of the Indians. As he had marched northward from Culiacán, Estevanico also had acquired a harem, several Indian girls he had found especially pleasing, and they had straggled along in his wake, much to the consternation of Fray Marcos.

Estevanico had been gone less than a week from Vacapan when an Indian arrived with a cross the size of a man. The friar's interpreter, a native of Culiacán who spoke Spanish, relayed to him an astonishing message.

Fray Marcos would send back a report, as Mendoza had instructed him to do as he proceeded: "This person told me that it was thirty days' travel from the place where Esteban was to the first city . . . which is called Cibola. . . . In the first province there are seven very large cities, all under one ruler, with large houses of stone and lime . . . and the ruler's house is four stories high. The doors have many decorations of turquoises, of which there is a great abundance, and the people are well clothed. There are other provinces further on, each one of which he claims to be more important than these seven cities."

This is the first time, as far as historians have been able to discover, that the word "Cibola" was heard by Spaniards. The legendary Seven Cities of Antilia now became known as the Seven Cities of Cibola.

Estevanico urged Fray Marcos to hurry forward. He would meet him in the village from which he had sent the cross. But Fray Marcos had not started before another cross as large as the first arrived.

A P R I L

Estevanico traveled with greater speed than Fray Marcos could manage, and it was the tenth before he reached the village from which the first cross had been sent. Estevanico had gone on, and although he was irritated, the padre was cheered when he met Indians who confirmed the black ambassador's report, and said they had gone many times to trade in the Seven Cities.

Doggedly Fray Marcos pushed ahead. The story was the same in each village through which he passed. Estevanico ignored the commands and pleas he sent to him to wait. At last came a message that Estevanico would wait for him in Pueblo de los Corazones, but that promise, too, was broken. When he reached the town of the deer hearts he was informed that Estevanico, with his harem and three hundred followers, had been gone for several days.

Perhaps Fray Marcos spat out a mild oath. He now understood that the Moorish devil had never intended to wait anywhere for him, and he was deeply perturbed. No telling what riches the unconscionable disbeliever might confiscate. He might set himself up as king of the new land, win fame and glory, not to mention the favor of Mendoza. It was very disheartening, but there was nothing to do but keep going.

MAY

From a great ridge in the Huachuca Mountains, up where the air is thin and sweet with the perfumes of evergreens and flowers, one may see in a magnificent panoramic view the place where Estevanico the Black passed out of Mexico into Arizona, unlocking for the world the first gateway to the Southwest of the United States.

His route was in general the ancient trade trail from the west coast of Mexico to Zuñi. It went down the San Pedro River. In the vicinity of Benson, Arizona, his Indian guides led him toward the northeast, across the Arivaipa Valley, to Eagle Pass, between the Santa Teresa and Pinaleno Mountains. In this vicinity was the prehistoric Indian ruin called Chichilticale (Red House), and near it the trail turned northward to the Gila River. From the Gila it continued northward across high mountain and plateau country to the Little Colorado, near St. Johns. Swinging to the northeast, it crossed Carrizo Creek and reached the Zuni River, which came out of Cibola.

Traveling with Cabeza de Vaca, Estevanico had passed through the eastern end of Gran Apacheria. Now he alone was the first man of the Old World to traverse its western reaches. The region between Chichilticale and the headwaters of the Little Colorado, rich in game and wild plant foods, was inhabited by several Apache bands, but there is no documentary proof that he encountered them. As he was accompanied by some three hundred Opata, the Apache may have deemed it wise not to show themselves, but that they were there is beyond question.

Estevanico the Black reached the end of his earthly trail at Hawikuh —on the Zuni River in New Mexico—the most westward of the pueblos of Cibola. He had sent ahead of him the sacred medicine rattle, a custom which had been followed by Cabeza de Vaca when approaching an Indian town. The head chief of Zuñi had thrown the rattle to the ground in anger, and had told Estevanico's emissaries to leave at once, or he would have them killed. They had returned to

Estevanico badly frightened, but he only laughed and went ahead.

Pedro de Castañeda, who lived in Culiacán at the time, would write that as Estevanico came boldly up to the gates of Hawikuh he was taken prisoner and lodged in a little hut outside the town. There he was questioned for three days by Zuñi leaders, and he told them that white men were coming behind him "who were sent by a great Lord, and knew about the things in the sky, and how these were coming to instruct them in divine matters."[5]

The Zuñi headmen did not swallow the tale. Above all else, one thing convinced them that Estevanico was a spy for some nation who wished to conquer them. They could not bring themselves to believe that there were "people who were *white* in the country from which he came, and that he was sent by them, he being *black.*"

After they killed him, to prove that he was not a man from the sky or a god, they cut him up in little pieces and distributed the bits of flesh and bone to other people of the region.

There is disagreement among students about how far Fray Marcos traveled. He was at least several days away from Hawikuh when runners brought him the news that Estevanico had been slain. The padre claimed that he went on until he could see the pueblo from a distant hilltop, but that he had not entered it because he feared that if he, too, were killed, "no information would be obtained regarding this land." He thought the country "the greatest and best of all that have been discovered," and after taking possession of it in the name of the king he had turned about and fled "with more fear than food" back toward Mexico.

There are good reasons for believing that Fray Marcos did not see Hawikuh at all, and that he never got farther north than the Gila River. In almost all its phases the report he wrote revealed him as an unmitigated liar.

JUNE

Near the end of the month Fray Marcos got back to Compostela and gave Governor Coronado an account of his mission. According to Castañeda, he told Coronado "such great things about what the negro Esteban had discovered and what they had heard from Indians, and about other things they had heard about the South Sea and islands and other riches, that, without stopping for anything, the governor set off at once for the City of Mexico, taking Friar Marcos with him, to tell the viceroy about it." Coronado "made the things seem more important by not talking about them to anyone except his particular friends, under promise of the greatest secrecy, until after he had reached Mexico and had seen Don Antonio de Mendoza."

AUGUST

Fray Marcos to Mendoza: "Hawikuh is larger than the city of Mexico."

Quickly the word spread that the Seven Cities had been found. They were inconceivably rich. The capital once again was in a state of delirious excitement. The viceroy had ordered preparations made for an expedition to conquer them. In command would be Coronado. Castañeda wrote that hundreds of noblemen, distinguished and wealthy citizens, and padres pleaded to be allowed to participate in the treasure hunt, "so many men of high quality . . . that such a noble body was never collected. . . ."

While it was true that Mendoza had authorized the conquest, it was also true that he was unable to quell his own suspicion that in some manner he was being deceived. There was only one way to find out.

SEPTEMBER

A courier was speeding westward from Mexico City over the long mountainous trail to Culiacán. He carried an urgent dispatch for Captain Melchior Díaz. It ordered Díaz, whom Mendoza knew to be unqualifiedly reliable, to go north as fast as possible and verify the claims of Fray Marcos.

NOVEMBER

Díaz left Culiacán with a small company of mounted soldiers and Indians—perhaps forty-five men in all.

His mission is of great historical significance for the reason that he took the first horses into the western United States.

Now there were days when the red peoples of northern Sonora and Arizona heard a new kind of thunder, a rhythmic beating on the earth in tempos they had never known, the sound of horses' hooves. Now there were nights when the lights of campfires caught on the sleek sides of the great beasts tethered about the mud and mat houses, and there were new sounds in the shadows, the sounds of them munching their fodder and stamping, and there were the strange smells of their sweat and their manure.

A new wonder and a new way of life had come to Apacheria.

DECEMBER

At Chichilticale Díaz encountered a number of Apache who gave him considerable information about the killing of Estevanico, and the customs of the people of Cibola and their environment.

Díaz was prevented from going farther north by extreme cold and deep snow. He and his men had not been equipped to withstand such weather. Two of them had died of exposure.

After huddling together for a fortnight in flimsy shelters, Díaz and his men turned back.

* * *

The Apache were one people, but they were not politically united nor universally governed. A love of independence and liberty was stronger in them than emotions arising from ties of kinship. There were no permanent supreme tribal leaders, although there were chieftains of both large and small groups. Chieftainships were hereditary, and were usually gained through clan and blood lineage. Bands united in wartime or for the purpose of conducting raids were controlled by recognized commanders, but when the purpose for which they had amalgamated no longer existed, dissolution occurred.

The names of clans—there were at least threescore among the Western Apache alone—were usually descriptive of natural features, such as *Water at Foot of Hill People, Between Two Hills People, White Water People,* and *In the Rocks People.* Some clans took their names from birds and plants, but not from animals. Descent was in the female line, and each person belonged to his mother's clan. Exogamy was strictly maintained, and marriages were prohibited between so-called related clans, even though the relationship was not consanguineous.

* * *

1540

MARCH

The pageantry rivaled the glory of the dream. The great army of Coronado was moving northward along the Pacific coastal road, two hundred and fifty men on horseback, nearly a hundred foot soldiers, several hundred Indian servants, and half a dozen padres in robes and sandals, led by the celebrated Fray Marcos.

At Chiametla the long-expected Melchior Díaz and his saddle-worn troopers appeared. The report Díaz made did nothing to bolster the spirits of Coronado and his lieutenants. The Indians with whom he had talked—the Opata at Pueblo de los Corazones and the Apache in Arizona—knew nothing of gold or other treasures. For that matter, they knew of nothing extraordinary to be found in Cibola. There were some turquoises, cattle robes, and cotton garments—that was about all. The assertion that Hawikuh was larger than Mexico City was nothing less than ridiculous.

Fray Marcos was angry. Díaz's report was an affront to his integrity. He denounced it as false, and promised Coronado that "what they should see would be good, and that he would place the army in a country where their hands would be filled. . . ."

JUNE

The Coronado Expedition was passing through a part of Arizona, following the trail Estevanico had taken, inhabited by Apache. Reports speak of the region as "uninhabited," but that was not true. Archaeologists have produced evidence showing that Apache were then living there. However, their villages would have been located some distance off any well-traveled trail and cleverly concealed, and they would hardly have exposed themselves to a column as large and imposing as that led by Coronado. The Western Apache saw Coronado in Arizona, even if he did not see them.

JULY

The hungry, weary soldiers of Coronado were stunned by disappointment when they gazed on the pueblo where Estevanico had died.

"Such were the curses that were hurled at Friar Marcos," said Castañeda, "that I pray God may protect him. . . . Hawikuh is a little crowded village, looking as if it had been all crumpled up together. There are haciendas in New Spain which make a better appearance."

Obviously news of the Spaniards' approach had been carried ahead of them, most probably by Apache who had continuously observed them along their line of advance. The Zuñi were fully prepared to do battle, and Coronado was forced to attack in order to occupy the pueblo. It was not an easy victory, and blood was shed on both sides before the Zuñi were subdued.

* * *

Considering that at the time of the Coronado Expedition no southwestern Indians owned horses, news traveled throughout the region with what justifiably may be termed remarkable speed. People living on the lower Colorado River, some five hundred miles to the west of Zuñi, knew of Estevanico's death and Coronado's fight with the residents of Hawikuh within a few days after those events occurred. Trading missions, hunting parties, and other groups moved frequently over the trails running east from Zuñi to such places as Acoma, Puaray, Santo Domingo, San Felipe, Cochiti, and Taos. Also, the gruesome details of Coronado's attack on the Cibolans obviously had been swiftly disseminated, not only westward but far to the east. While he was still at Zuñi, headmen came from as far away as the upper Pecos River, on the edge of the Great Plains, to tell him of the wonders of their own homelands and to assure him that he would be welcome if he chose to visit them.

Things did not turn out as might have been anticipated in view of the hospitable invitations. The march across New Mexico was marked by fierce fighting. By the time the Pueblos of the Rio Grande had been conquered, some of Coronado's officers and many of the soldiers were voicing strong doubts that anything worthwhile would be discovered. Hardships had been extreme. Spaniards had been slain by Indians struggling desperately to save their homes, families, and meager possessions, and others had died of exposure, malnutrition, infected wounds, and various illnesses. There was talk of abandoning the conquest, but Coronado held stubbornly to the conviction that somewhere in the vast land treasures were to be found. He shut his ears to the talk of turning back.

* * *

1541

MAY

Lured on by Indian tales that gold and other riches awaited him ahead, Coronado was leading his army across the grass sea of eastern New Mexico and western Texas. This was the land of the Plains Apache, the Lipan, the Llanero, the Teya. Coronado and his soldiers were the first white men to see these people.*

Castañeda would write vivid descriptions of the Plains Apache and their environment as he saw them on the march with Coronado in the dawn of recorded history. The Spaniards were overawed by the flatness and seemingly endless extent of the plains. Day after day they saw neither "a hill nor a hillock which was three times as high as a man. . . . The country is like a bowl, so that when a man sits down, the horizon surrounds him all around at the distance of a musket shot. . . . Several lakes were found at intervals; they were round as plates, a stone's throw or more across, some fresh and some salt. The grass grows tall near these lakes; away from them it is very short, a span or less. . . . There are no groves of trees except at the rivers, which flow at the bottom of some ravines where the trees grow . . . thick . . . they [the ravines] were not noticed until one was right on the edge of them. . . . There are paths down into these, made by the cows [buffalo] when they go to the water. . . ."

Horses and men, "in traveling over those plains, would leave no

---

*One exception should be noted in the case of the Teya. An old Teya told them that he and some others of his tribe had met Cabeza de Vaca. The place of the encounter is not known, but it undoubtedly occurred much farther to the south or southeast, for Coronado met the Teya at Tule Canyon in the Texas Panhandle, and Cabeza de Vaca did not get that far north.

more trace where they passed than if nothing had been there—nothing
—so that it was necessary to make piles of bones and cow-dung now
and then, so the rear guard could follow the army. The grass never
failed to become erect after it had been trodden down, and, although
it was short, it was as fresh and straight as before."

The number of bison seen was "something incredible." In one place
a group of soldiers came upon an enormous herd. They killed several
and the others broke into a wild stampede. As they fled "they trampled
one another in their haste until they came to a ravine. So many of the
animals fell into this that they filled it up, and the rest went across on
top of them. The men who were chasing them on horseback fell in
among the animals without noticing where they were going. Three of
the horses that fell in among the cows, all saddled and bridled, were
lost sight of completely." While hunting on the treeless plains "many
fellows were lost . . . and did not get back to the army for two or three
days, wandering about the country as if they were crazy. . . ." Every
night the soldiers in the main camp "took account of who was missing,
fired guns and blew trumpets and beat drums and built great
fires. . . ." The country was so level in places "that at midday, after one
has wandered about in one direction and another in pursuit of game,
the only thing to do is to stay near the game quietly until sunset, so
to see where it goes down. . . . There are great numbers of wolves on
these plains, which go around with the cows. They have white skins.
The deer are pied with white. Their skin is loose, so that when they
are killed it can be pulled off with the hand while warm, coming off like
pigskin. The rabbits, which are very numerous, are so foolish that
those on horseback killed them with their lances."

Castañeda wrote that the first Plains Apache encountered were
called Querechos. This was an identity by which they were known to
some Pueblo tribes, and may have derived from *Queros* or *Keres*, the
name of a Pueblo people with whom they maintained regular trade
relationships. The Querechos were undoubtedly the Lipan or some
subdivision of this large tribe.

Coronado thought their physiques "the best . . . of any I have seen
. . ." and noted that they subsisted "entirely on cattle, for they neither
plant nor harvest maize. With the skins they build their houses; with
the skins they clothe and shoe themselves; from the skins they make
ropes and also obtain wool. From the sinews they make thread, with
which they sew their clothing and likewise their tents. From the bones
they shape awls, and the dung they use for firewood, since there is no
other fuel in all that land. The bladders served as jugs and drinking
vessels." They ate the meat of animals slightly roasted, sometimes
uncooked, by "taking it in their teeth and pulling with one hand; with

the other [hand] they hold a large flint knife and cut off mouthfuls, swallowing it half chewed. . . . They eat raw fat without warming it and drink the blood just as it comes from the cattle. . . ."

Castañeda expressed the opinion that the Querechos had better figures, were better warriors, and were more feared by other Indians than the Pueblos. They traveled about like Arabs "with their tents and troops of dogs loaded with poles."* The Querechos' dogs also were equipped with "Moorish pack-saddles with girths. When the load gets disarranged, the dogs howl, calling someone to fix them right."

It was Castañeda's judgment that the Querechos, although they ate raw flesh and drank blood, were "a kind people and not cruel. They are faithful friends. . . . That they were very intelligent is evident from the fact that although they conversed by means of signs they made themselves understood so well that there was no need of an interpreter." The statement should be qualified with the explanation that the Spaniards knew nothing of the sign language, but had with them Indian guides well versed in it.

Castañeda: "The Querechos dry the flesh [of bison] in the sun, cutting it thin like a leaf, and when dry they grind it like meal to keep it and make a sort of sea soup of it to eat. A handful thrown into a pot swells up so as to increase very much. They season it with fat, which they always try to secure when they kill a cow. They empty a large gut and fill it with blood, and carry this around the neck to drink when they are thirsty. When they open the belly of a cow, they squeeze out the chewed grass and drink the juice that remains behind, because they say that this contains the essence of the stomach. They cut the hide open at the back and pull it off at the joints, using a flint as large as a finger, tied in a little stick, with as much ease as if working with a good iron tool. They give it an edge with their own teeth. The quickness with which they do this is something worth seeing. . . ."

Traveling toward the southeast from the Canadian River, where they found the Querechos, the expedition reached the Llano Estacado of western Texas and encountered the Apache Teya. They were now in the vicinity of Palo Duro Canyon, an area transected by numerous *barrancas.* The unbroken sweep of the Staked Plains, spreading over the curve of the earth on every side, astounded Castañeda even more than the flatness of the High Plains they had previously crossed. Whenever one looked at buffalo ahead "one could see the sky between their legs, so that at a distance they looked like trimmed pine tree trunks with the foliage joining at the top. When a bull stood alone he resembled four such pines. And however close to them one might be, when

---

*This was the means of transport to which later French *voyageurs* would give the name *travois.* It was used by most Plains tribes, even after they possessed horses.

looking across their backs one could not see the ground on the other side."

They came upon a large camp of Teya in one of the deep ravines, "and there were many groves of mulberry trees . . . and rosebushes with the same sort of fruit [flowers] that they have in France." The soldiers made a drink from grapes, and "there were walnuts and the same kind of [wild] fowls as in New Spain, and large quantities of prunes like those of Castile."

A Teya "was seen to shoot a bull right through both shoulders with an arrow, which would be a good shot for a musket. These people are very intelligent; the women were well made and modest. They cover the whole body. They wear shoes and buskins made of tanned skin. The women wear cloaks over their small under petticoats, with sleeves gathered up at the shoulders, all of skin, and some wore something like little *sanbenitos* with a fringe, which reached halfway down the thigh over the petticoat."

Coronado's credulousness matched his indestructible conviction that he would find treasure if he searched for it long and far enough. When an Indian who was a captive of a Pueblo leader told him that a fabulously rich kingdom could be reached by going farther across the plains, he had promptly acquired the prisoner as a guide to take him to it.

The Indian, dubbed the Turk simply "because he looked like one," had deliberately misdirected the expedition toward the southeast. Unaware that horses could thrive on nothing more than the nourishing buffalo grass, he had set a course toward the Llano Estacado, where he knew no grain or other fodder, except grass, would be found. Thus, the horses would perish, all the Spaniards would be afoot and lost and could be easily destroyed by Plains warriors, who would greatly outnumber them. Quivira, which spread along the Arkansas River in Kansas, was the Turk's homeland, and it was his hope that his plot to lead the expedition astray would provide him with an opportunity to escape and return to his own people.

There was a river in his country, said the scheming Turk, "which was two leagues wide, in which there were fishes as big as horses, and large numbers of very big canoes, with more than twenty rowers on a side, and that they carried sails, and that their lords sat on the poop under awnings, and on the prow they had a great golden eagle. He said also that the lord of that country took his afternoon nap under a great tree on which were hung a great number of little gold bells, which put him to sleep as they swung in the air. He said also that everyone had their ordinary dishes made of wrought plate, and the jugs and bowls were of gold." Farther inland, beyond Quivira, were even richer kingdoms, called Harahey and Guaes.

New hope filled Coronado. If what the Turk said was only half true, Montezuma's treasure and the gold and silver of the Incas would be mere pocket money by comparison. As he pressed on toward the southeast, across the plains beyond the Pecos, another guide, Ysopete, who also came from Kansas and had been a Pueblo captive, insisted that the Turk was lying and was taking them away from Quivira. Coronado ignored him. The Querechos confirmed Ysopete's claims, but Coronado continued to place his faith in the Turk. Not until the Apache had informed him that Quivira lay far to the northeast, and that he could not reach it in the direction he was traveling, was he convinced that he had been led away from his goal.

Only slightly diminished, however, was his belief that riches surpassing all others in the New World were to be found ahead. The Turk was placed in chains. Apaches volunteered to serve as guides. Although they would soon desert, they at least started him on the correct course to Quivira.

JUNE

The main army had been sent back to the Rio Grande to await Coronado's return. With only a small company—perhaps thirty horsemen—he pushed across the plains of the Oklahoma Panhandle and southern Kansas. This, also, was the country of Plains Apache, but they kept out of his way.

JULY

They had traveled for some thirty days toward the north-northeast from the Llano Estacado of the Texas Panhandle and had reached the Arkansas River where one day the town of Ford, Kansas, would stand. No royal barge with a golden eagle on its prow appeared.

Still Coronado refused to abandon all hope. Crossing the Great Bend of the Arkansas at the ford which had been used for countless centuries by Indians and buffalo, they went on toward the northeast as far as the Smoky Hill River in the vicinity of Lindsborg, Kansas. There Coronado gave up.

Ysopete had told him the truth. There were no large towns, no gold, no treasures of any kind—nothing but villages of Wichita Indians, half naked, heavily tattooed, and terrorized by the guns, the horses, and the men in armor—nothing but plains, buffalo, and sky. They garroted the hapless Turk.

SEPTEMBER

The aspens on the high mountains were turning gold when Coronado rejoined his men on the Rio Grande. For him and all of his

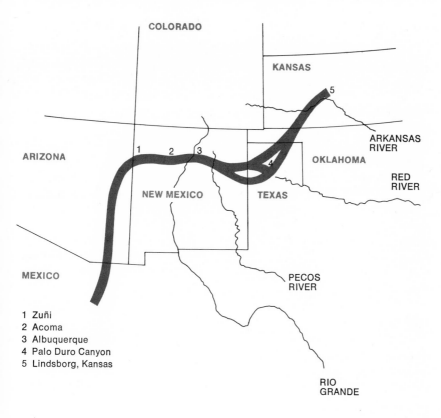

COLORADO

KANSAS

5

ARKANSAS
RIVER

ARIZONA

1   2   3

4

OKLAHOMA

RED
RIVER

NEW MEXICO

TEXAS

MEXICO

PECOS
RIVER

1 Zuñi
2 Acoma
3 Albuquerque
4 Palo Duro Canyon
5 Lindsborg, Kansas

RIO
GRANDE

approximate route of
CORONADO–1540/1541

In eastern New Mexico and the panhandles
of Texas and Oklahoma, and in Kansas,
Coronado and his lieutenants discover the
Plains Apache—Lipan and numerous other groups
and bands—whom they call Querechos.
They also met wandering Teya Apache, one of
whom remembered seeing Cabeza de Vaca
far to the south in 1535.

once powerful army—now tattered, weary, and completely dispirited —the great dream had been destroyed by stark reality. There was nothing to be done but wait through another bitter winter until the spring of 1542, when they would start on the long and sad march back to Mexico.

* * *

This was the way the Iron Age of civilization in Europe came to the Apache and other Indians of the Southwest, people still living then in the Stone Age. It had come gently at first, with four friendly men merely touching the southern fringe of the incredibly vast region, four men who took nothing, who left an inspiring memory, who vanished into the west as peacefully as they had come out of the east.

Suddenly the tempo had accelerated, sounded on the drums of insatiable desire and willful cruelty, creating a clash of mores, of beliefs, of values that were irreconcilable, and fomenting a fierce and uncontrollable conflict between materialistic gods.

The Plains Apache had known of the four men. They had known of the black man who had appeared at Zuñi and had met death there. Before they had heard the roar of the Coronado tempest, they had known how the Pueblos who made the tragic mistake of standing against its fury had been mercilessly slaughtered and burned alive. They had heard of such wondrous things as horses and armor and sheep before they saw them with their own eyes. They had been aware of the deadly power of the mysterious guns before they heard their thunder and saw their lightning and smelled their acrid fumes.

If the Apache could not understand the menace they understood its power, they knew what had happened and what could happen, and they could reason that by resisting it they could not hope to gain. The situation had not been the same for them as for the Pueblos. The Pueblos along Coronado's route lived in permanent structures, some of them very large and very old, and those buildings were their only homes, and in them were all their earthly possessions, their clothing, their food stores, their ceremonial kivas, the symbols of their spiritual beliefs, and around those towns were the little fields, the maize and bean and melon and cotton patches, on which they depended for their existence.

The Apache, following their nomadic way of life, could easily replace necessities, their skin tepees, their brush shelters, their garments, their utensils, for all those things were products of nature, of the realm of grass and animals through which they roamed.

The things coveted by the Spaniards were beyond their knowledge, but even if such things did exist, the Apache would not have known how to utilize or value them. They kept out of the way as much as they could, and when the soldiers had vanished, and the confusion and the clamor had subsided, they had gone on with the business of living as they had always lived. They remembered with vividness the magic they had witnessed, but not only with pleasure, for each memory was invested with a new hatred and a new anxiety. They could hope—perhaps the incomprehensible white men would never come again, perhaps—but always their gaze was toward the horizon.

Not everyone who had come north with Coronado, however, had failed to find treasure. In the eyes of three friars with the expedition the homelands of the Pueblos, the Plains Apache, and the Quiviras were the richest on earth, for in them were innumerable heathen souls to be saved. Their requests to remain and dedicate themselves to the service of God were granted.

They were the first missionaries to be stationed in the Southwest. All three would be martyred.

Fray Luis de Escalona made his headquarters at Pecos Pueblo, where many Plains Apaches came to trade. Coronado left with him a few sheep. There, said one report, he dwelt in a little hut, more like a cave. How long he survived is not known, for he was never seen again by white man, and later explorers could learn nothing of his fate.

Fray Juan de la Cruz also remained among the Pueblo people, making his residence, it is believed, at Puaray, a town on the Rio Grande (near Bernalillo). He was slain, probably at the instigation of jealous medicine men.

Fray Juan de Padilla went back across the plains to Quivira, and somewhat more is known of him than of the others. With him were three assistants, a Portuguese lay brother, Andres do Campo, and two Indians, Lucas and Sebastian, all of whom had accompanied him from Mexico. Coronado had supplied them with some equipment, religious articles, and a small band of ewes. After establishing a mission among the Quiviras, who had welcomed him, Fray Padilla had decided to explore country farther east, and with do Campo, Lucas, and Sebastian had set out, carrying supplies and baggage on the only horse they possessed.

They had traveled no more than a few days when they saw approaching at a distance a large party of warriors. Fray Padilla seemed to sense at once that his end had come. He commanded his companions to flee to safety on the horse, and they obeyed. Then, according to an early Spanish account, he "fell on his knees, and, beginning to pray, he awaited the fury of the barbarians . . . commending his soul to the Lord. . . . The cruel butchers in a twinkling filled him with arrows. . . ."

The site of the tragedy was in territory occupied by Indians the Quiviras called Guas, and who later would be better known as Kansa, from which the name Kansas derived. After they had gone, Lucas and Sebastian returned and buried Fray Padilla, then rejoined do Campo.

For almost five years the three men wandered in the wilderness, gradually making their way southward from Kansas to the Mexican state of Pánuco. They reached Mexico City in 1547, and a royal official reported to the Spanish Government:

"Very great are the things told of by a Portuguese who escaped from a province where the Indians killed a friar, and who, not knowing where he was going, by the will of God was brought to this city, with such great news of the land and its people that everybody marvels."

If the official's report was not as extreme or as glowing as those made by that master of fantasy, Fray Marcos, they had very nearly the same effect on the populace of Mexico City. Actually, do Campo and his Indian companions, being honest men, had made no claims that precious metals were to be found in Quivira or in any other region through which they had wandered. They had described the country factually as containing immense herds of game, a great many Indians, and very little else.

It did not matter. Once more the great dream was revived, and once more wild rumors circulated. Coronado had gone to the wrong places. Coronado had not gone far enough. A great new expedition was to be sent out to recover the fortunes Coronado had missed. The Portuguese and the two Indians, Lucas and Sebastian, had revealed to the viceroy in private where the treasures were to be found.

The talk was exciting and fired everyone's blood, but besides the fact that it was without a semblance of truth, there were very good reasons why nothing came of it.

In many respects, Mexico had become a land of turmoil. Indian uprisings, especially the Mixtón War, political dissensions, the discovery of rich silver mines, the opening of vast new grazing and farming areas, defiance of royal decrees and other forms of lawlessness had created internal problems that required the full attention of the provincial government. Much more had soon been forgotten about the daring exploits of Cabeza de Vaca, Estevanico the Black, and Coronado and his men than was remembered.

Steadily the frontier was being pushed northward from central Mexico. Towns mushroomed wherever minerals and cattle ranges were found. Although the Indians fought courageously to hold their homes and fields, tribe after tribe succumbed to the insuperable pressure. In violation of Spanish laws, uncounted thousands of them were enslaved and forced to work for mine owners, cattlemen, ranchers, and in other types of commercial enterprises. Always in the vanguard of the pioneers were priests. Missions and convents were established in the wilderness and soldiers were sent to protect them.

* * *

1567

Fabulous strikes of silver and other metals were made in Chihuahua (then called Nueva Viscaya) close to the southern border of Apacheria. Santa Barbara, a shabby, dirty town on the Rio Florida, was the trading center of the region and the wildest settlement on the northern frontier. To it and the surrounding country swarmed men of all stamp, miners, cattlemen, farmers, padres, slave traders, and outlaws.

Adventurers and missionaries talked of pushing farther north, wondering what riches, material and spiritual, might be found there. If they knew any details of the disastrous Coronado Expedition—which is doubtful—they ignored them. There were no printed histories or official reports available to them. Indeed, there were almost no printed books, except for a few religious tracts, to be found in all Mexico.

1573

Laws became effective which prohibited explorations and the establishment of new settlements without royal approval. The statutes contained strict requirements. Only persons of good character, known to be devout Christians, and who could be relied upon to treat Indians with kindness and justice, would be given permission to lead expeditions of discovery. Thus, it was one thing to think, or dream, of searching for treasure in the north, and another thing to accomplish the task. There were not very many persons on the frontier who could qualify under the new code, except missionaries, and it was required that even they must be accompanied by soldiers on any venture they wished to undertake. Sending padres and soldiers into the unknown was expensive, for the government was required by the new laws to furnish their food and other supplies, as well as to pay the wages of the military.

* * *

The Apache diet was greatly varied, and under normal conditions was well balanced. Except in the worst desert areas, big game abounded throughout Apacheria. The Apache hunted only to fulfill needs, never killing animals for sport. Fish, bear, and beaver were not consumed, a custom the genesis of which is not known but which undoubtedly was due to cosmogonic and religious views that had long been forgotten before the arrival of the Spanish in the New World. While deer, antelope, elk, and bison were preferred to other game, cougar, rats, hares, wolves, coyotes, squirrels, lizards, and snakes were eaten. Caterpillars were an ingredient of one type of gruel, and dishes containing bone marrow and blood were prepared. Certain parts of the viscera of large animals were considered tidbits. Wild fowl were not a staple, but were used on occasion of dire need, such as those which might be caused by reverses in warfare or unsuccessful raids.

As Spanish settlement pushed northward the Apache quickly acquired a taste for the flesh of domesticated animals, with the single exception of pork, which, for some unknown reason, they distinctly disliked. Mule meat was considered a delicacy, and they preferred roast horse to either mutton or beef. Not many years had passed before numerous Apache bands were sustaining themselves to a greater extent on stolen livestock than on wild animals, having found that raiding Spanish ranchos was easier and far more rewarding than hunting.

The Apache obtained a great variety of nourishing foods from wild plants. Among these were several species of cactus fruit, piñon nuts, bulbs and roots of many kinds, mesquite beans, mushrooms, greens, berries, acorns, and seeds. They made mescal and an extremely potent brew called *tiswin*. Drunken orgies were commonplace, and frequently resulted in women being beaten or otherwise abused, bloody fighting between men, and the commission of depraved acts. Some Apaches maintained small fields of corn and vegetables, but none engaged in agriculture sufficiently to make possible a sedentary existence.

* * *

1580

Fray Agustín Rodrigues had lived nearly ten years among the Conchos Indians of Chihuahua, and had been eminently successful in winning converts among them. His neophytes had told him of a large number of people who dwelt far to the north and who knew nothing at all of the Christian God. He had long been eager to visit the idolatrous nations, and now he wrote the viceroy proposing that he and two other padres, Fray Francisco López and Fray Juan de Santa María, be allowed to make the journey. His plan was approved, and Captain Francisco Sánchez Chamuscado, a veteran frontier officer, was ordered to accompany them with a military escort.

1581

JUNE

The Rodrigues–Chamuscado Expedition would reopen the northern gateway four decades after the heartbroken and ill Coronado had put Quivira behind him. But it would not follow Coronado's route. It would open a new trail through Apacheria.

In the company, which started from Santa Barbara, besides the three friars, were eight soldiers under Chamuscado and nineteen Indians who had been engaged as wranglers for the pack animals, a herd of ninety extra horses, and six hundred head of livestock.

Hernán Gallegos, Chamuscado's aide, would record that the purposes of the journey were "to carry out the discovery of New Mexico and the new lands—which had been sought for so many years," as well as to go "where God our Lord was pleased to direct them, in order that his Holy Faith might be taught and His gospel spread throughout the lands which they . . . might thus discover in His holy service and in the interest of the royal crown."

July

Turning up the Rio Grande from the mouth of the Rio Conchos they entered country inhabited by the Apache. One day, in an Indian town, Fray Agustín casually inquired if the people living there had ever seen a white man. The reply he received startled everyone. He was told, wrote Gallegos, that "a long time ago four Christians had passed that way." After forty-five years the memory of Cabeza de Vaca and his companions was still vivid among the Apache of the Rio Grande.

Above El Paso del Norte they entered country never before seen by white men, but that did not mean that the Indians did not know white men existed. They had heard of Coronado's trail of blood and death, and they fled from their pueblos. Fray Agustín was able to find some of them and convince them that he and his company wanted nothing but their friendship. Quickly the "news that we were coming in peace spread so widely that there was not a day or night when we were not surrounded and accompanied by more than three hundred souls."

August

They were camped in the Galisteo Valley, only a few miles south of the site of Santa Fe, near a large pueblo they called Malpartida. The surrounding area was mountainous, and according to Gallegos, ". . . we asked if there were many minerals in the region, showing the natives the samples we had taken along . . . . and requested them to lead us to the place where such riches might be found. They immediately brought us a large quantity of different kinds, including some of a coppery steel-like ore. This mineral appeared to be rich . . . they gave us to understand that there were many minerals near the province. . . . We went to investigate and discovered mines of different ores."

September

The first serious disruption of the smooth progress of the expedition came at Malpartida. Fray Agustín and Chamuscado had agreed that they should visit the buffalo plains which the Indians told them were to the east, but Fray Juan de Santa María had decided he would turn back "to report of what had been discovered to his prelate and to his Excellency, the viceroy." All efforts to persuade him to remain "until we had inspected everything" failed. He was determined to return, and he set out alone on the trail back to Mexico.

The company departed for the country of the Plains Apache. Regrettably Gallegos did not record their experiences among them. Presumably they traveled as far northeast as a branch of the Canadian River in eastern New Mexico. They encountered no difficulties—again the Apache stayed out of the way—and enjoyed buffalo hunting.

OCTOBER

When they returned to the Galisteo Valley they learned for the first time that the friendship displayed by the Indians was far from being sincere. Fray Juan de Santa María had gone only a short distance on his homeward journey when he was ambushed and slain. Inquiries brought the information that his killers, who were not identified, were convinced that the padre "was going to bring more Christians in order to put them out of their homes." Furthermore, the slayers were attempting to organize an attack on the entire company, for "seeing that they had killed the friar so easily, they thought they would kill us just as readily."

Fortunately a general assault did not materialize—nine armed men would have had little chance against hundreds of warriors—but trouble came in another form before the company was able to leave the area. Three valuable horses were stolen and slaughtered by residents of Malagon, an adjacent pueblo. Captain Chamuscado decided that in spite of the dangers involved, a show of strength had to be made, and he sent five mounted men to capture the horse thieves. Displaying boldness they probably did not feel, the soldiers rode up to the gate of Malagon, a large town "of eighty houses of three and four stories with plazas and streets," and found the Pueblos gathered on the roofs, prepared to defend themselves. When their demand that the culprits be surrendered was ignored, the soldiers opened fire, "although we incurred great risk in doing so, for we were only five men . . . attacking more than a thousand inhabitants." Terrified by the gunfire, most of the Indians concealed themselves in the buildings, but some attempted to flee. Two were captured and taken back to Malpartida.

Chamuscado ordered them beheaded. However, this was a ruse. He and Fray Agustín had agreed that just before the captives were put to death the two padres would rush out and save them. This scheme, it was thought, would demonstrate conclusively that Spaniards, and especially priests, harbored only good intentions toward Indians. The plan was carried out and appeared to have the desired effect, for on the following morning the people of Malagon "came heavily laden with turkeys and other foods for our use, entreating us not to be angry with them." The company moved on north, narrowly escaping a perilous situation.

DECEMBER

The high country of northern New Mexico was covered with deep snow, but the company rode ahead. From the pueblos on the Rio Grande they followed Coronado's trail as far west as Zuñi.

They returned by the same route as far as the pueblo of Puaray on the Rio Grande. There Fray Agustín and Fray Francisco López announced that they had chosen it as the site of the mission they wished to establish, and would remain. To no avail Chamuscado pleaded fervently with them to go back to Mexico with him.

1582

JANUARY

The two padres stood in their tattered robes before the gate of Puaray, made the sign of the cross, and waved good-bye to their companions.

FEBRUARY

In southern New Mexico "God willed that Captain Chamuscado should be stricken with an old ailment." Suffering great pain, and partially paralyzed, the veteran frontier soldier—he was more than sixty years of age—courageously kept on. "Since his condition was caused by exhaustion," said Gallegos, "we decided to bleed him. As the equipment had been left with the friars, we proceeded as soldiers do in time of need when they draw blood with a horseshoe nail and apply the medicines by means of a horn." The ministrations were ineffectual. With his hands and feet useless, Chamuscado was unable to stay in a saddle, and a litter was constructed for him and slung between two horses. By this means it was hoped that he could be taken "to Christian lands where the holy sacraments could be administered. . . . Burdened by this device, we traveled with great difficulty."

MARCH

Somewhere along the Rio Conchos trail Captain Chamuscado died.

APRIL

On the morning of Easter Sunday the residents of Santa Barbara were startled by the sound of guns being fired at the edge of town. They saw a ragged group of horsemen and Indians approaching, and "we were given an especially warm welcome because the inhabitants had thought us dead."

Couriers were soon on their way to Mexico City, carrying more misinformation than truth. Rapidly rumors spread that fabulous mines had been discovered by the expedition, that Gallegos had sent the viceroy incredibly rich samples of ore, that the friars and the dead Chamuscado had taken possession in the name of the king of an immense unknown territory that not only contained no end of minerals but endless grass pastures, lush valleys, immense forests, and great numbers of heathen Indians all eager to become Christians. A handful of soldiers had succeeded where Coronado, with an army, had failed, and the news "brought great relief and inspiration to many people in New Spain."

MAY

Not the least inspired by the glowing reports of Gallegos and his soldiers was Antonio de Espejo, a young adventurer of unsavory reputation and doubtful integrity who had arrived in Mexico from Spain in 1571 as a confidential officer of the Inquisition.

He devised a scheme by which he believed he could acquire the mines reported to exist in the country of the upper Rio Grande.

Espejo was possessed of a complex and many-sided character. Highly intelligent and clever, he was also tough but rarely crude, and he could be persuasive, diplomatic, and socially charming. He had considered his post as a spy for the Inquisition as no more than a stepping stone to greater things, and he was driven by an ambition to make a much greater fortune than was possible by exposing heretics and officials disloyal to the Church.

The opportunities in northern Mexico had soon attracted his attention, and he and his brother, Pedro, had moved to the vicinity of Santa Barbara. They had become successful cattlemen, but even in the wild and lawless country their ruthless and violent methods had got them into serious trouble. Antonio had murdered an Indian vaquero whom he accused of laziness, and the brothers had been involved in several other encounters in which blood was shed. During a roundup in the spring of 1581, several of their cowboys had deserted after Antonio had threatened their lives. A gunfight had followed in a nearby settlement, and Pedro had killed one of the deserters and wounded another.

Both Espejos had been charged with murder and taken to Mexico City for trial. Pedro had been sentenced to a term in prison, but Antonio —probably because he was still serving as an investigator for the Inquisition—was given a fine. Instead of paying, he had fled back to Nueva Viscaya.

Now aware that the Franciscans were profoundly anxious about the welfare of the two priests who had remained at Puaray, he offered to finance and lead a rescue party.

OCTOBER

After months of effort to obtain the required government approval of the plan, the patience of both the Franciscans and Espejo was exhausted.

Fray Bernardino Beltrán, who would represent the Order on the venture, at last volunteered to obtain the necessary permit by himself. He got it, but there is no certainty how he accomplished the feat. One account states that it was issued by his superior, but another record indicates that it was granted by the lieutenant-governor of Nueva Viscaya. In either case, its issuance would not have been in compliance with the law, which required the approval of no less a personage than the viceroy for any type of expedition to the north.

NOVEMBER

With Espejo and Fray Beltrán when they left Valle de Allende, a short distance east of Santa Barbara, were fourteen soldiers and a number of Indians engaged to care for a supply pack train and a herd of a hundred horses. It was a company prepared to travel with speed, and it did.

DECEMBER

One of the soldiers, Diego Pérez de Luxán, in a journal he kept of the journey, would write that while they were ascending the Rio Grande in New Mexico they were told by Indians that Fray Agustín and his colleague had been slain at Puaray.

Some of the men wanted to turn back, but Espejo refused, declaring that rescuing the friars had been only one purpose of the expedition. He had become excited by Indian tales that rich provinces lay both to the east and west. In several pueblos he had found "many ores of different colors," and he was convinced that his hopes would be fulfilled. He insisted, moreover, that "this was a good opportunity for me to serve his Majesty . . . while incurring no expense to him. . . ."

1583

FEBRUARY

The deaths of the two priests had been confirmed. From Puaray Espejo continued westward to Zuñi over the route traversed twice by Coronado and the Rodrigues–Chamuscado Expedition.

MARCH

Passing through Zuñi he continued on to the Hopi villages, which had been visited by two of Coronado's captains.

APRIL

The Hopi informed him that "riches of gold" were to be found far to the southwest, and he announced that he would go in search of them. Espejo's courage was never better illustrated than when, on the last day of the month, he set out with only four soldiers and several Hopi guides—the others were sent back to Zuñi to wait for him—after he had been told that "the mines were far away, that there was a scarcity of water, and that the route was over difficult ridges."

MAY

Now Espejo became a true discoverer. Crossing the Little Colorado near the site of Winslow, Arizona, he and his men pressed on through a magnificent country that was crisscrossed by gorges and great mesas that swept away under the blue spring sky, and reached the Verde River. Through this region ranged several bands of Western Apache, and they were the first white men to see them. The reverse was true of these Apache, but if they had never seen a Spaniard they knew something about them and they obviously understood their purpose in coming there. For Luxán, who was with Espejo, would write that many Apache, whom he called "mountain people," met them "with crosses painted on their heads, even the children. . . . They gave us ores as a sign of peace and many came to show us the mines . . . we found many mountain people who received us well."

Along the Verde River they found the mineral deposits about which the Hopi had told them. A deeply disappointed Luxán would describe them as being "so worthless that we did not find in any of them a trace of silver, as they were copper . . . and poor. We therefore determined to return at once."

Espejo would never know the magnitude of his mistake. He had discovered the great mines near Jerome, Arizona, which in later years would yield immense fortunes in copper and silver.

Returning to Zuñi, they found Fray Beltrán and several soldiers determined to leave at once for Mexico by the shortest possible route. A violent argument took place, with the result that the expedition was divided. Fray Beltrán and six men departed.*

JUNE

With the eight soldiers who had remained loyal to him—Luxán was one of them—and several Indian wranglers, Espejo traveled eastward on the trail to the Rio Grande. Pueblos who previously had been friendly now were openly hostile. Half a dozen skirmishes occurred in which several members of the party were wounded and one Indian servant was killed. According to Luxán, "so much news was brought to us to the effect that all the provinces were waiting to kill us, that it would have frightened any group of persons, even if they had been many, and the more so nine soldier companions, some poorly equipped. . . . Efforts were made to have the Indians come peacefully to us. . . . Instead, they remained in the hills and mocked us . . . shouting at us from the hills night and day."

At Puaray, Espejo's patience reached an end. Except for some thirty men on the roof, the town was deserted. A request for food was bluntly refused. Espejo ordered his men to attack and fire the pueblo. Luxán thought some persons "burned to death because of the cries they uttered. . . ." Men who sought to escape were driven into an underground kiva. When the battle ended, "we at once took out the prisoners, two at a time, and lined them up against some cottonwoods . . . where they were garroted and shot many times. . . . Sixteen were executed, not counting those who burned to death.

"This was a remarkable deed for so few people in the midst of so many enemies."

As they went on eastward they found most of the people friendly, for "news of what happened at Puaray spread through the provinces and the people were very much afraid and all served and regaled us."

JULY

Espejo was determined to see the buffalo plains, but his reasons were not revealed. From the Rio Grande he and his little band traveled eastward through Galisteo Valley to the Pecos River and turned southward, taking with them by force several Indians captured in the vicinity of Pecos Pueblo. Now they were once more passing through Apache Country totally unknown to white men.

---

*They would reach Mexico in safety, but no account of their homeward journey is known to have been written.

Apparently word of what they had done at Puaray had preceded them, for they saw no Plains Apache.

Luxán reported that the land was "all very level, containing fine pastures and many water holes . . . we found many buffalo tracks as well as bones and skulls. . . . In all this trip we did not find any buffalo, nothing but many tracks . . . we were greatly troubled by lack of food. . . ."*

AUGUST

As far as can be determined, they traveled along the Pecos River for several hundred miles until they were in the vicinity of Toyah Lake, in western Texas. There, fortunately for them, they met three friendly Jumano Apache, whom they were able to make understand that they wished to go to the junction of the Rio Grande and the Rio Conchos. The Jumano made it clear to them that if they followed the Pecos they would be going far out of their way, and offered to guide them directly "by good trails" to their destination, and "this brought us no little joy."

When they reached the confluence—called the La Junta area—"the people there gave us a great reception . . . and presented us with quantities of ears of green corn, cooked and raw calabashes, and catfish. They put on a great dance and festivities. . . . Our feeling of security was so great that we went about almost in shirt sleeves."

SEPTEMBER

After a journey of approximately ten months, they rode triumphantly into Allende, their starting place.

Espejo took pen in hand at once to prepare an account of his discoveries for the Spanish sovereign. It was even more glowing in its praises of the regions inhabited by the Pueblos and Apaches than the report submitted by Gallegos, and it left no doubt as to Espejo's personal ambitions. In part he wrote King Philip:

"The natives of all those provinces are large, more vigorous than the Mexicans, and healthy, for no illness was noted among them. Their women are fairer than the Mexican women, and they are an intelligent and orderly people. There are attractive pueblos with plazas, and well-arranged houses. This indicates that the inhabitants would learn quickly any matter dealing with good government.

"In the greater part of those provinces, there is an abundance of

---

*Espejo would write later that they had seen "great numbers of native cattle." However, Luxán's account is more reliable.

game beasts and birds: rabbits, hares, deer, buffalo, ducks, geese, cranes, and pheasants, and other birds. There are also fine wooded mountains with trees of all kinds, salines, and rivers containing a great variety of fish.

"Carts and wagons can be driven through most of this region; and there are good pastures for cattle as well as lands suitable for vegetables or grain crops, whether irrigated or depending on seasonal rains.

"There are many rich mines, too, from which I brought ores to be assayed and to determine their quality.

"I brought also an Indian man . . . and an Indian woman . . . so that they might enlighten us regarding those provinces and the road to that region, if its discovery and colonization are undertaken anew in the service of his Majesty. . . ."[6]

* * *

Everything the Apache made—implements, utensils, clothing, and other articles—was designed and developed to meet indispensable needs and was adaptable to their nomadic life. They made little pottery, but they were skillful and artistic basketmakers, producing them in a great variety of shapes and sizes. Pottery was heavy and difficult to transport. Baskets were comparatively light, could be borne on backs, and served efficiently as containers for foodstuffs and personal possessions. No Indians excelled the Apache in making arrowheads and arrows. Indeed, all their weapons were things of beauty and reflected their superb craftsmanship.

Their dwellings, or wickiups, were small, seldom more than ten or twelve feet in diameter and nine feet in height, and constructed of poles tied together at the top. The framework could be covered with various materials to make them comfortable under almost every climatic condition . . . rushes and leafy branches in hot weather, and the hides of large animals in winter. The ground within the wickiup was excavated to a depth of six or seven inches, and the earth was piled around the outside base to protect and reinforce the structure. Smoke escaped through a vent in the roof.

Nothing demonstrates better that the Apache were thorough students of adaptation than their main garments—the breechcloth of the men, the skirts of the women, and the moccasins. Drawing on several early sources, Ogle wrote of these articles: "The breechcloth was about two yards long. It passed between the legs and hung over the belt in front and behind, the rear part almost reaching the ground. A common buckskin skirt was composed of two buckskins hung over a belt, one in front and the other behind in the form of a kilt. The edges of the skirt were cut in deep fringe. The Apache moccasins were much like a boot. They reached nearly to the knees, and each was made of half a buckskin turned over in two or three folds, allowing them to be drawn up as a protection to the thighs; otherwise, the folds could be used as receptacles for implements, small arms and trinkets." The soles were made of undressed hide with the hairy side out, and the toes were turned up to protect the feet when running. Ogle points out that this type of moccasin "was a direct response to an environment of poisonous reptiles and xerophytic vegetation."

* * *

1584

King Philip disclosed an interest in taking steps to establish a permanent colony in the undeveloped country north of Mexico.

For more than forty years the Spanish Government had displayed very little official interest in the region, largely due to the failure of Coronado to discover any mineral wealth there. However, a series of menacing international incidents now forced it to give serious attention to this unguarded flank of Spain's immense New World dominion. British raiders had struck along the Pacific Coast, threatening the lucrative commerce which had been established between Mexico and the Orient. Explorers from other European nations were probing the opposite side of the continent. There were rumors that the Strait of Anian, long believed to reach from the Atlantic to the Pacific across northern North America, had been found, and that England was planning to fortify its western end.

King Philip expressed the opinion that the best method of procedure, and perhaps the most economical, might be to contract with some responsible person to undertake the northern conquest, a prominent and wealthy man who could be depended upon to abide by the laws controlling colonization and who had demonstrated his ability to serve as the first governor of the new province of New Mexico.

1585

As the trend of the king's thinking became known, a feverish competition developed throughout Mexico among wealthy cattlemen, mine owners, political and military officials of the various states, and other prominent men for the coveted post. More cognizant than the sovereign of the tremendous organizational, legal, and political complications involved in such an immense project, provincial authorities in

Mexico City moved with thoughtful deliberation and extreme caution.

1590

Almost no progress had been made toward undertaking the northern conquest. A new viceroy, Luis de Velasco, took office, and he, being totally uninformed about the problem, refused to make blind decisions or approve any of the actions taken by his predecessor. The delay continued.

One man who had strenuously sought the appointment decided he would wait no longer. He was Gaspar Castano de Sosa, a pioneer in the northern Mexican province of Nuevo León. Politically influential, he had been the first alcalde (mayor) of Monterrey and later the state's lieutenant-governor. Aggressive and unscrupulous, he had engaged in the Indian slave trade, had acquired mines and ranches, and had founded several settlements. Twice he had sent emissaries to Mexico City to obtain for him a license to conquer and settle New Mexico. The only reply he had received had infuriated him. The viceroy had ordered him to stop capturing and selling Indian slaves, and had warned him not to leave Mexico without permission.

Castano summoned townspeople and farmers to a meeting in Monclova, where he made his home. He had, he informed them, received confidential information about a bountiful land in the north, and he proposed that they join him in an expedition to occupy it. So great and rich was this land that all of them would quickly become wealthy. To prove that he was speaking the truth, he displayed some pieces of extraordinarily high-grade silver which he declared had come from unowned deposits on the upper Rio Grande. The settlers were won over by his salesmanship and the silver trick. They agreed to abandon their homes and go with him.

AUGUST

The Castano Expedition has its place in history for two reasons: (1) It was the first attempt to establish a permanent colony in New Mexico, and (2) it took the first wheeled vehicles into the homelands of the Apache and Pueblo Indians.

In the long column as it crawled toward the Rio Grande in the terrible summer heat were one hundred and seventy men, women, and children—virtually the entire population of Monclova—a train of supply wagons, a herd of horses and cattle, and two wheeled brass cannon. Riders were sent ahead to capture Indians and enslave them as servants and camp-tenders.

SEPTEMBER

Castano had not followed the familiar route down the Rio Conchos. It was his hope that if he broke a new trail he might discover treasures his predecessors had missed. As a result it took nearly six weeks of extremely difficult travel to reach the Rio Grande. The river was crossed at some point between the sites of the Texas towns of Del Rio and Eagle Pass.

OCTOBER

Moving toward the northeast, instead of taking the easier route that ascended the Rio Grande, the company was soon in Apache territory that in places proved to be impassable. Four more weeks were spent breaking through to the Pecos River, where they found a relatively easy line of march. They were now going north on the trail over which Espejo had returned. Undoubtedly the Apache observed them, but chose not to show themselves.

DECEMBER

The great Pecos Pueblo, about thirty miles southeast of Santa Fe, was reached on the last day of the year. Castano's overtures of friendship and his requests for food were bluntly rejected. He ordered an attack. Several Pecos were killed and the other inhabitants fled. Castano's men raided the pueblo and confiscated the supplies that were so badly needed.

1591

JANUARY

Despite the deep snow and bitter cold Castano explored the surrounding country. No ore veins were found.

FEBRUARY

Moving through Glorieta Pass, Castano led his colonists to the Rio Grande. He selected the ancient pueblo of Santo Domingo as his "capital."

APRIL

A company of soldiers commanded by Captain Juan Morlete rode into the plaza of Santo Domingo. After embracing Castano in the customary Spanish manner, Morlete read aloud the orders he carried. They were signed by the viceroy, Don Luis de Velasco.

Castano and all persons with him were to be brought back to Mexico as prisoners. All Indian slaves held by Castano were to be returned to their homes and assured that they would not again be harmed. The charges against Castano: engaging in an expedition of discovery, and attempting to establish a colony, in violation of royal decrees.

In the lovely full flowering of the New Mexico spring, the weary and hopeless colonists, the wagons, and the cannon, all guarded by soldiers, started on the long trail back to Mexico. Castano rode in one of the wagons, in shackles.*

* * *

Apache religion speaks of a class of supernatural beings who at one time lived as a people on the earth. Because of sickness and death they set out in search of a place without disease where they hoped to find eternal life. In Apache mythology the direction of all movements is from north to south. Today the Apache believe that these supernatural beings still exist in certain mountains and in realms underground which belong exclusively to them.

The Apache recognizes a Supreme Being—rather, a supreme power of creation—but he is neither benevolent nor punitive and is therefore not worshiped. The Apache has no conception of a hereafter, such as the Christian heaven and hell. His religion is a system of imitative and sympathetic magic aimed ritually at fulfillment of the requirements of life and living. It is not concerned with preparation for death and afterlife. Although, like any sane human being, the Apache attempts to prolong his life, he does not live in morbid fear of dying. Death is looked upon as the normal end of a life cycle for man, just as it is for plants or animals. When death comes, a man (or woman) becomes one with the cosmos, a condition in which he is neither punished nor rewarded—water poured into a river is no longer identifiable.

One may go into the remote Apache Country of today and—if fortunate—can witness a sing. They are still incomparably dramatic, beautiful, and inspiring. Every Apache ceremony is designed to accomplish a specific purpose. Some are prophylactic in nature, and conducted to ward off evil or attract goodness. The Apache endeavors especially to appease the Evil Spirit, which he believes controls their livelihood and their destinies. They live for the present, with little or no thoughts about what might happen to them in death. After more than four centuries of trying, the emissaries of Christianity have come nowhere near the goals they have always dreamed of reaching. The only victory they are justified in claiming is that by the divergent tenets of their faith they have succeeded in creating irresoluble confusion in Apache

---

*Before the year ended he would be sentenced to serve six years in exile in the Philippines. He would be killed there in a revolt of galley slaves.

minds. The picture of a God that is all good remains incomprehensible to the Apache.

* * *

1593

FEBRUARY

With a small contingent of cavalry, Captain Francisco Leyva de Bonilla ostensibly set out to hunt for Indians who had been raiding cattle herds along the upper Rio Conchos. He had schemed with a disreputable adventurer, Antonio Gutiérrez de Humana, to go to New Mexico and search for silver mines.

They were bold and reckless men, and in spite of the sad experience of Castano, they were unafraid to gamble their freedom and even their lives in an attempt to satisfy a craving for wealth and power in a manner forbidden by law.

Somewhere in the barren country along the Rio Conchos Humana joined Bonilla with a party of men who had been secretly recruited in Santa Barbara, and the united groups set off on their unlawful conquest.

APRIL

The Bonilla–Humana Expedition established themselves in the pueblo of San Ildefonso, about eighteen miles northwest of the site of Santa Fe. From Indians they heard the old story about the treasures to be found in a province called Quivira, and they swallowed it with no less gullibility than Coronado had done more than half a century earlier.

MAY

They passed Pecos Pueblo on their way to the buffalo plains.

JUNE

The route they took is uncertain, except that it ran generally toward the northeast, but it would become known that they passed without trouble through the area of eastern New Mexico inhabited by the Lipan Apache. After traveling about thirty days from the Pecos they came to "two large rivers, and beyond them many Indian villages with a large number of inhabitants. Farther on, in a plain, they came to a very large settlement . . . one of the two rivers they crossed earlier flowed through this town . . . in some places between the houses there were fields of corn, calabashes, and beans. The natives were very numerous but received the Spaniards peacefully and furnished them with abundant supplies of food."

These people may have been Wichita, Kansa, or Pawnee. The identities of the "two large rivers" have never been ascertained. They could have been the Arkansas and the Smoky Hill, the Kansas and the Republican, or even the North and South Platte.

At this point a chronological account of their travels becomes impossible, for reasons that will be explained. There are indications that for the remainder of the year they wandered great distances in their search for gold. Perhaps they remained for considerable periods in Indian towns. They may well have journeyed farther north than Coronado.

In any case, somewhere in the heart of the Great Plains Bonilla and Humana had a falling out, the cause of which is not known. After a bitter quarrel Humana sulked in his tent. At last he asked a soldier to summon Bonilla, "who came dressed in shirt and breeches. Before he reached the tent Humana went out to meet him, drew a knife from his pocket, unsheathed it, and stabbed Captain Bonilla twice, from which he soon afterward died. He was buried at once."

Fearful of their own fate under the leadership of the brutal Humana, five Indian servants deserted. Four of them perished while attempting to reach Mexico. The fifth, known only by the name of Jusepe, fell into the hands of a band of Plains Apache. After being held captive for a year, he escaped and found his way to a pueblo on the upper Rio Grande. The account he gave of his experiences, however, was not the complete story of the Bonilla–Humana Expedition.

After the death of Bonilla, according to one unsubstantiated report, Humana went farther northeast, but another story appears to be more in line with the truth. It says Humana traveled toward the southwest from the place of the murder, and eventually he and his men came to a small river in the area of western Kansas and southeastern Colorado that later would be called El Cuartelejo. One night, presumably early in 1594, a large band of Indians attacked them. One version of the tale states that a man and an Indian woman of the company escaped. Another says that every Spaniard was killed.

Whatever the truth, nothing more was heard of the Bonilla–Humana Expedition until years later when a party of Spaniards came upon a number of badly rusted guns and swords in a cottonwood grove beside the stream in El Cuartelejo. A padre gave it the name of *El Río de Las Ánimas Perdidas en Purgatorio*—the River of Lost Souls in Purgatory—for the rusted weapons allegedly were identified as having belonged to Humana and his men.

El Cuartelejo was Apache Country. Numerous bands, some quite large, ranged over the high plains that in this section roll like giant combers to break against the immense wall of the Rocky Mountains.

If the Indians who wiped out the Humana company were Apache—
and it would be unreasonable to think they were not—this is the first
record of an attack by the Apache on white men.[7]

* * *

The early Apache were not a people of large stature. Most men were
of medium height; those standing as much as two or three inches over
six feet were rare exceptions. They were spare, lithe, and possessed of
extraordinary stamina and remarkable muscular strength. Generally
females were shorter than males. In their early years many women
were physically attractive, but endless drudgery, childbearing, and a
precarious existence usually took a heavy toll on their looks long
before they reached middle life.

In the Southwest constant burning sunlight, dry desert air, almost
ceaseless activity, and a nourishing diet of proteins, fats, vegetables,
and fruits greatly contributed to their normal good health. Viral and
communicable diseases, such as smallpox, measles, scarlet fever, diph-
theria, tuberculosis, and syphilis, were unknown among them until
after the invasion of their homelands by white men and Indians who
had been exposed to these virulent afflictions. The Apache, however,
were no more free of native illnesses than any other red people. They
were not, for example, immune to arthritis, neuralgia, pleurisy, pneu-
monia, and various functional disorders. Ophthalmic conditions due
to smoke and sand, osteomyelitis and periostitis due to bone injury and
infection from wounds, were suffered by them.

Because they moved frequently in their hunts for game, to harvest
natural foods in season, and to protect themselves from enemies,
sanitation was not a problem. Indeed, wherever they stopped, either
for long or short periods, it was their custom to perform their bodily
functions at a distance from their wickiups and campgrounds. They
were not unclean until white men confined them in concentration
camps, forcing them to endure insanitary conditions which brought
severe sickness and death to many of them.

Although their life was normally arduous and always dangerous,
until Europeans and Americans destroyed their culture and their
economy they could not be characterized as a greatly disadvantaged
people. Intertribal conflicts, and adverse weather conditions which
caused wild foods to fail and scarcities of animals, brought inescapable
hardships, but these were temporary situations, and they invariably
found means of enduring them. Most of the time they lived well,
prospered from their labors, and, in the light of their own standards,
were generally content.

Not only their spiritual but their social activities were rich, rewarding, and pleasant. They held numerous ceremonies, engaged in many

communal dances, and were addicted to sports and games of chance, such as races of all types, a kind of ball contest, wrestling, and throwing dice. They were inveterate gamblers.

As was true of many Indian people, they attached great importance to what might be termed the family circle. They displayed profound affection for their children, but, being realists, they were unsparing in training their sons and daughters to counter and overcome the vicissitudes which they understood would surely confront them.

The young Apache was painstakingly taught to show no more compassion or consideration for a human adversary than for a bug or wild animal, to conceal all sensitivity to suffering, to subjugate emotion to coldblooded reaction. The law of the natural world was kill or be killed. The supreme law to which man must adhere was to retaliate in kind, and any deviation from this code was an invitation to disaster.

* * *

1598

M A Y

The Apache in the vicinity of El Paso del Norte gazed in wonder at a great moving dust cloud rising above the northbound trail along the Rio Grande. It was caused by nearly a hundred heavily loaded wagons, troops of horsemen, and an immense herd of more than seven thousand head of livestock strung out for nearly four miles.

In the awe-inspiring column were one hundred and thirty families of settlers, two hundred and seventy single men—soldiers, craftsmen, and hopeful young adventurers—eleven Franciscan friars, and scores of Indian and Negro servants, wranglers, and camp-tenders. In the lead rode a group of men splendidly arrayed in shining armor, plumed helmets, silk and lace shirts, and fine Cordovan boots with tasseled spurs.

The great prize had gone at last to Don Juan de Oñate of Zacatecas, a man of distinguished lineage and the heart of a beast. He was both the first governor and the first captain-general of the province of New Mexico.

The contract which Oñate had received over the understandably vigorous protests of jealous rivals provided that he would be granted title to a private estate of some two hundred square miles, with suzerainty of "all the vassals [Indians] thereon." He would receive an annual salary of eight thousand gold ducats (considered enormous at the time). Any mines he discovered and operated would be exempt from a royal tax. He and his officers would have the privilege of holding Indian workers in bondage *(encomiendas)* and profiting from their labors. Tribute could be exacted from all natives to be used in supporting the colony. The government would pay the expenses of all friars accompanying him. Besides supplying him with adequate quantities of arms and ammunition, the royal treasury would appropriate $4,000, and lend him another $6,000, to help defray the costs of his journey. Even more unusual than these generous provisions, and of greater significance, were the degrees of authority given him in other areas. In deciding problems of war and finance he could act independently of the Mexican Government, and he would hold supreme judicial powers —the right of life and death.

On two occasions at the El Paso ford of the Rio Grande, a few Apache, undoubtedly anxious to know the purpose and the destination of the formidable force, approached the column, signaling their friendly intentions. The itinerary of the expedition, written by one of the priests, notes that "... the first Indians of the river were brought into camp by the sargento mayor. After being clothed they were sent to tell their friends and to bring them in. That day about eight Indians came of their own accord. They were of a kind we call muleteers [*arreadores*], because to say *yes* they roll their tongues against their palates as we do when driving animals, *arre.*" Three days later the diarist recorded: "... we did not travel farther than to the pass of the river and the ford. Forty of these Indians came to the camp. They had Turkish bows, long hair cut to resemble little Milan caps, headgear made to hold down the hair and colored with blood or paint."

These Apache emissaries evidently found out what they wanted to know, for they told Oñate that the first of the Pueblo settlements he sought was eight days farther ahead. They were given "many presents, and they helped us to transport the sheep across the river." Then they vanished.

JUNE

En route up the Rio Grande, Oñate stopped at some twoscore pueblos. In each the inhabitants pledged their allegiance to the white man's God, to the Spanish king, and to him as their master.

JULY

The pueblo of Okhe stood on the east bank of the Rio Grande about twenty-five miles northwest of the site of Santa Fe. On every side beautiful hills and mesas rolled away, as if in support of the turquoise sky, and along the river fields of corn and other crops ripened in the warm sun.

(Eleventh)

Oñate proclaimed Okhe the capital of the province. Fifty-seven years before, a contingent of Coronado's army had visited it and left a cross standing in its plaza. In honor of them, Oñate changed the name of Okhe to San Juan de los Caballeros.

Mistaken in the belief that the Spaniards would not long remain, the people of San Juan graciously vacated the town, and the soldiers moved in. It was just as well, for had they objected to the intrusion they would have been forcefully evicted and everything they owned would have been confiscated.

Like all his predecessors in New Mexico, Oñate was consumed by a dream of discovering treasure, and he wasted no time in taking steps to fulfill it. He had founded the colony of New Mexico—an enormous realm of plains, mountains, and deserts, the boundaries of which, except for that on the south, extended only God knew how far—but he did not propose to burden himself unnecessarily with routine social, economic, religious, or political problems. He had brought along aides who in his estimation were qualified to assume these responsibilities. Of the greatest importance to him was the task of learning as rapidly as possible what riches might exist in the kingdom over which he ruled. Plans for extensive investigations were soon completed.

For the first time the name *Apache* appeared in written records. Early reports on the colonization of New Mexico would designate the Indians of the Plains as Querechos and Vaqueros. However, they also soon would be called Apaches.

One of Oñate's first actions was to divide the province into mission districts. Fray Alonso de Lugo was assigned to several pueblos "and, in addition, all of the Apaches and Cocoyes of the neighboring sierras and settlements." As Fray Lugo's station was in northern New Mexico, these Apaches and Cocoyes undoubtedly were the people who later would be called *Apaches de Navajo.* Besides the pueblos of Picuris, Taos, and adjacent towns on the upper Rio Grande, Fray Francisco de Zamora was to serve "all the Apaches from the Sierra Nevada toward the north and east." These Apache would come to be known as the Jicarilla, a Spanish-Mexican word meaning *little basket,* and given to them because of the expertness of their women in weaving baskets.

SEPTEMBER

The first exploring company Oñate sent out was commanded by his nephew, Vincente de Zaldivar, and was comprised of sixty men. In the middle of the month they were camped on the Rio Gallinas (near Las Vegas, New Mexico) and enjoying the trout fishing when "four Vaquero Indians came to see them. The Spaniards gave them food and gifts. One of them arose and shouted to many others who were hiding, and all came to where the Spaniards were. They are a sturdy people and fine bowmen."

These Vaquero Apache made it clear to the Spaniards "that they were very disturbed at seeing us in their land," but they complied with a request to guide them to the buffalo herds. The route over which the Apache took Zaldivar ran eastward across the plains to the Canadian River. Large herds of buffalo were seen.

One account of the journey gives the impression that no difficulties were encountered, but another version relates incidents that indicate the march was not accomplished without disruptions which further demonstrated that the Apache looked upon the white men as unwelcome visitors. In the vicinity of the Rio Gallinas, the Spaniards came upon "a ridiculous figure in human form, with ears almost half a yard long, a snout horrible in the extreme, a tail that almost dragged, dressed in a very tight-fitting pelico, which encircled the body and was all stained with blood; with his bow in his hand, and a quiver of arrows at his shoulder." The grotesque figure was captured and his costume removed. He was a "very frightened and embarrassed" Indian who confessed that he had thought he might scare "the Europeans so they would flee and leave their baggage."

On another occasion, according to an interpretation by Forbes, "Zaldivar's party came upon an Indian who was totally white, with blueish eyes and a graceful and respectable appearance. Behind him came a fair-sized party of Indian warriors. The white Indian advanced without a word, and in an extremely dignified manner he scrutinized the fifty Spaniards. Zaldivar, wishing to instill fear and astonishment in the Apaches, had one of his men discharge a musket. This apparently intimidated the Indians, and they agreed to furnish a guide for the journey ahead."

The guide, not relishing the job, soon vanished. Twelve other Apache were taken prisoners and forced to serve in his place.

OCTOBER

Vincente de Zaldivar, or perhaps one of his aides, conceived the idea of capturing a large number of buffalo, driving them back to San Juan, and domesticating them. In their translation of one report, Hammond and Rey provide a vivid account of the attempt to round up wild bison, a comedy that must have given no end of amusement to the watching and astounded Apache. When they came in sight of a large herd, the Spaniards "went on three leagues farther in search of a good location for a corral and the material with which to build it. Having located a site, they proceeded to build the corral of large cottonwood logs, which took them three days. It was so large and had such long wings that they thought they could enclose ten thousand head, because during those days they had seen so many cattle and they roamed so close to the tents and the horses. In view of this fact and that when they run they look as if they were hobbled, taking small leaps, the men took their capture for granted. . . .

"The corral being completed, they set out on the following day toward a plain where, on the preceding afternoon, they had seen about one hundred thousand head of cattle. As they rushed them, the buffalo began to move toward the corral, but in a little while they stampeded with great fury in the direction of the men and broke through them, even though they held close together; and they were unable to stop the cattle; because they are stubborn animals, brave beyond praise, and so cunning that if one runs after them, they run, and if one stops or moves slowly, they stop and roll, just like mules, and after this rest they renew their flight. For a few days the men tried in a thousand ways to drive them inside the corral . . . but all methods proved equally fruitless. This is no small wonder, because they are unusually wild and fierce; in fact, they killed three of our horses, and wounded forty others. . . ."

Unable to pen any grown buffalo, Zaldivar ordered his men to capture calves, but "of the many that were brought along, some tied by the tail and others carried on the horses . . . all died within little more than an hour." Abandoning the scheme of taking live buffalo back with them, the Spaniards slaughtered a large number, "and more than eighty arrobas of fat were obtained.* Without any question, it is far superior to lard. The meat of the bulls is better than our beef, and that of the cows equals our most tender veal or mutton."

Zaldivar's secretary provided a description of the Plains Apache as they were at the end of the sixteenth century that is of great value to historians and scientists. Remarking that they were many in number, he recorded that most ". . . of the men went about naked, but some wore skins of buffalo, and others blankets. The women wore a sort of chamois breeches, and shoes or boots. . . ." One rancheria visited contained "fifty tents made of tanned skins which were very bright red and white in color. They were round like pavilions, with flaps and openings, and made as neatly as those from Italy. They are so large that in the most common ones there is ample room for four individual mattresses and beds. The tanning is so good that even the heaviest rain will not go through the skin, nor does it become hard. On the contrary, when it dries it becomes as soft and pliable as before." Zaldivar "bartered for a tent and brought it to camp. And even though

---

*About two thousand pounds.

it was so large . . . it did not weigh more than fifty pounds.

"To carry these tents, the poles with which they set them up, and a bag of meat . . . the Indians use medium-sized, shaggy dogs, which they harness like mules. They have large droves of them . . . carrying a load of at least one hundred pounds. . . . It is both interesting and amusing to see them traveling along, one after the other, dragging the ends of their poles, almost all of them with sores under the harness. When the Indian women load these dogs they hold their heads between their legs."

The Vaqueros "eat meat almost raw, and much fat and tallow. . . . With the jerked beef in one hand and the hard fat in the other, they take a bit of one and then of the other. In this manner they grow healthy, strong, and brave. Their weapons consist of flint and very large Turkish bows. The Spaniards saw some arrows with long bone tips, although only a few, as the flint is better for killing the cattle. . . . They kill them at the first shot with amazing skill, while hiding in brush shelters built at the watering places. . . ."

That the Vaqueros were enjoying amicable relations with the Pueblos of the Rio Grande was apparent, but intelligence also was obtained which indicated they were at war with other Apaches. Through an interpreter Zaldivar informed them that Oñate would protect them from their enemies as long as they remained loyal to the king, but would deal harshly with any who were not obedient. Vaquero spokesmen promptly requested his "aid against the Xumanas, which is the name they gave to a nation of Indians who are striped like the Chichimecos [of the central Mexico plateau]." The "Xumanas" were the Jumano Apaches, who periodically traveled north along the Pecos River from western Texas to hunt buffalo, and were not infrequently hostile to other Apache. Zaldivar's reply to the Vaqueros' request for military assistance gave them no assurance that Oñate would act in their behalf. It was, he declared, the hope of the Spaniards that peace could be established among all tribes.

While Vincente de Zaldivar was still reconnoitering on the buffalo plains, Oñate set out with a large and well-supplied company. He had three purposes in mind: to look for metals, to obtain pledges of obedience from a number of pueblos he had not visited, and to reach the Gulf of California, from which it was hoped communications by sea could be established with Mexico. Left in command at San Juan was another nephew, Juan de Zaldivar, with instructions to follow him as soon as his brother Vincente had returned to the capital.

Oñate rode southward, passed through the Galisteo Valley, continued along the eastern slope of the Sandia and Manzano Mountains, visited the salines east of Estancia, the ancient town of Abo, and the Jumano pueblos near the northern end of Chupadera Mesa. The people in these places readily pledged allegiance to him.

Oñate now doubled back, crossed the Rio Grande near Puaray, and struck out westward. The people of Acoma, the Sky City, "furnished us liberally with maize, water, and fowls." Ironically it was this hospitality which was the primary cause of one of the most atrocious episodes in the history of the Southwest.

NOVEMBER

Oñate passed through Zuñi and continued on to the Hopi villages (in Arizona). As they had done with Espejo, the Hopi told him that mines existed some distance to the southwest. Oñate promptly dispatched Captain Marcos Farfan de los Godos and a small party to investigate.

Guided by Hopi, Farfan encountered bands of Western Apache. They willingly took him to the mineral deposits which they had shown to Espejo in 1583, and which Luxán had pronounced worthless. Farfan's examination, however, showed them to be extremely rich, and after taking a number of ore samples, he hurried back to Oñate. His encouraging report and the display of samples, which contained silver, "reanimated every man in this camp, who were languishing for want of metals to smelt."

DECEMBER

The weather was bitterly cold, snow had fallen, and Juan de Zaldivar had not appeared as planned. For these reasons Oñate decided to postpone his journey to the South Sea until the spring. He had been on his way back to San Juan only a few days when he met several soldiers who were looking for him. They brought bad news.

Setting out with thirty men to overtake his uncle, as he had been ordered to do, Juan de Zaldivar had reached Acoma on December 1. His demands for maize, flour, turkeys, and blankets were refused, the Keres of Acoma pleading that they had furnished Oñate large amounts of these products only a short time before and could spare no more or they would be without sufficient necessities for the remainder of the winter. Zaldivar argued and threatened them for a day or two, then attempted to take the requested supplies by force. The Keres were not easily intimidated, and resisted. In the fighting Zaldivar and fourteen soldiers were killed.

Filled with fury and grief, Oñate wasted no time getting back to San Juan. The people of Acoma, he declared, must be punished, not only to avenge the death of his beloved nephew but to teach them and all other Indians the folly of defying the "Christian representatives of the Spanish King."

1599

JANUARY

Defying the extreme cold and deep snow, Vincente de Zaldivar rode at the head of seventy heavily armed men toward Acoma. His orders reveal the viciousness of Oñate. The Keres were to be allowed to negotiate a peace settlement, but this offer was a mockery. Oñate was confident that the Acomas would not agree to the extreme terms which Zaldivar would insist they accept. These were : (1) The Indians must leave their pueblo; (2) they must surrender and be taken to San Juan for trial; (3) all their possessions must be relinquished; (4) their homes were to be completely destroyed; (5) should they refuse these conditions they were to be attacked.

"If God should be so merciful as to grant us a victory," Oñate told Zaldivar, "you will arrest all of the people, young and old, without sparing anyone. Inasmuch as we have declared war on them without quarter, you will punish all those of fighting age as you deem best, as a warning to everyone in this kingdom. All of those you execute you will expose to public view . . . . If you should want to show lenience after they have been arrested, you should seek all possible means to make the Indians believe that you are doing so at the request of the friar with your forces. . . ."

Zaldivar gave no thought to leniency. He offered no peace terms. Within a few days after reaching Acoma he and his men, none of whom was killed, had systematically murdered eight hundred men, women, and children.

When at last the Keres begged for mercy, proffered payments of food, blankets, and clothing, and offered to surrender, Zaldivar ordered the prisoners brought out. One by one they were hacked to pieces with swords in view of all others, and their remains thrown off a cliff. Five hundred women and children and eighty men were taken prisoner and conducted under guard to San Juan. The pueblo of Acoma was demolished.

In San Juan Oñate pronounced the punishment the prisoners were to receive. Males over twenty-five years of age were to have a foot cut off and labor "in personal servitude" for twenty years. Younger males and all women were sentenced to lives of slavery. Girls under the age of twelve were awarded to Fray Alonso Martínez, who was to distribute them to Spanish families "in this kingdom or elsewhere," and young boys were made the property of Vincente de Zaldivar, who could do with them as he wished.

It is improbable that an Indian lived between California and the Great Plains, between Colorado and Mexico, who did not know of the slaughter at Acoma before rains had washed the bloodstains from the rubble of the Sky City.

JULY

With twenty-five soldiers, Vincente de Zaldivar set out to discover a route to the Gulf of California. He rode southward to the east of the Sandia Mountains to the country of the Jumano Tompiros, and found them rude and inhospitable. His requests for food and blankets were refused. Apparently because these Apache greatly outnumbered the few men he had with him, Zaldivar chose not to press his demands, but he sent a message to Uncle Oñate about the affront.

Zaldivar went on to the west, but little is known of his journey. Apparently it was long, for he reported that he passed through many warlike nations, such as the Apache, "who are very numerous and extend for more than two hundred leagues to the west." There seems no doubt that he encountered the Western Apache in the mountains of the Flagstaff region, as another soldier stated they met "Apaches, Cruzados, and Tepeguanes." The "Cruzados" were Yavapai and the "Tepeguanes" were Pima of the Gila River, both in southwestern Arizona.

Insolence to any Spaniard and refusal to pay tribute were two things the governor would not tolerate, and he led a strong force to the Jumano pueblos. When only a few blankets were given to him in compliance with his orders, he announced that he intended to punish those who had refused to give supplies to Zaldivar. He did more than that. One pueblo was fired, and as the occupants fled six were slain, numerous others were wounded by gunfire, and two captured leaders were hanged. Because he thought the interpreter had not translated his words correctly, he also had him executed. Then feeling satisfied that he had taught the Jumanos a lesson, he marched back to San Juan. All Oñate had accomplished was to intensify the hatred of the Jumanos for all white men.

* * *

The theory advanced by some scholars that the Apache entered the Southwest only a short time before the arrival of Coronado and his gold-mad bandits has been disproven not only by archaeology but by established facts pertaining to their economy. For a great many years before the middle of the sixteenth century the Apache maintained relationships with dominant Pueblo tribes, among them the Pecos, Tewa, Taos, Jemez, Picuris, Keres, and Zuñi. These friendly affiliations could not have been established in a brief period. The Apache were among the most enterprising traders of the entire southwestern region, ranking in this respect with the notably commercial-minded Hopi and Mojave. They maintained a flow of buffalo robes, antelope hides, dried meat, tallow, and leather products from the southern Great Plains to other tribes scattered through the length and breadth of the Rio Grande watershed, and even beyond it. Their trading missions took them deep into Mexico, southern Texas, and westward at least as far as the Little Colorado. In exchange for their goods they received turquoise and other semiprecious stones, ornaments of a variety of materials, maize, cotton blankets, paint pigments, wooden and pottery utensils, and coral and shells from the Pacific, the Gulf of California, and the Gulf of Mexico.

It should not be inferred from this knowledge that the Apache were only infrequently embroiled in warfare. As was the case with Indians of all regions, territorial intrusions, disputes over trading rights, and other grievances, both real and imagined, sent them on the warpath. Often they were in violent conflict with the Pawnee, other Plains tribes, and the Pima, Papago, and Sobaipuri in Arizona, all of whom were from time immemorial their traditional enemies.

Sometimes the Apache took sides in clashes between Pueblo tribes, but almost always for economic reasons. Trade was vital to their existence, and they sought to keep the channels of commerce free of barriers which intertribal strife inevitably created. In many violent controversies between the Pueblos, however, Apache support came more often in the form of diplomatic recognition than as actual physical assistance. The Pueblos themselves were obliged to do most of the fighting, while the Apache remained at ringside and cheered for their favorites. Nevertheless, their moral encouragement and their known ability as vicious warriors were not without effect on the combatants.

The Spanish, of course, would disrupt intertribal trade and seek to dominate it for their own gain. Before that happened, however, events transpired which would establish the course Apache history would follow for more than two hundred years.

THE
SEVENTEENTH
CENTURY

1601

S P R I N G *(Probably April)*

Five soldiers deserted and set out for Mexico. They had not gone far before the Jumano, who had been watching for a chance to retaliate against Oñate, killed two of them. The other three managed to escape and return to the capital, no doubt praying that Oñate would be merciful to them. What punishment they suffered is not known, but it is a matter of record that because of the slaying of the two deserters Oñate declared war on the Jumano, and sent Vincente de Zaldivar against them with a large force.

Zaldivar augmented the reputation he held as butcher of the Acomas. In six days of fighting he and his soldiers killed six hundred men, women, and children, destroyed three Jumano towns, and took four hundred prisoners. Each soldier was awarded a male Jumano as his personal slave.

J U N E

Oñate had orders from the viceroy to arrest Bonilla and Humana. When he started for Quivira he knew that Bonilla had been murdered, for the lone survivor of the Bonilla–Humana Expedition, the Indian servant Jusepe, had given him an account of the fight and the slaying. Oñate, however, had no information regarding the whereabouts of Humana—the rusty weapons on the Purgatoire had not yet been found. The only evidence he had, besides Jusepe's tale, that the Bonilla–Humana company had traveled northeast across the Great Plains were several of their campsites which Vincente de Zaldivar had reported finding on his 1598 trip to the Canadian River.

How much Oñate was influenced by the old myth that great treasures existed in Quivira is not known, yet he hardly would have undertaken such a long and difficult journey if he had not believed that something of value would be discovered in the plains province. It is possible, of course, that because of the lack of knowledge of the country to the north, he may have been anxious to learn, if he could, how far it extended. There are indications that he believed he might be able to open a route to the North Sea, an accomplishment that would have been of surpassing value to Spain, and which would have brought him great honors, if not monetary reward.

He took with him seventy men, two padres, and a number of Indian servants. Several large carts drawn by horses and mules were heavily laden with supplies, and they would be the first wheeled vehicles on the central Great Plains. Serving as guide was Jusepe.

JULY

The trail followed took them across the Pecos and Gallinas Rivers to a branch of the Canadian River. Here they "were met by some Indians of the nation called Apache, who welcomed us with demonstrations of peace. The governor . . . treated them generously, so that, although only a few came to meet us, within a short time men, women, and children flocked to our camp and confirmed their peaceful disposition by raising their hands to the sun, which is their sign of friendship. They brought us some small fruit, black and yellow, which abounds everywhere along that river. These were the size of small tomatoes and gave every indication of being healthful, for although we ate them without restraint no one suffered any ill effects."

AUGUST

Going on toward the northeast, the account of the journey—prepared by a "reliable and trustworthy person," probably one of the priests—states: "Occasionally we found rancherias inhabited by people of the Apache nation. . . . We had no trouble with them, even though we crossed their land, nor was there an Indian who ventured to harm us in the least, a favor of God our Lord, wherefore we never tired of praising and thanking Him."

The situation, however, would soon take a turn for the worse.

Somewhere on the plains along the Arkansas River, in Kansas, Indians were encountered to whom they gave the name *Escanjaques*, because this word—or one that sounded like it to Spanish ears—was spoken when "these natives raised the palms of their hands toward the sun, which is a sign of peace among them."

The identity of these people has never been conclusively established. The guide Jusepe informed Oñate that they did not speak the same tongue as the Vaqueros, but the possibility that he was hearing a peculiar dialect of the Athapascan language which he could not understand cannot be arbitrarily dismissed. Moreover, Jusepe found among the Escanjaques several men who were unquestionably Plains

Apache, for he was able to converse with them in the Apache speech with which he was familiar.

I do not maintain that the Escanjaques were Apache, for I do not know, but I think certain similarities between their way of life and that of the Vaquero should be noted. The Escanjaques, states one account, "did not plant or harvest, depending entirely for their food on the cattle. They were governed by captains, and being free men obeyed them but little. They had large quantities of skins which they wrapped around the body for clothing, but, as it was the hot season, the men went about almost stark naked and the women clad only from the waist down. Generally they used bows and arrows, with which they were very skillful." The houses of the Escanjaques were made of poles "about ten feet high placed in a circle. Some . . . were so large that they measured more than ninety feet across. Most of them were covered with tanned skins, which made them look like tents."

The Escanjaques were at war with people living farther to the east who can be identified as the Wichita. This fact and the location of the Escanjaques along the Arkansas River makes some ethnologists think they were either Kansa or Osage. Others suggest that they may have been Tonkawan who had wandered north from Texas, but if this be correct it should be pointed out that they must have been in the area where Oñate came upon them for a good many years. They were full-fledged buffalo-hunting Indians, and their customs did not indicate a former affiliation with tribes who practiced agriculture and dwelt in permanent villages.

When the Escanjaques learned that Oñate was looking for Humana, they assumed that he wished to punish the Indians responsible for killing him and his men, and they declared that the Wichita had staged the ambush. It had occurred, they said, not a great distance to the west. The Wichita had crept up on the Spaniards in the night, had set fire to the tall grass around their camp, and had slain them as they tried to escape the flames. There was a major flaw in this tale, but Oñate, having no information about the date of the incident, would not have recognized it. Humana and his men most certainly were wiped out in the late winter or early spring when the grass would not have been tall and dry. Starting a fire such as the Escanjaques described would have been impossible. Nor would it have been likely that a large band of Wichita would have been as far west as southeastern Colorado during planting time, when hunting was good at home, and there was need of replenishing storage bins depleted during the winter.

The lying of the Escanjaques is understandable. They were eager to get the Wichita, their bitter enemies, in trouble, and they urged Oñate to let them join in an attack on them. As a diplomat to Indians Oñate left a great deal to be desired. He rejected the offer of the Escanjaques and settled the problem by seizing one of them, placing him in chains, and forcing him to serve as a guide. As the Spaniards moved on toward the northeast, Escanjaques warriors trailed them, making no attempt to conceal their anger.

SEPTEMBER

The Wichita in some manner, probably through their own scouts, had been warned that the expedition was approaching, and was followed by a band of Escanjaques. When the first large Wichita village was reached it was found to be deserted, "but well stocked with fine corn." The Escanjaques came up and wanted to sack the town, which contained more than twelve hundred houses, but Oñate permitted them to take nothing but a little corn, and then "ordered them to return to their rancheria, which they did."

Some Wichita were captured during the next few days in the surrounding country. They frankly warned Oñate that the entire tribe was gathering for the purpose of fighting him, and threatened that as there were so many of them "they would dispose of us in short order and not allow anyone to escape."

Oñate called his aides into consultation, and it was agreed that "in view of the fact that the horses and mules were exhausted from so much travel, that the main purpose of our trip had been accomplished, that his majesty would be better served by learning of the greatness of this land . . . and since it would be folly for the few of us to go ahead where more than three hundred were needed, we all decided to present a petition to the governor, explaining the just causes for not proceeding any further." To which it should be added that Oñate's scouts had verified the fact that several thousand Wichita were gathered nearby, prepared to do battle, and that the Spaniards were not only frightened but were badly discouraged; they had seen nothing of value on the long and hard journey, nothing, as Castañeda had so succinctly stated sixty years before, but plains and sky.

Oñate turned back toward New Mexico, but his troubles were far from ended.

OCTOBER

When the expedition neared the rancherias of the Escanjaques, a contingent of twelve men was sent ahead to reconnoiter. Near an Escanjaques village two soldiers were wounded in an ambush, and the others narrowly escaped injury.

"In view of this treachery . . . the governor ordered all men to put armor on their horses, as they themselves were always ready . . . and the whole army marched forward, with express orders to enter the settlement peacefully. . . . Although they did so, and entered with the signs of peace . . . the Indians began to attack with great fury."

Advancing in a semicircle, some fifteen hundred Escanjaques showered arrows on the Spaniards. Many of them fell under the fire of the guns, but the places of the casualties were quickly filled by other bowmen. Oñate ordered a retreat, and his men moved back to a more advantageous position and reorganized, "but the battle continued, and the Indians became more determined than ever and carried on for more than two hours with great bravery, although much to their cost, as they experienced the fury of Spanish power."

The position of the Spaniards had become untenable, and ". . . with most of our people wounded . . . and seeing the savagery of our enemy, that they could not be frightened or deterred . . . even though many of them had been killed . . ." Oñate ordered another retreat and "released some women that the soldiers had taken prisoners . . . retaining only a few boys, at the request of the friars, to teach them our holy Catholic faith . . . with this we returned to our camp to spend the night."

The next morning, ". . . after dressing our wounds, we started out with our customary care . . ."—a way of saying that their route continued with all caution and diligence until they had come once more to the land of the Vaquero Apache.

NOVEMBER

Oñate reached San Gabriel, now his headquarters (the pueblo of Yunque, at the confluence of the Rio Grande and Chama River). He and his men had come perilously close to suffering the fate of the Humana party. However, in the official report sent to Mexico City the battle was termed a triumph for Oñate, but it contained the admission that the "victory was granted by God our Lord. Without His aid it would have been practically impossible, in view of the way the natives kept increasing in number. . . ." Besides the aid of the Lord, Oñate and his soldiers had enjoyed a large measure of good luck. For some unknown reason, the Escanjaques had chosen not to pursue them as they fled homeward.

1605

Reports of Oñate's maniacal cruelties, of the economic distress of the colony, and of bitter dissension between him and the colonists reached the viceroy. He forwarded them to Spain.

1606

The king directed that Oñate be removed.

1607

The royal decision had reached Oñate's ears before it was officially executed. He submitted his resignation.

1608

Oñate was still waiting to be officially recalled.

1609

Oñate's successor, Pedro de Peralta, finally arrived at San Gabriel. He moved the capital to Santa Fe.

1610

In Mexico City, Oñate and several of his chief lieutenants, among them his nephew, Vincente de Zaldivar, were tried, convicted, and severely punished for inflicting barbarities on the Indians, dereliction of duty, and sexual immorality.

But the penalties they suffered would not reshape the mold they had made and left behind them in New Mexico, the die they had cut for corrupt government, for injustice, for unconscionable social practices, and it would be used by every Spanish governor to hold office in Santa Fe during the next two centuries.

As for the Apache, they, too, would adopt a new way of life, a pattern which, if they were to survive, they dared not change.

* * *

The Apache realized the power, value, and usefulness of guns and horses long before they acquired them. Indeed, it seems unquestionable that all Indians of northern Mexico and the Southwest knew that such wonders existed within a short time after the Spanish had begun to push northward from central Mexico. Word of them would have been carried rapidly over the trails that were arteries of commerce and communication between the Pacific and the Rio Grande, between the Great Plains and the Gulf of California.

The Apache did not acquire any horses or usable guns from the early explorers who penetrated Apacheria. They came into possession of them slowly, over a period of many years, as Spanish settlements gradually tightened a circle about them.

In the latter half of the sixteenth century the mining, agricultural, and religious frontiers pushed into the most northern provinces of Mexico, and the Indians began their war against the invaders that would continue for decades. Although Indian slaves were brought north to work in the mines and on the ranches, there were never enough of them to supply the demand of the steadily expanding developments, and strong bands of slavers scoured the region for more captives. The Indians struck back with the only effective means they possessed—raiding the Spanish settlements, missions, and *estancias.* They ate most of the livestock taken, but not many years passed before these Indians were mounted, with the result that their striking and raiding power was immeasurably increased.

Tribe after tribe joined in the conflict as the frontier was advanced, and certainly by 1580, and perhaps as early as 1570, some Southern Apache had become involved. Thereafter the northern spread of the horse was exceedingly swift, and it was so greatly prized that Indians were raiding each other to acquire them. By 1600 the Apache in western Texas, notably the Jumano, possessed enough to merit being called Horse Indians. By this time, however, the Indians of Mexico could obtain horses in another way besides stealing them from the Spanish or from each other, for, according to one report, there were large numbers of them grazing on the vast ranges, "so many that they go wild in the country, without owner, which ones are called *cimarrones* . . . some that live all their lives without an owner."

The seventeenth century was not very old when the Spanish gave up hope of preventing Indians from acquiring horses. The situation was far beyond possible control, and they concentrated their efforts on the more important—but in itself extremely difficult—task of staying alive under the burden of almost constant raids made against them.

Actually, the Spanish were themselves responsible, in a large measure, for the rapidity with which the horse reached the Great Plains. As they continued to push northward—not only treasure hunters but trading expeditions as well—each year they abandoned more mounts or lost them in stampedes caused by buffalo, cougars, wolves, and marauding Indians. Perhaps before 1650, and undoubtedly in the next two decades, Spanish expeditions of various types had traveled north of the Platte River, and there is evidence indicating that a hundred and fifty years before the Lewis and Clark Expedition Spanish traders out of Mexico had ridden northward along the eastern base of the Rocky Mountains as far as southern Montana. There among the Kiowas they saw horses, but not very many. However, within another twenty years the people of the northern Great Plains also had become mounted Indians.

Quickly realizing their opportunity, the Apache of the southern Great Plains spared no effort to acquire large numbers of horses, and not many years had passed before they were masters of the supply. They not only owned great herds but they maintained a barrier through which they funneled the animals to other tribes in profitable trade. Their struggle to monopolize this commerce would be one of the causes of their downfall as rulers of the Southern Plains.

The ranges of the Apache Country—indeed, of almost all of the American West—was a natural home for the horse. The grass was nutritious and dependable. If it failed or was destroyed by fire in one place, it could usually be found growing luxuriantly in other places not far distant. Instinctively the horse migrated, like the buffalo, following the grass and the seasons. Carnivorous enemies took a comparatively small toll, for the horse was intelligent and swift, both means of self-protection, and when cornered was a vicious fighter.

The gun came to the Apache with the horse, but its adoption, for obvious reasons, followed at a much slower pace. The Apache owned immense numbers of horses before they owned firearms, at least firearms that could be discharged. A gun without powder and lead was not as good a weapon as a war club with a flint spike in it. Guns could be stolen or captured, but obtaining sufficient quantities of powder and lead was extremely difficult. Moreover, solving the mechanics of these marvels and developing skill in using them were not easily accomplished.

The horse was easier to understand and to use. It was an animal. It ate grass, and it left droppings, and its meat was edible, and its hide could be tanned, and it propagated and took care of itself. No explosive and fire were needed to make them operate. The gun did not come into general use in hunting or war, nor was it a prized article of barter, until after white traders introduced them in quantity, accompanied with a dependable supply of powder and lead. Even long after Americans had begun to push westward from the Mississippi, the Apache and other southwestern Indians continued to use the lance, the bow and arrow, the hatchet, and the club, their traditional weapons, in intertribal conflicts and in resisting the destroyers of their hunting grounds.

But, although the gun came into general use long after the horse, the changes it wrought were hardly less significant. The horse made it possible for the Indian to travel long distances in commerce and war. The gun let him kill and defend himself with power equal to that of his antagonists. The horse allowed him to increase the quantity of his personal possessions. A pack pony could pull a travois loaded with a large tepee, robes, and utensils, and at the same time could carry a squaw and several papooses. On trading missions this incomparably strong beast of burden could travel from dawn until dark with a heavy pack of furs, hides, and other commodities, and in the evening it would roll and drink and refresh itself on grass.

The horse was a cultural force with which only one instrument invented by man may be equated—the gun. For it was the gun which made it possible for the Indian to make fullest use of the horse.

Together, the horse and the gun would transform the handicapped Stone Age Apache warrior into one of the most formidable and skillful fighters and raiders the world has ever known.

As early as the 1560's the southern Apache were aware of the growing menace of Spanish slave-hunters. Francisco de Ibarra, a rich mine owner, became the first governor of Nueva Vizcaya in 1563, and during his tenure of nine years numerous contingents were sent out to take captives. They went into territory north of the Rio Conchos, perhaps very close to the present international border, and northeast to the Rio Grande. At least one of them penetrated into Texas after crossing the Rio Grande in the La Junta area. This was in the country of the Jumano, Mescalero, and Lipan Apache. As these people maintained strong trade relationships with Indians along the river and numbers of them usually were in the river pueblos it is quite possible the slavers encountered them, but whether any of them were taken prisoner is not known. In any case, they were apprised of the danger moving toward them.

Ibarra himself took a strong company as far north as the Casas Grandes region of Chihuahua in 1565, and came upon people they called "Querechos," the name Coronado had given to the Plains Apache he had found several hundred miles farther north. These people, of whom they saw a large number, were undoubtedly Athapascan, but whether they were Querechos is uncertain. It seems more likely that they were Suma Apache. However, they were well informed about the "cattle plains" and the Querechos to the north, and they possessed buffalo robes. Two factors, as noted by Forbes, may account for their being identified as Querechos. Both Ibarra and the chronicler of his expedition, Baltasar de Obregón, thought they were nearer to the Great Plains than they were. Another of Ibarra's aides, Francisco de Carvajal, had been with Coronado, and may have recognized cultural and racial similarities between the Indians of Casas Grandes and the Plains Apache. On this journey, Ibarra was more interested in discovering new mines than in taking captives, and the Suma apparently were unharmed by his incursion.

Similarly, the expeditions to New Mexico in the 1580's and 1590's, previously described, were after treasure, not slaves, and the Apache through whose territories they passed were not seriously molested. However, this was a situation that would not long endure after the colonization of New Mexico.

Since the time the Spaniards had first appeared in Apacheria, the Apache, with few exceptions, had made every effort to avoid open hostilities with them, and to maintain trade with them as well as with the Pueblos. Although this commerce had been frequently disrupted by the greediness of officials and the internal strife of the colony, the Apache had been able to keep from becoming involved in the bloody and tragic conflicts between other peoples and the Hispanic conquerors. Had they chosen the opposite course, that is, to harass the Spaniards at the countless opportunities open to them and to unite in force with the suffering Pueblos, the province of New Mexico would have a different history. Indeed, Spanish control of the Southwest not only would have been achieved with far greater difficulty than was the case but would have been long delayed. However, an amalgamation of this type would never take place.

Moreover, even before they took possession of the lands north of Mexico, the Spanish had learned a great deal about the nature of the Indians. They realized the importance of capitalizing on their inherent weaknesses. And not the least of these were the independence so greatly valued by each tribe, their pride in blood lines, their unwillingness to join together for the purpose of fighting a common foe, their inability to organize, their deeply rooted jealousies, their constant attempts to take booty from each other, and their eternal feuds based on causes more often imaginary than real. In these respects the Indians were their own enemy.

Spanish law decreed that only Indians captured in warfare were to be held as slaves. But it was easy to start a war, to provoke Indians into committing hostile acts. All slave-hunters had to do was to confiscate Indian property, shoot an old man or two, or perhaps fire a village, and any retaliation by the victims could be termed an act of war and make them subject to capture and enslavement. Ibarra's lieutenant, Obregón, had clearly stated the policy of the invaders of Indian lands. A history written by another Obregón quotes him as saying: "Advantage should be taken of the enemy by setting those of one district against the opponents of another." The Spanish had much to gain and little to lose by fomenting Indian hostilities. Yet, every governor, priest, and military officer who served in New Mexico would falsely proclaim that his greatest hope, if not his only goal, was to establish peace and prosperity among all Indians under the tenets of Christianity.

The Apache learned the truth the hard way, and they never forgot it.

* * *

1627

SPRING

A large band of Plains Apache (Lipan) arrived in Santa Fe on a trading mission. Much to the delight of a padre, some of them admired a statue of the Virgin they saw in a chapel and expressed an interest in learning something of the Catholic religion. Then, as the priest would sadly relate, "the demon had recourse to one of the wiles he is accustomed to employ . . . choosing as his instrument the greed of our Spanish governor. . . ."

The governor was Felipe Zotylo. He conspired with a Pueblo headman whom he knew held a grudge against the Apache to organize and lead a surprise attack on their camp. The scheme was successful. More than a score of the friendly Apache, among them a chieftain, were killed, and perhaps twice that number were taken prisoner. The governor had intended to sell them as slaves, but priests and other Pueblos registered such furious protests that he was obliged to free the captives.

One padre who publicly condemned the governor for his treachery stated that the raid "provoked a revolt throughout the entire province." It did more than that.

Peace with the Spanish, a condition the Apache of New Mexico had striven to maintain in the face of repeated provocations for nearly ninety years, was no longer possible. Temporary disruptions of their commerce, swindling by traders and officials, and even the occasional confiscation of their goods were acts which the Apache had felt they could endure, injustices that they could learn to prevent without resorting to extreme violence, but slavery and wanton murders could be neither forgiven nor forgotten.

For the first time the Plains Apache sent word through the Southwest that they would henceforth wage unrelenting, all-out warfare against the conquerors of New Mexico. And it was soon raging on every front of eastern Apacheria. Although the conflict would be marked with periods of quiet during which the Apache, for reasons best known to themselves, would curtail their aggressions, the peaceful intervals would be deceptive in their appearance. If the fire of revenge burning in Apache blood was occasionally reduced to smoldering, it would never be extinguished.

1629

Fray Alonso Benavides was ministering temporarily in Santa Clara, a Tewa pueblo on the upper Rio Grande and close to the country inhabited by the Jicarilla Apache.

He had been a religious in the New World for more than three decades. Since 1621 he had held the office of Father Custodian of the province of New Mexico. Now he was thinking of returning to Mexico City, where he had been ordained and had long served, "to finish my days there if He will allow me to do so."

During his residency in New Mexico he had traveled extensively, and he had prepared a comprehensive report—he called it a "memorial" —for the king in which he described and located almost every Indian tribe of the province and recounted in detail the missionary work undertaken in his vast jurisdiction. He had demonstrated his own courage by assigning to himself the perilous task of attempting to propagate the gospel among the remote and purportedly savage Apache of the upper Gila River.

The locations in which Benavides placed the numerous Apache divisions—he included the Navajo—makes it clear that New Mexico was virtually surrounded by Athapascans. He spoke of them as "the huge Apache nation," declaring that "without exaggeration, it alone has more people than all the nations of New Spain put together." This, of course, was an absurd statement, for the Indian population of Mexico was no less than fifty times greater than that of the entire province of New Mexico. Nevertheless, the Apache occupied positions that were both economically and militarily advantageous to them.

Since the founding of the colony three decades earlier, attempts to win converts among the Apache had brought almost no success, and Benavides was understandably profoundly aggravated and disappointed. Now that the blunders and brutality of civil officials had created a schism which gave every indication of being irreparable he was not only deeply grieved but angered. However, he did not choose to place all blame for the distressing situation on the persons most responsible for it—the Spanish governors. He criticized them, but he also invoked the mitigating circumstance that the Apache were heathens manifestly unwilling to save their own souls through spiritual regeneration. He wrote of them, not entirely without praise but with some inaccuracy, that they were "a people very fiery and bellicose, and very crafty in war. Even in the method of speaking they show a difference from the rest of the nations. For these speak rather softly and deliberately, and the Apaches seem fairly to break their heads with the [spoken] word. They do not dwell in settlements, nor in houses, but in tents and huts, forasmuch as they move from mountain range to range, seeking game, which is their sustenance. However, each hut of a principal or individual has its recognized land on which they plant corn and seeds." Here he was making no distinction between the true Plains Apache and those in the south and west who were more sedentary and who engaged to some extent in farming.

Succumbing to more generalizations, he said: "They go clad in *gamuzas*, which are the skins of deer, very well tanned and adorned in their fashion, and the women gallantly and honestly clad. They have no more idolatry than that of the Sun, and even that is not general to all of them; and they scoff much at the other nations which have idols. They are wont to have as many wives as they can support; and upon her whom they [find] in adultery they irremissibly execute their law, which is to cut off her ears and nose. They are very obedient to their elders and hold them in great respect. They teach and chastise their children, which is a difference from the other nations, who have no chastisement whatever." This is contrary to numerous other accounts, which speak of Apache parents as showing patience and kindness toward their children.

In delineating the country of the Apache, Benavides permitted rumors to guide him more than known facts, for he declared that its southern boundary extended from the plains of Texas to the Pacific Ocean, and to the north the Apache domain "hits the Strait of Anian" (the illusive waterway believed to extend from the Atlantic to the Pacific through the Arctic region).

Benavides concluded his remarks with the ludicrous assertion that because of their bellicosity the Apache were a "crucible for the courage of the Spaniards," and that the Apache not only held the Spaniards in high esteem but "say that only the Spaniards merit the title of people, and that the nations of settled Indians do not."

Although scientifically valuable in many respects, the memorial of Benavides contains the elasticity of a propaganda document. He was campaigning to have more priests sent to New Mexico, and he consistently overstated the number of Indians to be converted and the number of towns in need of resident padres. If a historian can find no justification for his rash claims, it is possible to understand his reasons for making them. He was gazing hopefully into far-distant realms in which he envisioned countless souls to be saved, and, obviously, if no one could delineate the boundaries of New Mexico with even reasonable accuracy, no one could state with certainty how many Indians inhabited it.

It had been his hope for some time to capture an Apache warrior— preferably a Navajo—"but having seen that I could not catch one, to regale him and send him again to his land to tell his captains that I wished to treat for peace, I adventured and determined to send to them twelve Indians of my Christians. . . . I called the captains and the old men of the [Santa Clara] pueblo, and communicated to them the desire I had . . . and that we might by this road attain their conversion, which was my principal end."

Benavides thought—or at least he pretended that he thought—he was sending the Santa Clara delegation to carry his message to the Apaches de Navajo, who had rejected all missionary overtures made to them. It would have been a feather in his own miter if he could succeed, even to a small extent, where his colleagues had failed. He stated that his emissaries went to the Navajos ". . . with very great courage and spirit . . . God knoweth the constriction in which my heart was, seeing the manifest risk in which I was putting those Indians."

It was a dramatic, if somewhat unbelievable, episode that Benavides related for the Spanish sovereign. In it, however, he used the names Navajo and Apache indiscriminately, an unfortunate habit of other Spanish writers of the time, even though the two tribes, because of their contrasting ways of life, were considered to be distinct peoples and were so treated officially by the provincial government.

Benavides does not state the direction taken by the Tewas on their mission, nor does he intimate how far they went, but he does say that the Navajos lived only a day's journey away from Santa Clara, which was certainly untrue for persons traveling on foot, and most improbable even if the Tewas were mounted, which is unlikely, for Pueblos were prohibited from owning horses by the Spanish. To reach the Navajos the Tewas would have had to cross the rugged Jemez Mountains to the west. Moreover, Santa Clara had suffered from Navajo raiders. It seems irresponsible to accept the assertion that the dozen messengers would have walked into the country of people who had inflicted serious losses on them and had taken away Tewa women and children as captives.

But Benavides wanted a Navajo, and he claimed that the Tewas returned with not one but four.

They were undoubtedly Jicarilla, whom the Tewas easily could have reached by going up the Rio Grande to the vicinity of Taos. If Benavides were disappointed, he did not admit it. After all, the Jicarilla were Apache. Why be fussy about a small matter of identity and spoil a good story that would enhance his own record as a zealous servant of God? And that Benavides was. Assuredly the king, when he got around to reading Benavides's tale, was pleased. It was one of the most encouraging reports to come out of New Mexico.

The Tewa embassy had moved cautiously into the country of "that untamed and ferocious nation," and when in sight of a rancheria they signaled that they came in peace. Told that they might safely proceed, ". . . they went drawing nearer, although slowly and with mistrust." An Apache captain came forward and they delivered Benavides's message and gave him a packet of tobacco and a rosary. Having never seen a rosary, the Apache "asked what it signified that the thread had so many beads." It meant, explained the Tewas, that Fray Benavides was sending "word that he would be his friend." Putting the rosary about his neck, the Apache declared that he welcomed peace, but it was apparent to the Tewas that "he was suspicious that they might have some double dealing." To be certain that no trickery was involved, the Apache announced that "he would come and see us in our pueblo."

Here is an illustration of the haughtiness and boldness of the Apache. Despite the perilous situation, a captain—Benavides did not supply his Indian name—dared to go with only three companions to a pueblo that had been subdued and was controlled by the Spaniards. One wonders why they took the chance, for they had no assurance that they would not be killed or captured and sent into slavery, except the verbal promise of a padre that they would not be harmed—not to be depended upon under the prevailing conditions.

Excited and overjoyed by the way things had worked out, Benavides gathered "one thousand five hundred souls" to welcome the important guests. In order to assemble a throng of this size he would have been obliged to draw them from several pueblos. The population of Santa Clara was no more than three hundred.

The little Santa Clara church was suitably decorated, and "next to the altar I ordered a chair set upon a rug." Seated there he received them. Solemn and impressive ceremonies followed. A Pueblo Indian presented his bow and arrows to the Apache captain, declaring that "before God, who was on that altar . . . he gave those weapons in earnest of his word that he would never break the peace. . . ." Not to be outdone, the Apache proffered one of his own arrows with the pledge ". . . to that God, whoever he may be, I likewise give my word and faith, in the name of all my people . . . and that for my part and that of my people the peace and friendship shall never fail." Bells were rung and trumpets were sounded and hymns were sung, to the delight of everyone.

If he made it, one statement of the Apache captain is particularly significant. He informed Benavides that he wished to establish the "same peace with the Spaniards" that his people had with the Taos. The Jicarilla lived in close proximity to pueblos of the Taos.

However, not everything went smoothly. Try as he did, the Apache was unable to see the God which he had been told was on the altar. The explanation of Benavides that God would not be visible to him until he had been baptized was unsatisfactory, and he retorted that he "already took himself for a Christian," and therefore "he also wished to see Him." The argument ended by the Apache being asked to leave while Benavides sang mass. He went out in high dudgeon, but after a good meal and perhaps a few drinks his temper cooled, although he remained "very vexed, because he wished to have seen God in the mass."

When he found out that Benavides "was named Alonso, he said that I should give him permission to be named so. I told him that he should be named when he should be baptized." The Apache saw no reason to delay the matter. He took the name, and "from that moment the Tewas all called him Don Alonso."

Upon departing for his home the Apache promised to return in a few weeks with a large number of his people and many gifts "to make a big fair . . ." and that thenceforth not only would all Pueblos be welcome to hunt in his country but peace between the Apache and the Spaniards would exist, "and so it was."

So it was not.

Although he understood it very well, Benavides did not trouble to tell his readers that no Apache, no matter what his rank or position, could speak for all Apache or even for all the people of his own division. No Apache possessed the authority to negotiate single-handedly a treaty of peace. Like many western Indian tribes, the Apache maintained an almost pure democracy. Except on military campaigns or raids for plunder, decisions reached in councils ruled them, not chiefs. Although in many bands chieftainships were hereditary, most leaders were appointed, but in either case prerogatives could be rescinded. There was no permanent supreme governing body. Exigencies of the moment influenced policies, and every group or division had the power to act independently of all others.

The Apache captain who went to Santa Clara knew that every pledge he made was open to rejection by his own people and could have no influence on the actions of other Apache bands. He realized as well that there was no hope of a lasting peace between the Apache and the Spaniards. It is probable that for more than any other reason he had gone to Santa Clara to spy under the aegis of a truce proffered by a religious. He might have hoped that he could learn something of Spanish strength in the area, for not much time would pass before the Jicarilla would be raiding Spanish ranches and settlements in New Mexico. Yet he had been no more deceitful or hypocritical than his host. Benavides could not have been unaware of the futility of the show he staged. Unquestionably it bolstered his ego and gave him spiritual satisfaction, but he fully understood that no single effort of his own could bridge the chasm that his own people, falsely acting in the name of God, had created between the Apache and Spanish worlds.

* * *

1630

The Spanish population of Santa Fe was less than two hundred and fifty, yet these persons owned more than seven hundred Indian slaves. Children of mixed blood were not counted in any census, but reports indicate that the capital and its environs swarmed with them. Benavides had been pleased to inform the king that the Santa Fe presidio was not supported by "pay from your royal coffers, but by making the soldiers *encomenderos* of those pueblos."[8]

In the southern part of the province travel over the main road from Mexico along the Rio Grande was made extremely hazardous by mounted bands of Apache marauders. Caravans were attacked with regularity, and large numbers of livestock and quantities of supplies and equipment were lost. The dangers were not as great either to the west of the road, in the realm of the Gila Apache, or to the east of it, in the Plains Apache country. The reasons may be ascertained.

Most Western Apache were remote from any main routes of travel. If Benavides can be believed, he had a favorable encounter with some Gila who lived "fourteen leagues from the pueblo of San Antonio de Senecue, of the province of the Piros." This Apache rancheria was probably in the Sierra Magdalena, which marked the eastern boundary of Gila territory.

The enterprising padre recounted that a Gila leader, whom he called Sanaba, had come several times to hear him preach at Senecue, and had expressed a profound interest in Christianity. One day Sanaba arrived with a group of Gila and "ordered a servant to unloose a little bundle he was carrying, and took out from it a doubled-up *gamuza*, which is a tanned deerskin, and presented it to me. . . . I said to him that he already knew that I did not wish that they should give me anything; that what I desired of them was solely that with all their heart they should adore the Lord of Heaven and Earth. And smiling, Sanaba said to me, that I should undouble the deerskin and see what it contained. . . . I did so, and saw that it was very white and large; and painted in the middle of it was a sun of green color, with a cross on top; and below the sun was painted the moon in gray color with another cross on top. . . . I asked Sanaba what the painting signified."

Through an interpreter Sanaba explained that until this time the Gila Apache had considered the sun and moon their greatest benefactors, "but now that you have taught us that God is the Creator of the sun and of the moon and of all things, and that the Cross is the token of God, I ordered them to paint the Cross over the sun and over the moon." It was a gesture that made Benavides cry out with joy and thankfulness.

One of the Piro pueblos had been destroyed a short time before, and Benavides found its former residents wandering homelessly in the hills. He does not identify the attackers, stating simply that the town "had been depopulated through wars with other nations who burned it." Obviously the Gila were not guilty, as they were present among the Piro, and some of the homeless were living with them in the mountains. The most likely suspects are the Jumano Apache, who lived to the east, and the Manso Apache, who inhabited the El Paso region to the south. Both of these groups are known to have engaged in bitter trading quarrels with the Piro.

Although the Apache had made it clear that they were avowed enemies of white men, some of the Plains bands in eastern New Mexico and the panhandles of Texas and Oklahoma were still inclined to favor their old policy of avoiding the Spanish who made *entradas* into their territories. Behind this attitude was their loathness to give up entirely the lucrative trade which they had enjoyed for so long with the Pueblos, and they continued to take caravans to towns on the Rio Grande as often as possible. However, these journeys were far from safe for them at any time, and often they were forced to confine their missions to pueblos close to the western perimeter of the plains. Preferring barter to bloodshed, they displayed no belligerency when they found Spanish traders waiting to deal with them in such places as Pecos Pueblo for the valuable buffalo products. They completed their business, and vanished into the sea of grass.

The situation steadily deteriorated, not only for the Plains Apache but for the Pueblos who so badly needed any merchandise they could acquire to help them pay the tribute demanded of them. Captives in their towns, the Pueblos had become the main source of supply for the Spaniards. Without their forced labor and the expropriation of their farm products and the goods they manufactured, there would have been no colony, for the settlers could not have produced sufficient food and articles to sustain themselves and at the same time have borne the cost of raids by the Navajo.

Throughout the first four decades of the seventeenth century, had the Spaniards been smart enough they could have enjoyed commerce with the Apache, and lived in moderate comfort in spite of the onslaughts of the Navajo. With fair treatment they might even have succeeded in establishing peace with the raiders who swept upon them from western New Mexico. Instead they brought down their own economic roof by fighting among themselves. The basic causes of this catastrophe were the greed of both the Franciscans and the civil authorities, and each faction's consuming, irrepressible jealousy of the authority of the other.

The Plains Apache were cautious observers. Through the regimes of a series of governors, they watched the controversy between white men steadily become more bitter, until at last it had degenerated into actual violence. Still the Plains Apache sought to stay out of the fighting, taking no advantage of the unprecedented opportunity being afforded them. Had they chosen at this time to unite with the Navajos and Pueblos, the colony of New Mexico would have been obliterated.[9]

* * *

Two carriers were made for Apache babies, a temporary one at the time of the baby's birth, and a permanent one three months or so afterward. To make the baby comfortable a soft bedding of shredded bark or crumpled grass was placed on the face of the carrier. Over this bedding was laid the tanned, spotted hide of a fawn, the hair side up, or at times the skins of cottontail rabbits. The baby was then placed on this, and between its legs for a diaper was put soft, shredded bark. Another fawn skin, hair side in, was laid over it, the edges tucked in about the baby's body and up under its feet. It was then laced into the carrier with a strip of buckskin.

The baby's head was pillowed on Abert squirrel or sometimes a piece of beaver fur. The latter was thought to keep all sickness from the baby, for "Beaver" had power. Various things designed either to amuse the baby or to act as charms were attached to the hood. Sometimes the beard from the breast of a turkey cock was fastened where the baby could watch it swinging back and forth, or the turkey beard, the tail of an Abert squirrel, and the striped cones from the western yellow pine (thrown to the ground by these squirrels) were tied together and hung inside the hood of the carrier, near the baby's head. The squirrel tail was to make a baby a good climber, the striped pine cones so that it would not be injured in falling from trees, and the turkey beard merely for ornament. If the claw of a bear could be obtained, it might also be tied on the inside of the wooden part of the hood. This kept all sickness away because "Bear" has great power. Pieces of oriole's nest were likewise used to bring good luck, as it was believed they were composed of every known species of tree. Other objects tied to the hood were stone arrowpoints and bits of prehistoric shell beads or bracelets, all safeguards against disease or accident.

When the end of the navel cord dried up and dropped from the newborn baby, it was wrapped in downy turkey feathers or a small piece of buckskin and tied to the wooden part of the hood, inside and to either right or left of the baby's head. Later, the mother unwrapped this and, if the baby was a boy, buried it in a deer track to make him a good hunter.

When the baby's first temporary carrier was discarded for the permanent one, it was hung up on a tree. It was not supposed to be touched. Before it rotted and fell apart, the baby would be old enough to have the mother show it to him in the tree. She would tell the child: "Here is what you were in when you were a baby." If a baby had been sick in its permanent carrier, the carrier would be discarded, but if the baby had been exceptionally well in it the permanent carrier would be kept and used for as many as two succeeding babies.

A permanent carrier that was no longer to be used also was put away in a tree. A mother would take the carrier to the east side of a young tree. If the child were a girl, this was usually some food-bearing tree such as piñon, so that she would gather much wild plant food when she grew up. The mother removed the baby and hung the carrier high up on the east side of the tree, saying, as she did so, "Here is the baby-carrier. I put this on you, young and still growing. I want my child to grow up as you do."

When a mother could bear no more children, she hung the carrier up in thick brush, praying to it, "You have raised my children safely, so look after them from now on."

A special type of little buckskin shirt was worn by infants after they outgrew their carriers. This had a long, loose belt of buckskin attached about the waist and hanging down in back, by which the child could be lifted and slung over the shoulder of the mother, and, in later times, from the horn of a saddle.[10]

* * *

1639

The commercial-minded Plains Apache were forced to abandon their preferred position as noncombatants by the crimes of Governor Luis de Rosas. He had been in office in Santa Fe only a short time when it became clear that he had come to New Mexico with only one purpose in mind, and that was to get rich without undue delay. This was, of course, not a unique attitude, but Rosas's methods were extraordinarily stupid as well as cruel.

Accusing the Franciscans of attempting to gain monopolies of all Indian labor, the slave trade, and all wealth in the province, he threw several padres in jail. One of his next moves was to appear in a number of pueblos and order the inhabitants to disobey the fathers. The result was that some pueblos revolted and murdered both priests and Spaniards stationed in them. People in other towns began to assist the Navajo in making off with cattle and horses belonging to the missions. Rosas made no effort to punish the rebels, but sent soldiers to confiscate their possessions, and he took a large number of Pueblo children to be sold into slavery.

Forced to abandon their stations to save their own lives, the padres fortified themselves in Santo Domingo. In retaliation they adopted Navajo tactics, and conducted raids against the herds and ranches controlled by the governor and the colonists loyal to him. Chaos followed, with a three-pronged war raging in the colony, the Navajo raiding all Spanish establishments, the priests and the governor plundering each other, the confined and starving Pueblos striking where and when they could.

Next Rosas turned his attention to the Plains Apache. Informed that these people came regularly to trade in Pecos, he went there "loaded with knives" with the announced intention of exchanging them for buffalo robes. His real purpose was to capture Apache women and children to be sold in Mexico. Not an Apache was to be found in Pecos. In fact, many of the inhabitants had vanished from the town. Seething with anger, Rosas blamed a priest who happened to be there with warning the Apache of his approach and took him to Santa Fe in chains.

Rosas sent a strong band of men to take captives among the Apache on the Great Plains. The invaders enlisted the aid of Indians who were at war with the Vaquero (probably either Osage or Wichita), but this time the Vaquero put up a stubborn fight, instead of adopting the tactic of moving away they had previously used. A contemporary report stated that in the conflict the invaders "killed a great number of the said friendly Apaches . . . and they captured them [also] in this unjust war, and they took them to sell in Nueva Vizcaya . . . the people of Pecos have made a great demonstration of feeling in regard to this, because they were living with the Apaches and with them they had their commerce, by means of which they clothed themselves and paid their tributes."

Rosas had inflicted irreparable damage on the trade which the colonial merchants had been enjoying with the northern Apache, despite the strained relationship, and because of his attack on the Vaquero "the Apache nation remained with hatred and enmity towards the Spaniards." The grossness of this understatement was demonstrated a short time later when a party led by a Captain González attempted to trade with some Apache they called "Sumanas" in western Texas. They were attacked and forced to make a hasty departure from the area. In a running fight, González's son-in-law, Diego García, was killed. Thus the Apache warpath was now continuous all the way from Mexico to Kansas.

To escape from the *encomiendas* and factories which both priests and civil officials had established, hundreds of Pueblos found refuge among the Navajo and both the Eastern and Western Apache. The Taos revolted, and killed several Spaniards. Fearing Spanish retaliation, they abandoned their pueblos and fled to their friends, the Apaches of southeastern Colorado and western Kansas. They were welcomed, not only because they were allies but also because they brought with them a considerable herd of horses, which the Apache were making every effort to acquire in large numbers. In this area, called El Cuartelejo, the Taos built new towns. They would occupy them for a number of years before the Spanish military was able to force all of them to return to their ancient dwellings on the Rio Grande.

Indications of the situation existing in the region of the High Plains at the time have been unearthed by archaeologists. The ruins of the Taos towns in El Cuartelejo have been found, and the sites of villages, or rancherias, occupied by Apache have been discovered in western Kansas, western Nebraska, and eastern Colorado.* While the Apache still depended primarily on hunting for their existence, some of them had begun to grow maize, beans, and squash, crops the Taos, as well as the Quivira tribes to the east, cultivated. The finding of shards of Taos pottery in Wichita diggings, and pieces of Wichita shell-tempered pottery in Taos and Apache sites, suggests intertribal trading between these enemies. It would appear that at the time of the Taos exodus—if not before and afterward—at least some of the Apache bands were at peace with the Quiviras. Otherwise, the movement of trade goods could not have occurred, for the Apache were still in control of the High Plains from eastern New Mexico and Texas as far north as western Nebraska.

1641

Juan Flores de Sierra y Valdez arrived in Santa Fe to replace Rosas, but a short time later died. Although he was officially out of office, Rosas had not yet left for Mexico. The colony was without a governor. Taking advantage of this situation, the Franciscans stormed back into the capital, assumed control of the provincial government, clapped Rosas in prison, and plotted his death. Arrangements were made with a Señora Ortiz to be found by her spouse committing adultery with Rosas in his cell. Although Rosas was purportedly under guard, the

---

*The Athapascan sites have been termed Dismal River Culture.

allegedly outraged husband was permitted to enter the cell in the night and murder him.

1642

When Governor Alonso Pacheco de Heredia took office he made no effort to punish Rosas's slayer, but he drove the priests from political office and hanged eight Spaniards known to have supported their revolutionary *cabildo*.

Pacheco issued an order forbidding Pueblos to travel from one town to another without a license, and he doubled the taxes and tribute all Indians were required to pay. More Pueblos fled the country, going both westward to the Navajo and eastward to the Apache. Under the forceful restrictions, conditions steadily became worse.

1644

When Governor Pacheco left office, out of the one hundred and fifty pueblos occupied when Oñate founded the colony only forty-three contained inhabitants.

On the other hand, the population, prosperity, and power of the Apache throughout the province were increasing. The runaway Pueblos brought them new skills, military manpower, and intelligence regarding Spanish settlements, ranchos, defenses, and activities. Also, they were steadily acquiring horses and guns.

The Apache now thought it possible to put into operation a policy that had been debated in their councils for some time, but which they had been unable to act upon because of insufficient resources. Although it was a policy adopted independently by the many groups and bands—there was no representative government to initiate it and command its adoption—it soon would be universally applied, and it cemented the Apache both politically and militarily to a degree previously unknown.

It was a policy of retaliation and aggression, but its progenitors were endogenous compulsion, innate defiance, inherent pride, and sheer necessity. The Apache had come to understand that their only hope of survival was self-protection through attack, destruction, theft, and killing—their only means of defense was in offense.

They urged the Pueblos to rise, and offered to help them by attacking Spanish supply trains, traders, and ranchos. Their overtures were only partially successful.

1650

Governor Hernando de Ugarte y la Concho was informed that the Tewa, Keres, and Jemez were conspiring to revolt, were in league with the Navajo and Apache, and had "turned over to them in the pastures the droves of mares and horses belonging to the Spaniards, which are the principal nerve of warfare. They have already agreed with the said apostates to attack in all districts on the night of Holy Thursday, because the Spaniards would then be assembled."

Quick action by Governor Ugarte prevented the first organized Pueblo uprising from succeeding. Nine of the leading conspirators in Isleta, Alameda, San Felipe, Cochiti, and Jemez were captured and hanged, and several score persons from these towns were sentenced to serve ten years as slaves.

1659

Governor López de Mendizábal took office. The fire of the bitter feud between the priests and the civil authorities had abated somewhat, but he had been in Santa Fe only a brief time when he managed to fan the smoldering coals into flame.

López was openly anticlerical. The priests were attempting to halt all native religious ceremonials. López told the Indians to conduct their own rites whenever they desired. When the Franciscans started to rebuild the church at Taos which had been destroyed, López appointed a Taos Indian who had murdered a padre to be the governor of the pueblo. Fray Luis Martínez was sent to serve in Taos, but López told the Taos not to obey him, and charged that after raping an Indian woman Fray Martínez had cut her throat.

López quickly made his own reputation as a slaver. Although he had his eyes on the Navajo, his first quarry was the Apache. Perhaps it was carelessness on the part of the Apache that made his initial raid against them successful. Without fanfare he sent "squadrons of men to capture the heathen Apache [in eastern New Mexico]." The raiders "took many and sent them to the *reales* and mines [in Mexico] . . . to sell."

Some histories erroneously credit American military officers with having conceived the tactic of using friendly Indians to aid them in frontier warfare, the theory being that "only redskins understand the ways of redskins and can track them down." Two centuries before any American reached New Mexico, Indians themselves made it possible for the Spanish to enjoy this strategic advantage. Realizing the futility of defying the Spanish military, and with the hope of bettering their own lot, some Pueblos had volunteered to aid the Spanish in fighting and capturing Apache and Navajo. The Spanish were quick to understand the value of such assistance and provided horses, weapons, and supplies—and in some instances material rewards—for their Indian allies. Moreover, the plan was in accord with their policy, previously mentioned, of "setting tribe against tribe," which had been adopted for the purpose of preventing Indians from uniting to attack them.

The assistance they gave the Spanish benefited the Pueblos little, if at all. The Spanish usually confiscated all booty obtained, and sold all prisoners taken for their own profit. Exploitation of all Indians was their paramount motive, and no amount of friendship could weaken their greed. In the end, the Pueblos lost far more than they gained in their collaboration, for they not only became enemies of both the Apache and Navajo but the towns from which they came were special targets of Apache and Navajo raiders.

1661

Governor Diego de Peñalosa came upon the New Mexico stage to make his contribution to the calamitous conditions. Besides continuing the slave raids against so-called enemy Indians—meaning Apache and Navajo—and exacting tribute from the impoverished Pueblos, Peñalosa attempted to halt all intertribal trading. It was his theory that if commercial intercourse between tribes could be stopped they would not have an opportunity to plot against the Spanish. His real goal was to force the Apache to cease their attacks and to enter into trading pacts with him, whereby he could gain personal control of the flow of products produced on the plains. He also thought that if he could establish a commercial treaty with the Apache they would aid him in obtaining slaves from the tribes of Quivira. The scheme appeared to him to contain no insurmountable ramifications, but as things turned out it was not as simple as he was himself. Before he left office, the Apache, as well as the Navajo, had increased their attacks throughout the colony to such an extent that travel on any road, except by a large military force, was completely unsafe.

1665

Governor Fernando de Villanueva not only inherited from Peñalosa a land through which warfare raged but one which was stricken in many parts by famine. The normal exchange of food and commodities, upon which most people greatly depended, had been almost completely disrupted. The Apache, living on the Great Plains and in the mountains where game was always available, suffered little, but the Pueblos were prisoners in their own towns, and hundreds of them were dying of starvation. Also, a mysterious disease swept through New Mexico with devastating effect, killing both people and livestock.

Still the disastrous situation did not keep the Apache, Navajo, and Pueblos from continuing to plan for a united revolt. It was as if death and devastation were acting as fertilizer on the seeds of rebellion. To the east the Plains Apache maintained a strong defensive barrier, as did the Navajo to the west. The Gila and other Western Apache groups formed a strong front across the middle south and the southwest. The Apache of the Southern Plains and the El Paso region controlled the front east of the Rio Grande. The states of northern Mexico, Nueva Vizcaya, Coahuila, and Sonora were aflame with war. Bands from the north and the Apache inhabiting the Mexican regions ceaselessly raided Spanish settlements, missions, and ranchos. The military were unable to halt them, even though flying squadrons *(compañía volante)* of cavalry were organized for the purpose.

The fuse of revolt had been ignited, and neither Villanueva, the governors of the Mexican states, nor the military were able to extinguish it. They did their best, killing scores of Indians in battle, executing others suspected of plotting against the king and the Catholic faith, selling hundreds of captives into slavery, but to no avail.

1671

The Apache began an attempt to keep more Spaniards from entering New Mexico. They made their first strike against Governor Juan de Miranda as he was on his way to Santa Fe. The train with which Miranda was traveling up the Rio Grande road was largely destroyed and his livestock driven off by "a horde of Apache." Enough horses were saved to get him and his aides to the capital, but he was a badly shaken man. His efforts to strike back by sending out military contingents brought almost no results. A few Apaches were killed, but the burning of churches, the stealing of livestock, the murdering of civilians and priests continued throughout the vast region from Mexico to Kansas.

* * *

The refusal of most Apache to open their territories to priests who wished to establish missions was reason enough for a governor to declare them "heathen enemies." Under the designation they could legally be attacked, captured, and sold into slavery. Some officers and officials who conducted raids against them, not in defense of the colony but solely for the purpose of taking marketable captives, sought to amplify the justification for their actions by reporting that the Apaches were carrying off Pueblo converts to "cook and eat them." Under Spanish laws cannibals were subject to enslavement. If the dealers in human beings could make it appear that the Apache were eating "Christianized" natives, there would be even less chance of their being accused of waging unjust warfare against Indians. There was no proof whatsoever to support such a charge, and as intolerant and deficient in judgment as the high councils of the Spanish Government were, they never accepted it as having any basis in reality.

While taking captives in conflict was universally regarded as an achievement deserving of the highest praise, except in a few regions true slavery was not a common practice of Indians. Enemy prisoners were legitimate and valued spoils of war, and all tribes sought to obtain them, but only a few sought to hold them and to benefit from their labors. Some peoples, especially several inhabiting northeastern America, inflicted hideous tortures on a certain number of prisoners to glut savage passions, but by no means were all those taken so cruelly treated. Most tribes looked upon captives as resources from which they could profit. Enemy prisoners could be sold, traded, ransomed, and used as bribes or inducements in negotiating treaties.

True slavery was practiced by some peoples of far western Canada and the northwest Pacific Coast as far south as California, but there are few indications that it existed among Indians anywhere else north of Mexico. Early narratives and official documents are rife with references to it, but these are both misleading and of doubtful authenticity, as the words "slave" and "prisoner" were interchangeably and indiscriminately employed in them. Moreover, there existed another institution that colonial historians mistook for slavery. It was the institution of adoption, a custom found in the social structure of the majority of Indian tribes.

All Indians were involved periodically in intertribal warfare, and these conflicts were extremely costly in both resources and human lives. Causes of the fighting are generally attributed to disputes over hunting grounds and other lands, retaliation for acts of violence, and blood revenge, but, as Henshaw states, "underlying all was the fierce martial spirit of the Indian which ever spurred him from inglorious peace to stirring deeds of war." As a consequence, tribes suffered heavy losses of men killed, and women and children either killed or taken captive. Natural increase was not sufficient to overcome these losses. Also, infant mortality was high. Hence arose the institution of adoption. The human spoils of war were taken into clans, gentes, and families to replace lost members or relatives. As most tribes practiced polygamy, men customarily married female captives.

There is no reliable evidence to indicate that slavery existed as a permanent institution among the Apache before their discovery by white men, and certainly that was not the case in historical times. They took captives, but like most tribes they sought to market them for gain, and are even known to have disposed of them on occasion to white slave-traders. As was true of other types of trading in which they had traditionally engaged, this commerce was disrupted and finally halted by the course of events. With the spread of the Spanish invasion they were forced to consider captives in an extremely restricted manner.

Intertribal wars came and went, but the war with the Spanish was affected little by season or circumstance, a war for which the Apache envisioned no possible end. Under such conditions, unless captives contributed in some meaningful way to the success and welfare of the Apache, they were a heavy liability. The Apache needed fighters, not menials. Runaway Pueblos willing to fight the Spanish were welcomed into their ranks, but they proffered no haven for grown men with other intentions.

Unlike the Navajo most Apache had no permanent rancherias, and few fields in which slaves could be made to labor. The Apache moved frequently, changing their habitations to meet the demands of the moment. And unlike the Navajo, they were not thrifty and made little effort to build herds and maintain them. They continued to live as much as possible as they had always lived, on the natural bounties of their country. They consumed the cattle and sheep they stole without regard for possible future needs. They had a great liking for mule and horse meat, but mules and horses were valuable assets, and usually they ate only animals they considered expendable as surplus or those killed or made useless by injuries in battle.

But the Apache—and in this instance they adhered to a Navajo custom—saw the wisdom in building for the future by marrying young Pueblo women who fled to them and Mexican women who were captured in warfare, and giving them children. The progeny of these unions would grow up imbued with Apache beliefs, loyal to Apache causes—they would be Apache. Through these marriages the Apache blood became mixed, but it was not deleteriously affected. On the contrary it was strengthened, given new vigor, and otherwise improved, for in this transmutation the best characteristics of the participants seem to have been preserved.

* * *

1675

The fuse was burning. When Miranda gave way to Governor Juan Francisco Treviño, he faced an unprecedented situation. Instead of secretly conspiring to revolt, all Indians, even the Pueblos, were openly calling for it. The drums of war were heard on every side. Treviño received reports that priests were being "bewitched," perhaps a way of saying that they were scared out of their wits. Half a dozen had dropped dead, purportedly from fear. Treviño did what might have been expected of any Spanish governor under such circumstances. He hanged three Tewas suspected of defying the Faith, and lashed and sentenced to life slavery forty-three other "convicted and confessed idolators."

1679

Governor Treviño was happy to put Santa Fe behind him, and his successor, Antonio de Otermín, found himself faced with a profoundly discouraging prospect. Some seventeen thousand Pueblo Indians were still alive in New Mexico. How many Apache and Navajo there were was not known, for there was no way of obtaining a reliable count of them. All that could be said was that whatever their number, from the Spanish viewpoint, there were too many. Dutifully Otermín determined to combat them, for there was no longer any doubt that they were acting in consort with the Pueblos while at the same time continuing their raids of death and destruction against the Spanish and the Indians who had capitulated to the Franciscans or were aiding the military.

Reinforcements were believed to be on their way up the Rio Grande from Nueva Vizcaya. Otermín planned campaigns with which he would attack the Apache and Navajo on several fronts, and waited for the necessary support.

It was too late.

1680

O c t o b e r *(Tenth)*

The fuse reached the bomb.

Pueblo warriors from a score of towns and strong forces of Navajo, under the generalship of Popé, an influential medicine man of San Juan, swept through northern New Mexico in waves too powerful to be resisted. Apache bands struck simultaneously from the east and south. It was a well-executed uprising. Quickly more than four hun-

dred colonists and twenty-one priests were slain. A few of the more
attractive Spanish women were captured and turned over to Indian
captains for their pleasure. The settlers, soldiers, converted Indians,
slaves, and servants who escaped the initial onslaughts fled to Santa
Fe and barricaded themselves with Governor Otermín and residents
of the capital in government buildings, one of them the Palace of the
Governors, which still stands today.

There for ten days they successfully withstood assaults by several
thousand Indians. The bravery of the Spaniards was extraordinary.
On one occasion, near the end of the siege, a hundred soldiers and
daring civilians broke out in a surprise counterattack. Under the
fusillades of their guns, the besiegers, armed only with bows and
arrows, lances, and knives, were routed. Three hundred of the attackers were slain, and forty-seven taken alive were hanged in the
Santa Fe Plaza.

Yet the Spaniards understood that they had won only a temporary
victory, that there was no hope of containing the revolt, and that to
remain in their present position meant slow starvation and death.

(Twenty-first)

As the first light appeared in the eastern sky, within the sight of
Indian campfires and the sound of drums, they emerged in a close-
order column and moved as swiftly as possible along the road to the
south. The Apache and others harassed them day and night, but
launched no massive attacks. After a fortnight of hard riding, they
arrived, exhausted and half-starved, in the safety of the El Paso garrison. En route they had met no reinforcements coming north to help
them.

The province of New Mexico was abandoned to the Indians. And
they, determined to destroy every remaining trace of the invaders,
continued to rampage through the land, burning the Spanish churches
and missions and factories and farms and homes, making off with all
livestock and all articles considered useful or which delighted their
eyes. And every Indian who had been baptized by priests was vigorously scrubbed with yucca suds.[11]

* * *

There is no doubt, as Lummis would observe, that Leonidas and his
three hundred were very worthy citizens; but it is evident that they
missed their vocation. Their military intentions were creditable but
crude. If Leonidas had been an Apache, he would have killed off the
Persian myriads a handful at a time, without once being seen by them.
Three hundred Spartan wives and mothers would each have been a

husband or a son ahead . . . and we should have lost one of the most brilliant examples we are wont to call heroism.

Uncelebrated in song, unappreciated by history, and thereby denied his due place on Fame's canvas, the Apache has been the most notable and the least noted of warriors. It was not numbers that gave him his reputation. He was not of imposing height. Most Apache warriors were of medium stature, straight (without the stiffness generally displayed by Americans who attempt to be erect), compact, and strongly built, but seldom heavy; and always of that easy carriage which belongs alone to perfect physical condition. There was never the classic protuberance of knotted muscle so affected by our athletes; nor were they in fact so powerful in foot-pounds as highly developed Caucasians. Their arms and legs were smooth and round; rarely scrawny and rarely fat. A grand depth and breadth of chest and generous substantiality of back were observable in all.

The Apache warrior's head was fairly well molded and of good size. The straight black hair was generally trimmed at the level of the shoulder blades. The features were strongly and rather sharply marked; the aquiline nose not generally heavy, nor the lips over-full. The eyes were sparkling, restless, and unfathomable. The face was never blank, yet never legible. It seemed as if the nerves and muscles by which, in civilization, the brain reflects its images upon the countenance, had all been cut. There was not a twitch, a shade, a change by which the keenest could read what was behind.

Meantime, through this impassive mask he was searching your very soul with indifferent eyes which never looked at you. He could come very near telling you what you had for breakfast. He kept the senses which nature gave man, and he educated them as few of us are ever educated in anything. No sound was so faint, no trace so delicate, as to escape his notice; nor, noticed, to elude his comprehension. A pebble with its earthward side turned up, a broken marguerite, the invisible flash of a gun ten miles away—he noted and understood them all. He would stoop to a trail so dim that the best Caucasian observer would not dream of its presence, and tell correctly how long ago that imprint was made. The arid hillside or the dusty maze of the highway were an open book to him, with full detail of when and how many passed, Indians or whites, men or women, by night or day.

The secret of the Apache warrior is chiefly his physical training. He is born out-of-doors, and until his comrades pile above his clay the rocks which cheat the prowling coyote, he draws no breath elsewhere. The mother who bore him was a sturdy animal capable of tiring out the flower of the white usurpers. He was always learning from nature at firsthand, and his livelihood and his life depended upon his observant receptivity.

To the natural acuteness of all his kind, the country of his nativity added a finish that was peculiarly the Apache warrior's own. In the grassy, well-watered, game-populous regions the aborigine was comparatively a lazy, fat-bodied, and fat-witted brute. In the grim deserts of the Southwest he became the most tireless, acute, and terrible man. His whole existence a hardship, a struggle with a nature from whose gaunt fist only the most persistent and skillful wrenching can wring bare life, the Apache was whetted to a ferocity of edge, an endurance of temper, which were impossible in more endurable country.

The Apache warrior earned the eye of the kite, the ear of the cat, the cunning of the fox, the ferocious courage and tirelessness of the gray wolf. Over the crags of his arid ranges he could travel farther in a day than the world's champion on a cinder track, and keep it up for more days.

He would ravage along a zigzag line for hundreds of miles with soldiers in hot chase, and never once be seen by his pursuers. But he would be felt. From behind cactus, from behind boulders, from behind a tuft of bear grass, would rise sickly little curls of smoke, and for each faint spiral a soldier tumbled. It was not a place to stop and fight—as well put your head under a triphammer. The only thing to do was to get out of that death-trap, and those who were left got out. By the time they were ready to continue pursuit, the pursued were ten miles away.

Had he been a civilized soldier, the Apache's elusiveness would have availed him little; but he was not. Civilization sacrifices the individual to the aggregate. The Apache warrior was not socially drowned. He was the essence of individuality. He was always a warrior and never a soldier. He turned war into a science. He was self-reliant, self-contained, and self-sufficient. He needed nothing which the Saxon had to have—from food to a leader. He was equal by himself to every emergency of the desert and of battle.

A military expedition against the Apache was conducted by a pack train carrying rations for the probable length of the campaign, as well as water, ammunition, and cooking utensils. If long cut off from this slow-moving base the command would perish in such a wilderness. The Apache needed no pack train. His ammunition was stored in numerous belts about his body. He carried no pots, no frying pans, no canned goods, no cases of hardtack and salt meat. If he moved at leisure he carried a load of jerked meat, roasted mescal, and other desert dainties, but these were discarded without hesitation in time of need.

When his belt hung loose from his hunger, an Apache warrior might extract from a tangle of leaves and twigs a score of fat prairie mice. With a long and supple switch he might lash through sand hillocks and obtain gracile lizards. A rattlesnake was a delicate entree. On the run, when his horse at last succumbs, its services are not yet ended. The tenderest portions would be hacked off and would dangle in sun-cured strips across the back of his next mount. The dead horse's long intestine would be cleaned and would become a water keg. If transportation were adequate, twenty feet or so of this unique canteen would be wound around a led horse. If at the moment horses were scarce, four or five feet of it would be slung, life-preserver fashion, about the neck of some brave. By this means enough water could be carried to supply a family for a week. The mescal gave the Apache a quasi-bread, two intoxicants, thread, and even clothing, and countless minor staples. Roasted mescal was very nutritious, and it could be stored for six months. The valuable plant could be found in very nearly every part of the Apache range. There were as well the fruit of the Spanish bayonet, the mesquite bean, the acorn, and there was wild game. After the Spanish came, of course, there were, besides horses and mules, sheep and cattle to be stolen and devoured.[12]

* * *

1681

New Mexico once more belonged to the Indians, but it soon was no less a land of turmoil than it had been under the Spanish. Word reached El Paso, where the refugees had been saved by the timely arrival of a supply train, that the tribes were fighting each other. Revolt leaders were attempting to form a central Pueblo government, but their demands for tribute with which it was to be supported were being rejected in many towns. Many pueblos were deserted. Bloody clashes were occurring. The Apaches on the south, and the Utes on the north, took advantage of the situation by raiding for plunder through the war-torn country.

It was the same old story of the inability of tribes to amalgamate, act in unison, and maintain peaceful relationships and orderly conditions. Barbarism worse than that of prehistoric times spread throughout all the northern land.

Orders came from Mexico City to retake the province. In El Paso the refugee Governor Otermín had no enthusiasm for the undertaking, but he had no alternative but to obey or resign. He had difficulty enlisting a force, but at last obtained the manpower and supplies he thought adequate for the attempt.

NOVEMBER

Otermín started up the Rio Grande from El Paso with one hundred and forty-six soldiers, one hundred and twelve Indian allies, nine hundred and seventy-five horses, and a supply train of carts and mules. He found that all Piro pueblos in southern New Mexico had been abandoned, and all ranchos along the route had been pillaged.

DECEMBER

Although they were now enemies, both Pueblos and Apaches independent of each other had ravaged the land and destroyed churches and every vestige of Spanish occupation.

In northern New Mexico most of the Indians had vanished, but the Tiguas had remained to give battle. However, they had not offered much resistance, and under Spanish assault they capitulated. Many of them fled, but several hundred swore allegiance to the conquerors. Otermín moved on. Although the pueblos were deserted, considerable amounts of food were found in them, and this was systematically destroyed. Captured Indians testified that the tribes were reorganizing to launch a concerted attack.

At Christmas time Otermín held a *junta de guerra*. The final decision: In view of the natives' bitter hostility, the smallness of the Spanish force, the weariness of the soldiers, the bad condition of the horses, the deep snow and intense cold, a retreat was the wisest course.

1682

JANUARY

Otermín gave up his attempt to recapture New Mexico and started back to El Paso. With him went nearly four hundred Indians of Isleta.

1683

Otermín resigned, ill in health, and severely condemned for his failures. His successor was Domingo Jironza Petris Cruzat.

The king urged that efforts to regain the lost colony be renewed.

1684

Cruzat conducted numerous campaigns northward from El Paso, giving special attention to the Apache, who were raiding from Texas to Arizona and often deep into Mexico. He and his soldiers killed a number of warriors and took prisoners the women and children of several bands.

1686

Cruzat was replaced by Don Pedro Reneros de Posada. He led one assault against the Keres.

1689

Posada was charged with being inefficient, and Cruzat was reappointed governor. He also attacked the Keres and several other Pueblo tribes who had fortified themselves at Cia, killing six hundred, taking seventy prisoners, and burning to death a number in their dwellings.

1690

Cruzat was prepared to launch another campaign against the Pueblos, but was forced to forgo it and fight the Suma Apache, who were on the warpath through northern Mexico and southern New Mexico.

Cruzat might have restored New Mexico to the Crown if he had been given more time, but before reports of his successes against the rebels had reached Spain the king had awarded both that task and the governorship to Diego de Vargas Zapata Luján Ponce de León.

1691

Although he took office de Vargas was delayed for more than a year from starting for Santa Fe by the Apache. Every man available was required to prevent them from taking over the provincial governments of the northern Mexican States. As well as attacking Spanish settlements they conducted offensives against the Pima and Sobaipuri as far west as Arizona.

1692

The Apache were far from being defeated, but there were urgent reasons why the reconquest of New Mexico could no longer be delayed. The French, both the Jesuits and La Salle, were on the Mississippi and looking westward. *Voyageurs* were pushing out on the Great

Plains. The northern possessions of Spain, the boundaries of which were still undetermined, were obvious goals of these invaders. And who could say what Russia had in mind, or what the British were planning? Not only the colonies of Texas and New Mexico were menaced, but Mexico was also endangered from the north Pacific.

AUGUST

Reinforcements were en route to him, but de Vargas did not wait for them. He started up the Rio Grande with only sixty soldiers, one hundred Indian auxiliaries, and three padres.

The Apache made no attempt to disrupt him. Every soldier who went to the Pueblo Country was one less to contend with. Indeed, on his march up the Rio Grande, de Vargas encountered no Indians at all. The pueblos were deserted.

SEPTEMBER

A strong group of Tanos from Galisteo held Santa Fe. De Vargas cut off the water supply and stationed his men in strategic positions around the villa. After several hours of defiance, the Tanos accepted his offer of forgiveness for their offenses against the king. The capital fell without a blow being struck, and de Vargas occupied the old Palace of the Governors.

OCTOBER

De Vargas and his soldiers displayed their power to the Pueblos, going as far west as the Hopi villages in Arizona, and numerous peace pacts were obtained. Many of the towns were deserted, however, and he learned that the people who had lived in them would not submit to him. He made no effort to find them. It would be easier, he would write, to defer the Jews from the Inquisition than to reduce runaway apostate Indians without stronger military forces than he had with him.

NOVEMBER

No attempt was made to open negotiations with the Navajo, for de Vargas was aware that an *entrada* into their country would result in warfare that might be disastrous to him. The Navajo watched him, but did not attack, although one night they stole a number of his horses.

From Zuñi, de Vargas set out directly across country for El Paso, confident that his reconnaissance had brought the desired results. Although his actions had been restrained and he had succeeded in avoiding violence, he left no doubts among the Pueblos that he would soon return to resettle the colony, and that he would expect all Indians to obey Spanish laws and accept Catholicism. No exceptions would be permitted.

But he had not consulted any Apache. When he reached that part of the road known as the *jornada del muerte*—between Cristobal and El Paso—the Apache were waiting for him. He was obliged to engage them in a running battle to the end of his journey. The casualties were light. One Spanish officer was killed and a soldier was wounded. One Apache was slain and one was captured.

Under questioning that was accompanied by a beating, the captured Apache admitted that he had participated in raids on El Paso. De Vargas ordered him shot, but the execution was delayed long enough to let a priest baptize him. Thereafter, de Vargas announced, he would shoot all Apache captured unless the whole nation submitted to Spanish authority. It was not a policy conducive to an improvement in relations. Actually it had no effect at all on the Apache. Since the revolt of 1680 they had never ceased their raids and attacks, and they had no intention of curtailing them now. Many areas of northern Mexico were in desperate condition. Some settlements, missions, and ranchos were reduced to poverty, their livestock herds depleted to such an extent that they were threatened with hunger, mines had to be closed because they were without the manpower to defend them, and even some presidios had lost so many horses that they were unable to mount enough soldiers to launch counterattacks.

1693

Impatiently de Vargas waited to begin his march back to Santa Fe. Several factors prevented him from starting. The warfare with the Apache had not abated. Soldiers had been taken away from him to fight them—there were only fifty left in El Paso. The colonists he was to take with him were arriving in piecemeal fashion. A strong military contingent would be needed to protect them, for they would be subject to possible attack from at least six Apache groups on the journey up the Rio Grande.

The viceroy, the Conde de Galve, realized the importance of reestablishing New Mexico as soon as possible, but he considered the stopping of the Apache destruction in northern Mexico more urgent. Therefore, he sent orders to de Vargas to undertake a joint campaign with Captain Francisco Ramírez of Casa Grande. De Vargas replied that his soldiers were needed in El Paso. In defending that place he had been forced to divide his command into three contingents, one to protect his own headquarters and the settlement, one to guard his horse herd, and one to pursue any Apache who came to the Rio

Grande. He advanced another reason why he believed pacification of the frontier should be undertaken after New Mexico had been reestablished: the Pueblos were apostates and for a dozen years none of their children had been baptized. To save the souls of all of them they should be brought back into the Faith. The Conde de Galve was unimpressed by this argument, and his order stood. De Vargas had no alternative but to obey.

De Vargas and Ramírez merged their small forces and carried on a campaign against the Apache which took them through much of Sonora and northward as far as the Gila River (presumably at some point in far western New Mexico). This was the realm of the Gila Apache, and de Vargas considered them the most powerful and important enemies. Gila Apache rancherias were found on both sides of the river, but Gila scouts spotted the Spaniards in time to let most of their people flee, and "although . . . we tried to give a surprise attack at dawn . . . because of the forests and the rough land, nothing could be accomplished but the capture of twenty-three women and children with two warriors. . . ." The prisoners apparently were unwilling to be enslaved without a fight, and a "brawl" ensued in which "as many as sixteen persons died."

In a snowstorm the Spaniards left the remote high country and started back to Mexico. Captain Fernández would complain that the offensive, which had been commanded by Captain-General de Vargas, had not been "made against the Indians that infest the neighborhood of El Parral but against Apache who used to make war in the Kingdom of New Mexico when the Spaniards were settled in it. . . ." It was his opinion that the campaign should have been made against Apache and other Indians attacking the hard-pressed presidios and settlements of northern Mexico. As a result of the strike on the Gila, the Apache had "made a formidable union of all the people of their nation . . ." and were uniting with other tribes to destroy El Paso, Janos, and Sonora. He was right.

A large band of Jano, Jocome, Suma, and Gila had gathered near the presidio of Janos. The Spaniards had attacked them with such success that they had asked for peace. It was granted, and nearly three weeks passed without further hostilities. Then a group of Apache appeared at the presidio, ostensibly for more talks and giving no indication of violating the previous truce. The soldiers gave them presents of clothing and food. Suddenly they produced weapons, and before being driven off, killed and wounded ten or twelve Spaniards. The war on the Apache frontier went on with unabated fury.

Military officers and civil officials of the northern Mexican States strenuously protested the plan to send a strong force north to retake New Mexico when soldiers were so badly needed by them. De Vargas went ahead with his plans, however, and he had backing now which no colonial government authority could overcome. It came from the king. The motives of the sovereign in overruling the opinions of the viceroy and the state governors and favoring de Vargas were, as Forbes (1960) notes, several in number. Although it was true the colony had contributed nothing to the royal treasury, ". . . the French menace was considered very real; and the desire to exploit the Sierra Azul mines, the ache to get revenge for the 1680 defeat, the feeling that continued freedom of the Pueblo Indians gave hope to other rebels, and the wish to save the souls of apostates and their pagan children all worked together to promote the enterprise."

OCTOBER

De Vargas left El Paso for Santa Fe. With him were a hundred professional soldiers, fourscore families of settlers, eighteen padres, a large contingent of half-breed Indians, and an odd assortment of other persons that included mercenaries, ex-convicts, a few men and women of good birth, lawyers, notaries, and hopeful shopkeepers and craftsmen. The ever-watchful Apache sent word up the Rio Grande that he was coming. Messengers sped from pueblo to pueblo, and throughout the Apache territories, councils were held, and within a short time most of the main Pueblo tribes and all but one of the Apache groups had pledged themselves to fight the invaders. The Pecos adopted a policy of attempting to make peace with them. Commercial ties influenced the decision of the Faraon Apache. They were good friends of the Pecos and enjoyed a profitable trade with them. The Faraon, therefore, feared that by siding with the others they would antagonize their best customers, and chose to make every effort to stay out of the coming fight.

DECEMBER

Apparently the Apache and their Pueblo allies had agreed not to attack the expedition before it reached northern New Mexico, and without any serious difficulties de Vargas brought his company to the gates of Santa Fe. They found that the town was strongly fortified, and as de Vargas and a group of priests entered it singing hymns, several hundred warriors stood at battle stations, silent, their weapons poised.

There was no sign that the defenders might be willing to negotiate. There were no responses to de Vargas's demands at all. Still hoping that he and his colonists could make a peaceful entry, de Vargas announced that he would allow the Indians the time they needed to evacuate the town, and he ordered a camp established on the outskirts. It was bitterly cold and snow covered the ground.

For two weeks de Vargas waited. The suffering of his people and soldiers was extreme, and twenty-one of them died. As the year 1693 ended so did his patience, and he attacked. Bit by bit the soldiers took Santa Fe. After two days of fierce fighting the Indians fled. Seventy who were captured were hanged.

1694

The fall of Santa Fe did not signify that the reconquest of New Mexico had succeeded. Indeed, it marked the beginning of the fight. The bloody struggle which had occurred in the capital was repeated in other places as de Vargas led his troops in campaigns up and down the Rio Grande. All but four pueblos had to be taken by assault. Hundreds of Indians were slain, and many fled to the Navajo, Apache, and to other tribes. The Apache made the road north from El Paso a bloody gauntlet, but more troops and colonists were able to get to the upper Rio Grande and help to strengthen de Vargas's defenses.

"With full sails we forge ahead," de Vargas wrote with a confidence that must have been slight. At the time both Apache and Navajo raiders were striking close to Santa Fe. Soldiers were pursuing them with small success, for on most occasions they disappeared like wraiths before they could be intercepted, leaving behind dead herders and farmers.

1695

Reports reached de Vargas that most of the tribes were once again organizing to launch a united revolt. Yet, while he girded to meet the expected assault, he moved some sixty newly arrived families to a new settlement near San Juan. As more colonists arrived, Bernalillo was established.

Now a prolonged drought added its burden to the precarious situation. The crops of the Pueblos failed, which meant that they could not pay tribute in food. No rains fell in the high Navajo Country to the west, nor in the country of the Plains Apache to the east. Game disappeared. The specter of starvation stalked the land beside its ally, death.

JUNE

The long-expected offensive of the combined Pueblos and Athapascans came. Some padres abandoned their stations and found haven in Santa Fe. But within a few days five priests and twenty-one soldiers were slain, and once again most of the churches and all their furnishings were destroyed.

De Vargas moved fast and without mercy against the rebels. Some help came to him now from Pueblos who realized the futility of attempting to fight both the Spanish and drought at the same time.

OCTOBER

On a thrust up the Rio Grande, de Vargas learned that a large group of Taos and Picuris, with all their possessions and a number of stolen horses and other livestock, were attempting to join the Plains Apache in northeastern New Mexico. He set out in hot pursuit. When he passed the Picuris Pueblo, which was deserted, Indian scouts told him he was only three days behind the fugitives, who were obliged to move slowly because of the band of stolen sheep and goats they had with them.

Obviously aware that the Spaniards were after them, the runaways abandoned unnecessary equipment, and de Vargas found their trail littered with discarded tepee poles, equipment, and household goods. The weather turned cold, and snow fell, but pressing on, the soldiers found many of the Picuris and Taos huddled together in a ravine, and during the next two days other women and children came in to the Spanish camp to surrender.

NOVEMBER

No Apache had been encountered, but their campsites had been found, and scouts had reported they were not far away. Deep snow and high winds prevented de Vargas from continuing. Some horses had been frozen to death. Their meat was fed to the captives, who numbered eighty-four, among them several suckling babes. When he reached Santa Fe, de Vargas gave all the prisoners as slaves to the soldiers and civilians who had accompanied him. He was profoundly aggravated when he learned that many of his quarry, despite the blizzards, had succeeded in uniting with the Apache. One of those who had escaped was Lorenzo, head chief of the Picuris, the greatest prize of all. This brief winter sally of de Vargas was the first military expedition to enter northeastern New Mexico in almost two decades, and although it harmed the Plains Apache not at all, they looked upon it as a forewarning of what might be expected in the near future, an attitude that would soon illustrate their shrewdness in analyzing the strategy of the Spaniards.

* * *

Meanwhile, warfare on the Mexico frontier had brought serious reverses to the Apache. In the last six years of the seventeenth century some seven hundred, the great majority warriors, had been killed by Spanish soldiers, and hundreds of women, children, and young persons had been captured and sold into slavery. Some historians attribute the Apache attacks in Mexico solely to an insatiable craving for booty, but that is patently untrue. They were motivated to a far greater extent by an irrepressible hatred for white men, a burning desire to gain revenge for past injustices, and an indestructible determination to protect their homelands and maintain their independence. It is unreasonable to believe that in the face of such grievous losses they would have continued their raiding only to obtain plunder which could have been of little value to them.

As the seventeenth century drew to a close the situation was this:

The Apache tribes of the northern Mexican States had been largely destroyed, although they were still fighting, and other Apache from the north were keeping the region aflame with raiding.

The Spanish in Texas were attacking Apache with the aid of Indian forces.

Troops were patrolling the Rio Grande north of El Paso and pursuing Apache raiders who came in from both the east and west to sack pueblos friendly to the Spanish and to attack caravans.

In Arizona and western New Mexico the Pima, Papago, and Sobaipuri were fighting Apache raiders in consort with Spanish troops.

De Vargas had failed to put down completely the rebellion of the united Pueblos and Apache, but they had suffered serious punishment at his hands, and when he left office in 1697 he was justified in declaring that the colony was reasonably secure. During the regime of his successor, Pedro Rodríguez Cubero, the Pueblos became subdued to the extent that they were no longer considered dangerous enemies. Rodríguez successfully negotiated treaties with most of the Pueblo tribes, but not with any Apache group.

Contrary to reports, the French were not yet presenting a real threat to the Southwest, but a few French traders had reached the Pawnee and other tribes on the Great Plains.

Apache and Navajo were appearing in Taos and Pecos with articles of French manufacture which they had obtained either in trade from other Indians or in raiding their old enemies, the people of Quivira.

It seems apparent that the Apache realized the fear which the Spanish held of the French, for they spread false stories that French troops were advancing in large numbers toward New Mexico from both Texas and Kansas and were accompanied by hordes of Pawnee, Osage, Wichita, and Caddo.

THE
EIGHTEENTH
CENTURY

As the eighteenth century began, the Apache of the High Plains were faced with a new and swiftly growing danger. It was the southward migration of the Comanche.

The Comanche belong to the Shoshonean linguistic family. Their tongue is virtually identical with that of the Shoshoni of the northern Rocky Mountains and the Great Basin. Horses were in possession of northern Indians to some extent when the Comanche began migrating southward from Wyoming. This was not a mass movement. It was an offensive sustained over a considerable period of time, perhaps as much as three or four decades, and its sole purpose was to obtain large numbers of horses, and thereby acquire great economic and military powers. Band followed band from the north until at last they became a formidable Plains people. They were warriors of extraordinary courage and skill, and as mounted fighters they steadily overcame tribes which stood in their way.

The Spaniards were the first white men to use the name Comanche in written documents, but until recent years its origin remained a puzzle. It could not be shown to have derived from any Spanish or Indian word. Then in 1943 the distinguished scientist Marvin K. Opler successfully traced it to the language of the Ute, who also are of Shoshonean stock. It came from the Ute word *Komantcia*, which in its fullest sense means *anyone who wants to fight me all the time*. The Spanish got it from the Ute, and to Spanish ears it sounded like Comanche.

The Pawnee of Nebraska evidently owned horses in fairly sizable numbers by 1630 or 1635, and at this time the Comanche apparently were their neighbors. Whether the Comanche went around the Pawnee or were permitted by them to pass without prolonged fighting is not certain. The fact remains that they pushed on south and eventually established themselves close to the northern borders of present New Mexico and the Texas Panhandle. There they created what became known as the Comanche barrier and made numerous northern tribes dependent upon them for the invaluable horses. And out of the barrier they began to raid southward, striking at both Indians and Spanish alike. Gradually the Plains Apache were forced to fall back, their position steadily becoming more untenable with the Spanish pressing upon them from the west, several enemy tribes from the east and south, and the Comanche from the north. By the year 1705 the Comanche dominated parts of northern and northeastern New Mexico, and were making successful raids throughout an immense region of the High Plains eastward and southward of Pecos.

Early in the eighteenth century some strange events occurred in the province of New Mexico.[13]

* * *

1706

The Pueblo Picuris who had fled only a few years earlier to live among the Apache in El Cuartelejo, as well as some Apache bands of that region, appealed to the Spanish for assistance in the conflict with the Comanche and Pawnee.

Francisco Cuervo y Valdez, now governor, recognized the unprecedented opportunity to bring the apostate Picuris and the previously intractable Apache—or at least some of them—to terms, and he assigned Captain Juan de Ulibarri to undertake the mission.

Negotiating peace with the hard-pressed groups who had asked for protection, however, was only one of Ulibarri's assigned duties. Presumably with other Apache and the Comanche in mind, Cuervo ordered Ulibarri to make a show of force before any Indians he encountered and warn them that further attacks on Spanish settlements would mean a campaign to annihilate them. Also, Ulibarri was to spare no effort to find out how far the French had penetrated into Spanish territory.

JULY

With a well-equipped force of about one hunderd and forty men—only twelve were professional soldiers, the others being civilians experienced in fighting Indians, and recruits from friendly pueblos—Ulibarri reached Picuris, about forty miles north of Santa Fe. The inhabitants, eager to have their relatives and especially their distinguished leader, Lorenzo, return from exile, willingly supplied him with blankets and additional horses.

From Taos Ulibarri followed the ancient trail over Palo Flechado Pass. On Magdalena Creek, some forty miles east of Taos, he encountered Jicarilla, Conejero, Ocho, and other Apache. A council was held, and when they learned the nature of his mission these Indians, who since the founding of New Mexico had been considered deadly enemies of the Spanish, warmly welcomed him. They demonstrated their new friendship by warning him that Comanche were waiting to attack him in Raton Pass, which was on the customary route to El Cuartelejo. He rewarded them with gifts of tobacco and knives.

Having no intention, despite his orders, of attempting to make a show of force to Indians lying in ambush in a mountain defile, Ulibarri turned sharply north. More Jicarilla came to talk with him, invited him to visit their villages, and offered him maize, beans, and pumpkins. So convinced was Ulibarri that they could be trusted that he left his tired and weak horses in their care.

August

Following a course that took him through rough country and across the Purgatoire, Apishapa, and Huerfino Rivers, he reached the Arkansas opposite the mouth of Fountain Creek.* Against the sky in the northwest a great blue pile could be seen. (More than a century later it would be unjustly given the name of Pike's Peak.)

It was up Fountain Creek that the main north-south Indian trade trail of the region immediately east of the Rocky Mountains wound its way, eventually reaching the most important prehistoric crossroads of the West, the junction of the Laramie and North Platte Rivers. Undoubtedly some Spanish traders had reached this confluence (in southern Wyoming), but no Spanish military force had ever gone farther north than Ulibarri's camp on the Arkansas River.

Going on toward the northeast, Ulibarri found more Apache ". . . who came without weapons, very happy and elated. They brought us much buffalo meat, roasting ears of Indian corn, tamales, plums, and other things to eat." As he camped at an Apache village in El Cuartelejo, people crowded about shouting a welcome, and ". . . out of the huts came Don Lorenzo and the rest of the Picuris Indians, men and women who were with him . . . we embraced him and gave them to understand why we were coming, having been sent by our governor. . . ." Here was the unique situation of people who had revolted and refused to submit to Spanish control wildly greeting a Spanish soldier.

The Apache pleaded with Ulibarri to lead them in a raid on the Pawnee and French. Perhaps that could be done at a later time, he told them, and questioned them as to the whereabouts of the French. They

---

*Site of Pueblo, Colorado.

were, replied the Apache, not a great distance to the northeast. A few weeks earlier some Pawnee and French had been defeated by them. Besides a Pawnee chief they had killed a white man and a white woman in the fight. They had scalped the woman, but the man was bald. An Apache leader stepped into a hut and returned with an obviously new gun, announcing with pride that it was part of the loot taken from the defeated Pawnee. Examining the flintlock Ulibarri saw that it was of French manufacture.

Although they fully understood the value and the power of guns, and sought to obtain them, most Indians of the time mistreated them and gave them no care at all. They used them as clubs, as digging tools, as tepee pegs, decorated them with studs, scalps, paint, and gewgaws, and took them apart, using the plates as hide scrapers. Had the weapon displayed by the Apache shown signs of such abuse, it would have given Ulibarri less concern than it did, but it was still shiny, unbattered, and unbroken. If it had been obtained from the Pawnee, it had not been in their possession for any length of time.

September

Ulibarri was unable to ascertain how close the French were, or how many of them were known to be among the Pawnee, but that they had reached the region there no longer could be any doubt. He set out on a forced march for Santa Fe, taking with him Lorenzo and "sixty-two persons, small and grown, of the Picuries who were living as apostates, slaves of the devil. . . ." When he reached the Jicarilla he learned that soon after he had left them they had suffered from two raids by Utes and Comanches. However, they had protected his horses, and the animals were turned over to him.

When he informed Governor Cuervo what he had learned about the French, dispatches marked *secreto y urgente* were sent at once to the viceroy in Mexico City.

* * *

If some of the Apache of southeastern Colorado and western Kansas, through necessity, had shown a willingness to remain at peace with the Spanish, the Plains Apache of eastern New Mexico and western Texas, with the exception of the Faraons, had never ceased their attacks on the colony. Several expeditions were made against them, but with small success, mainly for two reasons: (1) The Navajo were an even greater menace, ravaging the country in sweeps from the west almost without surcease, and the colonial government was obliged to use most of its military forces in counteroffensives against them, and (2) the necessity of maintaining a line of defense on the north to repel

Comanche raiders. To aid them on this salient the government made alliances with the Jicarilla and Cuartelejo Apache, both of whom were suffering from Comanche attacks. Spanish manpower was spread extremely thin. All of these operations not only required the maintenance of troops and negotiators in the field but were costly and frequently depleted food supplies and equipment to dangerously low levels.

The Faraons, as previously noted, had abstained from joining the Pueblos and other Apache groups in a united attempt to prevent de Vargas from reconquering New Mexico. It had been their hope that by avoiding a direct confrontation with the returning Spanish they would be able to preserve their profitable commercial relations with Pecos and other towns. They had not been altogether scrupulous in adhering to this policy. The temptations to raid, especially for the Faraons inhabiting the territory directly east of the Sandia Mountains, often had been too great to be resisted. Although they were not a major menace, bands had struck against caravans and ranchos with no little success from time to time. When men could be spared from other fronts, punitive expeditions had been sent against them, but on almost every occasion they had managed to slip away without sustaining serious losses.

Several factors caused the Faraons to make an about-face after some twelve or thirteen years of doing no more than spasmodically bedeviling the colony. They could no longer follow their traditional life customs and no longer conduct their trading under conditions advantageous to them. That time had gone, its end brought about by Comanche inroads on the eastern New Mexico and western Texas plains, by the steadily increasing military strength of the Spanish, and by the growing number of armed civilians and Indians available for campaigns against them.

The Faraons now became full-fledged relentless raiders, striking against both Spanish settlements and pueblos with devastating fury. Two of their main targets were Picuris and Taos, the people of which they now condemned as Indian traitors who had aligned themselves with white men. Reports began to reach Santa Fe that immense droves of stolen horses and mules were being held in Faraon rancherias.

* * *

1715

Governor Juan Ignacio Flores Mogollón of New Mexico decided that the time had come to teach the Faraon Apache a lesson they would not soon forget.

AUGUST

A campaign was planned and forces were assembled at Picuris under the leadership of Captain Juan Páez Hurtado.

The extent to which many of the Pueblo tribes had aligned themselves with the Spanish to fight the Apache is illustrated by the roster of Hurtado's expedition. It was composed of thirty-nine soldiers, twenty civilian settlers, and one hundred and fifty-one Indian men who came from the pueblos of Pecos, San Juan, Nambe, San Ildefonso, Santa Clara, Pujuaque, Tesuque, Taos, and Picuris. Seventy-six of the warriors had guns. Every member of the force possessed two or more horses or mules.

Starting from Picuris, Hurtado crossed the mountains and descended the Mora River, en route being joined by thirty Jicarilla and an Apache guide from El Cuartelejo. Thus, there is further evidence that in order to hold the favor of the Spanish and protect themselves the Jicarilla were willing to fight other Apache.

In traveling more than one hundred and fifty miles east of Santa Fe the expedition saw not a single Plains Apache. Faraon camps were found, but they were deserted. Tracks made by the horses of numerous bands were followed, but these trails split and ran away in all directions, vanishing into the sky. Hurtado was correct in concluding that the Faraon had been notified by Indian spies of his campaign against them in time to let them escape. He took his anger out on his guide, accusing him of negligence and sentencing him "to be given fifty lashes with a whip. For this reason I called the place the Arroyo of the Whipping."

He returned to Santa Fe, his campaign a complete failure.

1717

Antonio Valverde, now governor, was a man of many enemies, but contrary to the old adage this was not a reliable measure with which to judge his qualifications or his character. He was corrupt, cold-blooded, and cowardly. He falsified his accounts, stole government stores, and cheated soldiers by charging them outrageous prices for the supplies they required to feed their families.

Valverde had been an army captain before being sent as chief executive to Santa Fe. Regarding his cruelties to the Indians, one report to the viceroy stated: ". . . the Manso and Suma [Apache] rose up, and leaving their pueblos, went to the mountains because of bad treatment given them and because their land had been taken away for cultivation . . . he [Valverde] maintains possession of them, having profited from them since 1711 from the very expensive crops of wine, wheat, maize, beans, and other grains. The poor Indians, because they have no lands nor pueblo where they can sow, go about perishing, acquiring bad habits, and are obliged to rob to maintain themselves.

". . . his own soldiers are and have been kept so badly disciplined that they do not even merit the name of soldiers. Because he does not look after anything else than the provisioning of the soldiers, the interests which he was advancing in the increased prices he was charging for them, the collection of their salaries, the ranches which he had acquired and the herds of cattle which he had formed, the soldiers do not have any other occupation than . . . service directed to his affairs and profits. This work is paid for with the wages of the king."

The Comanche were driving the Jicarilla Apache from their homelands north of New Mexico, and they made new and frantic appeals for aid from the Spanish. Fray Juan de la Cruz, stationed at Taos, informed the viceroy of the opportunity to send priests among these people, convert them, and maintain them as a buffer against the French. From Mexico City came orders to Valverde to adopt the priest's plan, send out an expedition to chastise the Comanche, and at the same time make a new attempt to discover the exact position of the French.

SEPTEMBER

Valverde started on his assignment from Taos with the largest military force to enter the Great Plains since the founding of New Mexico. According to Thomas (1935), who translated Valverde's own report of the journey, he had under his command, besides sixty regular soldiers, "forty-five settlers, and four hundred sixty-five [Pueblo] Indian allies, later augmented in La Jicarilla by one hundred ninety-six Apaches. So poor were the settlers that Valverde himself had to furnish them with leather jackets, guns, powder, shot, and seventy-five horses. How many animals were taken along is unknown. Besides these seventy-five, the soldiers undoubtedly possessed both horses and mules. The Pueblo Indians had six hundred eighty beasts, and the Apaches from Jicarilla added one hundred three, making an imposing known total of over eight hundred fifty animals. A drove of sheep, great quantities of pinole, chocolate, tobacco, and presents for the friendly Indians to be met en route completed the supplies. . . . The governor himself took several casks of wine, 'a small keg of very rich spiritous brandy,' some glasses, and rich melon preserves for important saints' days. To replenish their larder from time to time, hunting of fine fat turkeys, bears, deer, and buffalo supplanted the more serious pursuit of [Comanche] Indians."

Apache bands continued to join Valverde as he made his way in leisurely fashion on a course that took him from the Canadian River over the divide to the Purgatoire and on to the Arkansas, which he reached some distance southeast of Fountain Creek. By this time he was surrounded by a horde of Apache—Jicarilla, Cuartelejos, Palomas, Calchufines, Carlanas, and others—whose leaders poured out tales of their sufferings at the hands of the Comanche. The desperate plight of these people was made evident by the sight of destroyed Apache villages. In one rancheria alone more than sixty Apache had been killed by raiders, who also carried away "many women and children." The fighting and killing was occurring with greater frequency each year, and they would not be able to bear it much longer unless the Spanish helped them to defend themselves. On numerous occasions the Apache danced in honor of the governor and demonstrated their shrewdness and diplomacy by displaying crude crosses they had made of sticks and reeds. One afternoon the Carlana, led by the chief from whom they took their name, "circled the camp on their horses, jubilantly singing and shouting. In the evening they danced according to their custom, some covered with red and others with white paint. They came to the tent of the governor, who received them with great kindness. After they had danced for a good part of the night, he ordered them entertained and feasted." Valverde thought that the Apache were "very close to embracing our holy faith . . . they only lack priests to instruct and convert them."

The Apache lacked a great deal more than priests. They were on the verge of being driven from the region they had occupied for countless centuries. In his responses to their pleas Valverde was generous with his sympathy and promised them unstinting support, but he took no action to demonstrate the sincerity of his words. Indeed, he did nothing at all for them.

OCTOBER

Several Comanche trails were discovered, but Valverde's trackers judged them too old to be worth following. At one place they came upon a campsite of a very large band in which the ashes of more than two hundred cooking fires were counted. Guides estimated that considerably more than a thousand Comanche had stopped there only a few days earlier. As they proceeded "the track of the enemy was recognized, which left a clear trail wherever it went, both on account of the great number of Comanche and their multitude of horses, as well as the tent poles they carried dragging along behind. Their road went northeast . . . the governor ordered a halt."

Valverde would state that he had been strongly in favor of pursuing the Comanche "until they should all be punished," but that he was dissuaded from so doing by Chief Carlana, who advised him that "it would not be possible to follow them because they had changed direction and had taken another route along which there were very few springs, and those too scanty to support the main body of his horseherd and the command." In another discussion of the problem, according to Valverde, he was reminded that the weather was turning cold, some snow already had fallen, "and that by continuing to follow the Comanche there was a manifest risk that all the cavalry, which was the principal means by which the kingdom was sustained might be lost [in a blizzard]." Valverde would maintain that he was greatly displeased at not being able to come to grips with the large Comanche band but as he was "familiar with the rigor of the snow and cold weather, which in these lands is so extreme that it benumbs and annihilates," he was constrained to abide by the counsel of his advisers.

Thereafter he gave his full attention to the task of trying to obtain intelligence regarding the activities of the French. As more Apache came to his camp on the Arkansas he questioned them closely, and his efforts bore some fruit.

Informed that an Apache had arrived who had suffered a gunshot wound that was not yet fully healed, he had him brought to his tent. There, said a report, "the governor examined the wound and asked him who had given it to him. . . ." Through interpreters the wounded Apache, a Paloma, "answered that while he and his people were in their land . . . the French, united with the Pawnees *and the Jumanos,* attacked them from ambush while they were planting corn. Placed on the defensive, they fought, and it was then that they gave him the oblique wound in the abdomen which was still healing.* The Apache also said that had not night settled on them, so that they could escape from their rancheria, none would have been alive. The Comanche seized the Paloma lands . . . and held them from that time on."

The reference to the Jumano Apache being in league with the French and Pawnee presents a puzzle that ethnographers have never been able to solve. The same statement had been made by Indians in Santa Fe on at least two other occasions, but there is no documentary evidence to support it. In the eighteenth century the Jumano Apache ranged over southwestern Texas and southeastern New Mexico. There is no known reason to believe that they were enemies of their Athapascan relatives in El Cuartelejo, and there is no record to show that El Cuartelejo Apache ever invaded Jumano territory. The probable explanation is that a band of Jumano, probably small in size, either were driven from their people or chose to separate from them, perhaps after a quarrel, became outlaws, and eventually found a

---

*It must have been infected, as corn was planted in May or June, and this was mid-October.

haven with the Pawnee, but of this there is no proof.

The story told by the wounded Paloma Apache got better as it progressed. Said the report of his interrogation: "The French have built two large pueblos, each of which is as large as that of Taos. In them they live together with the said Pawnees and Jumanos Indians, to whom they have given long guns which they taught them to shoot. . . . They also carry some small guns suspended from their belts." At the time of the fight the Paloma had shouted at the French that they would ask the Spanish for help, and "to this the French responded that they would be greatly pleased to have them notify the Spanish and bring them there, for the Spanish were women."

Valverde appeared to be unperturbed by the insult, as he understood "that these are words, however rude, that the Indians are accustomed to use to incite ire." But he was disturbed by the wounded Paloma's assertion that besides the two Taos-sized towns, the French "have three other settlements on the other side of the large river, and that from these they bring arms and the rest of the things they bring to those they have recently constructed. The Apache know this because they were told by some women of their own tribe who were made captives among the French . . . but who had fled and returned." The "large river" was the Missouri, and from it the French followed the Platte on their trading journeys to the Great Plains.

NOVEMBER

Valverde returned to Santa Fe. There he was given even more alarming news than he had learned on his trip. It was that the French were marching toward New Mexico six thousand strong. He wrote excitedly to the viceroy that French "troops are drawing nearer, chiefly across open land, without Spanish forces or trained men able to resist them. Accordingly, they will come closer swiftly and easily." He pleaded for reinforcements.

Either Valverde was gullible or he was ignorant of the geography of the Great Plains. Perhaps he was both. If France had managed to send an army of six thousand soldiers overland anywhere in the Southwest, all hope of Spanish dominion continuing to prevail north of Mexico was futile. Yet, even if such a miracle had been accomplished, French troops advancing from the lower Mississippi—the only possible place of origin for a force of such size—hardly would have bothered to go as far north as the Platte, then cut hundreds of miles southwest and struggle through high mountain passes in a campaign to take Santa Fe. The trails up the Red, lower Arkansas, and Canadian Rivers, which *voyageurs* apparently were already using, would have led them over a comparatively easy route directly to their goal.

1719

Viceroy Valero ordered Valverde to establish a presidio in El Cuartelejo and form a firm alliance with the Apache of that region, but Valverde thought it too far from Santa Fe. Invaders could easily circumvent it. He advised that the fort should be located among the friendly Jicarilla, only some seventy miles from the capital. His argument, undoubtedly sound, prevailed, and he was instructed to proceed with his own plan.

J U L Y

Meanwhile, deeply worried, Valverde decided he had better send out another scouting party to obtain the latest information on the activities and intentions of the French. The officer he selected to lead it was Captain Pedro de Villasur, who recently had come to Santa Fe from Nueva Vizcaya. It was an unwise choice, and would never be adequately explained. Valverde had available to him men thoroughly trained and experienced in fighting Indians, yet he placed full responsibility for the hazardous reconnaissance on the shoulders of a young soldier who had "not the least knowledge of the land [El Cuartelejo and the Great Plains], nor was practiced nor experienced in war, nor understood that [Comanche, Pawnee, and French] which he was to fight, much less govern and direct." One critic testified that Villasur, "a visionary," never understood "in what manner he had won the pleasure" of the New Mexico governor, or why he had been chosen. Captain Don Felix Martínez would charge Valverde with cowardice and declare under oath that because the governor "did not wish to expose his person to danger, he adopted the pretext of sickness," yet after Villasur had departed, the governor "himself went out on an inspection."

Villasur was permitted to take with him only forty-two soldiers, one priest, three civilian settlers, and sixty Pueblo Indians, hardly a sufficient number in view of the perilous nature of his assignment—another of Valverde's mysterious actions. Ironically, the civilian who was to serve as Villasur's interpreter was Juan de L'Archeveque, a Frenchman who had taken part in the murder of La Salle in Texas, had escaped to New Mexico, sworn allegiance to Spain, and had become an Indian trader. Villasur's chief scout was the veteran Naranjo, who spoke several Indian tongues and had served with previous expeditions. The padre was Fray Juan Minguez.

Villasur left from Santa Fe, crossed the mountains near Taos, and was guided over the usual trail to El Cuartelejo by Jicarilla and Carlana Apache. No enemy Indians were encountered, and he could learn nothing from the Apache of the whereabouts of the French.

AUGUST

From the Arkansas the intrepid Villasur led his company toward the northeast. Reaching the Río Jesús María (South Platte River), they pressed steadily on to the North Platte, which they called the Río Saint Laurent. Scouts were sent out, and they returned to report having sighted Indians moving toward the confluence of the Platte branches.

Villasur forded the North Platte and turned down its left bank. He had now gone farther north than any previous Spanish military force —west-central Nebraska—and he was on the main east-west trade trail from the Missouri River. After descending the North Platte for four days, he made camp on the main river a short distance below the confluence, and across from an immense village of Pawnee.

An emissary was sent with gifts to arrange a smoke with the Pawnee, but he was held a prisoner. In view of this cold rejection of his friendly efforts, Villasur took his troop back up the North Platte above the confluence, recrossed it, and made camp on the slender tongue of land separating the two streams in what he considered a safer place.

(Fourteenth)

At dawn several hundred Pawnee warriors attacked with such suddenness and fury that Villasur and a number of his men were slain before they could fire their guns. The Pueblo Indians panicked and escaped with the horse herd, but not before eleven of them had died. The professional Spanish soldiers fought with great bravery. They took a heavy toll of the Pawnee, but only twelve of them, almost all badly wounded, would break out of the ambush and live. Among the thirty soldiers and eleven Pueblos dead on the field were Naranjo, Father Minguez, L'Archeveque, and the other civilians. Many of the Pawnee had been armed with guns, and not a few of them had been wearing "French clothes."

SEPTEMBER

The reports of the survivors who straggled into Santa Fe caused consternation throughout the colony. Governor Valverde knew no more than he had before Villasur's departure. That the French were among the Pawnee there could be no doubt, but where was the great French legion that was supposed to be moving toward New Mexico?

* * *

Eventually the truth would reach Santa Fe in official dispatches from Mexico City. The story of the impending French invasion had been a myth, and the end of the Franco-Spanish War had removed all danger of a French military conquest on the Rio Grande. French traders, however, would continue to push out to the Rocky Mountains along the Arkansas and the North and South Platte Rivers, not to claim territory for their country but to obtain furs and sell goods to the Indians. They wanted to establish trade with the Plains Apache, but this ambition would be thwarted, not by the Spanish but by the Comanche who blocked their way.

Yet the colony of New Mexico would remain in a precarious situation. The defeat of Villasur had sent Spanish prestige tumbling to an unprecedented low level. Capitalizing on the inability of colonial arms to retaliate effectively, the Comanche and the Ute would steadily increase their ravaging of the northern and northeastern frontiers. The El Cuartelejo Apache, having abandoned all hope of receiving Spanish assistance, would fall back under the Comanche onslaughts. The Ute would hold the north along the sources of the Rio Grande, and the Comanche would take complete control of western Kansas, southeastern Colorado, and the panhandles of Oklahoma and Texas. The Navajo would dominate the vast region west of the Jemez and south of the San Juan, their raiders sweeping out of it great distances the year round to pillage and kill and take captives and drive off livestock.

But if the danger to the colony from the Apache had been shifted because of the intertribal warfare it had not been eliminated. In their new positions they composed a strong barrier in the southeast, the south, and the southwest, from Texas to Arizona.

A truism often heard was: "You can't count money you don't have, and you can't kill or capture Apache until you find them."

Then there were two questions which never left the thoughts of Spanish soldiers in their grubby barracks on the Apache frontier, questions which had been just as appropriate and reasonable in 1650 as they were in 1750. Where will they strike next? When?

In the early decades of their conquest of Mexico the Spanish had won swift and decisive victories with traditional European military tactics. In addition, they had possessed material, technological, and psychological advantages that were beyond the comprehension of their primitive adversaries. Hernán Cortés and his soldiers encountered in the Aztecs, as Moorhead succinctly states, "a sophisticated Indian civilization concentrated in a relatively small area, tied by religious devotion to permanent temples, by economic dependence to tilled fields and established market places, and by social organization and sentimental attachment to fixed townsites. The defenders could not retreat." Moreover, the Spanish ". . . had horses for mobility; cannon for destruction; armor for personal protection; the strangeness that inspired fear; and a talent for creating confusion."

As the frontier was pushed northward, conditions made it necessary to adopt some new practices. Mexico steadily grew wider. The Indians became progressively less settled in their way of life, roaming over large areas. The vast ranges running into nothingness were arid. Settlements and presidios could be established only in locations where productive soil and water existed, and these were seldom close together, thus the problems of communications and logistics became increasingly complicated and difficult. Indian mercenaries from subdued tribes in the south were brought north to support the inadequate number of soldiers, but, understandably, they were not always trustworthy, and in some cases proved to be more of a liability than an asset. Flying squads were organized, but more often than not they found themselves chasing ghosts. The farther north the Spanish went in Mexico proper the less effective became their military operations.

When at last they began their drive to conquer the Apache it was brutally made clear to them that they were facing the strongest opposition they had ever known. No longer would the classical tactics and methods with which they had conquered so much of the New World suffice. Nor were material and technological superiority the advantage they had been in years past. As for psychological advantages, they were no longer possessed by them. They were held by the Apache. Now it was the Apache who could create confusion, who could inspire fear, not with strangeness but with total unpredictability.

As the second half of the eighteenth century began, the thirty-second parallel of north latitude passed approximately through the center of the immense theater of the Apache-Spanish war. From east to west this imaginary line was more than seven hundred miles in length, extending from the Colorado River in Texas beyond the Santa Cruz River in Arizona. For some two hundred miles north and south of it the fires of conflict alternately flamed and died away without pattern, but always smoldering in their coals, in no place completely extinguished.

Few prisoners were recovered by either side. The Spanish captured were killed, clubbed or knifed to death, sometimes maimed and left to expire in terrible agony. The Apache captured were sold into slavery, and ended their days broken by labor in mines and mills. Young men and women and children brought the highest prices, the young men because they were strong and could be expected to survive for several years, the young women not only because they could labor but also because they were desirable as prostitutes, the children because they were more tractable and could be trained as servants and more easily converted by priests. But the Spanish would never seem to realize the great price they paid for every Apache captive. For each one they took, perhaps as many as a dozen settlers and soldiers were sacrificed in Apache raids of revenge.

Some idea of the tragic toll of the conflict may be gained from official reports which stated that between 1748 and 1770 the Apache killed more than four thousand persons and stole or destroyed property valued in excess of twelve million pesos. In a period of less than three years one hundred and forty settlers were murdered, more than seven thousand horses and mules were stolen, and large numbers of sheep and cattle which the Apache had been unable to drive off were slaughtered by them in pastures. The Apache casualties could not be counted with accuracy, for they often carried away their wounded and dead, but they could not have been a tenth as great. Yet, the Apache could not be said to be winning, for there were far fewer of them. The death or capture of a few hundred would have been a serious loss.

The bloody fortunes of war flowed back and forth, one side winning today and the other victorious tomorrow. If the Apache had been weakened, they showed no sign of it, but that could not be said of the Spanish. The Apache could live off the land, they could move at will, they could strike wherever and whenever they pleased, they could take advantage of an opportunity without regard for supplies or equipment. And they did. They slipped away through trackless deserts, vanished into canyons and mountains, sometimes going great distances without water, splitting into small groups and disappearing as if they had been swallowed by the earth.

The Spanish had been successful in negotiating treaties of peace with tribes which were ruled either by a supreme chief or a council of leaders. This was impossible in the case of the Apache, for they had no government with which a treaty could be negotiated and enforced. As Moorhead notes: "The fragmented nature of the Apache nation reduced peace pacts to mere truces; what the Apache people held as liberty the Spaniards considered license. . . . If the amorphous Apache groups were lacking in central authority, the more unified Spaniards were lacking in central policy. They did have a national government in structure, but in operation it allowed for such a large measure of local autonomy that no concerted attitude or action was possible. . . ."

Until the year 1772 provincial governors and garrison commanders dealt almost independently with hostile Indians. Treaties were made with some Apache, but they contributed nothing toward the solution of the problem. Moorhead continues: "One governor might negotiate peace with an Apache band or tribe, grant it protection, and provide it with food and clothing. But this merely gave security to the women and children while the warriors rode off to raid in a neighboring province where no such pact was in force. And when these marauders returned, they were not only safe from pursuit and punishment, but were also free to barter their booty . . . among the obliging provincials with whom they were at peace. If they should choose to break their treaty, they were free to do so in the full knowledge that another provincial government would grant them the same protection. In a sense the Apaches held the Spanish frontiersmen in tributary vassalage, extracting from the settlers and their subject Indians a never-ending subsidy. Yet neither side was satisfied with the arrangement, and both preyed upon the other when occasion permitted."

The stalemate would never be completely resolved. Apache groups would amalgamate, but almost entirely for purposes of augmenting their ability to wage war. If a group sought peace, it was done usually because it had suffered adversities and needed time to reorganize and recover. There would be no supreme Apache government. Bands might fight together, but they would never give up their independence. The Spaniards would enact standard policies, but they would prove to be in the larger degree unworkable or unsuitable under the existing conditions.

This was not a war that could be settled with diplomacy. Its issues and causes were irresolvable, for they sprang from contrasting ways of life, of demands, of beliefs that could be reconciled only through death.[14]

* * *

1775

The Spanish Government had become fully aware that it was threatened with the loss of its possessions north of central Mexico. The dire situation had been growing steadily worse for more than two decades, and during this period, although officials on both sides of the Atlantic had been cognizant of the developing disintegration, no actions had been taken to prevent a complete collapse. Obviously decisions could no longer be delayed. The time had come for drastic reorganization of administrative, political, and military policies.

The problems contributing to the crises were complex and numerous. The vastness of the region, its aridity and roughness, and the ever-present threat of attacks by Apache and other Indians made it extremely difficult, and often impossible, to maintain regular communications. Supply trains frequently were captured or destroyed by marauders. For months at a time troops were so short of ammunition that they could do no more than defend themselves and were unable to protect mines, haciendas, and settlements. Paymasters were required to purchase supplies in local distributing centers, and whenever money did arrive, merchants conspired to raise their prices, with the result that foodstuffs obtained were inadequate. Large parts of the funds intended for soldiers were stolen by presidio officers, and were irretrievably lost in gambling casinos or spent on fancy women. Most soldiers did not receive enough pay to purchase bare necessities for their families; they went deeply in debt, and their only hope of escaping from bondage was desertion.

When supplies, equipment, horses, ammunition, and manpower were available at the same time, campaigns were launched against the Apache and other unfriendly people. These offensives were undertaken in the hope they would discourage the Indians from making future raids. Usually they did no more than cause temporary interruptions in the depredations, and not infrequently the soldiers returned to a settlement that had been left defenseless to find it in ruins, the women and children carried off or murdered.

Social, economic, and religious factors created conflicts that sped the deterioration of affairs in the north. The mining, cattle, military, missionary, and Indian frontier society, Thomas (1941) writes, "was governed by the prevailing ideas of social organization that dominated the colonial period of Hispanic America. Its basic economic character found its expression in large land grants . . . to the privileged members of the Spanish aristocracy. . . .Likewise the Church received outright vast tracts of land for purposes of its support. . . ." Sheepherders, cowboys, and domestic servants ". . . were largely drawn from the *mestizos*, offspring of Spanish and Indian unions principally fostered through the missions. On the lands of the Church the same social blends existed." Labor in the mines was performed by "condemned prisoners, runaway Indians or Indians seized on the ground of being cannibalistic, and by the *mestizo* group available in nearby towns and haciendas."

The wealthy mine- and landowners resented interference from the provincial government. The lands of common settlers were confiscated on various ruses by the holders of grants. Governors sought to reclaim the illegally acquired lands for the king. The result was an endless flood of litigation. Every high military officer proposed new measures for countering Indian attacks. The result was never-ending confusion over policies. "In conflict, too," says Thomas, "with the central authority was the Church. Constant bickering characterized the relations between the local priests and the presidial captains and soldiery who, infringing the rights of the Padre's mission Indians, attempted to deprive them of lands or made more personal attacks. Higher up, the governor and the bishop waged endless war over questions of jurisdiction involving land, taxes, and control of the Indian communities which furnished the Church with important income and the governor with a source of labor supply in the royal mines, or in his own. Paralleling this conflict was that carried on by the Church with the powerful Creole landowners over identical issues."

Ironically, at the time the northern colonies were in the deepest trouble, the course of international affairs made them more valuable than they had ever been to the Spanish Crown. Ostensibly California had been occupied to create a barrier against Russia's movements on the Pacific Coast. In the Seven Years' War Spain had acquired the immense territory of Louisiana. Thus, countless thousands more Indians had been brought under Spanish jurisdiction. To establish peaceful relations with them far greater sums of money would have to be expended. The newly acquired and immense regions could never be successfully controlled if the older provinces, lying between them, were lost.

The Comanche had accomplished in a few decades what the Spanish had been unable to do in more than a hundred and fifty years, and that was to drive the Apache from the plains of western Kansas, southeastern Colorado, eastern New Mexico, and northern Texas. Groups of Apache, once strong, had vanished, and even their names were no longer to be found in official dispatches. If they had not been annihilated, they had been absorbed by other groups farther to the south and west.

The Jicarilla, victims of both the Utes and the Comanches, remained close to the stronger presidios of northern New Mexico for their protection, and some of them served with Spanish troops. The once numerous and powerful Lipan of the plains had taken refuge close to the Mescalero in the mountains of western Texas and along the Rio Grande in both Texas and Mexico. The Jumano were broken and scattered, as were the Manso. The Natagee drifted between western New Mexico, where they aligned themselves with the Gila Apache, and allies in Nueva Vizcaya, with whom they carried out raids on Spanish settlements. The Lipan and Mescalero frequently united to strike far below the Rio Grande, raiding haciendas and towns in the regions of Saltillo and Monterrey, sometimes going as far south as Durango. On other occasions they raided Spanish missions and settlements in Texas, striking as far east as San Antonio.

The Comanche conquest of the plains had not, however, been helpful to the Spanish. It meant in reality simply that instead of the Apache they had the Comanche to fight in that region. Moreover, the Comanche were mounted and well armed, and, therefore, were far more formidable foes than the Plains Apache had been before the advent of the horse and the gun.

Deprived of their traditional source of sustenance, the buffalo herds, and forced to live in the arid lands of southwestern Texas and northern Mexico, where game was scarce, the former Plains Apache steadily increased their raiding of Spanish ranchos to steal cattle, horses, and sheep, to supplement the natural foods they were able to obtain. It was obvious to the Spanish that before they could hope to wage a successful war against the Apache, they must first strive to make peace with the Comanche. The task was undertaken first in Texas, and after a decade of negotiations considerable headway was made, although the cost in human lives and money was great.

The Spanish-Comanche alliance achieved in Texas created an eastern barrier which the Apache could not penetrate, and they turned the full force of their attacks on northern Mexico. Thus, west of the Rio Grande the Apache became the predominant antagonist of the Spanish. Nor was the Texas pact with the Comanche effective in the Northern Plains regions held by that tribe. There the Comanche remained a constant and dangerous menace, attacking not only other tribes but Spanish settlements, and not infrequently raiding in force deep into Mexico.

1776

King Charles III, after long consultations with the Council of the Indies and provincial officials, approved a drastic measure which it was hoped would open the way to alleviating the desperate conditions, and serve as the means of resolving the major problems, of the northern frontier.

The interior provinces were taken from the control of the Mexican viceroy and placed under a separate military government. Don Teodoro de Croix, a veteran officer, was named commanding general, and awarded almost supreme powers.

1777

De Croix traveled on an inspection trip through a large part of his enormous jurisdiction. He brought into his administration many men of ability, integrity, and experience. One of them was the famed explorer and colonizer of California, Don Juan Bautista de Anza.

The king appointed Anza to the governorship of New Mexico. However, if de Croix lost a capable field commander in Mexico he gained a brilliant executive and diplomat in New Mexico in whom he could place his complete trust.

1778

De Croix continued his tour of inspection. He knew that the danger to the interior provinces from foreign powers had been greatly exaggerated, and the real threat to them came from the Apache. The problems they had created were formidable. From every quarter reports poured in telling of destroyed towns, settlers murdered, women and children slaughtered or carried into captivity, supply trains taken, missions burned, troops defeated, livestock stolen. From Texas to the California border, from northern New Mexico deep into Mexico, the Apache and their allies controlled the country.

1780

By this year de Croix had put into operation a sweeping plan, but he had been seriously hampered by the incredible red tape of the Spanish Government, by political jealousies, by the failure of promised funds to arrive. Not all the measures he proposed could be put into effect, yet he was successful in strengthening the defenses to a degree never previously achieved, and his accomplishments were noteworthy in other respects. He forced commercial establishments, mines, and the aristocratic owners of great haciendas to pay taxes for the support of his troops. He proposed a system that would assure the paying and supplying of soldiers with regularity. He built a new presidial line, keeping strong patrols moving between stations, guarding the most vulnerable sectors.

De Croix's strategy was to keep the Lipan, Mescalero, Gila, and other Apache bands under attack as much as possible. In numerous offensives his troops were victorious. Then, to his utter dismay, he received orders from the king that open warfare against hostile Indians was to be waged only under extreme necessity, and that no efforts were to be spared to obtain peace through negotiations and treaties. De Croix said bluntly that such measures would never succeed, for hatred of the Spanish had been instilled in the Apache through many generations. Yet he dutifully informed the state governors of the sovereign's commands, and instructed them to make every attempt to abide by them.

1783

De Croix was appointed viceroy of Peru.

The protective measures he had executed had brought new prosperity to many sections of northern Mexico. For the first time there was reason to believe that the Apache menace was on the wane. Then influential officials in Spain, who had never seen an Apache and knew little, if anything, about actual conditions in the New World colonies, persuaded the king to divide the military government of the interior provinces of New Spain into several sub-districts and restore control of all of them to the viceroy in Mexico City. These moves, of course, opened the gates to patronage, which was what the politicians wanted, but it created administrative chaos. The policies of de Croix, which had been effective, were soon rendered unworkable by internal conflicts. The final result was that unified strategy was impossible.

Not unaware of the confusion and the absence of cooperation between military authorities, the Apache struck viciously on all salients, and the interior provinces once again suffered from their destructive, murderous raiding.

1786

Bernardo de Gálvez became viceroy of Mexico. He was a veteran frontier Indian fighter, and, drawing on his extensive experiences, he composed his notorious *Instructions for the Governing of the Interior Provinces of New Spain.*

The instructions were in many respects a compromise, containing elements of several previous policies. They called for the vigorous prosecution of warfare against Apache, or any other Indians, who refused to submit, while at the same time urging field commanders to adhere to the king's "peace-by-persuasion" strategy. Fundamentally, however, they comprised the most dishonest and brutal plan for the pacification of Indians ever devised by a supreme commander since the first Spaniards set foot on the North American mainland.

The Apache, Gálvez told Ugarte and other frontier officers and governors, would never, in his opinion, voluntarily capitulate. Therefore, while relentless warfare was to be carried on against them, year round, they were to be notified that any of them who surrendered would be established in towns adjacent to military stations, fully protected and furnished with all the necessities of life.

Diabolical trickery was concealed in the offer. The Apache were to be given attractive gifts and assured of adequate food supplies as inducements to surrender, but were also to be furnished guns and liquor.

Regarding the firearms to be furnished the Apache who agreed to accept peace terms, Moorhead interprets Gálvez's instructions in this way: ". . . the muskets should be long ones. These would be awkward for the Indian to use while on horseback. They should also have weakened barrels, stocks, and bolts, making them easily damaged and in continuous need of readjustment, repair, and replacement by skilled Spanish gunsmiths. Having accepted firearms, the Indians would abandon their native weapons, lose their skill with them, and become dependent upon the Spaniards for both the supply and maintenance of their new ones."

Previously the Spanish had attempted to prevent Indians from obtaining intoxicating liquors, but Gálvez ordered that the Apache be furnished with as much as they desired. As translated by Worcester, Gálvez stated: "After all, the supplying of drink to the Indians will be a means of gaining their goodwill, discovering their secrets, calming them so they will think less often of conceiving and executing their hostilities, and creating for them a new necessity which will oblige them to recognize their dependence upon it more directly." In plainer English, the Apache who submitted were to be destroyed by liquor.

Gálvez died shortly after issuing his instructions, but frontier officials, notably Ugarte, continued to abide generally by them, and from the Spanish point of view the results were beneficial. The Franciscan missionaries registered strong complaints against the policies, charging that their true purpose was corruption and not Christianization. Numerous Apache groups in northern Mexico and southern Arizona had accepted sanctuary. They were given weekly rations of corn, meat, tobacco, candy, and enough liquor to keep them stupefied most of the time. As one padre in Tucson vehemently complained, no effort was made to instill Spanish virtues in them. They lived in terrible squalor, and soon adopted all the vices of the white man, such as gambling, cursing, immorality, and drunkenness.

1787

Manuel Antonio Flores became viceroy. He did not approve of the methods of his predecessor. The cornerstone of his own announced Indian policy was extermination. He was critical of the plan to grant asylum and protection to Apache bands in one area while other areas were suffering from their ravages. He reshuffled the military organization, transferring the capable Ugarte, and divided jurisdictions, with the result that cooperation between frontier military leaders was all but destroyed.

Anza retired as governor of New Mexico. His record was marked by extraordinary achievements. Among them:

1. After long and arduous efforts he had succeeded in inducing the Ute and Comanche, traditional enemies, to cease their hostilities against each other and agree to the terms of a treaty he proposed.

2. He had broken up an alliance between the Navajo and Gila Apache which had existed for five years. The agreement had opened to both tribes vast areas for plunder, and formidable forces of the united warriors had conducted raids into Mexico.

Anza had driven south from Santa Fe and had established a military line between the territories of the two tribes at the Río de la Laguna (Río San José). Forces moved north from Mexico and inflicted serious defeats on the Gilenos.

Anza thoroughly understood not only the perfidious nature of the Navajo but also their economic and political structures, and he was fully aware of their precarious situation as a result of pressures from enemy tribes, especially the Ute. He added another pressure on them by stationing a force on the Río de la Laguna and notifying the Navajo that any of them found in Gila territory south of the stream would be considered "declared enemies," seized and taken to Santa Fe, and punished.

The pincers campaign had brought the desired results.

3. Anza forbade all trade and communications between Navajo, Pueblo, and Apache, warning all colonists and peaceful Indians that violations of the order would bring severe penalties.

The strategy was effective. Trade was vitally important to the economy of the Navajo, and their leaders soon appeared in Santa Fe to pledge that they would sever their ties with the Gila Apache and to request that the trade barrier be removed. Some of the Navajo even offered to join the Spanish in attacking the Gilenos. Anza accepted the offer and rescinded the order preventing them from bartering with other tribes. On several occasions the Navajo carried out raids against their former allies, the Gila Apache, and drove them southward.

4. In several campaigns Anza inflicted such severe losses on the Comanche that not a few of their leaders were convinced of the wisdom of making peace. Anza and his superior in Mexico, Captain-General Jacob Ugarte y Loyola, insisted that all branches of the Comanche must be represented in any negotiations undertaken. Their demand was met.

In the spring of Anza's last year in office the headmen of the Comanche Nation affixed their signatures to a treaty of peace with the Spanish Government.

When Anza left Santa Fe, Comanche, Pueblo, Ute, and even some apostate Apache were serving as auxiliaries under the Spanish flag.

* * *

Under the changes wrought by Gálvez and Flores the system of alliances which Anza and Ugarte, working as a team, had constructed began to disintegrate. Nevertheless, for a time the northern frontier knew unprecedented quiet. As more Spanish troops were sent to the territory, more Apache sued for peace. Spanish settlers began to reestablish farms and ranchos in places that the Apache menace had made uninhabitable for decades. Bands came from the mountains of New Mexico and Arizona to live near the presidios of Tucson and Tubac, although the great majority of the Gila Apache refused to capitulate. Some three hundred Chiricahua accepted Spanish protection in Sonora. Some Mimbreno and Mescalero surrendered in Nueva Vizcaya. The Lipan had asked for sanctuary in New Mexico, but the Comanche prevented an accord being signed between them and the Spanish. It was the contention of the Comanche that if the Lipan were permitted to surrender they would be forced to cease their attacks on them. Fearful of antagonizing their Comanche allies, the Spanish refused to negotiate with the Lipan.

Fortunately for the northern colonies, ill health forced Flores to resign after only two years in office. His successor, the Conde de Revillagigedo, promptly restored the competent Ugarte to the post of supreme military commander of the interior provinces. Ugarte had formed peace pacts with several thousand Apache, and although during Flores's brief tenure most of them had violated their pledges—largely due to neglect and broken promises—and had fled to resume their raiding, Ugarte was able to win many of them to new alliances.

By 1796 some high Spanish officials permitted themselves to believe that the long war with the Apache might be nearing an end. They were to be sadly disappointed. In the last years of the eighteenth century pressures began to arise that would deliver a death blow to the policy of sustaining all Apache who surrendered. They came from several sources. Maintaining villages for peaceful Apache and supplying them with food, clothing, and liquor was an expensive program. Considerable numbers of presidial troops had to be provided, both to protect them from hostiles and to keep them from running away. Settlers and other civilians did not like to have numbers of indolent Indians living in close proximity to them, and they resented having to pay taxes to help support savages who contributed little or nothing to the economy.

As the nineteenth century began it was clearly apparent that peace with the Apache through subsidization could not be successful, and the program had to be abandoned. But this would not be done by official action. It would be accomplished by several momentous events which would leave the Spanish Government no prerogatives in formulating a new Indian policy.

THE NINETEENTH CENTURY

PART I

1800–1845

1803

Despite the seriousness of the Apache menace, as Spanish official-dom viewed the situation, an even greater threat faced New Mexico. It arose with the sale by France to the United States of the immense and inadequately defined Louisiana Territory.

1804

The first American traders, defying Spanish regulations, began to appear in Santa Fe.

Rumors that American military forces were pushing westward and were attempting to induce Great Plains tribes to join them in attacking Spanish settlements came with the regularity of the moons.

1807

The first American spies, Zebulon M. Pike and Dr. John H. Robinson, and a small group of American soldiers, were captured on Spanish territory.

Governor Joaquin del Real Alencaster, after interviewing them in Santa Fe, sent them under military escort to Chihuahua.

Intelligence of Aaron Burr's conspiracy with General James Wilkinson, commander in chief of American forces in Louisiana, to launch a filibustering expedition against New Mexico and Texas gave nightmares to the harassed Alencaster. Patrols were sent along the northern Louisiana boundaries claimed by Spain to search for the invaders. Fortunately for them they encountered only more traders eager to open commerce between St. Louis and Santa Fe. Had a strong American military contingent been approaching, the sparse forces of New Mexico would have been quickly overcome.

Pike got a glimpse of Apache en route as a prisoner to Chihuahua.

On the lower Rio Grande he saw a large group of them encamped near San Elizerio, and he wrote: "Around this fort were a great number of Apaches, who were on a treaty with the Spaniards. These people appear to be perfectly independent in their manners and were the only savages I saw in the Spanish dominions whose spirit was not humbled, whose necks were not bowed to the yoke of their invaders."

1810

The Mexicans launched their revolution to win independence.

The beleaguered Spanish provincial government withdrew troops from the northern frontier to fight the rebels in the south. The remaining small garrisons were no longer able to control, much less supply, the Apache who had made peace. These people were forced to steal to sustain themselves, and there were too few soldiers to pursue and punish them.

Once again the flames of Apache warfare raged out of control across the desert and mountain regions of Apacheria and northern Mexico.

1811

This was the picture:

East of the Rio Grande, in the mountains of southeastern New Mexico, were the Faraon, survivors of Comanche onslaughts on the Great Plains. They raided Spanish settlements to the north and to the south in Nueva Vizcaya, often uniting with their close relatives, the Mescalero.

The Mescalero inhabited the region between the Pecos River in Texas and the Rio Grande in New Mexico. Barred by the Comanche from traveling northward to hunt, they preyed on the herds of livestock in Coahuila and Nueva Vizcaya.

Directly east of the Mescalero were the Llanero, the Lipiyane, and the Natagee, constituting a single tribe. On their north was the Comanche barrier, and they concentrated their attacks on the Spanish towns and ranchos of Coahuila, frequently uniting on raids with the Mescalero and the Faraon.

The Lipan dwelt southeast of the Llanero. They attacked the Spanish in lower Texas, but often joined the Mescalero and Llanero on raids into Coahuila.

In southwestern New Mexico were the Mimbreno. Bands of them joined the Faraon in raiding New Mexican settlements and the Gileno and Chiricahua on forays into Mexico.

The Gila Apache lived along the river from which they received their name, in southeastern Arizona. They ranged on their raids as far north as the Zuñi and Hopi Countries and far south into Nueva Vizcaya and Sonora.

South of the Gileno was the homeland of the Chiricahua, in the rugged mountains of southeastern Arizona. They attacked ranchos, mines, and towns in southern Arizona and in the northern Mexican provinces. In raiding they joined the Mimbreno and Gileno, and these united bands were feared more by the Spanish than any other Apache. They not only struck in well-organized and superbly directed attacks, but wreaked more devastation, killed more people, stole more live-stock, and destroyed more property than any other raiders.

In the Pinal Mountains and the Tonto Basin were the Tonto (Coyotero), and because of their isolation they seldom had been the targets of Spanish campaigns. However, they frequently emerged from their remote range to join the Chiricahua on raids into Mexico.

* * *

In its early stages the Mexican Revolution had no significant effect on that part of New Mexico that would become known as Arizona, but that was not the case with the eastern part of the province containing the Rio Grande watershed. There serious new problems were added to the burdens with which officials had long contended. A New Mexico governor in Santa Fe had little time to concern himself with a rebellion taking place some fifteen hundred miles away. Its outcome—whatever it might be—would shape the course of events, but meanwhile, his struggle must be directed against the pressures mounting closer to him, that is, if he were to continue to perform his sworn duty of protecting and preserving the colony, as well as his own neck.

These pressures, originating both internally and externally, came from all sides. The colonists obviously cared little whether Spain or Mexico was victorious. The raiding of the Navajo from the west and of the Apache all across the southern perimeter had forced the aban-donment of mines, ranchos, settlements, and missions. The with-drawal of troops to fight in the Mexican uprising had so weakened defenses that there was no hope the remaining soldiers could halt the onslaughts of the Indians.

It is improbable that the ignorant settlers of the upper Rio Grande realized in their fears that one factor alone provided them with a large measure of security. That was the inability, or the unwillingness, of the Indians to organize. If no more than five thousand Indians had over-come, even temporarily, the prejudices and hatreds that normally dominated them, had merged their forces, and had attacked in unison, New Mexico would have known the same fate it suffered as a result of the uprising of 1680. It would have become once more a vast theater of warfare between tribes, with the Comanche and others sweeping in from the plains to fight the Navajo and the Apache for the prize, and with the virtually helpless Pueblos caught in the middle. As it was, although the small garrisons left on the upper Rio Grande, with the aid of Indian mercenaries and civilian militia, were frequently successful in inflicting punishment on raiders, their strikes had little lasting effect, and the fighting seldom halted for more than a few months at a time. Their efforts, nevertheless, saved New Mexico.

* * *

1821

News that Mexico had won independence from Spain reached Santa Fe.

Ceremonies and gay parties were held, there was dancing in the streets, guns were fired, and the last Spanish governor, Facundo Melgares, made a fervent speech which showed that he knew very well the side on which his bread was buttered.

"New Mexicans," he shouted, "this is the occasion for showing the heroic patriotism that inflames you . . . with our last drop of blood we will sustain the sacred independence of the Mexican Empire!"

1822

The Apache problem was thrown squarely on the shoulders of the incoming New Mexico authorities representing the new Mexican Republic. They could be excused for shaking their heads in dismay. It appeared to them that little, if anything, had been accomplished toward resolving it since the first Spanish soldiers and missionaries had pushed into the northern wilderness. A few things had changed, but nothing of great significance. The Plains Apache had been driven far south of the great grass ranges over which they roamed when Castañeda wrote of them. Many bands had been broken and scattered, but the survivors had found havens among their people in other areas on both sides of the Rio Grande. One of the greatest of all difficulties facing the Mexicans was that in the political and social structures of the Apache Nation nothing at all had changed. Each group still retained the autonomy enjoyed since the first Apache had migrated southward from northern Canada. No single leader could speak for all Apache. Nor was there a council composed of representatives of the innumerable bands. Negotiating a treaty with the Apache as a people was still an impossibility.

Yet the Apache were a people held together by indestructible bonds. In warfare, in their raiding, they were in every sense a united nation, inspired by the same motives, with a common objective—preservation of their independence and their enormous homeland.

Moreover, in other ways the Apache problem with which the Mexican Government was forced to contend was more difficult, more menacing, more complicated, than it had been when the Spanish began their long and desperate struggle with it. Now the Apache were mounted, the possessors of countless thousands of horses and mules. They were armed with guns, as well as bows and arrows. They understood Spanish customs, were trained in combating Spanish military tactics, many of them spoke the Spanish language, and they had increased in number.

The Mexicans had to begin all over again, almost exactly where the Spanish had begun, but under far more difficult circumstances.

* * *

If there was any difference between a Spaniard and a Mexican the Apache were unable to discern it. The change of flags brought no changes in policies that were beneficial to them. Indeed, the opposite was true. If the Mexicans had any plans at all for dealing with the Apache they were comprised of only two objectives: (1) Take captives to be sold into slavery, and (2) Kill all Apache who refused to surrender.

Apache children were worth one hundred fifty pesos on the open market. Priests "saved the souls" of captured small boys and girls by baptizing them before they were sold as servants to affluent Mexican families. Records are vague, but mission documents indicate that several hundred captive young Apache were baptized in the first few years after New Mexico became a Mexican dominion. Because they had few soldiers at their command, the Mexican provincial governors engaged friendly Ute, Comanche, and unconscionable civilians to conduct slave raids for them, paying for their services with booty, which included both human beings and livestock. Repeatedly Mexican governors sought to induce Apache to capitulate by promising them gifts and a treaty of peace under which they would be sustained and protected— the old Spanish policy. Whereas the Spanish, in numerous instances, had abided by similar agreements, the Mexicans had no intention of honoring them. A few Apache succumbed to the trickery, but once the insincerity of the Mexicans had been made manifest, an offer of amnesty was answered with bloody raids on Mexican presidios and settlements.

Now, suddenly, the Apache were confronted with a new foe.

The men whom they saw trapping on the clear, cold streams in the mountains of southwestern New Mexico and southeastern Arizona were a breed completely strange to them. They spoke an incomprehensible language, appeared to have little in common with Mexicans, and seemed to be bent upon a single mission, to take pelts and move on their way to a mysterious destination.

They were American beaver-hunters, members of that rare fraternity of wild adventurers, the Mountain Men, who within a few years after the American acquisition of Louisiana Territory would penetrate every valley and range and desert of the West.

It is doubtful if the Apache understood that most of the Americans they came upon trapping the streams which flowed into the Gila and other rivers had no right to be in Mexican territory. Nor could they have determined in the beginning that some of them were desperate outlaws. There are numerous records to show that the Apache at first were inclined to be friendly, to let them go about their business, and disappear. The Apache's fight was with the Mexicans, and there was cause enough for that, but they had no reason for committing hostile acts against a handful of strange men who gave every indication that they wished only to pass through Apache Country, taking some skins as they went.

The Apache would soon come to understand how wrong was their thinking and their attitude. They would soon learn that the Mountain Men had an Indian policy of their own. It was: Shoot first and talk afterward.

* * *

1824

The first American fur trappers known to have reached the interior of Apacheria were a small group led by Sylvester Pattie who in this year took beaver on the Gila River in New Mexico. With Pattie was his son, James Ohio Pattie, whose published account of his adventures would be a best-seller in the United States and in several European countries.

The beginning of the war between Apache and Americans is traceable to the exploits of the Patties, father and son, and their companions. Imbued with a hatred of all Indians, held by so many Americans of similar frontier background, they made no attempt to be friendly with the Apache they encountered. They exhibited their true feelings by aligning themselves with Mexicans. The result was that the Apache soon recognized them as the enemy they were, and blood was shed. In the fighting, the actions of the Pattie band—and this may be said as well of the Americans who followed them in Apacheria—were no less barbaric than those of the Apache. Neither side surpassed the other in deceit, brutality, or fiendishness.

After trapping down the Gila to its confluence with the Salt River in Arizona, the Pattie party cached their furs and turned back upstream, their destination the Santa Rita copper mines near the present Silver City, New Mexico. Located in the very heart of Apacheria, the mines had for years been targets of Apache raids, and they had continued to operate only under perilous conditions. Abandoning all hope of Christianizing any Apache in the area, the resident padre some time before had departed to carry on his crusade elsewhere under more promising conditions. En route up the Gila, Pattie recounted:

"We found a man [Mexican miner] the Indians had killed. They had cut him up in quarters, after the fashion of butchers. His head, with the hat on, was stuck on a stake. It was full of arrows, which they had probably discharged into it, as they danced around it. We gathered up the parts of the body, and buried them."

1825

Fearing that he and his workers would not be able to withstand Apache attacks much longer, much less be able to get any of their metal out of the country, the mine operator, Juan Unis, persuaded the Patties to remain as guards. Sylvester Pattie directed his men in building strong new defenses. Two Apache who apparently had been observing the work in progress were pursued and captured. After being held a night one of them was freed with instructions "to tell his chief to come in, with all his warriors, to make peace. We retained one of the prisoners as a hostage, assuring the other that if his chief did not come in to make peace, we would put the hostage to death."

Within a day or two an Apache leader appeared, and signaled that he was there to negotiate for the release of the prisoner and agree to peace terms. Behind him were eighty mounted warriors. While the council was being held, the Apache were kept at a distance by riflemen in a trench that had been excavated before the wall which enclosed the main mine and village.

Four Apache representatives sat about a blanket with the Patties, and "we asked them if they were ready to make a peace with us; and if not what were the objections? They replied that they had no objections to a peace with the Americans, but would never make one with the Spaniards. When we asked their reasons, they answered that they had been long at war with the Spaniards, and that a great many murders had been mutually inflicted on either side. They admitted that they had taken a great many horses from the Spaniards, but indignantly alleged that a large party of their people had [once] come in to make peace with the Spaniards . . . and the Spaniards had decoyed the party within their walls, and then commenced butchering them like a flock of sheep."

The Apache counselors were told the mines were now being worked jointly by the Spanish and the Americans, "and that if they would not be peaceable, and allow us to work the mines unmolested, the Americans would consider them at war and would raise a sufficient body of men to pursue them in their lurking places . . . and that we could shoot a great deal better than either they or the Spaniards. . . ."

The Apache agreed not to attack. The hostage was restored to them. They vanished into the magnificent high country. If there had been any question in their minds as to whether Americans were staunch allies of the Mexicans, it no longer existed. "All this farce," said James Ohio Pattie, "of bringing the Indians to terms of peace was of infinite service to the Spaniards,* though of none to us; for we neither had any interest in the mines, nor intended to stay there much longer. But we were glad to oblige Juan Unis."

Juan Unis was appreciative, but he understood the Apache, and he had had enough fighting. He knew that as soon as the Americans departed, the attacks would be resumed. In the hope of saving them from destruction, he proposed that the Americans "rent the mines for five years, at a thousand dollars a year. He was willing to furnish provisions for the first year gratis, and pay for all the improvements we should make . . . this was an excellent offer. My father accepted it." However, his son would not agree to remain, "feeling within me an irresistible propensity to resume the employment of trapping." When a band of French trappers arrived, James Ohio Pattie and several other Americans left with them.†

The Apache kept their pledge not to attack the mines as long as the Americans operated them, but they retaliated in other ways which forcefully demonstrated their anger. They almost continually harassed the American trappers and their French companions, shot at them from ambush, stole their horses, and robbed their caches of furs and supplies. And one day "our sentinels apprized us that savages were at hand. We had just time to take shelter behind the trees, when they began to let their arrows fly at us. We returned them the compliment with balls, and at the first shot a number of them fell. They remained firm and continued to pour in their arrows from every side. . . . At length one man was pierced, and they rushed forward to scalp him."

As he tells the story, James Ohio Pattie darted from behind a tree

---

*He makes no distinction between Spaniards and Mexicans.
†The elder Pattie would continue to operate the Santa Rita mines until his son returned a year later. Together they would journey to California, where Sylvester would die in jail, charged with entering the country without permission.

to help the wounded man, and was "assailed by a perfect shower of arrows, which I dodged for a moment, and was then struck down by an arrow in the hip. Here I should have been instantly killed, had not my companions made a joint fire at the Indians . . . by which a number of them were laid dead. But the agony of my pain was insupportable. . . . A momentary cessation of their arrows enabled me to draw out the arrow from my hip, and to commence re-loading my gun. I had partly accomplished this, when I received another arrow under my right breast, between the bone and the flesh. . . . I snapped it off, and finished re-loading my gun."

The trappers retreated to a river bank, and after "we had gained this security, the Indians stood but a few shots more, before they fled, leaving their dead and wounded at our mercy.

"Truth is, we were too much exasperated to show mercy, and we cut off the heads of all, indiscriminately."

An appendix to Pattie's narrative states that the "arrows of the Apaches are three feet long, and are made of reed or cane, into which they sink a piece of hardwood, with a point made of iron, bone, or stone. They shoot this weapon with such force, that at the distance of three hundred paces they can pierce a man. When the arrow is attempted to be drawn out of the wound, the wood detaches itself, and the point remains in the body. Their second offensive weapon is a lance, fifteen feet long. When they charge the enemy they hold this lance with both hands above their heads, and, at the same time, guide their horse by pressing him with their knees. Many of them are armed with firelocks. . . . The archers and fusileers combat on foot but the lancers are always on horseback. They make use of a buckler for defense. Nothing can equal the impetuosity and address of their horsemen. They are thunderbolts, whose stroke it is impossible to parry or escape.

"We must cease to feel astonished at the invincible resistance which the Apaches oppose to the Spaniards, when we reflect on the fate to which they have subjected those other Indians who have allowed themselves to be converted."

Whether the latter statement reflects Pattie's sentiments is not made clear. It is attributed to a work called *Universal Geography*, for which no publisher is given, but it should be noted that the language is strikingly similar to that of Pattie's ghostwriter, Timothy Flint, who besides being an editor was also a Protestant minister.

Pattie is credited with stating that the Apache in the fight in which he suffered two wounds were a band of Mescalero who possessed no firearms, and "the men, though not tall, are admirably formed, with fine features and a bright complexion inclining to yellow. Their dress is a buckskin belt about the loins, with shirt and moccasins to match.

Their long black hair hangs in imbraided masses over their shoulders, in some cases almost extending to the heels. They make a most formidable appearance when completely painted and prepared for battle."

If James Ohio Pattie's narrative can be believed—and there are good reasons for believing a large part of it—he saw more of the West than any other American of his time, with the exception of Jedediah Smith. He was the first American to journey up the Colorado River from its mouth on the Gulf of California to the mountains of Colorado State. He was the first American to look into the depths of the Grand Canyon. Certainly he and his companions were the first Americans to fight the Apache.

* * *

With the new nation embroiled in political turmoil, administrative chaos, and bitter jurisdictional disputes, officials in Mexico City, none of whom could be certain of holding his job from one day to the next or of the extent of his authority, gave little attention to the problems of the northern states. Statutes were enacted and often revised or revoked before they became effective. Chief executives and military commanders were sent north and recalled on the heels of each other.* Every official messenger arriving in Santa Fe brought directives, legislative rulings, and judicial decisions which conflicted with those previously received. The resulting state of constant confusion afforded governors a free hand to do much as they pleased. Without exception they directed affairs in ways personally advantageous to themselves. All of them kept their snouts in the public trough.

Santa Fe was the fountainhead of the corruption which spread throughout New Mexico. The arrival of American trappers and gold hunters and the development of the Santa Fe Trail trade provided sources of revenue which enriched high and low officials. The Mountain Men and the prospectors increased in number each year. Some of them took the trouble to pay a fee for a permit to operate in the country, but many did not bother with this formality, international borders meaning no more to them than to Apache, Navajo, and Comanche. The law—or as individual governors chose to interpret it —required American interlopers to deliver a certain percentage of any furs they took or precious metals they discovered to the chief executive in office, but few, if any, of them complied with it.† If they were lucky enough to have survived attacks by Indians and Mexican bandits, they simply disappeared at the end of a season's work, but many of them were robbed and killed before they could escape from these occupational hazards.

---

*Between 1822 and 1846 nineteen governors held office in New Mexico.
†On several occasions New Mexico had two, or even three, governors at the same time.

La entrada de la caravana! was a cry which caused great excitement and rejoicing on the highest and lowest levels of Santa Fe society. Temporarily freed of their duties, the wagoneers, wranglers, guards, and traders, craving entertainment and lustful after ten weeks' journey from Missouri across the Great Plains, swarmed into the gambling dens and houses of prostitution. A session at a card table usually cost them the wages they had earned on the hard and perilous trip. A silver dollar got them a few minutes in bed with a senorita. No charge was made for the gonorrhea and syphilis they contracted.

The customs inspectors received their bribes, but the bulk of the duties went directly to the governor, who enjoyed the prerogative of establishing the tariffs to be paid on each type of merchandise. Not infrequently, goods—in some cases an entire caravan—were confiscated on the charge, usually without foundation, that they had been brought illegally into Mexican territory. On some occasions the owners were sent as prisoners to Mexico, where they languished for months in prison before being expelled from the country. Losses as high as thirty thousand dollars are known to have occurred.

"The *derechos de arancel* (tariff imposts) of Mexico," wrote the prominent Santa Fe Trail trader, Josiah Gregg, "are extremely oppressive, averaging about a hundred per cent upon the United States' cost of an ordinary 'Santa Fe assortment.'

"For a few years, Gov. Armijo of Santa Fe, established a tariff of *his own*, entirely arbitrary—exacting five hundred dollars for each wagon-load, whether large or small—of fine or coarse goods! . . . As might have been anticipated, the traders soon took to conveying their merchandise only in the largest wagons, drawn by ten or twelve mules, and omitting the coarser or more weighty articles of trade. This caused the governor to return to an *ad valorem* system, though still without regard to the *Arancel general* of the nation. How much of these duties found their way into the public treasury, I will not venture to assert."*

Campaigns against the Apache by both civilians and the few soldiers in the garrisons were almost totally ineffective. A few were killed and some were captured and sold into slavery, but these modest successes only stirred the Apache to greater vengeance. At certain times they held almost absolute control over large parts of the region. Their raiding so greatly devastated southern Arizona that only two settlements, Tubac and Tucson, existed there. This area at the western end of Apacheria would enjoy a respite from their attacks simply because

---

*Manuel Armijo, born of a poor family, was governor of New Mexico three times, 1827–1829, 1837–1844, 1845–1846. As a youth he was employed as a sheepherder by a wealthy rancher near Albuquerque, and stole and sold so many of his employer's animals that he became prosperous, if not rich.

there was little left to be stolen. Some other parts of Apacheria fared
not much better. Settlers were forced to abandon most of the Rio
Grande Valley in southern New Mexico and Texas. In the vicinity of
El Paso, farming and livestock-raising could be conducted only under
the shadows of presidio walls. Commerce with Chihuahua was possible
only with strong armed escorts. Occasionally a supply caravan would
disappear—wagons, livestock, cargo, and personnel—as if it had been
swept from the earth. Searchers sometimes found wreckage, but seldom anything of value remained to be salvaged, and the bleached
bones of the defenders lay among the burned skeletons of the vehicles.[15]

* * *

1835

With no hope of receiving from Mexico City the military forces
needed to combat the Apache, the state government of Sonora inaugurated its own *Proyecto de Guerra.* Under the terms of this war project,
which was to be financed by a special fund created for the purpose,
Apache scalps would be paid for on the following scale:

One hundred pesos for the scalp of an adult male.

Fifty pesos for the scalp of a female.

Twenty-five pesos for the scalp of a child.*

Within a short time bands of bounty hunters were combing Apacheria as well as surrounding regions, their trails marked by a terrible
carnage.

Juan José's Indian name has been lost to history. He was a Mimbres
Apache who, as a youth, had been sent to a mission school. His high
intelligence soon attracted attention, and he was induced to study for
the priesthood. He had progressed rapidly, became fluent in the Spanish language, and soon demonstrated that he possessed qualities that
could make him an able wilderness emissary of the Church. However,
this career had been abruptly terminated when Mexicans murdered his
father. Juan José went back to his people, filled with hatred and a
consuming desire for vengeance. As the leader of a powerful group of
warriors, he conducted terrifying and devastating raids on Mexican
settlements and haciendas. His education gave him an advantage other
Apache leaders did not enjoy. By robbing the mails and waylaying
messengers he was enabled to put to good use the intelligence contained in official communications. Plans for military operations against

---

*At this time the peso and the American silver dollar were almost equal value. The
state of Chihuahua would adopt a similar reward system two years later.

the Apache were thwarted by him, and not infrequently troops rode into deadly ambushes.

For some time Juan José had maintained friendly relations with James Johnson, an American who operated a trading store at Oposura, in Sonora. Johnson agreeably exchanged firearms and foodstuffs for livestock and other goods stolen by Juan José and his band. They gave him no trouble, considering his post as an outlet through which they could safely and profitably dispose of surplus booty, of which they usually had a large amount.

Purportedly in the spring of this year, but perhaps a year later, Juan José intercepted a letter from the Mexican Government to Johnson in which the trader was offered a large reward for his scalp. Juan José confronted Johnson with the written evidence, but was convinced by him that he had no intention of committing the dastardly deed. After inviting the trader to visit his camp, Juan José departed.

A short time later, Johnson arrived with a pack train in the rough and remote territory of southwestern New Mexico in which Juan José made his home. With him were several Missourians who ostensibly had come to Sonora to obtain mules, and who had agreed to accompany him after he had told them that Juan José might be able to furnish them with the animals they sought. Two of these American adventurers can be identified by the names of Gleason and Eames, but how much they knew of the plot Johnson had in mind is not a matter of record. They, nevertheless, would take part in one of the most infamous events, involving Americans, ever to occur on the Apache frontier.

Johnson established a camp, and sent word to Juan José that he had brought gifts for him and his people. He arranged a large pile of blankets, sacks of flour and pinole, saddles, and kegs of whiskey. Concealed under them was a small howitzer loaded with bullets, slugs, nails, and pieces of broken chain. Juan José and some thirty-five Apache men, women, and children appeared, and the festivities began. Johnson had placed the gifts so that they would be obliged to stand in front of the gun to accept them. With the guests all assembled and shouting their pleasure at receiving the presents, Johnson touched a lighted cigar to the fuse.

More than twenty were killed under the rain of shrapnel. Juan José, although badly wounded, grappled with Gleason, and was on the verge of cutting his throat when Johnson saved him by shooting Juan José in the back. Two or three of the Missourians were slain as the Apache who had escaped the blast fought their way out of the camp. The wounded Apache, among them several women and children, were shot or clubbed to death by Johnson, and all victims were scalped. He took his pack train of goods back to his trading post, and presumably collected the bounties for some twenty-five scalps, a considerable sum. However, his days as a trader soon came to an end. His post was destroyed by Apache raiders, but he managed to elude the attackers and find safety in a distant Mexican settlement.*

About the same time as the Johnson massacre a similar atrocity was perpetrated in El Paso. Mexican soldiers captured several Apache, one of them the wife of an influential Mescalero. Gregg tells of the tragic event in this way: "The bereaved chief, hearing of their captivity, collected a band of about sixty warriors, and, boldly entering the town, demanded the release of his consort and friends. The commandant of the place, wishing to gain time, desired them to return the next morning, when their request would be granted. During the night the forces of the country were concentrated; notwithstanding, when the Apaches reappeared, the troops did not show their faces, but remained concealed, while the Mexican commandant strove to beguile the Indians into the prison, under pretense of delivering to them their friends. The unsuspecting chief and twenty others were entrapped in this manner, and treacherously dispatched in cold blood; not, however, without some loss to the Mexicans, who had four or five of their men killed in the fracas. Among them was the commandant himself, who had no sooner given the word, '*Maten á los carajos!*' (Kill the scoundrels!), than the chief retorted, '*Entonces morirás tu primero, carajo!*' (Then you shall die first!), and immediately stabbed him to the heart!"

Innumerable instances in which lone and defenseless Apache were shot as if they were wild animals were reported. A typical case occurred in Chihuahua City. Up to the front of the Palacio (Government House) rode a Mexican officer, on the tip of his lance a fresh Apache scalp. Proudly he explained that he and his men, while pursuing a small band of raiders, had come upon a young squaw with an infant in her arms. She was immediately slain and scalped. As neither milk nor other suitable food was available for the infant, it had quickly perished, and its body had been thrown into the brush. The Chihuahua newspaper commended the officer for his gallantry.

Within a few days after the slaughter in Johnson's camp Americans throughout the length and breadth of Apacheria had begun to suffer the consequences of his barbarism. On the Gila River, not far distant from the scene of Juan José's death, a company of twenty-two trappers under the leadership of Charles Kemp were attacked by a horde of warriors and wiped out. A few miles away three other beaver hunters were surrounded. Two of them were killed, but the third, Benjamin D. Wilson, by some miracle escaped, and succeeded in reaching Santa

---

*Later he went to California, where, unfortunately, he lived in comfort to old age.

Fe.* Mexican patrols frequently reported coming upon the remains of *norteamericanos.* Usually they had been cut up and the bloody pieces of their bodies had been hung on stakes and filled with arrows. In most instances the hats of the victims had been replaced on their battered heads. More was signified by this macabre practice than an intent to produce horror in the eyes of a white beholder.

1836

A great new leader had risen to power among the Western Apache. He would become famous under the identity of Mangas Coloradas (Red Sleeves), but the name given him by his people, if it were ever known to white men, has not survived. It was he who was responsible for the custom of leaving hats on the bloody heads of the Americans and Mexicans he and his men killed. Apache men did not wear hats. White men did. "Shoot anyone who wears a hat," Mangas Coloradas told his warriors. "Then everyone will rejoice in knowing that we have killed another enemy, even when no flesh and no hair remains on the bones."

Mangas Coloradas was an immense man, standing six inches over six feet, and possessing extraordinary physical strength. He was highly intelligent, shrewd, skilled as a negotiator, an accomplished orator, fearless, and a clever strategist—in every respect qualified to be a leader. Thrapp described him fittingly as a "giant stalking the desert mountains, who made his own legends and whose fame and the terror of whose name reverberated from Durango in the south to the Navajo country in the north, from the Davis Mountains of West Texas to the Santa Ritas below Tucson."

Previous to the passage of the bounty law, Mangas Coloradas had counseled his people to keep out of the way of the American trappers as much as possible. His reasoning had been based on the fact that Americans were not attempting to establish permanent settlements, nor were they building forts, in Apacheria. They were interested only in taking beaver, which Apache did not eat, perhaps finding some gold, and then moved on in their searching. The Mexicans were the great enemies of the Apache, declared Mangas Coloradas, and the war against them should be continued with all possible fury. Then it soon had become tragically apparent that Americans, although there were not many of them, were no less uncompromising enemies of the Apache than the Mexicans.

It is improbable that any Apache leader was more successful in

---

*Wilson would be the first American mayor of Los Angeles.

organizing the many bands of his tribe into a formidable unified force. Mangas Coloradas convinced the Mimbreno, his own people, that by forming a military alliance to carry on a war of vengeance under his leadership they could drive all white men from their country. Granted unusual powers to develop and execute his plans, he named as his lieutenants men who for years to come would comprise the most capable and redoubtable group of field leaders in Apache history. Accounts identify some of them as Delgagito (The Slender), Poncé, El Chico, Pedro Azul, Coleto Amarillo (Yellow Jacket), and Cuchillo Negro, but there were others equally as notorious. Three young men for whom Mangas Coloradas was a mentor and to whom he was an inspiration would earn undying fame as Apache chieftains—Cochise, Victorio, and Geronimo.

The Mimbreno were one of the largest and strongest Apache divisions, but Mangas Coloradas understood that as united as they were under his command they would need the cooperation and friendship of other independent groups. He recognized divisiveness as the greatest weakness of the Apache. There was no hope of inducing some chieftains to submit to his jurisdiction, but he found a way of establishing strong bonds between three of the most powerful and himself. He had several wives. One of them was a beautiful young Mexican whom he had married after capturing her. By her he had three exceptionally comely daughters. Suitors swarmed like flies about his lodge, but Mangas Coloradas had his own plans for their futures. As soon as the eldest became of marriageable age, he presented her to the great Cochise of the Chiricahua. The second was given to Katu-hala, leader of the White Mountain Apache, and the third to the Coyotero chief, Cosito.

1840

Mangas Coloradas was probably in his late forties when he began his campaign against the copper mines at Santa Rita. The mines then had been operating under an agreement reached between the owners and Mangas Coloradas's predecessor, Juan José. The understanding provided that the long pack trains which carried the almost pure ore to a government mint in Chihuahua must follow a specified trail, going and coming, that no travel was to be conducted over the route without the permission of the Apache, that the number of inhabitants was not to be increased, and that Santa Rita was not to be developed as a permanent presidio.

Mangas Coloradas contended that while the Mexicans had honored some of the restrictions they were guilty of violating others. Specifically he pointed out that the population at the mine had increased from a few score miners to some four hundred persons. Women and children had been brought in, the town had been enlarged around a plaza, and defenses had been strengthened. Santa Rita was becoming a bustling and growing town. Moreover, the mine operators were providing havens for scalp hunters, a fact that undoubtedly galled him more than anything else.

The strength of Santa Rita—amounting to more than two hundred Mexican rifles and a number of heavily armed Americans—made it unwise to attempt to sack it with a direct offensive. Even if such an assault were successful, Apache losses would have been heavier than Mangas Coloradas was willing to sustain.

The town was entirely dependent upon Chihuahua for its foodstuffs, ammunition, and all other types of supplies. These necessities were brought in by *conductas,* the long mule trains which carried out the copper. The arrival and departure of these trains had been maintained with such regularity that no effort had been made to retain provisions to meet possible emergencies. Also, because no serious troubles with the Apache had occurred as the trains went back and forth, the mining company gave little thought to the matter of protecting them. The Apache had abided by the agreement, and there was no reason to believe that it suddenly would be broken.

In a mountain valley far to the south of Santa Rita, Mangas Coloradas's warriors attacked and burned a large *conducta.* Every man with it was slain, the lucky ones being killed in the fight, and those unfortunate enough to have been only wounded at last succumbing to death under terrible tortures. No word of the destruction got out. A second *conducta* carrying among provisions a supply of new guns and quantities of ammunition was soon obliterated.

From their concealed observation points in the hills surrounding Santa Rita the Apache watched the villagers. Production had halted in the mine. Little knots of people stood in the sun-drenched plaza. Men were out hunting deer, turkeys, any game, and, much to the satisfaction of the Apache observers, with every shot using precious powder and lead.

Within a fortnight Santa Rita was facing starvation. At first it was proposed that a strongly armed group of men be sent to learn why the *conductas* had not arrived, but protests that those who remained would be without adequate means of protecting themselves in the event— God forbid—of an Indian attack forced the abandonment of this plan. At last it was decided that all would leave together.

The Santa Rita mines were deserted. Across the arid hills on the long trail to Chihuahua crawled a strange caravan of some four hundred men, women, and children. Wellman states that every kind of vehicle obtainable was in it, and that the people "tried to take along

their most precious possessions, sacrificing speed with useless treasures, adding weight to the burdens. Even wheelbarrows from the
mines were requisitioned. Mules and burros staggered under towering
packs. And many of the men and even the women and children walked
with their shoulders bent under heavy bundles."

For a good reason there are no documents to recount the story of
the trek. Only a few persons, perhaps no more than five or six, lived
to tell of their ordeal. It is believed, however, that on the fourth day
after leaving Santa Rita the Apache attacked without warning as the
long column was passing through a narrow gorge. Some—how many
is not known—managed to fight their way out of this trap, only to meet
death in another defile through which they were obliged to pass. Some
days later the handful of survivors straggled into the presidio of Janos,
leaving behind them the bleaching bones of nearly four hundred men,
women, and children—another payment Mangas Coloradas had taken
in his war of retaliation.

Because of the unique method in which he slaughtered his guests
and his betrayal of the trust Juan José had placed in him, James Johnson is accorded more space than other bounty hunters in the accounts
of the time. However, he took no more scalps than many others among
the swarm of unconscionable, ferocious men—Americans, Mexicans,
Englishmen, and Frenchmen—who were engaged in the wanton business. Some of them were only "part-time killers," shooting an Indian
or two when an opportunity arose, but others, usually operating in
groups, devoted their entire time to hunting for human quarry. Fabulous sums were expended by the governments of Sonora and Chihuahua, placing heavy burdens on their financial resources. Rewards paid
to individual bounty hunters of ten to forty thousand pesos were
commonplace. Perhaps the most successful of all was an American
Mountain Man named James Kirker. In one year he reportedly collected one hundred thousand dollars.

The bounty system had created an intolerable situation, but not only
in Apacheria. It had intensified and spread warfare between all Indians
and all white men to such an extent that all of northern Mexico was
a gigantic field of slaughter, and was dangerously close to complete
economic collapse. It had united the red people to a degree that had
never before existed. Groups normally inhabiting widely separated
areas moved great distances to combine forces and pour out of mountain strongholds with a single purpose—to wreak vengeance. Not a few
presidios and settlements were virtually under a state of siege. Even
the larger towns were not safe from their vicious onslaughts. Hundreds
of Mexican men, women, and children were killed in their homes by
strong bands of raiders who swept suddenly upon them in the night,
and disappeared before either military or civilian forces could be orga-

nized to repel them. The streets of Mexican communities, large and small, were splotched with blood.

Another factor predominantly responsible for the law's failure was the insatiable, deplorable greed of the bounty hunters. Committees appointed to examine the grisly evidence and authorize rewards were confronted by sacks of scalps. They were unable to tell the difference, as Faulk states, "between the hair of hostile savages and that of friendly Indians. Soon almost all natives were on the warpath." Moreover, there was little difference between the hair of countless Mexicans and Indians. On several occasions bounty hunters wiped out Mexican villages, scalped their victims, young and old, male and female, and delivered the scalps to the authorities for payment with the claim that they had been taken from Apache.

Apparently, Mexican authorities, at least in the state of Chihuahua, had not abandoned the Spanish policy of attempting to bring individual Apache groups under control by signing local treaties with them. Noting that northern Mexico continued to suffer from their depredations, Gregg states: "Such is the imbecility of the local governments, that the savages, in order to dispose of their stolen property without even a shadow of molestation, frequently enter into partial treaties of peace with one department while they continue to wage a war of extermination against the neighboring states. This arrangement supplies them with an ever-ready market for the disposal of their booty and the purchase of munitions wherewith to prosecute their work of destruction."

He tells of witnessing in 1840 "the departure from Santa Fe of a large trading party freighted with engines of war and a great quantity of whiskey, intended for the Apaches in exchange for mules and other articles of plunder which they had stolen from the people of the south. This traffic was not only tolerated but openly encouraged by the civil authorities, as the highest public functionaries were interested in its success—the governor himself not excepted."

Thus, it is seen that some Mexicans, among them high officials, were not averse to entering into trade with Apache for property stolen from other Mexicans. The Apache themselves, whenever they thought it advantageous to them, "proposed a truce to the government of Chihuahua, which it generally accepted very nearly upon their own terms. It has on some occasions been included that the marauders should have a *bona fide* right to all their stolen property. A *venta*, or quit-claim brand, has actually been marked by the government on large numbers of mules and horses which the Indians had robbed from the citizens. It is hardly necessary to add that these truces have rarely been observed by the wily savages longer than the time necessary for the disposal of their plunder. As soon as more mules were needed for

service or for traffic—more cattle for beef—more scalps for the war-
dance—they would invariably return to their deeds of ravage and
murder."

Gregg's inquiries brought him the information that the Apache
numbered in excess of fifteen thousand persons, of which two or three
thousand were warriors. These figures undoubtedly are incorrect, although the latter may be more accurate than the former. Ethnologists
estimate that there were no more than five thousand true Apache in
1680. It is not improbable, however, that their population was increased considerably during the eighteenth century by absorption into
their ranks of captives and refugees from other tribes. A band of
raiders seldom numbered more than a hundred, rarely as many as two
hundred, and most forays were carried out by no more than forty or
fifty men. Records are rife with hundreds of instances in which ten or
twelve men, and not infrequently no more than four or five, succeeded
in stealing large herds of livestock.

Commenting on the desperate situation of the Mexicans because of
constant Apache attacks, Gregg reported that "beyond the immediate
purlieus of the towns, the whole country from New Mexico to the
borders of Durango is almost entirely depopulated. The haciendas and
ranchos have been mostly abandoned, and the people chiefly confined
to towns and cities. To such a pitch has the temerity of those savages
reached, that small bands of three or four warriors have been known
to make their appearance within a mile of the city of Chihuahua in open
day, killing the laborers and driving off herds of mules and horses
without the slightest opposition."

He recounted that occasionally "a detachment of troops is sent in
pursuit of the marauders, but for no other purpose, it would seem,
than to illustrate the imbecility of the former, as they are always sure
to make a precipitate retreat, generally without even obtaining a
glimpse of the enemy. And yet the columns of a little weekly sheet
published in Chihuahua always teem with flaming accounts of prodi-
gious feats of valor performed by the 'army of operations' against *los
bárbaros:* showing how the 'enemy was pursued with all possible vigor'
—how the soldiers 'displayed the greatest bravery, and the most unre-
strainable desire to overhaul the dastards,' and by what extraordinary
combinations of adverse circumstances they were 'compelled to relin-
quish the pursuit.' Indeed, it would be difficult to find a braver race of
people than the *Chihuahueños* contrive to make themselves appear on
paper."

Gregg did not neglect to record the Indian side of the conflict. He
cited numerous occasions on which Apache had been robbed of their
resources, cheated by traders—both Mexican and American—lured
into negotiations and wantonly murdered, and, speaking generally of

frontier Indians, he wrote: ". . . they are continually preyed upon by the unprincipled harpies who are ever prowling through their country, ready to seize every opportunity of deceiving and defrauding them. . . . The most depraving agencies employed to this end are the ministration of intoxicating drinks, and gaming, both of which the Indians are passionately fond, and by which they are frequently robbed of their money almost as soon as received."

* * *

1845

The perilous conditions created by Apache aggressions and the bounty system were overshadowed by an even more ominous situation —the rapid deterioration of relations between the United States and Mexico.

Mexico owed the United States money which it refused to pay, boundaries were in dispute, and irresponsible officials in Mexico City were making stupid statements and inane threats, warning that if the United States sought to force settlement of its demands and claims the Eagle and the Serpent would soon be flying over Washington. These were, in reality, minor questions and, although extremely provocatory, undoubtedly could have been settled in time without either side resorting to open hostilities.

The basic dispute driving the two nations apart was the unveiled ambition of the United States to acquire more territory. An expansionist, James K. Polk, was in the White House. He advocated the annexation of Texas, and the taking by aggression of an enormous region, containing some six hundred thousand square miles, and embracing the present states of Utah, Nevada, California, New Mexico, and Arizona. His expansionist and war policies were opposed by such prominent men as Henry Clay, Daniel Webster, and John C. Calhoun, as well as by a young Whig Congressman named Abraham Lincoln. President Polk defended them as being in line with America's "manifest destiny," and won strong support of individuals and commercial interests eager to exploit the bountiful resources in the Southwest and on the Pacific Coast.

THE
NINETEENTH
CENTURY
PART II
1846–1886

1846

Mr. Polk sent General Zachary Taylor with an army to the mouth of the Rio Grande, obviously with the hope of intimidating Mexico. This was considered an act of aggression by the Mexican Government, which maintained that the Neuces River was the border between the two countries. Mexican troops crossed the Rio Grande and shelled the Americans at Fort Taylor. Mr. Polk asked Congress for a formal declaration of war, and it was issued on May 12.

In justification of the President's policies and his belligerent action, Secretary of State James Buchanan wrote: "The truth is, that we had endured so many insults and grievous wrongs from Mexico, with such unexampled patience, that at the last she must have mistaken our forbearance for pusillanimity. Encouraged, probably, by this misapprehension, her army has at length . . . invaded the territory of our country—and has shed American blood on the American soil."

August

In New Mexico, Governor Manuel Armijo had no time to think about Indian problems. Scouts had brought him the alarming news that a great American army was marching south from Bent's Fort on the Arkansas. The intelligence made it clear that resistance would be utterly futile and could only result in useless bloodshed and death.

Armijo was thoroughly terrified, but even under less menacing circumstances neither his patriotism nor his loyalty to the Mexican Government would have been sufficient to inspire him to endanger his own life in any attempt to prolong the loss of the colony. He had the means of waging guerrilla warfare that would have given the Americans considerable trouble, but the fact that he did not utilize them was not attributable to a praiseworthy desire to prevent the shedding of the blood of either civilians, Indian mercenaries, or the presidial troops under his command.

Armijo concluded, however, that it would be advisable to leave on the record some manifestation, if no more than a pretense, of demonstrating his responsibility as a Mexican officer. In a fiery outburst he appealed to the people to rise and repel the invaders. The response was decidedly halfhearted. Word of the approaching army's strength had been widely disseminated, and not many citizens enthusiastically answered the call to arms. But some did, and with his regulars and the volunteer auxiliaries—perhaps two thousand persons in all—Armijo boldly marched out to Apache Canyon, a short distance southeast of Santa Fe, with the avowed intention of making a desperate stand.

On the eve of the arrival of the first American contingents he suddenly changed his mind. The civilians, most of whom were poorly equipped, were ordered to disperse and return to their homes. An aide, Juan B. Vigil, was appointed acting governor, and left to welcome alone the conquerors to the capital. With his few hundred presidial troops Armijo fled south by way of Galisteo, where he abandoned his cannon in order to speed his rate of travel.

(Eighteenth)

The Army of the West, commanded by General Stephen Watts Kearney, entered Santa Fe. The American flag was raised above the old Palace of the Governors, in which Kearney established his headquarters. He had occupied New Mexico without encountering resistance, indeed, without a shot being fired.

The Apache had seen Armijo and his troopers, as well as soldiers from other Mexican posts, fleeing southward along the Rio Grande to El Paso. They had seen other Mexican forces moving northward to establish battle lines in Chihuahua. If they were not apprised of the causes of the war between the United States and Mexico, they were able to recognize the significance of the conflict. Moreover, although they were not in any remote sense responsible for it, they would soon come to realize that they were inescapably involved in it, that a powerful new enemy confronted them, that Apacheria was as much an American prize as any other part of the immense territory to which Mexico had held claim.

General Kearney told the people of New Mexico that the American Government would forthwith halt all Indian depredations. No longer would Navajo and Apache "come down from the mountains and carry off your sheep and your women whenever they please." The lives and property of all "quiet and peaceful inhabitants," as well as their religious institutions, would be protected against the onslaughts of savages, and New Mexicans would be granted the privileges of political and religious freedom enjoyed by all other Americans.

He said nothing about stopping the slave raids conducted against the Apache and Navajo by New Mexicans. He said nothing about stopping the unscrupulous white traders who sold firearms and liquor to Indians, encouraged them to raid settlements, and bought the livestock and merchandise they stole. He said nothing about punishing the white men guilty of mass killings, nothing about stopping local governments from paying bounties to persons who shot helpless Indians for their scalps.* He said nothing about restoring the freedom of hundreds of Indians held in peonage by wealthy landowners. He said nothing about protecting the homelands and property of Indians, nothing about according them the privileges of free men.

In an official proclamation issued at Santa Fe, General Kearney said: "The undersigned hereby absolves all persons residing within the boundary of New Mexico from further allegiance to the Republic of Mexico, and hereby claims them as citizens of the United States." He did not trouble to state that Indians were excluded. Perhaps he thought it unnecessary to explain that under federal laws the granting of citizenship to Indians was prohibited, that they were held to be foreigners, that the tribes were foreign nations, and, therefore, could be dealt with only through diplomatic relations and the instruments of negotiated treaties. They, the Indians, and they alone, the only strictly native-born Americans by race, were the only people from any quarter of the globe who could not become American citizens through birth, residence, or naturalization.†

* * *

The only Americans the Apache had seen in previous years had been the comparatively few beaver trappers, traders, and bounty hunters. Now they watched columns of infantry, cavalry, and artillery snaking through Apacheria, officers and civil officials alike claiming all the land under the sky. The only contrasts they could recognize between Mexicans and Americans were on the surface, discernible only to the eyes and the ears—their respective flags, uniforms, weapons, languages. Goals, motives, demands, spiritual beliefs were similar, if not identical.

There was one very significant difference between Americans and Mexicans, however, although years would pass before the realization of its existence would penetrate the Apache consciousness and it would be even partially understood. The Mexicans—and before them the Spanish—had been united under the banner of a single faith. It had

---

*Some counties established after the American occupation of the Southwest would enact statutes under which bounties were paid for Apache scalps. Such a law was in force in Grant County, New Mexico, as late as 1866.

†The legal fiction that Indian tribes were independent nations would be set aside in 1871, but not until the passage of the Dawes Act in 1887, after long opposition, could Indians legally be allotted lands in severalty, granted homesteads, and accorded other rights as full-fledged citizens.

been woven into their political and social structures, in many respects given the force of law, and it had wielded a powerful influence on their thinking and their actions.

Among the conquering Americans, be they soldiers, civilian settlers, farmers, tradesmen, government officials, or persons of any other calling, were to be found advocates of several faiths—the Protestant with its many divisions, the Catholic, the Mormon, and others. This disunity, as the Apache eventually would learn, did not mean the absence of a universal intolerance. Americans might display bigotry and prejudice in their relations with each other, but—with rare exceptions—they were united in the conviction that the spiritual persuasions and rituals of Indians should be condemned and destroyed.

The Americans—again with a few notable exceptions—manifested no interest in any consideration, except the physical conquest of the territory to which they had been assigned. Indians were animals and should be dealt with accordingly. Indians were ignorant savages, ludicrous pests. Indians had no rights, either legal, civil, or moral, and were entitled to none. The Americans laughed at them. They derided them. They aped them in crude and cruel pantomime. They supported, even encouraged, the slave trade. They raped Indian women. They scalped Indian men, and on furlough took the bloody mementos back to their homes, eager to enjoy the shudders of friends and relatives. They swept into Indian villages and stabled their horses in Indian houses and cornfields. With ghoulish delight they robbed Apache graves, and stripped the corpses of Apaches they killed. "Lookee here, I taken this string o' doodads offen the naked body of a dirty squaw, still warm."

The Americans smashed into New Mexico and on into Apacheria harboring the erroneous assumption that with proclamations, manifestos, and regulatory demands they could effect a tripartite peace among themselves, the Mexicans, and the Apache. With almost inconceivable naïveté they took it for granted that signatures and marks on a piece of paper would bring an end to hostilities and dissipate hatreds that had endured for centuries. A document duly executed in the shade of a cottonwood tree would seal the doom of outlawry, inaugurate an era of peace, tranquillity, and economic progress, and induce warring factions to forgive and forget.

Even before the Apache had come into direct contact with American soldiers to any great extent, the conquered Mexicans held them in condemnation and bitterly resented the treatment received from them. The rag-tag and bobtail contingents that plunged through the country were boisterous, ill-mannered, undisciplined, and lawless in their conduct. Writing from personal observation, a British explorer, George F. Ruxton, described the volunteers from the American Midwest as "the dirtiest, rowdiest crew I have ever seen collected together." The American soldiery, said various newspaper dispatches, had rapidly degenerated into a military mob, were the most open violators of law and order, and daily heaped insult and injury on the people. Many of the captains did not know the number of their men nor where they were to be found; and they themselves were to be seen nightly in fandangos and even less reputable places. The troops were seldom drilled or mustered; all was insubordination, misrule, and confusion. About a fifth of the whole command had soon died from venereal diseases, and many more were incapacitated by them.

The Apache were recipients of the false intelligence that the Americans were scheming to join with the Mexicans and the Pueblo tribes in a campaign to exterminate them. The rumors derived from three sources, from Mexican loyalists who hoped the Apache would attack American garrisons, from traders who wished to gain by trading guns to the Apache for stolen livestock and other plunder, and from some Pueblos who had suffered from Apache raids. Results of the propaganda were detrimental to its disseminators. The Apache increased their attacks on Mexican settlements and ranchos, trading caravans, and the unfriendly Pueblos. The Navajo, who had been deceived by similar information, reacted to it in the same way. Mexican residents of New Mexico alone bitterly complained that within a few weeks after the arrival of the Americans, Apache and Navajo raiders killed or carried off into captivity fifty citizens and stole some sixty thousand cattle, horses, and sheep. The figures may have been exaggerations, but they had the effect of spurring the American military into action against both the Navajo and Apache.

It was a situation for which the shrewd Mangas Coloradas could see no good end, at least no end that would in any way be beneficial to his people. He set about devising a plan by which he might be able to bring at least a semblance of order out of the maelstrom. It was his theory, certainly founded on logic, that if everybody continued to fight everybody, the chaos could only increase. Therefore, the interests of the Apache could best be served by choosing a side. He summoned Apache leaders from far and wide, and a plan of action he proposed received their endorsement.

Original American military strategy called for General Kearney to proceed from Santa Fe to California with three hundred dragoons, and for Colonel Alexander W. Doniphan to lead troops down the Rio Grande and engage the Mexicans below El Paso. Indian attacks, however, necessitated a postponement of Doniphan's campaign.

SEPTEMBER

General Kearney left Santa Fe on his famous march to the Pacific Coast, traveling by way of the Gila River route.

OCTOBER

At San Lucia Springs, not far from the Santa Rita copper mines, scouts told General Kearney that Indians were signaling from a nearby hill requesting a talk with him. He ordered a reply granting the conference and assuring the signalers that they could come to his camp in safety. A short time later the scouts reported, not without some astonishment, that Mangas Coloradas had arrived with a delegation of Apache headmen.

If a verbatim record of the talk between the American commander and the great Apache was written, it has not come to light. However, the essence of the exchanges, made through interpreters, was recounted verbally by men who were present and has been preserved in printed narratives.

Exhibiting his talent as a diplomat, Mangas Coloradas praised the Americans for their bravery. The Apache had fought them—not American soldiers but American trappers and gold prospectors—and had seen them display courage and ability as fighters that every Apache warrior admired. The Apache held great respect for Americans.

Kearney thanked him.

It was clear to the Apache that the Americans would be victorious in their war with the Mexicans.

Kearney thought there was no doubt about that. He asked questions which revealed that he was striving to determine the underlying purpose of the Apache in asking for a meeting.

Mangas Coloradas was not to be hurried. The Apache wanted peace with the Americans.

That was good. The Americans wanted peace with the Apache. If the Apache were sincere, there was only one way they could show it. That was by ceasing their raiding.

Mangas Coloradas stated a few facts. The Mexicans, and before them the Spanish, had for two centuries invaded the Apache's own country, had tried to drive them from it, and take it for their own. The Apache had defeated both the Spanish and the Mexicans.

KEARNEY: The Apache could not defeat the American Army.

MANGAS COLORADAS: Perhaps that was true, but the Apache's war was with the Mexicans, not the Americans. Now the Americans had come into Apacheria. Was it the intention of the Americans to drive the Apache from their homeland, as the Mexicans had attempted to do?

KEARNEY: All lands occupied by Americans belonged to the United States Government. All Indians within the territory claimed by the United States must abide by American laws. Those who did not would be considered enemies of the American people. If the Apache wanted peace, they must halt their attacks on all people residing in American territory, including the people of Spanish descent.

Mangas Coloradas thought it was a strange situation. The Americans were fighting the Mexicans, yet they were demanding that the Apache stop fighting them. The Americans were protecting people who had for many lifetimes persecuted the Apache.

That was not true, said Kearney. The United States was at war with the Republic of Mexico. It was not at war with Mexicans living within the occupied territory, for they were now Americans.

MANGAS COLORADAS: The Apache did not wish to think of themselves as either Mexicans or Americans. They were Apache.

KEARNEY: Then they must suffer the consequences.

Not necessarily, Mangas Coloradas thought. If the Americans were intent upon occupying the Apache's country, then the Apache would soon face a desperate condition. Their lands, their hunting grounds, everything they were dependent upon, would be lost. Under such circumstances they would have to defend themselves as they had done against the Mexicans. They would be forced to raid and to steal to sustain themselves.

KEARNEY: If the Apache took such a course, they would be destroyed.

Mangas Coloradas did not argue the point. The Apache desired friendship and peace with the Americans, and they were prepared to prove it.

Proof could be manifested in only one way, as Kearney had explained.

Mangas Coloradas thought there was another way. The Americans and the Apache had a common enemy, the Mexicans. Why should not they be allies? The Apache knew Mexico much better than the Americans. They could be very helpful. The Apache stood ready to join the Americans in defeating the Mexicans. Would not that be a demonstration that they wanted peace with the Americans? Several thousand Apache warriors were ready. When the war had been won—and that would be quickly accomplished by the combined forces—then the Americans would know that the Apache were not their enemy, and they would let the Apache live in their country in security. The Apache and the Americans would have no reason to fight each other.

The offer of the Apache, said Kearney, was rejected.

Mangas Coloradas rose, stood very straight, towering above the other Apache emissaries. Moving over the faces of the officers before him his eyes spoke the words that did not cross his lips: there could be no peace with the Americans. He and his counselors mounted their horses and vanished into the hills surrounding San Lucia Springs.

1847

Pinda Lickoyi, the White Eyes, continued to come, stirring up dust clouds on the trails through Apacheria. They came in military columns, with rolling guns and caravans of wagons creaking under heavy loads of stores and ammunition and equipment. Always the Apache watched them, but gave them little trouble. Apache leaders counseled restraint. Let them go, for as long as they did not intend to remain they could do little harm. The main fighting between Mexicans and Americans was taking place far to the south. It wasn't the Apache's war. But occasionally some of the Apache couldn't resist the temptations which the passing forces proffered. Now and then some took a few potshots at them. Now and then some ran off a few horses and mules and got away with supplies. The strikes were of little consequence, but the White Eyes were unwilling to ignore them and go on about their business of whipping the Mexicans. Almost invariably when a theft occurred troops were sent to recover the stolen goods and chastise the culprits. Once, not far from El Paso, a small group of Mescalero got away with twenty or thirty horses and oxen. Troops followed their trail for seventy miles. At last they came upon the oxen speared to death in a ravine, but the Mescalero and the horses had vanished into the sky. It was like that in most cases. Seldom were the Americans more successful than the Mexicans had been in overtaking Apache raiders.

1848

Two provisions of the Treaty of Guadalupe Hidalgo, which ended the war between Mexico and the United States, had a direct effect on the fortunes of the Apache.

Even before the treaty was signed, they had seen themselves in a position in which they had no alternative but to continue in the role of independent belligerents. The very idea of entering into an agreement with Mexico was unthinkable and repugnant. No pact, even though its terms were advantageous and it was offered with every evidence of good faith, was possible between themselves and their traditional enemy. Now, with American soldiers occupying their country, fighting them, and showing every intention of establishing permanent garrisons, it appeared obvious that there was no possibility of reaching an understanding with the United States which would give them the security they required and to which they believed they were entitled. As they understood their situation, if they were to survive as a people, they had no recourse but to fight all invaders of the territory they claimed with all the means, strength, and determination they were capable of commanding.

In the treaty Mexico recognized the American claim that the Rio Grande was the boundary of Texas. Westward from Texas for some distance the southern boundary of the immense territory (New Mexico and Arizona) ceded to the United States was the parallel of thirty-two degrees north latitude, and thereafter the meandering course of the Gila River.

Thus, the border between Mexico and the United States passed in large part through the heart of Apacheria.*

The arbitrary division of the homeland of the Apache between the two nations might have been of little concern to them—at least not for some time to come—if the treaty had not contained Article Eleven.

This provision obligated the United States: (1) To prevent the Apache (or any other Indians) who resided in the territory ceded by Mexico from raiding south of the border; (2) When the United States was unable to prevent such incursions it was to punish the raiders and exact satisfaction from them "with equal diligence and energy as if same incursions were . . . committed within its own territory. . . ."; (3) Citizens of the United States were forbidden to purchase any livestock or goods stolen in Mexico; (4) The United States was to indemnify Mexicans for losses inflicted by Indian raiders who invaded Mexican territory from north of the border.

1849

S U M M E R

The first Indian agent assigned to New Mexico reached Santa Fe. He was James S. Calhoun, a close friend of President Zachary Taylor, and a self-pronounced rabid Whig. In the Mexican War he had served with distinction and had risen to the rank of lieutenant-colonel. Although he had no previous experience in handling Indian affairs, he would soon demonstrate that he was qualified to fill his office. His reports to Washington were unusually blunt, objective, critical, and devoid of political mumbo-jumbo. He would make his share of mistakes, but his sincerity in struggling to resolve problems in ways he

---

*Under this initial agreement El Paso and extreme southern New Mexico remained in Mexican territory. This area was considered a vital section of the most practicable route for a southern railroad to the Pacific.

considered just, and his personal integrity, were unquestionable.

Meanwhile, as Calhoun was familiarizing himself with his duties, a different kind of American was arriving in Apacheria. There was nothing military about them. They wore every conceivable type of dress, and they traveled in every conceivable type of vehicle—buggies, wagons, carts—and some were on horseback and muleback, and some were on foot. There were young men and old men, young women and old women, boys and girls and infants. They came from the Gulf of Mexico ports, straggling across the plains and the deserts and the mountains, in long trains and short trains. They were weary and sick and ragged and hungry, but nothing could stop them. Their numbers steadily increased, a swelling wave of humanity washing through the arid country. At one time more than four thousand of them were huddled close to the tents and clapboard buildings of Fort Bliss, which had been established hurriedly on a ranch near El Paso in an attempt —which proved to be largely futile—to afford them some protection.

If they were persons of countless callings, if they were laborers and farmers and desperados and moral degenerates and preachers and prostitutes and gamblers and swindlers, they had one thing in common. It was a dream, a dream that filled their eyes with a strange look, a reflection of both an incurable madness and an indestructible hope, a dream of finding gold in California.

The road of the Forty-Niners that passed through Apacheria was a road of devastation and death. The members of each new train were repeatedly confronted with terrifying spectacles: the twisted frames of burned vehicles; the rotting carcasses of horses, mules, oxen, and cows; skeletons of men, women, and children bleaching in the searing desert sun. For hundreds the journey ended to the accompaniment of an Apache war cry, and with the deadly whizzing strike of an Apache arrow. And the desert took its own toll, murdering all living things, human and animal, who were not adequately prepared to overcome the rigorous demands it made of them. Yet, incredibly, somehow, most of them lived to reach the promised land—only to know that their ordeal had been in vain. Few of them found the treasure that for so many months had glowed, an irresistible golden magnet, in their great dream.

OCTOBER

By no means all troubles involving Apache with which Calhoun was obliged to deal arose in southern New Mexico. The northern part of the territory had its share, and not a few of these were the result of wanton acts committed by troopers and civilians.

One tragedy attracted national attention. Assistant Indian Agent

John Greiner reported to Calhoun that near Las Vegas, east of Santa Fe, a group of soldiers had fired "without sufficient cause or provocation" into a small band of Jicarilla Apache, wounding several of them. The outraged Jicarilla awaited an opportunity to gain revenge.

One report stated: E. J. White, with his wife and child, was on the way to Santa Fe, where he had formerly engaged in trade, in company with a wagon train. . . . They had passed the country considered dangerous, and the Whites went ahead, accompanied by a German named Lawberger, an unidentified American, a Mexican, and a Negro. The Jicarilla attacked them, killing all the men, and taking Mrs. White and the child captive. Soldiers were soon in pursuit of the Jicarilla. They were found and several were killed, but Mrs. White was murdered and the child was carried away. The Federal Government offered to pay a thousand dollars to the Jicarilla if they would return the White child, but without success. Presumably it, too, had been slain.

James A. Bennett, who took part in the search for the slayers of the Whites, would recount that one evening "a noise was heard near our camp. At first we supposed it to be an animal of some kind. Three or four of us made an examination through the willow bushes and found an Indian child which I suppose was about eight months old. It was strapped to a board as all Indian babies are. I found it. An old gruff soldier stepped up and said, 'Let me see that brat.' I handed it to him. He picked up a heavy stone, tied it to the board, dashed baby and all into the water, and in a moment no trace of it was left. The soldier's only comment was, 'You're a little feller now but will make a big Injun bye and bye. I only wish I had more to treat the same way.' "

1850

Calhoun expressed the belief that, judging from past and present events, any attempt to conciliate the Apache would fail. It was his conviction that they must be "properly chastised" before peace could be established. Yet, while he advocated a policy of meeting force with force, he thought that a strong invasion of their country might have the effect of "awing them into submission," and in this way extreme violence might be averted. His theories were soon put to the test.

The Jicarilla, aided by Utes, kept up their attacks on small wagon trains on the trails near Santa Fe and Taos. In one fight eleven men carrying United States mail met death. Troops were constantly in the field. On several occasions they overtook and killed raiders, but their operations failed to gain any lasting results. The assaults continued spasmodically.

Calhoun at last was able to persuade Jicarilla leaders to meet with him under a white flag for the purpose of discussing a peace. After several talks he succeeded in convincing them that they were fighting a losing war, and they signed a treaty. Under its terms they were to be awarded lands on which they could develop farms, and the government was to supply them with agricultural inplements, instructors, pay them a monthly annuity, and furnish them with rations and clothing until they were able to sustain themselves. It was a noteworthy accomplishment.

Calhoun sent the treaty to Washington. That was the last he ever heard of it.

* * *

Although the chronology of this narrative will be briefly interrupted, it seems appropriate to complete the story of the Jicarilla at this point.

The treaty Calhoun made with the Jicarilla was never ratified. His successor found himself in the unenviable position of having to tell the Jicarilla—more than two hundred and fifty of whom already had moved to their new treaty home—that the promises made to them would not be fulfilled. Hungry and desperate, they promptly returned to the warpath. Within a few months their depredations had become so extensive that a large force of troops had to be kept in the field in a campaign against them.

They would suffer a severe defeat by United States troops in 1854, and be forced to live on the immense Maxwell grant in northeastern New Mexico. They were still there in 1870, when, according to the distinguished authority Swanton, "sale of the grant necessitated their removal. In 1872 and again in 1873 attempts were made to move them to Fort Stanton [New Mexico], but most of them were permitted to go to the Tierra Amarilla, on the northern confines of the territory, on a reservation set aside in 1874. Their annuities having been suspended in 1878 on account of their refusal to move southward in accordance with an Act of Congress of that year, they resorted to thieving. In 1880 the Act of 1878 was repealed, and a new reservation was set aside on the Navajo River, to which they were removed. Here they remained until 1883, when they were transferred to Fort Stanton. On February 11, 1887, however, a reservation was set aside for them in the Tierra Amarilla region by Executive Order. They removed to this territory. . . ."

And there they are today.

* * *

A band of Gila Apache attacked the town of Doña Ana on the Rio Grande about fifty miles north of El Paso. After a short fight in which one man was killed and several were wounded, the raiders fled east. A contingent of cavalry commanded by Major Enoch Steen soon arrived from Fort Bliss and set out in pursuit of the raiders. Steen's scouts were able to keep on their trail for some distance before losing it. The Gila had scattered, and had returned to a rendezvous near Doña Ana. While the troops were searching for them far to the east they again raided the town and stole all the livestock of the inhabitants. This time they went west, escaping into the mountains with the animals.

Although his quarry had eluded him, Steen decided to continue on and search for renegade bands of Indians in the wild, rough country of the Organ Mountains and the Tularosa Basin. After riding nearly two hundred miles he picked up a fresh trail, and scouts were sent ahead. Just how or from whom they obtained their information is uncertain, but the scouts returned to report that the Indians being followed were Sierra Blanca Mescalero led by a notorious chief named Santana.

Steen would report to his superiors: "I was informed that there were about two thousand warriors in waiting for me; and my command not being sufficient to engage so large a band of Indians, I thought it more prudent to retire. . . ." He had been badly misinformed. According to Sonnichsen, "the Sierra Blanca Apache never numbered a thousand, including women and children. Santana probably had no more than two or three hundred fighting men, but he made his bluff stick."

When he learned that the Doña Ana raiders were Gila Apache, Major Steen recommended that a garrison be established at the Santa Rita copper mines "to overawe the hostiles." Captain A. W. Bowman was sent with a troop into the area to appraise the situation. Mangas Coloradas kept his warriors in check, and held a parley with Bowman. The giant leader bluntly explained that his people could not depend entirely for their sustenance on wild game. For several years the supply had been steadily dwindling, due to the mass migrations of California-bound emigrants, the invasions by troops, and continual hunting by bands of settlers and trappers from the Rio Grande Valley. "We must steal from somebody to survive," Mangas Coloradas is reported to have stated. "You tell us we must not rob the Mexicans south of the border. If we cannot do that, we must steal from Americans, and fight you."

Bowman did not discount the seriousness of the threat. There were, he reported, some eleven or twelve hundred warriors in the immediate area of Santa Rita and probably three times that number of women and children. These people had to be controlled and fed or be exterminated. The situation was explosive, and he strongly advised the establishment of a post with no less than six companies of cavalry.

The proposal was in line with Calhoun's thinking. He urged that an experienced agent be assigned to the Mimbreno and other Apache of the upper Gila River country. It was his conviction that with a strong garrison at Santa Rita and the establishment of an adequate reservation the Apache of the region could be contained . . . that is, if Congress would authorize the necessary expenditures. He sent his recommendations to his superiors, and announced that meanwhile he would go to the Mimbreno to commence negotiations for a treaty. However, when he requested a military escort for the mission, Colonel E. V. Sumner, commander of the Army's Department of New Mexico, refused to cooperate with him. He could not very well go alone, and he angrily wrote the Commissioner of Indian Affairs that in view of Sumner's attitude the military thenceforth would have to be held responsible for settling the dire problems in southern New Mexico.

The clash between Calhoun and Sumner was not unique, rather it was a commonplace. Similar situations existed throughout the entire West as a result of jurisdictional disputes in Washington. The War Department was adamant in its contention that, since warfare was involved, the conduct of Indian affairs was properly its business, and it was openly resentful of what it held to be unwarranted interference by the civilian Indian Bureau. The Bureau no less stubbornly maintained that it had been created for the express purpose of inaugurating and executing procedures which would bring a halt to Indian troubles. As tribes were foreign nations, approval of any treaties consummated had to be obtained from the State Department before ratification was possible. Congress, of course, made all final decisions, and invariably these were shaped more by political considerations than by a desire to see justice prevail. The bitter wrangling continued while thousands of homeless and hungry Indians desperately attempted to defend themselves against the onslaughts of their white persecutors.

1851

Calhoun was appointed governor of New Mexico, but he continued to serve as superintendent of Indian Affairs.

No action was taken on the proposals made by Captain Bowman and Calhoun for the establishment of a garrison in the Santa Rita area.

SPRING

The United States Boundary Commission and the Mexico Boundary Commission, charged with surveying and marking the international border agreed upon in the Treaty of Guadalupe Hidalgo, were pushing westward from the Rio Grande.

In the American force of three hundred men, directed by John R. Bartlett, were a company of infantry commanded by Colonel Lewis S.

Craig, topographical engineers, technicians, scientists, craftsmen, laborers, cooks, packers, clerks, guides, hunters, and at least one medical doctor. The Mexican group was smaller, but similarly composed.

Chief interpreter of the American commission was John C. Cremony, a Boston newspaperman who had been a captain in the Mexican War. He spoke Spanish, and in the few months he had been in the field among the Apache had acquired considerable knowledge of their difficult tongue and of the sign language. He would spend years in the Apache Country, both as a civilian and an army officer, and he would publish a narrative of his experiences.[16]

* * *

APRIL

The entire force reached the abandoned copper mines at Santa Rita, which had been selected as summer headquarters. The commission camp had been no more than established before an imposing delegation of Apache appeared for a consultation with the "American chiefs." Led by the giant Mangas Coloradas, its other members were Delgagito, Poncé, Cuchillo Negro, and Coleto Amarillo.*

Bartlett, with Cremony interpreting, welcomed the visitors, and presented them with gifts of tobacco and food.

MANGAS COLORADAS: Our people have watched you for many days.

BARTLETT: Yes, we knew that.

MANGAS COLORADAS: We wished to learn where you were going. It was our hope that you would pass through our country. Now it seems that you intend to stay. What do you wish to do here?

BARTLETT (after explaining the work of the commission): We do not intend to stay any longer than necessary. If all goes well, we will be gone west before the snow comes again.

CUCHILLO NEGRO: These are great medicine men. They have guns that shoot five times without reloading. They have many other things of magic.

BARTLETT: We are very strong, but we want no trouble. We want to be friends, and we hope you will be our friends. When the border between Mexico and the United States is marked, we will go.

MANGAS COLORADAS: This is our country. We need no border.

BARTLETT: We recognize that this is your home, but to the north the land belongs to the United States, and to the south the land belongs to Mexico.

MANGAS COLORADAS: We do not agree. The land belongs to us.

BARTLETT: It is not our intention to take the land from the Apache.

---

*Their Spanish names. Cremony did not learn their Indian names.

CUCHILLO NEGRO: Why do you build log houses if you only will be here a short time?

BARTLETT: I have told you the truth.

MANGAS COLORADAS: We will camp two miles from here with our families. There will be no trouble, if you speak the truth.

BARTLETT: The Apache are welcome to come into our camp at any time during the day. At night it is closed.

MANGAS COLORADAS: We extend the same privilege. Our camp is open to you.

It was a beginning that gave rise to hopes for an amicable relationship during the summer months, but this pleasant prospect soon faded under the shadows of profound concern. Succeeding events strikingly illustrated—at least in the reasoning of the studious and intelligent Cremony—the basic differences which underlay the conflict between Apache and American ways of life. Previously he had entertained a belief that they might be resolvable, but now he began to realize the impossibility of reconciling them. Between the two peoples were social, economic, and cultural chasms that might be bridged by force but which would never be obliterated.

Bartlett conceived the notion that the friendly relations he and the Apache had agreed would be preserved might be enhanced if he could demonstrate that he considered Mangas Coloradas a man worthy of the highest respect. In a consultation, he and his aides agreed on the means they believed would most readily succeed. From the commissary Bartlett withdrew a pair of blue pants ornamented with a bright red stripe on the outside of each leg, a field officer's tunic, a pair of epaulets, a white linen shirt, a black cravat, and a pair of rugged new shoes of the kind usually furnished soldiers of the infantry. If the assortment violated regulations, it was at least colorful. Cremony was assigned to deliver the gifts.

Mangas Coloradas was delighted. Cremony helped him to don the gala attire, "but some difficulty was experienced in getting him to wear the shirt inside the pants. . . . After a time he made his appearance in *grande tenue*, evidently in love with his own elegant person. During the whole day he strutted about the camp, envied by all beholders, and as vain as a peacock. . . ."

As dusk fell Mangas Coloradas departed. When he reappeared two days later, obviously having partaken of too much *tiswin*, the pantaloons "were wrapped around his waist; his shirt, dirty and partly torn, outside; his uniform coat buttoned to his chin; one epaulet on his breast, and the other fastened, bullion down, between the hind buttons of his coat. In this guise he fancied himself an object worthy of universal admiration; and as he walked along, he would turn his eyes over his shoulder to relish the brilliant flashes of his posterior ornament."

A few days later Bartlett was grieved by the sight of another Apache wearing the coat, shirt, pants, and epaulets in much the same fashion. Mangas Coloradas had lost all his symbolic regalia in a gambling game.

* * *

Traders—American, New Mexican, and Mexican—were a constant source of trouble to authorities on both sides of the border. They acted as agents in the slave trade, bartered weapons, munitions, whiskey, and other goods to Indians for stolen livestock, and often disrupted peace negotiations by spreading false rumors. Enforcement of the provisions of the Guadalupe Hidalgo treaty would have had a crippling effect on their commerce.

The struggle to halt their illegal activities was made more difficult by the attitudes of both Mexican and New Mexican landowners, especially operators of mines and cattle and sheep ranchos, who held large numbers of persons in peonage. In Mexico these rich and prominent citizens were politically powerful. In New Mexico, although slavery and peonage were prohibited by federal statutes, the state legislature, comprised almost entirely of "American" New Mexicans, consistently refused to cooperate in halting these practices. Legislators and other officials were themselves slaveowners and held workers in bondage.

Calhoun registered vehement protests against the unscrupulous traders, writing: "So long as these wandering merchants are permitted a free and unrestrained access to the wild and roving Indians of this country, just so long are we to be harassed by them and their allies." When he was informed by Indian friends that white traders in western New Mexico were telling the Apache—obviously for the purpose of increasing their trade with them—that Americans and New Mexicans were organizing an immense force to kill all of them without mercy, he took a drastic step which he hoped might help to drive them out of business. On this occasion the military supported him.

He issued a regulation requiring all traders to obtain federal licenses. Its provisions were stringent: "An applicant must be a citizen of the United States, produce satisfactory testimonials of good character, and give bond in the penal sum of five thousand dollars . . . that he will not trade in fire-arms, powder, lead, or other munitions of war. . . . No license will be granted authorizing trade with Navajos and Apaches. . . ."

The regulation failed to improve conditions, for the traders were hardly less elusive than their customers, and Calhoun had no means of enforcing compliance with it in such a vast territory.

* * *

MAY

The complications involved in the illicit trading and the vicious traffic in human chattels were forcefully revealed to the members of the boundary commission. Four traders were discovered selling guns and whiskey to Apache near Santa Rita. They had with them an attractive young Mexican woman whom they were taking to Santa Fe where they believed, because of her charms, she would bring a good price as a prostitute. At Bartlett's request, Colonel Craig sent a squad of soldiers to rescue the girl.

The young captive was Inez Gonzales. Her home was at Santa Cruz, on the frontier of Sonora. About nine months earlier she had set out to attend a religious fiesta in Magdalena with her uncle, aunt, a young woman friend, and her friend's brother. "They were protected," Cremony wrote, "by a military escort of ten soldiers and an ensign. The second day of their journey they were ambushed by a large party of El Pinal Apaches, who killed her uncle and eight soldiers, including their officer, and carried off her and the other two females, and the boy. For seven months she had been in their power. . . . Her companions in captivity were subsequently purchased by a band of New Mexican traders. . . . She never heard of them afterwards. A second party had seen and had purchased her, with a view to taking her to Santa Fe. . . ." (Inez would be protected until some weeks later when Bartlett would return her safely to her home.) The traders were told "that any delay in getting out of Santa Rita would be attended by imminent danger. In less than twenty minutes they had left. . . ."

Cremony had pitched his tent "some six hundred yards distant from the rest, and shut out of sight by an intervening hillock. At this place the stream widened . . . and with a little labor I had built a sort of dam, which raised the water . . . and formed a delicious bathing pool, which was shaded by a very large and spreading cottonwood tree. At this place the Apaches frequently congregated in considerable numbers, maintaining a lively conversation, and enabling me to make many observations I could not otherwise have done. As I was the only member of the Commission with whom they could converse, my tent became their headquarters during their visits, which were almost daily. . . ."

And Cremony would note:

"Although the Copper Mine, or Mimbres Apaches, have signalized themselves by many of the boldest and most daring exploits, they are not physically comparable to the Mescalero, Jicarilla, and Chiricahua branches of the same tribe. But what they lack in personal strength they make up in wiliness and endurance."

"No amount of cold, hunger, or thirst seems to have any appreciable effect upon an Apache."

"Ten Apaches will undertake a venture which will stagger the courage and nerve of a hundred Yumas, or Pimas, or Navajos. . . ."

"The cunning of the Apache is only equaled by his skill and the audacity with which he executes his projects, and every success is chuckled over with undissembled gusto by the whole tribe. . . ."

"Their conversation is always carried on in low tones, and only one person ever presumes to speak at a time. There is no interruption to the speaker's remarks; but when he ceases another takes the word, and either replies or endorses the opinions of his predecessor. During a general conversation on indifferent topics they separate into several small knots, and in each the above rules are strictly observed."

J U N E

On a hot sultry afternoon shortly after the rescue of Inez, Cremony was reading a book. His aide, José, was washing clothes in the pool. Suddenly two boys burst into his tent and concealed themselves beneath a cot. From under the blankets they whispered to him that they were Mexican captives of the Apache, and pleaded with him to save them.

"Indians coming this way," José said as he came in the tent.

Cremony thrust two six-shooters into his belt, took two more, one in each hand, ordered José to arm himself with a carbine and a double-barreled shotgun, "and telling the boys to keep close to my side—one on the right and the other on the left—I sallied from the tent with the determination to take these captives to the Commissioner. . . ."

They had proceeded only a short distance when they were surrounded by forty Apache warriors, who angrily demanded that the boys be released to them. Cremony "told José to place his back to mine, cock his gun, and shoot the first Indian he saw bend his bow or give sign of active hostility; while, with a cocked pistol in each hand, we went circling around, so as to face all parts of the ring in succession, at the same time warning the savages to keep their distance."

None of the Apache disobeyed, and in this manner the two men and the boys were able to continue their advance until several others ran to their assistance with drawn guns. The Apache disappeared. Bartlett delivered the boys to General García Condé, leader of the Mexican members of the commission. (They would be restored to their families in Mexico.)

For four days no Apache appeared in the Santa Rita camp. Then word came from Mangas Coloradas that he wanted to have a "big talk." Told that he would be welcome, he arrived with two hundred warriors. With him before Bartlett and Cremony sat Poncé, Delgagito, Cuchillo Negro, and Coleto Amarillo. "The mass of Indians formed themselves in a semicircle, facing the door of the room . . . pipes and tobacco were handed round and a cloud blown. . . . About a hundred and fifty of the Commission were near at hand with their arms ready," said Cremony.

MANGAS COLORADAS: Why did you take the boys from us?

BARTLETT (with Cremony interpreting): They came to us and asked our protection.

MANGAS COLORADAS: You came to our country. You were well received. Your lives, your property, your animals were safe. Our wives and children have visited in your cabins. Believing we were friends, we came among you with these boys. We did not conceal them. We showed them to you. We trusted you. Why did you take them away from us?

BARTLETT: We fought the Mexicans. When we won the war, we made peace with them. Now they are our friends. The peace treaty binds us to protect them. We told you this, and we asked you to stop your hostility against Mexico. We promised to protect Mexicans from the Indians living on our side of the border, and we are doing it as best we can. We promised friendship and protection to you, and we will give it to you.

PONCÉ: We did not know of this promise to give captives back to Mexico. It is not our promise. Mexican captives are our property. The Mexicans have taken many of our people captive. If we had known of this promise, we would not have come here in friendship. We would not have trusted you.

BARTLETT: It is our duty to fulfill our promises to both the Mexicans and you.

DELGAGITO: The owner of these boys is poor. He took them at great risk of his life, and paid with the blood of his relatives. He wants them back, and it is just that they be given back to him.

BARTLETT: Our great chief in Washington has told us: 'You must take all Mexican captives you meet among the Apaches and set them at liberty.' We must obey. The boys cannot be returned. No American can buy them from you. But there are Mexicans with us, and they want to buy them and send them to their homes. We would have no objection to that, and if they cannot afford the price, we will advance them the money.

DELGAGITO: The owner does not want to sell them. He has raised them from babies, and he loves them. They speak our language. They are Apache. Money cannot buy affection.

BARTLETT: Make up your minds.

DELGAGITO (after a brief consultation with the others): The owner will take twenty horses for them.

CREMONY: You are trying to take advantage of us. You think we are foolish. Speak again.

DELGAGITO: What will you give?

BARTLETT: I will show you.

Calicoes, blankets, sheetings, and other goods valued in excess of two hundred dollars were spread before the delegation.

"This was more than Apache cupidity could stand," said Cremony. "The bargain was soon closed, and the affair passed away in peace. But it was never forgotten, and I felt positive that the time would come when they would endeavor to wreak their ill-concealed vengeance."

He was right. But the case of the Mexican boys was not the only issue responsible for the disastrous events which were soon to occur.

JULY

A Mexican, Jesús López, employed by the commission, shot and critically wounded an Apache in a dispute over some trade merchandise. López was arrested and placed in the guardhouse. His victim was taken to the camp hospital. He lingered for a time, reported Cremony, "and then died, surrounded by his friends. He was buried in secret by his own people, who declined a coffin and interment at our hands."

Before a large crowd of Apache, Bartlett declared: "We are all sad. The dead man was our friend, and we regret his loss. I know that he committed no offense, that he even did not provoke the attack upon him. . . . It is my duty to see justice done you, and the murderer punished. A great chief of the Americans lives in Santa Fe. He is the governor of all New Mexico. This great chief administers the laws of the Americans. He alone can inflict punishment when a man has been found guilty. To this great chief I will send the murderer. . . . He will try him, and if found guilty, will have him punished according to American laws. That is all I can do. . . . It is all I have a right to do."

PONCÉ: The Apache know you will keep your word, but we will not be satisfied to know he has been punished in Santa Fe. We want him punished here. We want to see him put to death.

BARTLETT: I will make another proposal. The murderer will be kept in chains. Each month that we are here his wages will be paid to the widow of the dead man. This will be paid in blankets, in cotton cloth, in corn, and anything else the family wants.

PONCÉ: Money will not satisfy an Apache for the blood of a warrior. Goods will not drown the grief of this woman. Would money satisfy an American for the murder of his people? No. This woman demands the life of the murderer.

BARTLETT: I understand. What I propose is for the good of this man's family. I want to give them the aid of which they have been deprived by the loss of their protector. If the prisoner's life is taken, your desire for revenge is satisfied, law and justice are satisfied, but the dead man's family gets nothing. They remain poor. Would it not be better to provide for them?

PONCÉ: It is not satisfactory.

BARTLETT (with sternness): Let me tell you this. American laws will be upheld. If you do not obey them, we cannot be friends. War will follow. Thousands of soldiers will take possession of your lands. They will destroy every Apache warrior they find, and take your women and children captives.

The menacing statement, in Cremony's words, "brought the Apache to a proper sense of the case." On the advice of Poncé and other leaders the family of the dead man accepted Bartlett's offer, but it was obvious that as the Apache left the conference they were deeply resentful and far from being appeased.

AUGUST

After the murder of the Apache, Mangas Coloradas appeared only once more in the camp of the commission. He was seen there one morning among a throng of Apache men, women, and children.

The observant Cremony noticed that a small group of strangers were there, too. The strangers stayed together, as if they were uneasy. They were fine-looking men, and they rode about on their small, wiry horses with remarkable ease and grace. They were Navajo.

At Cremony's suggestion, two scouting groups were sent through the country to the north. They returned with the intelligence that several hundred Navajo were camped along the Gila River, some thirty miles from the commission's camp.

Cremony gave Bartlett and Colonel Craig his analysis of the situation: The Apache did not have enough food stored to feed such a large number of visitors for any length of time. The Navajo would not have come without a predetermined reason. The hunting grounds around the copper mines offered no special inducement. The Navajo must have passed through a hundred and fifty miles, or more, of country in which the hunting was better. Trade with the Apache would not have attracted them. Mangas Coloradas must have asked them to help him in carrying out some scheme. That could be only one thing: an attempt to drive the commission out of the country.

The truth was, as Cremony would learn, that Mangas Coloradas "had sent messengers to tell the Navajo that a large body of Americans had come into his country; that they were very rich in horses, mules, cotton cloth, beads, knives, pistols, rifles, and ammunition; that he was not strong enough to raid and kill them himself, and therefore required their aid . . . one half the plunder was to be theirs. . . . Lured by these promises, and urged by their chief, who was the son-in-law of Mangas Coloradas, four hundred of them had come down to help. . . . They had met in council with the Apache, and agreed to come in and spy out the land before commencing operations. . . . Should matters promise well, a sudden attack was to be made by their united forces; but if that was not practicable without great loss of life . . . then the system of harassing us by stealing our animals and cutting off small parties was to be adopted."

It soon became apparent which tactic the allied Apache and Navajo had chosen to employ. Twenty-five of the commission's mules disappeared. In the course of searching for them, trackers led Colonel Craig and a contingent of soldiers to the camp of Delgagito on the Mimbres River. He denied knowing anything of the theft, and promised to return the stolen animals if he found them. Colonel Craig continued his search, but to no avail. A few days after he returned, some forty more horses and mules were stolen.

About this time a report circulated through New Mexico that gold had been discovered at Pinos Altos, a few miles northwest of the copper mines. Two hundred miners were soon in the area, and a new settlement had been established. The Apache were deeply distressed by the sudden influx.

Concluding that infantry was no match for the mounted Apache, Bartlett had requested cavalry reinforcements, and a company of dragoons had been sent from Doña Ana to serve under Colonel Craig. Shortly after they arrived, Apache got away with a number of their fine horses.

Detachments of troops continued to comb the mountainous region, but no animals were recovered and no thieves were captured.

On a morning toward the end of this month, a miner on a horse that was nearly exhausted dashed into the commission camp with word that Apache had attacked the mining settlement and had stolen a number of cattle. A platoon of dragoons and several commission members, among them Cremony, immediately set out in pursuit. The raiders were "overhauled in a thick forest, and one party, numbering about fifty warriors, stood to give us battle, while others hurried on with the cattle."

During the fighting, "all doubt as to the identity of the robbers was set at rest, for they were headed by Delgagito, who kept at a safe distance and poured out torrents of the vilest abuse upon us."

Cremony had with him a new Wesson rifle fitted with fine sights, and "with this weapon at three hundred and fifty yards a good marksman could hit the size of his hat eight times out of ten." Pointing out Delgagito, Cremony handed the gun to "Wells," Bartlett's carriage driver, "an excellent, brave, and cool man, and a crack shot."

Wells cautiously worked his way forward, gliding from tree to tree, "until he got within two hundred and sixty yards of Delgagito, who was slapping his buttocks and defying us with the most opprobrious language. While in the act of exhibiting his posterior—a favorite taunt among the Apache—he uncovered it to Wells, who took deliberate aim and fired. This mark of attention was received by Delgagito with an unearthly yell and a series of dances and capers that would put a ballet dancer to the blush. . . . The ball from Wells' rifle gouged a neat streak across that portion of Delgagito's person denominated in school parlance as the *seat of honor*. His riding and general activity were spoiled for several weeks."

The Apache, awed by a gun that could be fired with accuracy at such a great distance, broke into a swift retreat, and after a pursuit of thirty miles abandoned the cattle and disappeared. This was one of the few times stolen animals were recovered.

SEPTEMBER

Despite the precautions taken, Apache raids continued to be successful. When the commission left Santa Rita, more than three hundred horses and mules had disappeared as if they had vanished in the air. Almost the entire force was obliged to depart on foot. Some of them went southward through Sonora, intending to take passage on a ship in Guaymas for California. Others, among them Cremony, set out on the perilous route which passed through Tucson and Yuma to the Pacific Coast.

Mangas Coloradas had never believed that the White Eyes would abandon Santa Rita in the fall, as Bartlett had promised, and now he knew that he had been right. When the Boundary Commission departed, the old buildings were occupied by one company of the Second Dragoons and one company of the Third Infantry. The post was given a new name—Fort Webster. He ordered his warriors to stay away from it and to make no attempt to fight the soldiers.

Mangas Coloradas reasoned thus: The Boundary Commission had been forced to leave when most of their horses and mules had been stolen. If the Apache refrained from troubling the troops at Fort Webster there would be no campaign against them. Under such conditions he could give his full attention to getting rid of the miners at Pinos Altos. This, of course, had to be achieved by pacific means. Another raid could only result in bringing the military against the Apache.

He put his shrewd mind to work on the problem, and eventually devised a scheme he believed would achieve his purpose. The Pinos Altos miners wanted only one thing—gold. Therefore, he would offer to show them where it could be found in much larger amounts than in the hard rock of the field in which they were working.

On a fall day he boldly rode alone into Pinos Altos. Snow had already capped the high peaks, he told the miners. Soon the country would be white and the weather would be bitterly cold throughout the high country. It was much warmer down in Mexico. There much *oro* could be obtained. He knew where it was, and he would guide them to it. They would all be rich.

It would be reasonable to believe that Mangas Coloradas was telling the truth. However, the miners, some of whom were drunk, suspected his motives. One of them shouted: "You're a filthy redskin lyin' son of a bitch. You want to get us off down there away from the soldiers, out of our own country, and murder us."

"Let's teach the bastard a lesson he won't forget," another miner yelled, and picked up a bull whip.

It took a dozen men to wrestle the giant Apache to the ground. He was tied to a tree. The bull whip cut the flesh of his broad back to bloody ribbons. Not a cry passed across his lips. When he was on the verge of collapsing from the torture, he was freed. The miners howled with glee as he staggered to his horse, pulled himself on it with great difficulty, and rode reeling out of the camp.

"Better for the whole white population of the Southwest would it have been had they finished by killing him," wrote Wellman. "Deeper than the wounds on his lacerated back were the wounds in his heart. It was the greatest insult that could be inflicted even on an ordinary Indian. And Mangas Coloradas was a great chief."

Thereafter even the mention of his name struck terror in Americans, Mexicans, and peaceable Indians alike throughout Apacheria, and even far beyond its limits. His raiders swept deep into Mexico, as far east as the plains of Texas, as far west as western Arizona, and throughout all of New Mexico, plundering, burning, killing.

The miners of Pinos Altos knew his terrible wrath. The soldiers of Fort Webster were unable to protect them—they had all they could do to defend themselves. The miners' horses and cattle were slaughtered. Their supply trains were robbed and destroyed. They were hungry. Some took refuge in the fort. Others attempted to get out of the country, but few of these escaped.

Troops attempting vainly to halt the Apache scourge on a front hundreds of miles long frequently came upon scenes of horror. They found Americans and Mexicans suspended by their feet from tree limbs and wagons, their heads perhaps eighteen inches from the ground. Under each head were the ashes of a fire. As they had screamed in agony their brains had been slowly roasted until their heads had burst, giving them relief in death.

DECEMBER

The members of the Boundary Commission, reunited in San Diego, were informed that all the work they had done the previous year was wasted effort. Negotiations were under way between the United States and Mexico which, if successful, would move the international border considerably south of the line they had surveyed.

* * *

Cremony: "There are cases where an individual Apache will conceive a personal regard for a particular white man, and will do him almost any act of kindness in his power, but this is far, very far, from being a general rule.

"From earliest infancy they are instructed to regard every other race as natural enemies. Their suspicions and savage distrust are aroused and cultivated before they ever come in contact with other people. An Apache child of three years will run and yell with fear and hate from a white man. Apache mothers hush their children by naming an American. To rob or kill a Mexican is considered a most honorable achievement; but to commit successful outrage upon an American entitles the perpetrator to the highest consideration.

"The most adroit thief is precisely the man who is best capable of maintaining his wives in plenty and bedecking them in meretricious finery, of which they are inordinately fond. The Apache woman who is saddled with the least work and the most ornaments is the envied of her sex. For this reason, the young girls prefer to become the fifth, sixth, or seventh wife of a noted robber, rather than the single spouse of a less adroit thief.

"A really brave man does not rank as high as a really clever, thievish poltroon. His gallantry is admired, and in times of danger all flock around him for protection; but at other periods the young squaws give him the cold shoulder, and he is regarded as little better than a fool. . . . 'He is a very brave warrior,' they say, 'a man who will fight and shed his blood in our defense; but he is little better than an ass, because he is always poor and don't know how to steal and not be caught.'

"I am not too sure that something of this characteristic does not obtain among people who profess to rank much higher than the Apaches in the scale of mankind. It might be as well, perhaps, to pull the mote out of our own eyes before we attempt to extract the beam from those of our savage brethren.

"Nevertheless, the Apache character is not lovely. In point of natural shrewdness, quick perception, and keen animal instinct they are unequaled by any other people. They know what is just and proper, because in all their talks they urge justice and propriety, and profess to be guided by those virtues; but all their acts belie their words. Deceit is regarded among them with the same admiration we bestow upon one of the fine arts. To lull the suspicions of an enemy, and then take advantage of his credence is regarded as a splendid stroke of policy. To rob and not be robbed; to kill and not be killed; to take captive and not be captured, form the sum of an Apache's education and ambition, and he who can perform these acts with the greatest success is the greatest man. . . .

"They are far from cowardly, and they are exceedingly prudent. Twenty Apaches will not attack four well-armed and determined men, if they keep constantly on their guard and prepared for action. In no case will they incur the risk of losing life, unless the plunder be most enticing . . . they will track a small party for days, waiting an opportunity to establish a secure ambush or effect a surprise.

"A celebrated warrior once told me: 'You Americans are fools, for whenever you hear a gun fire you run straight to the spot; but we Apaches get away, and by and by steal round and discover the cause.' "

* * *

1852

APRIL

James S. Calhoun to Colonel Edwin Vose Sumner, commander of American forces in New Mexico: "You are perhaps advised of my weak, feeble, and almost helpless condition—and I feel that I am speaking almost as a dying man. . . . For the last four weeks I have been unable to stand alone."

MAY

Because of Calhoun's illness, John Greiner was acting Indian agent. On the last day of the month, he wrote the Indian Bureau in Washington: "On Wednesday last Governor Calhoun left Fort Union for the States with very little probability of ever reaching there alive—he takes his coffin along with him."

JUNE

Calhoun had made known his fervent hope that he might live to be buried in Washington. He died on the Great Plains.

Building on groundwork laid by Calhoun, Greiner sent Indian messengers asking leaders of the Gila Apache bands to meet him in council at Acoma Pueblo to discuss a treaty. Several accepted the invitation. One of them was Mangas Coloradas. Colonel Sumner announced that he would conduct the negotiations, and he and Greiner had a dispute.

Sumner threatened to force Greiner to accompany him if he did not go voluntarily, and the agent capitulated.

JULY

The Apache delegates refused to agree to halt their war against the Mexicans, but were willing to sign a treaty of peace with Americans. It was signed on the first day of the month.

Greiner justly claimed credit for having made the pact possible.

SEPTEMBER

William Carr Lane, former army officer and an ambitious Missouri politician, arrived in Santa Fe as governor and ex-officio superintendent of Indian Affairs. Knowing nothing whatever of conditions, he expressed the belief that Indian problems could be resolved "by feeding them, not fighting them." He quickly learned that he had not struck upon a panacea.

1853

Governor Lane announced that he would seek the office of delegate to Congress from the territory of New Mexico. He formulated and executed Indian policies in ways he thought would help his campaign. They did not follow a pattern. It was his belief that he could gain votes by demanding a strong military offensive against the Navajo. Colonel Sumner rejected the plan, contending that only a few Navajo renegades were causing trouble, and that it was unfair "to hold an immense tribe of ten or twelve thousand Indians responsible for the crimes of four or five uncontrollable outlaws. . . . All that would be accomplished would be the destruction of Navajo crops, homes, and herds belonging to people who in no way could be held responsible for the killing of some Mexicans, and who in all probability did not even know that the killings had occurred." However, under continued public pressure from Lane, Sumner at last agreed to send a column on a swing through Navajo Country simply "to make a show of force."

Keeping politics in mind, Lane signed several treaties with other northern bands under which he promised to supply them with corn, salt, beef, and breeding stock, and to furnish them with "reasonable subsistence" for three years. Without waiting for approval from the Senate, he collected a large number of Mimbreno near Fort Webster, and appropriated federal funds to buy supplies and other things for them.

Defeated in the race for Congress, Lane suddenly lost all interest in

New Mexico and Indians, resigned the governorship, and went back east.

MAY

The Mescalero—at least some bands of them—were trying valiantly to keep out of the warfare. Chief Josecito and several other prominent Sierra Blanca Mescalero went to Santa Fe to report that their people were "making crops" and remaining peaceful. They voiced the hope that the government would build a fort in their country and protect them from unscrupulous whites and renegade Indians. Sonnichsen states that "it was the last visit of this kind the Mescaleros would ever make. Grief and destruction were in store for them."

AUGUST

A man who knew a great deal about the West and about Indians became governor of New Mexico. He was David Meriwether, a veteran frontiersman and former trader with John Jacob Astor's American Fur Company. In 1819 the company had sent him with a band of Pawnee to attempt to open trade with New Mexico. Captured by the Spanish, he had been taken to Santa Fe and accused of being an American spy. Lacking evidence to substantiate the charge, the Spanish had released him after he had spent a month in jail.

Meriwether advocated a policy of "containment" in dealing with Indians. He wanted "buffer zones" established between "Indian country" and white settlements, with the Federal Government holding title to intervening lands in order to prevent them from being occupied by either white ranchers or Indians.

When he took office, Meriwether found that Indian funds had been exhausted during the tenure of Lane. A short time later he received word that the Senate had refused to ratify Lane's treaties or approve his unauthorized expenditures.

Washington also ignored Meriwether's recommendations. The bands with which Lane had signed pacts, infuriated by the bad faith of the government, resumed their depredations.

* * *

For five years, between 1848 and 1853, both the American Army and the Indian Bureau of the Department of the Interior had failed in attempts to enforce the provisions of Article Eleven of the Treaty of Guadalupe Hidalgo. At one time more than two thirds of the entire army, some eight thousand troops, had been stationed along the southwestern frontier. Yet, Indian depredations—committed not only by Apache but also by Comanche, Kiowa, Ute, and Navajo—had continued to increase. These tribes had soon come to understand that the international border, as originally defined in the treaty, could be used to their own advantage. When pressed by American troops they fled into Mexico, where their pursuers could not go.

Mexico had suffered to a far greater extent from Apache raiders than New Mexico, although their attacks north of the line had been constantly severe enough to keep thousands of troops campaigning against them. The dire situation in Mexico, however, had been largely the fault of Mexican officials. Garber wrote: "In order to prevent revolution in the northern states of Mexico, the government disarmed the inhabitants after the treaty of Guadalupe Hidalgo and left them, until the fall of 1853, without the means to protect themselves from Indians."

A plan to establish eighteen garrisons in Mexico along the border had not been executed. Retaliation by Mexican forces against raiders had been spasmodic and ineffective. General Carrasco's campaign had been typical of the few offensives undertaken. With some four hundred soldiers he had pushed north, boasting that he would exterminate the Apache on the Gila River. He had found no Apache to exterminate.

The Indian policy of Texas also had hampered American efforts to enforce Article Eleven. As Garber notes, under the terms of the "compact by which Texas was admitted to the Union, she retained the ownership of all vacant lands within her limits, but the Indians became wards of the federal government. No portion of the state was assigned to the Indians, and as fast as the settlements advanced, counties were formed and the land was sold." The Indians were compelled to plunder to sustain themselves.

Texas had paid dearly for its refusal to accept any responsibility in dealing with Indians. In one year, more than two hundred persons had been killed and property valued in excess of one hundred million dollars had been destroyed by raiders.

The Federal Government was precluded from awarding Texas lands to Indians, nor could Texas be forced to establish reservations. President Millard Fillmore feared that unless Texas took steps to resolve its Indian problems they would become a serious embarrassment to the government. The army could not protect the Texas frontier as long as Indians were free to roam wherever they wished. Moreover, bands of lawless white men were complicating the situation by plundering both Americans and Mexicans. Secretary of State Daniel Webster advised Congress that there was little hope of enforcing Article Eleven on the Texas border unless the hostile incursions of Americans into Mexico were stopped. Texas had refused to alter its original policy, considering Indians intruders on Texas lands. They must be removed, driven from the state. The means used did not matter.

The Mexican state of Coahuila, virtually devastated by Apache raids emanating from the United States, had devised a scheme by which it hoped to gain relief from the menace. It had sent emissaries to negotiate an agreement with Wild Cat, leader of a strong band of Lipan Apache. Under its terms, if he and his people would migrate from the United States to Coahuila, each family would be given ten acres of farm land. In return for this generous gift, Coahuila expected them to pledge themselves to protect the state from all Indian raiders. Wild Cat had accepted the offer, and had crossed the Rio Grande with some three hundred warriors and their women and children. Coahuila had gained some relief, but Texas had paid the bill. Wild Cat had construed the understanding as giving him unlimited license to conduct raids into the United States. Angrily American officials had complained that seldom a month passed in which Wild Cat and his warriors did not kill Texans, destroy property, and steal livestock and merchandise. After perpetration of these barbarities they recrossed the Rio Grande and found security from pursuit and punishment in Mexico. Coahuila had made no effort to convince Wild Cat that his interpretation of the pact was based on an erroneous assumption.

Charging that the American Government had failed to enforce the provisions of Article Eleven, the Mexican minister in Washington had repeatedly demanded that Mexico and its citizens be indemnified for the losses they had suffered as a result of raids by Apache and other Indians from the United States. Not a few members of Congress and several cabinet officers had contended that Article Eleven was a solemn treaty obligation, and the United States was bound to abide by it. However, when Mexican claims continued to mount by millions of dollars each year, their attitude had begun to change. Obviously the United States had failed to halt the depredations, and there was little hope that it could succeed in halting them. General Winfield Scott had declared that it would cost more than ten million dollars a year for at least ten to fifteen years to defend Mexico from American Indians.

Manifestly a way had to be found to relieve the United States of the onerous, unenforceable, and costly obligation. Mexico's desperate need of money at last had provided the opportunity. The American minister to Mexico, James Gadsden, succeeded in negotiating an agreement under which Article Eleven of the Treaty of Guadalupe Hidalgo was abrogated, and for ten million dollars the United States acquired the lands it coveted in southern New Mexico and south of the Gila River.

All that the Gadsden Purchase meant to the Apache was that the international border had been moved farther south—hardly an inconvenience.[17]

* * *

1854

MARCH

The Jicarilla and Ute continued to ravage the northern New Mexico plains. A contingent of soldiers under a Lieutenant Bell killed several in a skirmish, but another command under a Lieutenant Davidson suffered a crushing defeat. With sixty men Davidson rode into a Jicarilla trap. Only he and eighteen of his troopers, almost all of them wounded, were able to fight their way to safety.

APRIL

The Jicarilla and Ute continued their raids, and troops engaged them in several running fights.

JUNE

Mescalero attacked wagon trains in the Eagle Springs area. These raids were made by Chief Gomez and his warriors from the Big Bend country of Texas, but the more peaceful Sierra Blanca Mescalero were blamed for them.

Governor Meriwether, sorely aggravated by the dire situation and by Washington's failure to supply funds, revealed his feelings with the statement that since the government had reneged on its promise to feed the Indians, only a single alternative remained to him—to whip them.

General John Garland, the new commander in New Mexico, agreed with him. He launched two strong campaigns, one against the Jicarilla and Ute, and the other against the Mescalero.

JULY

Acting on the erroneous intelligence that the Sierra Blanca were guilty, several companies invaded their territory. "This band has been infesting the road from El Paso to San Antonio, committing murders and robberies," Garland reported. "The steps I have taken will, it is believed, put an end to their depredations in that quarter." The drive was a failure, not only because Garland had selected the wrong target, but because the Sierra Blanca Mescalero, deeply discouraged by the unjustified action against them, avoided the troops, and no fighting took place.

Congress appropriated thirty thousand dollars "for the purchase of goods, tools, and presents to be used in making treaties with the hostile tribes of New Mexico." Governor Meriwether spent the money sparingly and postponed indefinitely plans for making peace with the troublesome Gila Apache.

JULY

General Garland reported that the Jicarilla had been subdued. One band had escaped and had taken refuge among the Ute, but others had asked for peace. The drive would be continued until all had been conquered.

OCTOBER

Unidentified Apache attacked a wagon train on the El Paso–San Antonio road. Troops pursued them to the south, overtook some of them, and killed "a chief and six warriors."

All Mescalero bands were thoroughly aroused now. Even the Sierra Blanca group, hopeless in the face of military pressures, resumed raiding. They stole large numbers of horses, drove them to northern New Mexico, and easily traded them for other mounts which had been stolen in other regions. Thus, if they were imprisoned by the military the mounts they possessed could not be identified as animals stolen by them in southern New Mexico and western Texas. Several Mescalero bands deserted their homelands and took refuge in Coahuila and Chihuahua, where American troops could not follow them. From these havens they could easily cross the Rio Grande and continue their depredations on caravans and stages traveling the road to San Antonio. And they did.

Indian Agent E. A. Graves: "These Indians must live, and when the mountains and the forests cease to supply them with food they will doubtless seek it from those who have it; and if not to be had peaceably, they will attempt to obtain it by force. No animal creature, whether civilized or not, will perish for want of food when the means of subsistence are within his reach."

Sonnichsen: "Like many Americans at this time, Graves was not much worried about the Indian as a long-term menace. He was of the opinion that it would not take long for all of them to starve to death, and felt no discomfort over the idea. 'That this race,' Graves phrased it, 'are destined to a speedy and final extinction, according to the laws now in force, either civil or divine, or both, seems to admit of no doubt, and is equally beyond the control or management of any human agency. All that can be expected from an enlightened and Christian government, such as ours, is to graduate and smooth the pass-way of their final exit from the state of human existence.'

"The year 1854 was the turning point for the Mescaleros. Under Governor Meriwether the government had grown deaf and hostile. Harried by the army, hungry, and disappointed, the Apaches no longer hoped for peace; before the year was out actual fighting had begun. . . ."

"This time . . . military leaders were not going to be satisfied with punitive expeditions."

1855

JANUARY

While strong forces were carrying on their campaigns in the north, contingents of cavalry began to advance through the heart of the Mescalero Country from several directions. The main detachment, commanded by Captain Richard S. Ewell, started from Fort Thorn on the Rio Grande, with orders to advance eastward to the Pecos River, some two hundred miles distant, where Mescaleros were reported to be raiding cattle ranches. A rendezvous with other units proceeding toward the same area from other posts was planned.

At the little town of Anton Chico on the Pecos it was learned that the Mescalero raiders had fled southward. Ewell led his men down the river, and in a few days was joined by Captain Henry W. Stanton, who had with him a troop of dragoons and a company of infantry. The united forces proceeded up the Peñasco River into mountainous country known only to Indians who inhabited it.

The Mescalero launched their attack at night, and the fighting continued for the next two days as the troops pursued the enemy farther up the Peñasco. In the running engagement Captain Stanton and two troopers were killed. Indian deaths were estimated at fifteen. Before turning back from the chase Ewell and his cavalry had reached an altitude of nine thousand feet. The country was covered with deep snow, and the cold was so extreme that the exhausted horses were "dying fast, eight to twelve per day."

Returning down the icy, swift-flowing Peñasco, Trooper Bennett would note in his diary: "Came to where we buried Captain Stanton and the two men. Found the bodies torn from the grave; their blankets stolen; bodies half-eaten by wolves; their eyes picked out by ravens. . . . Revolting sight. We built a large pile of pine wood; put on the bodies, burned the flesh; took the bones away."

FEBRUARY

The Mescalero again attacked the soldiers in camp on the Peñasco, but were driven to flight.

Ewell returned to Fort Thorn by a circuitous route up the Rio Bonito, passed the sites of Lincoln and Carrizozo, and along the edge of the Manzano Range to the Rio Grande. He would report: ". . . a winter march of four hundred and fifty miles had reduced the horses too much to catch Indians on their fresh animals."

MAY

Nevertheless, the campaign was considered highly successful, and General Garland sent three hundred troops to the Rio Grande to make a second strike. Before it was launched, however, Dr. Michael Steck, newly appointed Indian agent to the Mescalero, reported that they were prepared to negotiate a treaty.

JUNE

Governor Meriwether met with Mescalero leaders and scores of warriors, their wives and families. The terms of the treaty were settled and it was signed.

The Mescalero were frightened, badly beaten, and hungry.

Meriwether: "I found these Indians in the most destitute condition imaginable. I relieved their immediate wants, and directed Agent Steck to issue them a limited amount of provisions, from time to time, as they might apply for relief and their necessities seemed to require it."

JULY

The severe punishment inflicted on the Ute, Jicarilla, and Mescalero by General Garland's campaigns had succeeded in intimidating the Gila Apache. They sent word to Dr. Steck that they, too, would sign a treaty and would agree to become farmers. The pact was signed.

OCTOBER

Both the Gila and the Mescalero were still waiting for the promised relief. Meriwether could get no more funds. Washington had ignored the treaties.

The Gila remained peaceful.

Some of the Mescalero resumed their depredations.

1856

Dr. Steck was sent to the Gila to direct agricultural developments. Few implements and little seed were available, but they managed to plant some crops on a small amount of land which were successful. They were encouraged, and Dr. Steck assured them a larger harvest would be enjoyed in the next year.

Apache west of the Gila, angered by the growing number of troops sent to patrol in the Gadsden Purchase area, began to attack settlements along the Rio Grande. A band of fifty of these raiders, who came from the Mogollon Rim area, was pursued by a strong command under Lieutenant Horace Randall for more than three hundred miles westward into Arizona. Although a number of stolen animals were recovered, the Apache eluded capture.

Dr. Steck found the means to hire several men and send them to start a small farming project for the Mescalero. Some seventy acres were planted in corn and vegetables. Like the Gila, the Sierra Blanca Mescalero were enthusiastic, and voiced the hope that they might soon become self-sufficient, and troops would no longer harass them.

NOVEMBER

Some supplies began to arrive at Dr. Steck's agency headquarters in Doña Ana, and he asked the Sierra Blanca band to meet him at Fort Stanton. There he distributed blankets, knives, shirts, tobacco, and food, and promised them that as long as they behaved they would receive beef and corn every full moon.

Chief Cadette gave his word that he would halt the depredations, and he did all he could to keep his pledge. But Cadette could not control all Mescalero. Some of them refused to submit to "the white way of life," although most of the rebels lived in the Davis Mountains, and followed other leaders. Moreover, it was these Texas bands, not the Sierra Blanca Mescalero, that had done most of the attacking along the San Antonio road.

Coyotero and Mogollon Apache made several raids on Zuñi and Navajo herds. Major H. L. Kendrick was sent with a cavalry contingent to track them down. With the troops was Henry Linn Dodge, Navajo agent, who had been extremely successful in holding the Navajos in line. Dodge, a former army captain, was the son of Senator Henry Dodge of Wisconsin and a brother of Senator Augustus Caesar Dodge of Iowa. He was a staunch friend of the Navajo, had married a Navajo squaw, and was thoroughly trusted and highly respected by all the tribe, except a few outlaws.

While hunting deer near Zuñi, Dodge was ambushed and killed by a group of Apache stock thieves.

1857

The Gila Apache, holding to their agreement to remain peaceful, raised almost enough corn and other products to sustain them through the year. Pointing with pride to their achievement, Steck sent them other provisions, and predicted that if the program could be continued at least the Gila problem would soon be resolved. He was overly optimistic, as he would soon learn.

Mimbres, Chiricahua, and Tonto bands increased their raiding, and extended their onslaughts deep into Mexico. A number of Mexican haciendas were destroyed, many persons were slain, and large numbers of livestock were stolen and driven northward into the United States.

Progress was being made in establishing farms in the country of the Sierra Blanca Mescalero. The commander at Fort Stanton, Major T. H. Holmes, reported: "These people have all along shown the most friendly disposition, and are doing all they can to prevent the other Mescaleros from depredating." At last the identity of the Mescalero committing attacks on the San Antonio road was established. They were warriors led by the intractable Chief Gomez from the Davis Mountains. A dispatch to General Garland from Major Holmes cleared the Sierra Blanca band of any connection with the raids in Texas, and stated that "this abstinence on their part is entirely to be ascribed to the beneficial influence exercised by means of the small amount . . . the commissary . . . at this post was authorized by Dr. Steck to issue."

Colonel Dixon S. Miles, with four hundred troopers, was sent to punish the Apache who had killed Dodge and stolen animals from the Zuñi and Navajo.

JUNE

In the high mountain wilderness of the upper Gila River Miles trapped a large band of Apache, killed forty-two warriors and captured thirty-six. Almost at the same time a detachment of Miles's command, under Colonel W. W. Loring, encountered another band, killed seven Indians, and recovered a thousand head of livestock. One of the Apache slain in the fight was Mangas Coloradas's lieutenant, Cuchillo Negro. Ten soldiers lost their lives in the campaign.

Badly frightened by the Miles Expedition, which had come close to them, the peaceful Gila farmers scattered into the wild, abandoning their growing crops. The disappointed Dr. Steck wrote his superior that in his view ". . . a pacific policy characterized by a liberal distribution of subsistence was best if the Indians' methods of a century were to be radically changed."

The promising agricultural project among the Gila, however, had been destroyed.

Dr. Steck urged that a reservation be established on the Gila River, where, he believed, the Apache could be contained if properly supplied and taught to develop farms and livestock herds of their own. The new superintendent of Indian Affairs for New Mexico, James L. Collins, agreed with him, and declared that the Indian Bureau must choose between "peace and subsistence or total extermination." Collins thought the peace policy preferable, and that the Gila reservation should be located "far from white settlements and vested interests."

Some officers vociferously disagreed with Steck and Collins, and advocated total extermination of the Apache. Others thought that whatever Indian policy was adopted it should be shaped to allow the greatest leeway in building an overland railroad and highway through Apacheria, and should assure the greatest possible development of mines and agriculture by white Americans in the Gadsden Purchase area. Lieutenant Sylvester Mowry, a strong supporter of railroad interests, frankly stated that he favored "extermination," but as an alternative he believed that properly located cavalry posts could keep the Apache confined north of the Gila, and prevent them from interfering with commercial enterprises.

Secretary of War John B. Floyd recommended that a strong line of cavalry and infantry posts be built at close intervals along the entire Apache frontier. Congress ignored all proposals.

Meanwhile, conditions were rapidly deteriorating in the Mescalero Country east of the Rio Grande. New Mexican and American settlers from the East arriving in the area wanted Mescalero lands, and they were sharply opposed to Dr. Steck's efforts to make the Indians self-sustaining. They wanted all Apache driven out of the region and left to starve. Mescalero were beaten, robbed, and otherwise abused to the extent that they feared to enter settlements or even to visit the Indian Agency. White bootleggers were a great source of trouble. They traveled through the country selling and trading rotgut whiskey, and law enforcement officers made no attempt to stop them. As Congress had not ratified a treaty with the Mescalero, and they were not living on lands officially designated as a federal reservation, the military had no authority to drive bootleggers out of Mescalero villages or camps.

The flood of whiskey destroyed the Mescalero's initiative. They bartered their horses, saddles, harness, implements, and even their personal belongings for drink. Feuds developed. Fights in which Indians were killed frequently occurred. They were sliding down the path to hell.

* * *

United States marshals estimated from reports they received that in one period of five years Apache stole from New Mexico ranches approximately four hundred and fifty thousand sheep, thirteen thousand mules, seven thousand horses, and thirty-two thousand horned cattle.

Both Apache and Navajo used the same unique method for making off with large flocks of sheep. They would shape the stolen flock into an oblong pattern never wider than thirty feet, and as long as necessary. The strongest sheep were lashed together, two by two, and formed into a living fence that enclosed the flock on each long side until the sheep within could not stray. Drivers strode along beside and behind the flock, and at its head hardy young men set the pace.

Traveling at a run night and day in this way, an enormous flock could be moved as much as fifty miles without stopping. The hardy sheep of the arid country could travel long distances without water or food. Often a flock containing several thousand sheep would be moved several hundred miles, far beyond the reach of pursuers.[18]

* * *

1858

FEBRUARY

The New Mexico Territorial Legislature petitioned Congress to remove all Indians north of the thirty-fourth parallel, that is, into the northern parts of New Mexico and Arizona. Congress took no action on the request. Instead, to the dismay of the legislators, the military forces assigned to Apacheria were reduced.

A band of peaceful Mescalero came to Doña Ana to confer with Dr. Steck, and set up their tepees near his agency. A group of New Mexicans from the nearby settlement of Mesilla, who called themselves the "Mesilla Guards," suddenly swept down on the camp, killed nine helpless Mescalero men and women, and in a drunken state pursued Mescalero women and children who fled into Doña Ana for protection.

More slaughter was prevented by soldiers from Fort Fillmore, and the commanding officer of the post recommended to General Garland that since the "Mesilla Guards" appeared determined to handle all Indian problems the army troops should be withdrawn from the area.

A few days later Chief Gomez rode into Doña Ana at the head of a hundred heavily armed Davis Mountain warriors. Without hesitation he announced that he had come to kill every "Mesilla Guard" that could be found.

Dr. Steck was able to convince him that an attack on Mesilla would result in bringing army forces into action against him, and nothing would be accomplished. He promised Gomez that he would make every effort to prevent a recurrence of the tragedy. Gomez took Dr. Steck's advice and departed.

MARCH

Settlers of Doña Ana and Mesilla, alarmed at the possibility that the proposal to withdraw soldiers from the area would be accepted, frantically sent General Garland a petition urging him to keep Fort Fillmore in operation and to increase the size of its garrison.

General Garland replied that while he had no intention of closing Fort Fillmore he felt that it was unnecessary to send more troops there. He warned the petitioners, however, that ". . . citizens who perpetuate acts of violence and outrage . . . have no claim to the protection of the military and will receive none."

APRIL

Well aware that no court in the territory would punish a person for killing an Indian, the "Mesilla Guards" attacked a Mescalero camp at dawn, slaying a score of men, women, and children before troops could arrive and stop them.

Juan Ortega, leader of the "Guards," and thirty-six of his followers were arrested and confined in the fort jail. Town officials immediately got off posthaste letters to the Secretary of War, and town and civil officials in Santa Fe protested that the imprisonment of Ortega and the other "American citizens" was "a gross outrage" committed by the commander at Fort Thorn. The protesters charged that several hundred head of livestock had been stolen from them by Mescalero in the last six months.

That, reported the Fort Thorn commandant, was not the truth. If any animals were stolen, they were not taken by the Mescalero, but by other raiders from another area. "For the last four or five months," he declared, "the Apache at Fort Thorn have been at peace and on friendly terms with all in the vicinity; have been daily in and about the garrison, quiet and well behaved, and have given no cause for this cowardly outrage."

Civil officials demanded the release of the "Mesilla Guards," and, having no orders to the contrary, the commander was obliged to free them. They were never punished; indeed, they were never charged with having committed some thirty murders.

Dr. Steck continued to urge that a large reservation for the Gila and other western Apache groups be established north of the Gila River, but his appeals went unheeded.

JUNE

Chiricahua, Mimbres, and Tonto Apache carried out a series of costly raids in the Gadsden Purchase and northern Mexico. Troops were unable to prevent the attacks. Special Indian Agent George Bailey was sent to study the situation.

OCTOBER

Bailey reported that the raids emanated north of the Gila, and recommended that large military posts be located on the Arivaipa, the San Pedro, and at old Fort Webster near the copper mines. Forces from these posts, he believed, would be able to cut off the raiders and recover their plunder. This system of controls would be less expensive than paying the "depredation claims" that were flooding Washington.

President James Buchanan expressed to Congress his opinion that rapid development in the Gadsden Purchase demanded the establishment of forts not only north of the international border but south of it in Mexico as well. Diplomats did not favor the idea of demanding that Mexico assume the cost of protecting itself against Apache from the United States—relations were strained enough.

DECEMBER

The Indian Office, fearing that its adversary, the War Department, would be given authority to establish military control in Apacheria, sent the able and courageous Dr. Steck to council with the Chiricahua. He met them near Apache Pass, but the best he could do was to obtain their promise not to molest commerce moving over the Overland Trail through the Gadsden Purchase. Once again he registered a plea that the Apache be moved north of the Gila. It fell on deaf ears.

* * *

Captain Cremony: "The territory over which the Apache roam is more than three times larger than California.

"No great expenditure of arithmetic is necessary to prove that to dominate over a region so vast, to guard all its passes, to keep watchmen on all the principal heights overlooking the plains usually traveled, to keep up a regular system of videttes over its expanse, to strike a half dozen places two or three hundred miles apart at the same time, to organize parties for scouring the wide valleys and attending the movements of travelers, and to be a terror and a scourge throughout its whole area, must employ the utmost resources, activity, and energy of a numerous people, exceedingly vigilant and rapid in their movements."

Estimating that at least five thousand Apache were "capable of taking the field and bearing an active part in their system of warfare," Cremony added: "A boy of fourteen is quite as formidable an antagonist as a man. . . . From behind his rocky rampart or wooded covert he speeds a rifle ball as straight to the heart of his foe. . . .

"Many of the women delight to participate in predatory excursions, urging on the men, and actually taking part in conflicts. They ride like centaurs and handle their rifles with deadly skill. . . . In the estimate made, no account is taken of the fighting women, who are numerous, well trained, and desperate, often exhibiting more real courage than the men.

"If anyone indulges the idea that the Apaches are weak and few; that they can be reduced to submission by the establishment of scattered forts in the regions occupied by them; that they can be tamed, and rendered peaceable under any circumstances; that they are to be bound and holden by treaty stipulations; that they are susceptible to any law or code, except retaliation and homicide-for-homicide, is wonderfully in error.

"I was in every way predisposed to offer every kindly act toward that race. Admiring their unyielding resistance; their acknowledged prowess; their undoubted intelligence and native force of character; acquainted with their language, traditions, tribal and family organizations, and enjoying their confidence to a degree never before accorded to any but an Apache, I strenuously used every effort in consonance with my orders and plain duties to better their condition, and instill such information as would best conduce to their future peace and happiness.

"These facts will appear . . . together with the lamentable failure of all conciliatory schemes. . . ."

* * *

1859

The indefatigable Dr. Steck met at Cañón del Oro with Pinal Apache leaders who purportedly represented more than three thousand Indians. Settlers and civil officials were bombarding the authorities with demands that these Apache be forcibly removed somewhere—anywhere, just so it was out of the southern parts of Arizona and New Mexico. Dr. Steck stood firm in his belief that such drastic measures would serve no good purpose. If properly treated, the Pinals would adopt peaceful ways.

JUNE

General Garland's successor, Colonel Benjamin Louis Eulalie de Bonneville, distrustful of such humanitarians as Dr. Steck, made a swing through the Gila River country, purportedly to form his own judgment of conditions there. He went, however, with the preconceived belief that all Apache were hopelessly addicted to outlawry, and that the only means of controlling them was by force of arms. He would learn nothing that changed his mind.

Bonneville was nearing the end of a long military career that was marked by unsavory episodes for which he had been publicly criticized by both military colleagues and prominent civilians. In 1831 he had obtained a two-year leave from the army under the pretense that he would, without cost to the government, explore the unknown West. His true purpose was to engage in the fur trade. Without troubling to ask for an extension of his leave he had overstayed it by two years, and had been dropped from army rolls. When he arrogantly applied for reinstatement, the War Department refused his request, but was overruled by President Andrew Jackson. Bonneville had shown Mr. Jackson some maps of the West, and the President had praised them as significant contributions to the geographical knowledge of the country. Bonneville had copied the maps from several prepared by outstanding authorities, among them former Secretary of the Treasury Albert Gallatin, and the famous explorers General William H. Ashley and Jedediah Smith. On one of the maps he had given his name to the Great Salt Lake Basin, a brazen assumption, "when," as Chittenden stated, "we consider the utter lack of any connection which his work had with that body of water."

The great historian H. H. Bancroft wrote of Bonneville that "being in his coarse way a *bon vivant* and voluptuary, he preferred lording it in the forest with a troop of red and white savages to his heels, and every fortnight a new unmarried wife flaunting her brave finery. . . . To shoot buffalo was rare fun; but men were the nobler game, whom to search out in their retreat and slaughter and scalp were glorious." From a business standpoint, Bonneville's fur-trading venture had been a total failure, but he had been made famous by Washington Irving's fictional account of his adventures during the four years he had spent roaming the western mountains with an expedition of trappers.

On his journey of inspection through Apacheria, Bonneville met the Mimbreno near the old Santa Rita copper mines. The mines were once more operating, and he was surprised to discover that the Mimbreno had not caused trouble for the miners, although Fort Webster had been closed since 1853. He questioned Dr. Steck about the matter, and the agent frankly admitted his doubt that the peaceful situation would long prevail unless the Mimbreno were placated with substantial quantities of provisions and an annuity. Bonneville had no authority to provide the Mimbreno with anything, but he had the power to take whatever military measures he deemed necessary. He assigned a lieutenant and twenty men to remain at Santa Rita to protect the miners.

Going on west into Arizona, Bonneville was surprised a second time to learn that the Chiricahua were adhering to an agreement they had made with Dr. Steck not to raid travelers on the Overland Trail, although they were continuing to raid ranchos in Mexico. Settlers and miners were occupying the San Pedro and Santa Cruz Valleys, and Bonneville feared that these areas could not be properly developed without military protection. He recommended the establishment of two new posts, one in the mountains near Tucson and another on the Rio San Pedro.

A U G U S T

A band of unidentified Apache—perhaps Chiricahua—attacked the mining town of Patagonia, southeast of Tucson, killing a prominent white man and wounding several other persons. Bonneville had gone on his way, and the military in the area made no attempt to track down the raiders. It was feared that if a punitive campaign were undertaken the Chiricahua would break their agreement with Dr. Steck and would retaliate by attacking emigrant caravans and stages on the Overland Trail.

S E P T E M B E R

Fully realizing the precariousness of the situation, Dr. Steck gathered all supplies, clothing, and other articles he could find in the region, and set off into the wilderness to hold talks with the Apache.

O C T O B E R

Dr. Steck met with eight hundred Apache in the Burro Mountains, and gave presents. They promised to be peaceable.

N O V E M B E R

At San Simon Dr. Steck held a council with Cochise and some four hundred Chiricahua. Cochise denied that his warriors were responsible for the Patagonia attack and assured the agent that he could control them.

Dr. Steck was severely criticized by the military for treating with perfidious savages, but he carried on with his mission. Near the site of Safford, Arizona, more than two thousand five hundred Coyotero, Mogollon, Pinal, and Mimbreno assembled to "smoke" with him. In this vicinity many Apache had developed such good farms that he felt they would soon become self-supporting if provided with adequate implements. He wrote Indian Superintendent James L. Collins urging that a reservation be established in the area, and expressed the belief the Apache easily could be persuaded to remain on it.

However, there was no doubt that some of them, especially the Pinal, might not willingly submit. This problem, in Dr. Steck's opinion, could be resolved by the establishment of a military post. However, the soldiers should be stationed there only for the purpose of chastising the few Apache who would attempt to foment trouble. If the troops engaged in long patrols and treated the Apache like prisoners, breakouts would surely occur, and settlements and travelers would suffer grievously.

Once again Dr. Steck pleaded for an enormous reservation comprising the mountain wilderness region north of the Gila—once again in vain.

Colonel T. T. Fauntleroy, an officer generally suspected of secretly dealing with land development companies, took command of the department in New Mexico. He ignored Dr. Steck's advice and sent Colonel I. V. Reeve with two hundred troopers to punish the Pinal, whom he accused of committing depredations in the San Pedro Valley. The Pinal, of course, vanished. Reeve pursued them on a zigzag course through the wilderness for more than three hundred and fifty miles before he gave up the chase. Many of the cavalry horses succumbed to exhaustion, and others were stolen by Apache before Reeve could get back to his base on the Rio San Pedro.

In reporting the failure of his offensive, Colonel Reeve unnecessarily expressed the belief that if troops were to be successful against the Apache they should be stationed close to them, and not long distances from their camps and villages. A number of others, both officers and agents, had already proffered the same idea innumerable times.

Dr. Steck went back to his agency to see how things had gone with the Mescalero during his absence. He found the people of Mesilla and other settlements in the Rio Grande Valley still yelling for relief from the "Indian menace." The Mescalero were doing everything they could to protect themselves and survive, but the odds were overwhelmingly against them. Squatters were taking their best farming lands and cattlemen were moving herds onto their ranges. They were accused of stock thefts committed by white rustlers, not a few of whom were "respectable citizens" seen in church every Sunday in Mesilla and other communities. Mescalero women and children were abused, cursed, and threatened in their homes and on town streets. Indian men were shot at in their fields and while riding to military stations to plead for provisions. Utterly discouraged and helpless, many Mescalero sought relief in drink. The bootleggers were always handy with an "alcoholic spring."

A small band of young Gila Apache attacked a rancho near San Tomás, killing two or three persons, and making off with some stock. The Mescalero were accused of the raid, although they had nothing to do with it.

The dishonest editor of the *Mesilla Miner:* "How long, oh! how long are we to endure these outrages. Will Congress never give us protection?" He knew how to hold his circulation.

Sonnichsen: "The Mescaleros were neither willing nor able to do much harm at that moment. They were hungry and hopeless. The white man had not been successful in his effort to exterminate them, but his diseases and his whiskey were rapidly getting the job done. They could thank Congress for that. Since the treaty they were living under had not been ratified, the Intercourse Laws did not apply to them. The government could give little protection against the human vultures who preyed upon them."

1860

Although they made raids into Mexico, the Chiricahua, Mimbreno, and most other Western Apache bands were extraordinarily peaceful most of the year in the Gadsden Purchase. The reason is known.

It is improbable that any powerful Apache leaders were greater friends, or trusted and admired each other to a greater extent, than Mangas Coloradas and Cochise. Perhaps it was Cochise, although it could have been Mangas Coloradas, who first advocated a policy of permitting the coaches of the Butterfield Stage Line and freight caravans to pass unmolested along the Overland Trail. In any case, they agreed that if they attempted to disrupt the traffic, strong military forces would be sent against them. The plunder they might gain for a short period would not be reward enough to justify taking a chance on suffering serious losses in the warfare that inevitably would follow any attacks they made.

They would not, of course, cease their raiding into Mexico—there could be no peace under any conditions with Mexicans as long as an Apache of any band was alive—but they could, at least for the time being, hold their high mountain sanctuaries with greater ease if they allowed the overland coaches and wagon trains to go on their way unharmed.

Being realistic men, they looked upon their decision only in the light of an expedient. Its wisdom would have to be demonstrated. There was not in their shrewd minds any thought that it might lead to a general truce between them and Americans. The day when that might have been possible had long since passed. Peace could be achieved now only with dishonor to their people, for Americans had made it clear they would not permit it under any other circumstances.

Stage drivers and agents and freighters soon understood what Mangas Coloradas and Cochise had done for them, and they did not fail to place the credit where it was deserved. Mangas Coloradas was seldom seen, but Cochise went out of his way to make friends with operators and drivers. Halfway up Apache Pass, in the Chiricahua Mountains, was a stage relay station. Cochise was a frequent visitor there, and held the implicit trust of the agent, a man named Wallace. The horses were turned out to graze without fear that they would be stolen. Cochise and a number of Apache families often camped near the station, and Wallace paid them to keep him supplied with firewood.

OCTOBER

A band of Pinal carried out a series of raids on settlers along Sonoita Creek, south of Patagonia. On one foray they carried off a boy of eleven, Felix, the adopted son of a squatter, John Ward. Soldiers from Fort Buchanan, sent after the raiders, returned empty-handed, reporting that the Pinal had split into three parties and their trails had been lost in desert sands. The commandant at Fort Buchanan, probably as the result of garbled intelligence, became convinced that the boy had been kidnapped by Chiricahua. However, no further attempts were made to rescue him during the balance of the year, inactivity for which there is no explanation in military records.

1861

JANUARY

The stupidity, pigheadedness, and uncontrolled temper of a young shavetail, fresh out of West Point, were responsible for fighting in which hundreds of persons died. He was Second-Lieutenant George Nicholas Bascom, and he was assigned to make an effort to recover Felix Ward.

Acting on the erroneous belief that the Chiricahua had stolen the boy, Bascom led fifty-four troopers and an interpreter up Apache Pass and made camp at the stage station where Wallace was on duty.

Wallace didn't believe that Cochise or any of his people were guilty. Bascom disagreed, and demanded to know the location of Cochise's winter camp. Wallace told him that it was nearby and offered to go to it and inform Cochise that the soldiers had arrived, although he had no doubt that the chief already knew of their presence.

A short time later Cochise appeared with a number of his warriors, one of whom carried a white flag. He greeted Bascom cordially, and unhesitatingly entered the lieutenant's tent.

Without preliminary conversation or ceremony, Bascom bluntly accused Cochise of leading the Sonoita raids and stealing the boy and a number of cattle. Cochise appeared to be completely surprised, but he remained calm as he stated that he not only was not responsible for the depredations but that he did not know they had occurred.

Bascom became furious, charged Cochise with lying, and told him that unless the boy and the cattle were surrendered he and his men would be held as hostages, taken to Fort Buchanan, and imprisoned.

It is probable the inexperienced and cocky young lieutenant did not realize that he was dealing with one of the shrewdest, most powerful and dangerous leaders of the entire Apache Nation. At this time Cochise was thirty-eight or thirty-nine years of age. He was not a tall man, standing about five feet, nine inches, but his shoulders were broad, and he gave the appearance of being lithe and muscular. His forehead was high, his nose large, his eyes and straight hair correspondingly black, his mouth a thin slit in a face that might have been molded of dark red stone.

Bascom repeated his threat and ordered the tent surrounded by soldiers. Suddenly Cochise whipped out a knife, whirled and slit the tent wall, and dashed out. Troopers fired at him as he raced toward a hillside. A bullet struck him in the arm. It was a superficial wound. He disappeared into a thicket.

Some of the warriors who had accompanied him to the conference also got away, but six were taken prisoner. This had no more than been accomplished before heavy rifle fire came from nearby trees. Several soldiers went down, others ran for the protection of the station's log horse corral. Three more were wounded there. The fighting continued until nightfall. Lieutenant Bascom now realized that he was in deep trouble. He had a dozen wounded men on his hands. Wallace warned him that several hundred Apache warriors probably would be in the vicinity before morning, and that if he wanted to get any of his men out alive he had better find some means of getting more soldiers to come to his rescue.

The name of the daring cavalryman who volunteered to attempt to reach Fort Buchanan has been lost to history. In the darkness he quietly led a mule up the steep slope of Apache Pass and vanished into the wilderness night.

A short time later, according to Wellman, "the Overland Mail coach from California struggled up to the corral. One horse had been left dead on the trail behind, the driver's leg was shattered by a bullet, and a passenger was shot through the chest. Apaches had attacked it down the pass. By a miracle the plucky driver succeeded in cutting the dead horse loose and getting the rest of the frightened animals to pull the stage up the pass."

So the month ended.

FEBRUARY (First)

Near the western entrance of Apache Pass, Chiricahua attacked a small wagon train which had received no warning of the fighting ahead. Three of the teamsters were taken prisoner. The others were killed.

The next day Cochise approached the station under a white flag and signaled that he wanted to talk with the lieutenant. Wallace offered to act as interpreter, and he, Bascom, and two stage company employees, Jordon and Lyons, walked out to meet the chief.

As they conferred, a lookout on the station roof suddenly shouted that Indians were creeping toward them through the surrounding brush. Bascom immediately broke into a run for the station. Four bullets clipped his uniform, but he reached safety unharmed. Wallace, Jordon, and Lyons, still believing that their friend, Cochise, would not turn against them, had made no attempt to get away. They were quickly surrounded and taken prisoner.

There was no water in the corral, and the cavalry horses held there were suffering from thirst. The nearest small stream was some six hundred yards away in a ravine. Bascom assigned men to lead half the animals to it. The Apache were waiting. They allowed the horses to drink, then opened fire. Several troopers were wounded and had to be carried to safety while the others returned the fire as they retreated. The horses fell into Apache hands. A few hours later Bascom ordered the other horses turned out of the corral to save them from perishing. The troopers were afoot.

Shots were exchanged at intervals during the next two days. Some soldiers managed to crawl to the spring at night and return with filled canteens. Several men had died of their wounds. The situation was rapidly becoming desperate. An attempt to escape without mounts would have been suicidal.

On the seventh day of the siege, Cochise again appeared within speaking distance under a white flag. He offered to exchange Wallace, Jordon, Lyons, and the three white captives from the wagon train for the six warriors being held prisoner. With a curse Bascom refused, and ordered his men to open fire. Cochise disappeared. In a desperate attempt to escape, three of the six warriors being held captive were slain.

The messenger had got through to Fort Buchanan. Fifteen troopers commanded by Captain B. J. D. Irwin, a surgeon, started at once to Bascom's relief. They were all the men the commander, Colonel Morrison, could spare, but he sent couriers to Fort Breckenridge, a hundred miles to the north, requesting that two companies of cavalry be sent to Apache Pass. The Fort Breckenridge troops were soon in the saddle and riding hard down the San Pedro Valley.

As they neared the pass entrance Captain Irwin and his men came upon a small band of Apache driving a herd of cattle. They attacked, killed several warriors, and took three prisoners. Continuing on as rapidly as possible after the fight, they soon came upon the remains of the caravan Cochise had plundered and destroyed. Lashed to the burned wagons were the charred remains of eight men.

Strangely Cochise made no effort to prevent Irwin from reaching the besieged men at the station.

Twenty-four hours later the troops from Fort Breckenridge arrived. The firing ceased. The Chiricahua disappeared into the high mountains, Cochise apparently concluding that he could gain nothing by fighting such a strong force.

By the eighteenth the wounded were able to travel, and with the most seriously hurt lashed on horses Captain Irwin, the senior officer, ordered the retreat begun. The six Chiricahua prisoners were taken along. As they traveled slowly down the pass the next day, they saw a flock of buzzards circling a short distance from the trail. Scouts sent to investigate found that the birds were feasting on the bodies of Wallace, Jordon, Lyons, and the three teamsters from the destroyed wagon train.

Captain Irwin ordered the immediate execution of the six warrior prisoners. Lieutenant Bascom, to his credit, argued that they should be delivered for trial to Fort Buchanan, but he was forced to obey his commander. When the troops went on they left the six Chiricahua hanging from trees.

"The punishment was an extreme mode of reprisal," Irwin would write, "but was demanded and justified by the persistent acts of treachery and the atrocious cruelties perpetrated by the most cowardly tribe of savages infesting the territory."

This was neither a complete nor an accurate report. He did not mention that three of the executed warriors had been taken captive by Bascom under a flag of truce, and the other three had been captured in the fight over the herd of cattle, a considerable distance from the stage station. Nor did he trouble to state that none of them had anything to do with the killing of the stage company men, the teamsters, or the attack on the wagon train.

(*Note:* It would be learned in time that three of the Chiricahua hanged were close relatives of Cochise. Within sixty days one hundred and fifty white men attempting to travel the Overland Trail had been killed. Thrapp: "No traveler, no settler, no miner, no small party of soldiers, no small community was safe from the avenging warriors." The Overland Trail was a road of almost certain death.)

SEPTEMBER

During the summer the Mimbres, joined by groups of Chiricahua and Tonto, had made a series of devastating raids in Mexico. Now Mangas Coloradas thought the time had come for him to give his attention to the miners who had reoccupied Pinos Altos. Despite the Apache peril the settlement had grown, and strong defenses had been built. With most of the Mimbres area swept clean of white men, the presence of these defiant intruders in the very heart of his country was gall in both his heart and his memory. He determined to sack the plague spot and kill everyone in it.

On the twenty-seventh, with some two hundred warriors, he attacked, but he had waited one day too long. The previous evening a contingent of heavily armed men calling themselves Arizona Guards had ridden into Pinos Altos. The warriors met a heavy fire from breech-loading rifles. Although the fighting continued through the day, Mangas Coloradas had soon realized that he could not hope to overcome the defenders, and in the darkness he ordered a withdrawal.

A wagon train moved out of Pinos Altos the next morning on the road toward the Mimbres River. Mangas Coloradas sent his warriors against it, but the Arizona Guards swept upon them, forcing them to scatter in retreat. Several Apache were killed. For the next fourteen hours the Mimbres sniped at the train, and although they kept it from moving, they were unable to get close enough to do any serious damage. Mangas Coloradas gave up, and the wagons went on their way.

The two setbacks were bitter pills for Mangas Coloradas to swallow. He resumed his raiding on both sides of the international border during the winter, but always uppermost in his mind was his determination to find a means of wiping out Pinos Altos.

* * *

The Civil War in Apacheria

From the Big Bend Country of Texas, across New Mexico, to the Rio Santa Cruz in Arizona, in the early summer of 1861, the Apache were mystified. Strange events were taking place. Soldiers were leaving some posts in the Gadsden Strip. In some valleys settlers, left without military protection, were fleeing to the east, to Mexico, toward California, abandoning livestock and growing crops. Mines were being deserted. Tucson, Mesilla, Doña Ana, and El Paso were filled with refugees.

If any Apache had heard of the fall of Fort Sumter, which was doubtful, he would not have understood what it meant. If any Apache had heard of the Confederacy or the Confederate States of America, which also was doubtful, he could only have wondered what they were, and even if he had been told he would not have understood.

There was one thing, however, that soon became apparent: the Americans were fighting each other. And if that puzzled him, too, if he were not certain of the causes for the fighting, he was absorbed by the realization that it was taking place. He would soon come to understand its significance, and how it would influence his own life.

Colonel Edward R. S. Canby was in the Navajo Country when word came that the War Between the States had begun. With him was his brother-in-law, Major Henry Hopkins Sibley. He had successfully negotiated a treaty with Navajo leaders, and had sent it to his commanding officer in Santa Fe, Colonel Thomas T. Fauntleroy. The belief was general that if the treaty were ratified and the government adhered to its provisions—all of which were reasonable and just—the war with the Navajo would be over. But that was not to be.

In the twenty years since he had graduated from West Point, Canby had been in almost constant combat from the Florida Everglades to the western frontier. He had distinguished himself in the Mexican War, and his competence as a field strategist had been demonstrated in campaigns against Indians on the plains and in the mountains. Highly respected by officers serving with him, he was known as the "prudent soldier," a term intended to denote both wisdom and shrewdness in his conduct of practical affairs.

Now he was faced with a type of conflict and a problem he had never encountered. Hundreds of privates, noncoms, and officers serving under him in the southwestern Indian campaigns were deserting to take up arms for the Confederacy. His troops were becoming scattered, organization was collapsing, demoralization had set in, and, worst of all, he found himself powerless to halt the disintegration. Colonel Fauntleroy resigned, leaving the Ninth Military Department (New Mexico) without a head. Major Sibley said farewell and told the soldiers who had chosen to remain loyal to the Union: "Boys, if you only knew it, I am the worst enemy you ever had."

Orders came to Canby from Washington to abandon Fort Defiance, the main post in the Navajo Country. He was to leave a small garrison at Fort Fauntleroy (which would be renamed Fort Lyons), and move the remaining troops to the Rio Grande.

Similar changes were taking place throughout Apacheria and elsewhere. Apache, Navajo, Ute, and Comanche raiders were sweeping through the entire Southwest, and the skeleton forces were powerless against them.

Most of the citizens in Tucson and Mesilla were southern sympathizers. They created the Confederate Territory of Arizona, defining its northern boundary as the thirty-fourth parallel between Texas and California. The Confederate Congress, meeting in Richmond, Virginia, subsequently would recognize the new territory and would seat its first delegate, Granville H. Oury of Tucson.

Mescalero raiders, swooping down from the Guadalupe and Davis Mountains, had all but halted civilian traffic on the San Antonio–El Paso road. Suddenly they saw a strange kind of soldier wearing gray instead of blue and carrying a strange flag.

The Texas Mounted Rifles, commanded by Colonel John Robert Baylor, were the first to appear. Fort Bliss already had been abandoned by Union forces. Baylor led his cavalry into southern New Mexico "to

protect the citizens of Confederate Arizona." Union soldiers still occupied Fort Fillmore near Mesilla, but instead of making a stand, their
commander, Major Isaac Lynde, ordered a retreat up the Rio Grande.
Colonel Baylor pursued and overtook the Fort Fillmore troops near
San Augustine Pass, some twenty miles north of Mesilla. Major Lynde
surrendered without a shot being fired.

The headline of the *Mesilla Times:* ARIZONA IS FREE AT LAST.

Colonel Baylor announced the establishment of a temporary military government for Arizona Territory, and appointed himself governor.

Captain B. S. Roberts, the Union commander at Fort Stanton, on the
Rio Bonito, received orders to take his troops to Albuquerque and join
Colonel Canby. He tried to burn the post as he departed, but heavy
rains put out the fire. Sierra Blanca Mescalero and some Mexicans
from adjacent settlements quickly plundered the storerooms, and
completed the destruction.

Lieutenant John R. Pulliam had been assigned to take Fort Stanton.
When he and his cavalry arrived there they found nothing left. Pulliam
sent four men out to scout for Union troops. The Mescalero killed
three of them. Another band of Apache attacked the little settlement
of Placitas. Pulliam raced after them and killed five warriors, but the
others got away with the booty. As Fort Stanton was destroyed, Pulliam
took his contingent back to Doña Ana. The settlers who were dependent on Fort Stanton to protect them poured out of the area, abandoning all they possessed.

A band of Davis Mountain Mescalero led by a treacherous chief
known as Nicolas attacked the Confederate beef herd at Fort Davis,
killed two guards, and got away with a large number of animals. A
Lieutenant Mays and fifteen cavalry were sent to run down the raiders.
Mays and his men were young Texans without experience in fighting
Indians. Displaying more bravado than good sense, they rode into a
draw and were wiped out.

Sonnichsen: "The Mescaleros were left for a little while in complete
and undisputed possession of the mountain region. It was like the old
days. There was not an American or a Mexican in the country, and
many of the Apaches supposed, as did other Indians in the Southwest,
that the white men would be too busy murdering each other from now
on to interfere with the normal activities of the red men. Bands of
warriors headed for the sheep ranches of the Pecos country, for the
traditional ambush site at Point of Rocks on the Jornada del Muerte,
and for exposed ranches and settlements in the Rio Grande valley.
Happy days had come again. . . .

"It was probably true at this time, as always, that wiser heads among
the Indians knew that the white man would eventually punish the

whole tribe for the sins of its more violent members. But this was no time for counsels of moderation. The young men felt that their hour had come and they meant to make the most of it."

Colonel Baylor was confirmed as governor of Arizona by President Jefferson Davis of the Confederacy. It was Baylor's belief that Arizona was already safe in Confederate hands, and the immediate task to be undertaken was to combat the Apache who were terrorizing the entire region. For this purpose he organized the Volunteer Arizona Guards around cadres of experienced soldiers. Robert P. Kelley, editor of the *Mesilla Times*, didn't agree, and criticized him for not moving north and fighting Colonel Canby. He shot Kelley to death.

Baylor had his own Indian policy, and he proclaimed it in orders to the Arizona Guards: ". . . use all means to persuade the Apaches or any tribe to come in for the purpose of making peace, and when you get them together kill all the grown Indians and take the children prisoners and sell them to defray the expense of killing the Indians. Buy whiskey and such other goods as may be necessary for the Indians and I will order vouchers given to cover the amount expended. Leave nothing undone to insure success, and have a sufficient number of men around to allow no Indian to escape."

Faulk states that "Baylor was charged with ordering poisoned food left for Indian consumption. . . ."

Not only the Arizona Guards but most residents of Confederate Arizona, including the leading merchants of Tucson, heartily endorsed Baylor's policy.

Colonel Canby had been placed in supreme command of all federal troops in New Mexico. He increased the garrison at Fort Craig, on the Rio Grande near San Marcial, and strengthened the defenses of Albuquerque and Santa Fe. Reinforcements were sent to him from Colorado. On the way from California was a brigade of volunteers, commanded by General James H. Carleton.

While Canby was preparing to make a stand and save New Mexico for the Union, his brother-in-law, the former Major Henry H. Sibley, was making plans to invade the Southwest. In an audience with Confederate President Jefferson Davis, Sibley had presented a grandiose scheme of securing New Mexico, Arizona, and California for the Confederacy in one sweeping blow. These regions, he argued, contained not only great mineral wealth but countless thousands of Indians and Mexicans who might be enslaved. Sibley had visions of vast new plantations reaching from the plains of Texas to the rich valleys of the Pacific Coast. Davis thought well enough of the idea to commission Sibley a general and authorize him to raise a brigade of fighting men in Texas, march west, and start badly needed western gold flowing into the South's treasury. Within a few months Sibley had recruited a force of three thousand eight hundred mounted Texans, who, he proudly reported, were "the best damn fighters that ever threw a leg over a horse."

Reaching El Paso, General Sibley sent two hundred cavalry to Tucson, and continued up the Rio Grande with his main force. Canby attacked him near Fort Craig, but the Confederates held strong positions and the next morning the Union troops were forced to retreat to the post for ammunition and provisions. Within a matter of hours Canby moved them out again, and launched an assault at Valverde. Throughout the day the fighting was fierce. The turning point came when five companies of New Mexican militia refused to obey orders to advance, with the result that Canby's strongest and best battery of field guns was captured by Confederate cavalry. The Union troops broke before a charge by the Texans, "more like a herd of frightened mustangs than men." General Sibley was regrouping for a new advance when Canby sent out a truce party asking for a cease-fire to permit removal of dead and wounded. It was granted by Sibley and the battle was over.

Canby withdrew to Fort Craig in utter defeat. Ignoring him, and making no attempt to take over the post, Sibley moved on north. Three days later he was outside Albuquerque. This would prove to be a mistake, for Fort Craig had been well supplied with food and ammunition by the "prudent soldier."

After restocking at Fort Craig, the Union troops destroyed the supplies that could not be taken with them, and fled toward Santa Fe. Sibley took Albuquerque without firing a shot. Soon afterward Santa Fe fell to him in the same manner, Canby's force there destroying stores and retreating toward Fort Union, on the Santa Fe Trail northeast of Las Vegas. "It is needless to say that this country is in critical condition," read a dispatch sent by a Union inspector-general to army headquarters in St. Louis.

For two reasons, the situation was not as critical as the retreating inspector-general had painted it: first, Canby's strategy and plans of battle; second, logistics.

Canby had well-armed cavalry and infantry, as well as several batteries of artillery, in strong positions between Fort Union and the mountains west of Las Vegas. These could be quickly shifted to meet contingencies. With his battered troops rested, reorganized, and well supplied, Canby waited. He knew the Confederates would soon be desperately in need of rations and ammunition. He could cut off any provision trains that attempted to reach them from El Paso. Forces at Fort Union, his strongest post, could delay, if not destroy, Confederates approaching from the east. All Union stores at Albuquerque and Santa Fe had been burned before the towns were evacuated.

Canby not only knew the country but also its resources. The Confederates might obtain enough food to keep them going, but Fort Union was the only remaining depot where they might obtain adequate supplies of munitions. Even the capture of supplies from Union troops in the field would not long sustain them.

Fort Union, as Canby had anticipated, became Sibley's objective. Union scouts observed a picket column of six hundred Texans leave Santa Fe and take a position at the western mouth of Apache Canyon. Sibley's strategy was to have this force guard the eastern approach to the New Mexico capital until joined by the main body of Confederate troops. Then the united forces would sweep on to Las Vegas and Fort Union. Their victories had filled the Texans with confidence, and, as one of them wrote his wife, they all "felt like heroes . . . Fort Union was ours already; and then New Mexico would belong to the new government of the south and it would then be so easy to cut off all communication with California."

Scouts brought word to the Confederate picket that a small force of two hundred New Mexicans and two hundred regulars from Fort Union were moving up Apache Canyon. They raced forward to "dispose of the foolhardy Union troops." What they did not know was that the intelligence they had received was incomplete.

The Confederates soon came in sight of the Union column, which was advancing at double time, and opened fire. The column halted and took a defensive position. The Texans continued to advance, and suddenly were caught in devastating fire that rained upon them from both slopes of the canyon. Union infantry, one Texan recounted, "were upon the hills on both mountains jumping from rock to rock like so many mountain sheep."

The Union column had been a decoy, and the Texans were caught in a trap. They fled in disorder, leaving more then seventy dead and scores of wounded behind them.

Sibley rushed his full force—except for a few soldiers who remained with him to hold Albuquerque—and his main supply train into the canyon. Now Union troops poured westward from Fort Union and Las Vegas. The two armies met head on in Glorieta Pass. Throughout the day the battle raged without either side gaining an appreciable advantage, but late in the afternoon the Confederate colonel in command received news that made victory for him an utter impossibility. Union cavalry had circled the canyon without being discovered and had swept down on the supply train. They had captured the men guarding it, destroyed the wagons and all munitions and foodstuffs in them, and killed the animals.

The Confederate colonel asked for an armistice until the following noon to allow his dead to be buried and the wounded removed to safety. Canby readily granted it, but when the hour for its expiration arrived, the Confederates were gone.

Leaving their sick and wounded in Albuquerque, "without attendance, without medicine, and almost without food," the Texans continued their retreat down the west bank of the Rio Grande. Down the east bank moved Canby and several companies of Union troops. For a week the two forces were within gun range of each other, but there was no firing from either side. Officers urged Canby to cross the river and "wipe out the Confederates, once and for all," and they wondered if his refusal were based more on personal than humane reasons. Through his field glasses he could see his brother-in-law riding at the head of the Texans. There was no doubt they were almost helpless, and Canby was not the type of officer who would have found glory or satisfaction in attacking defenseless men, no matter who they were.

When Sibley and his weary column disappeared into the San Mateo Mountains, taking the hardest but shortest route to Texas, Canby turned back to Santa Fe.

For New Mexico and the short-lived Confederate Territory of Arizona the Civil War had ended less than a year after it had begun. But throughout the vast reaches of Apacheria another war was still raging, its deaths mounting, its fury rising, as Union troops from California and Santa Fe, townspeople, the few ranchers and miners remaining in the region, and the rampaging Apache struck viciously at each other.[19]

* * *

1862

JUNE

The troops from California commanded by General James H. Carleton reached Tucson. They had made a grueling forced march in terrible summer heat across the Mojave and Arizona Deserts, but they were under no pressure now. Colonel Canby had already saved the Southwest for the Union.

Carleton established a camp at Tucson, planning to continue to advance and join Canby after several weeks' rest for his weary, tortured men and horses, and gave his attention to civil matters. He issued a proclamation:

"In the present chaotic state in which Arizona is to be found: with no civil officers to administer the laws: indeed with an utter absence of all civil authority: and with no security of life or property within its borders: it becomes the duty of the undersigned to represent the authority of the United States over the people of Arizona."

Thus the abortive territory of Arizona, which had been carved out of the Southwest by southern sympathizers, and included the larger part of Apacheria, had its second military government. Carleton was no less demanding than the Confederates who had briefly ruled the region. He required every citizen to take an oath of allegiance to the United States. Some who refused were either imprisoned or forced to leave, and their property was confiscated. He imposed heavy taxes on merchants, saloon-keepers, and gamblers to help defray war expenses. His policy regarding the Apache was very simple—kill them where you find them.

JULY (Fourth)

The first of the California troops left Tucson on the march to Santa Fe. They consisted of two companies of cavalry and a small battery of howitzers under Captain Thomas Roberts. Roberts was to travel ahead as an advance guard, and he would be followed by Captain John C. Cremony with a supply train guarded by a company of infantry and a company of cavalry.

On the fifteenth Roberts began the climb up Apache Pass. It was his plan to camp at the abandoned stage station near the top, where water was available, and await the arrival of Cremony and the supply train. Apparently fearing no danger, Roberts advanced without scouts or flankers.

From a high pinnacle two men were watching him. They were Mangas Coloradas and Cochise. In various positions on both sides of the pass were some five hundred Chiricahua and Mimbres warriors.

Mangas Coloradas had come there to ask Cochise to join him in another assault on Pinos Altos. Apache patrolling the trail had spotted the dust cloud being raised by the approaching soldiers, and the two leaders had gone to the observation point. Pinos Altos was forgotten.

As they watched word was brought to them that a party of fourteen mounted miners with several heavily laden pack animals was approaching the pass from the east. Cochise and Mangas Coloradas agreed that it would be to their advantage to cut off the miners before they could reach a good defensive position in the pass, otherwise they would have enemies on two sides, and might sustain unnecessary casualties.

With fifty warriors Mangas Coloradas rode swiftly to the sloping plain just east of the pass. It was open country, but he and his men were able to conceal themselves in a shallow gulley without being detected. The ambush was successful. Several of the miners fell under the first volley. The others fought desperately, killing several warriors before they died.

The fourteen bodies were filled with arrows. The hats of the victims were replaced on their heads. Pack animals carrying pouches containing gold dust estimated to be worth forty thousand dollars were led away. Mangas Coloradas had come to understand the value of the yellow metal. It would buy many guns and large quantities of ammunition from both Mexican and American traders. Savoring his triumph, he led his warriors back to rejoin Cochise.

The careless Captain Roberts had permitted his troopers to string out as they moved up the pass. They were almost to the stage station when the weird Apache screams were heard, and lead and arrows rained on them. The soldiers, although badly disorganized, fought their way forward until the stage station was reached. They were still some six hundred yards from the nearest water. The Apache had built rock defense works overlooking the stream. Roberts brought up two howitzers.

This was the first battle in which American troops used artillery against the Apache. The shells exploding among them took a heavy toll, and the others attempting to keep the troops from the water, terrorized by the noise and fire and the sight of their dead, broke and fled.

Soon after the attack had begun, Roberts had sent a small detachment back to warn Cremony and the supply train. The Apache had anticipated the maneuver, and attacked the messengers. Three were wounded and fell from their horses, but others pulled them up behind their saddles and plunged on. The running fight continued for several miles. Private John Teal's horse was shot from under him. The others saw it go down, but with the Apache close upon them they had no chance to rescue Teal. All were wounded when they reached the wagon train. Teal was reported to have been slain.

But Teal was very much alive. Late at night he staggered into Captain Cremony's headquarters, carrying his saddle, which his thrifty nature would not permit him to abandon to the Apache.

When his horse fell, Teal had got behind the dying animal. He estimated that fifteen Apache were circling him, but the rapid fire of his breechloader kept them at a distance. In the gathering dusk a huge man rode into his view and appeared to be giving orders to the others. Teal took careful aim and fired. The huge man fell from his horse.

It was the shot that won the battle for the troops. Teal did not know it then, but he had wounded Mangas Coloradas. In his report to Cremony, he said: "He must have been a man of some note, because soon after that they seemed to get away from me, and I could hear their voices growing fainter in the distance. I thought this a good time to make tracks . . . I have walked eight miles since then."

Captain Roberts and Cremony and their troops passed safely through Apache Pass. Some Indians were sighted, but there was no more fighting. They counted the bodies of sixty-three Apache war-riors. The American losses were two killed and a number wounded.

When their great leader fell the Apache lost all desire to continue the fight with the soldiers. They thought only of saving the life of Mangas Coloradas, and for that they were unwilling to depend on the magic of their own medicine men. They wanted white man's magic, the skill of the white man's physician, for they knew its power, they had seen it work.

A special big litter was constructed and slung between two strong horses. The immense old chief was placed on it. With several hundred warriors as an escort, Mangas Coloradas, conscious but suffering ex-cruciating pain, was carried nearly a hundred miles over mountains and deserts to the little Mexican town of Janos. The Apache knew— or perhaps it was Mangas Coloradas himself who knew—that a doctor lived there.

AUGUST

A small garrison of Mexican soldiers was at Janos, but they did not leave their barracks when the hundreds of Apache rode into town. The people stayed in their houses.

An Apache spokesman, perhaps Cochise, told the doctor: "You make him well, and everybody lives. If he dies, everybody in Janos dies."

For some ten days the Apache held Janos. No one was permitted to leave, and those who arrived were forced to remain there. Seldom in that time did the desperate doctor leave the bedside of his patient.

Mangas Coloradas's strength rapidly returned after he was permit-ted to get up and move about. On a hot summer day he rode out of Janos at the head of a long column of happy Mimbres and Chiricahua, on the trail back to his own country.

During his absence, General Carleton had built Fort Bowie near Apache Pass, and then had gone on to Santa Fe. Canby was called east to receive a general's star and a new assignment.

Carleton was the commander of all forces in the Southwest. He continued to search out and arrest known southern sympathizers, but his real trouble came not from them. It came from the Apache and the Navajo.

* * *

General Carleton quickly became the absolute ruler of New Mexico. The vast territory had a governor, and it had other civil officials and Indian agents, but they were puppets in his hands. There was a reason for this situation. Only the military, only force of arms, could control affairs in the torn and bloody land. Only troops could enforce laws, give any protection to white people, and stand against Indian attacks.

Any number of uncomplimentary adjectives may be used to describe Carleton, whose nickname was Mogul. He was merciless, cold, stubborn, unconscionable, arrogant. He was a hypocrite. Many of his letters and reports were maudlin and sickly sentimental.

Sonnichsen describes him as "a down-east Yankee from Maine, forty-eight years old at the time, spare and durable and ramrod straight in his Army blues. His glance was penetrating, his thick hair tended to bristle, his wide mouth, surmounted by a military moustache and flanked by heavy sideburns, drooped at the corners and shut like a rat trap. With his arms folded and his head thrown back, he was a picture of indomitable self-confidence."

Perhaps his greatest failing was that he would never admit that he had misjudged a situation, that he had made an error. Once he had made up his mind he refused to change it, no matter what the consequences. He refused to admit that he had been wrong.

* * *

September

General Carleton had a plan. As he revealed it, it appeared to be constructive and practicable, and it received both the sanction of the War Department and the approval of Governor Henry Connelley. In reality, its success depended upon barbaric tactics which if not unprecedented ranked among the most hideous devised by any American military commander in the campaigns against western Indians.

Carleton's strategy, at least as he explained it, was to force the Indians, tribe by tribe, onto lands set aside for them as far as possible from white settlements, where, in his own words, they would be "away from the haunts and hills and hiding places of their country" and where the army would be "kind to them; there teach their children how to read and write; teach them the arts of peace; teach them the truths of Christianity." There, too, in these comfortable havens, they would be taught to farm and support themselves. The plan was not new. Indeed, it had been advocated by government authorities and civilian groups since the American occupation of the Southwest. Carleton, however, was not hesitant in intimating that the idea was a product of his own ingenuity.

The first step was to obtain the services of a field commander who not only knew the country but the Indians and was thoroughly experienced in fighting them. The logical choice—perhaps the only man in New Mexico fully qualified in all respects to undertake the assignment—was the noted Mountain Man and scout, Kit Carson. When approached on the matter, Carson frankly expressed the doubt that full-scale military operations were necessary to achieve the desired goal. It was his belief that if permanent and adequate reservations were established, the Indians could be moved to them without fighting.

If things worked out that way, Carleton said, well and good, but he would not be dissuaded from sending soldiers in large numbers to execute his program. His troops had been given little to do, except policing operations, and morale was low. They had made a forced march across the deserts from California, only to find that the Confederates had been driven from New Mexico. Their disappointment had been great, and they were eager for action.

Carleton disclosed that a contingent of army officers was already at work planning a reservation on the Pecos River in eastern New Mexico, lands personally selected by himself. The campaign would be directed first against the Mescalero. After they had been removed to the Pecos, the offensive would be concentrated against the Navajo, and in turn against any other troublesome Indians, until all had been driven to confinement under conditions in which they could be effectively controlled.

Both Governor Connelley and Carleton put heavy pressure on Carson to accept the command, and at last he agreed. Holding a commission as Colonel of Volunteers, he set out for the Mescalero Country. The orders he carried, issued by General Carleton late in September, 1862, said:

"Fort Stanton, on the Bonito River, in the country of the Mescalero Apaches, will without delay be reoccupied by five companies of Colonel Christopher Carson's regiment of New Mexico volunteers."

O C T O B E R

Colonel Carson had not yet reached Fort Stanton when he received additional orders from General Carleton. The veteran scout was appalled to learn that the Mescalero were not to be taken peaceably to the reservation on the Pecos. Said Carleton:

"All Indian men of that tribe are to be killed whenever and wherever you can find them. The women and children will not be harmed, but you will take them prisoners, and feed them at Fort Stanton until you receive other instructions about them. If the Indians send in a flag and desire to treat for peace, say to the bearer that when the people of New Mexico were attacked by the Texans [Confederates], the Mescaleros broke their treaty of peace, and murdered innocent people, and ran off their stock; that now our hands are untied, and you have been sent to punish them for their treachery and their crimes; that you have no power to make peace; that you are there to kill them wherever you can find them; that if they beg for peace, their chiefs and twenty of their principal men must come to Santa Fe to have a talk there."

Although he was shocked by the savagery of the order, Carson saw no alternative but to occupy Fort Stanton. Troops were already deployed against the Mescalero. One company which had penetrated the Guadalupe Mountains found only a number of abandoned camps, and the commander reported that all his men were disappointed, "but none so much as myself, in not getting a fight out of the redskins." Another company had more success. A band of ragged and hungry Mescalero—men, women, and children—armed mostly with bows and arrows were encountered. The leader was the aging Manuelito. He informed the company commander, a Captain James Graydon, that he and his people were on their way to Santa Fe to beg for peace and protection. Captain Graydon opened fire. Manuelito, another leader, José Largo, nine other men, and several women were instantly killed. A number of others were mortally wounded and left to die lingering deaths. Some of the band escaped. Captain Graydon, pleased with his "victory," rode triumphantly back to Fort Stanton.

It wasn't a "victory" to Carson, and he did not hesitate to say as much in a dispatch to Carleton. The general replied: "If you are satisfied that Graydon's attack on Manuelito and his people was not fair and open, see that all horses and mules . . . are returned to the survivors."

NOVEMBER

The slaughter continued. The Mescalero, terrorized, were fleeing as best they could, seeking hideouts from troops converging on them from three directions. Several score men, women, and children were murdered by soldiers during the month. A large number trapped in a place called Dog Canyon were shot to death.

The Mescalero, knowing the famed Colonel Carson well, would not believe that he would wantonly murder them, and they began to flock to Fort Stanton. Those who reached the post safely were saved. Carson seemed to forget his orders to kill Mescalero "whenever and wherever" he found them. He fed and protected several hundred survivors.

Carleton had instructed him that "if they beg for peace, their chiefs and twenty of the principal men must come to Santa Fe to have a talk there." Carson took advantage of this part of his orders. There weren't twenty bona fide "leading men" at Fort Stanton, but there were four and one prominent chief, Cadette. With Indian Agent Labadie and a military escort he sent them to Santa Fe.

Captain Cremony recorded and translated Chief Cadette's appeal to General Carleton in this way:

"You are stronger than we. We have fought you so long as we had rifles and powder; but your weapons are better than ours. Give us weapons and turn us loose, and we will fight you again; but we are worn out; we have no more heart; we have no provisions, no means to live; your troops are everywhere; our springs and waterholes are either occupied or overlooked by your young men. You have driven us from our last and best stronghold, and we have no more heart. Do with us as may seem good to you, but do not forget that we are men and braves."

General Carleton displayed no compassion. The Mescalero could either surrender and go to the new reservation on the Pecos or be killed. Cadette would be given a safe escort back to his people to tell them they had no other alternative.

Cadette returned to Fort Stanton. Some warriors, perhaps a few more than a hundred, rejected Carleton's ultimatum, and fled westward to join the Gila. But most of the Mescalero resigned themselves to imprisonment on the Pecos . . . if they could live long enough to get there.

West of the Rio Grande in southern New Mexico, along the Gila and the San Pedro and the Santa Cruz Rivers in southern Arizona, along the Rio Verde and Agua Fria in the Tonto Basin, and along the Mogollon Rim the fighting continued to rage, with troops hard-pressed to hold their stations and protect white settlements against almost constant raiding by Apache bands.

* * *

A hundred and seventy-five miles southeast of Santa Fe the red muddy Rio Pecos twisted through the western reaches of the vast Llano Estacado, a dry, barren land, treeless except for the ragged cottonwoods that lifted tortured limbs along the edge of the alkaline stream. Coronado's chronicler, Castañeda, had written: "It is impossible to find tracks in this country, because the grass straightened up again as soon as it was trodden down. In two hundred and fifty leagues was seen not a hillock which was three times as high as a man. The country is like a bowl, so that when a man sits down, the horizon surrounds him all around at the distance of a musket shot."

This land had not changed at all when Carleton came to know it, more than three hundred years later. It suited in almost every particular the plan the general had in mind. It was isolated, far from every white settlement, a part of the public domain, and inhabited only by a few New Mexican cattlemen, wandering Indian hunters, buffalo, wolves, coyotes, and jackrabbits.

Both the War Department and the Bureau of Indian Affairs had agreed to Carleton's plan to set aside the necessary agricultural lands and to build a new post, Fort Sumner, so that troops would be present to maintain order among the Indians to be settled there. The site

Carleton had selected was known as Bosque Redondo, where cotton-wood groves stretched for several miles along the Pecos.

A board of army officers assigned to inspect the place vociferously disagreed with Carleton's choice, reporting that Bosque Redondo was "remote from the depot of supplies, Fort Union, and from the neighborhoods that supply forage. Building material will have to be brought from a great distance. The water of the Pecos contains much unhealthy mineral matter. A large part of the surrounding valley is subject to inundation by the spring floods." The board recommended another site closer to Las Vegas and Fort Union, "where the supply of good timber for building and firewood is convenient, the water is pure and abundant, the grazing is very fine. . . ." Carleton overruled the inspectors and was sustained by the War Department.

Acting upon the advice of Secretary of the Interior John P. Usher, President Abraham Lincoln would sign an order creating a forty-square-mile reservation at Bosque Redondo. The President was told that it would be large enough to serve the needs of the Mescalero and other small Apache bands inhabiting eastern New Mexico. He was not informed, however, of General Carleton's plan to confine thousands of Navajo in the small area. Thus, through no fault of the President, two cabinet departments would become engaged in a vicious jurisdictional dispute and a bitter controversy over conflicting interpretations of regulations and policies. It would be a contest lasting for years, but the persons who would suffer most from it would be the hungry, diseased, ragged Indians forced to live in filth and squalor, terrible heat and terrible cold, in the mud huts, while the supplies and clothing and medicines which might have relieved their suffering either failed to arrive because of War Department red tape or were stolen from them by crooked contractors and thieves in the Indian Bureau.[20]

* * *

It would be difficult, if not impossible, to find in the long history of Apacheria a record of a more motley group of adventurers than the Walker Party. Among the forty or more members, led by veteran Mountain Man Joseph R. Walker, were renegades of many types—thieves, wanted murderers, trappers, miners, Confederate rebels, farmers, some men of education, some who had received technical training, and a few whose instincts and habits were above those of animals. Despite the diversities of their characters they had two things in common, an indestructible dream of finding gold and an inveterate hatred of Indians.

By the time they had reached southwestern New Mexico they had traveled far. Starting in California they had crossed northern Arizona, prospected in Colorado, and traveled south to Santa Fe. No written account of this portion of their journey had been found, but as they continued their wandering it must be assumed that they had discovered no veins promising enough to hold them. The company alternatively decreased and increased as it progressed. In northern New Mexico it was joined by Daniel Ellis Conner, a Kentuckian twenty-five years of age who had gone out to Colorado in 1859. For three years Conner had prospected with little luck. In 1861 he had obtained employment at a military post near Pueblo. Because of avowed loyalty to the Confederacy, he had been forced to flee to escape imprisonment. Conner had attended Hanover College, studying civil engineering. He also aspired to be a writer, and, although his literary talents were limited, he would leave an account of the adventures of the Walker Party in Apacheria that eliminates historical gaps which might well have remained unfilled.

In 1863 Walker was sixty-five years old. As trapper, prospector, explorer, guide, he had wandered through the western wilderness for more than thirty years. A big man with a snowy mane and bright blue eyes, he was renowned as a Mountain Man from the Yellowstone to the Rio Grande, from the Platte to the gold fields of California. In Santa Fe in 1862 he had quickly gained the confidence of General Carleton, to whom he revealed the plan he had in mind.

It was to take his company south along the Rio Grande, turn westward near Cook's Spring, pass through the mountains in the vicinity of Pinos Altos, descend Apache Pass, and from Tucson turn northwest to the Gila River, and search for gold in the rugged country about the present site of Prescott. Some authorities maintain that Walker, in the company of Kit Carson and another notorious Mountain Man, Pauline Weaver, had visited western Arizona as early as 1842, that he had always believed gold was to be found there, and that he had always wanted to return to make a thorough search for it.

Whatever the case, Walker's plan, for two reasons, met with Carleton's approval. The first, and probably the most important, reason was that Carleton himself held an unshakable conviction that both the Navajo Country and western Apacheria were rich in minerals, and he wanted to get a finger in the pie. The second reason was that Walker's project was in line with Carleton's Indian extermination policy. At every opportunity he encouraged miners and settlers to emigrate to Arizona. If more settlements, ranches, and mines developed, the government would be forced to send more troops to protect them. Thus, the task of destroying the Indians would be more easily accomplished.

Carleton and Walker formed some kind of a partnership.

Details of their agreement are not available, but under it Carleton was to receive a certain percentage of any discoveries Walker made. In return, Walker and his company would be relieved of any burdens imposed by the martial law by which Carleton governed New Mexico and Arizona, and would be given a license to travel, prospect, and file claims wherever they wished without any restraints whatsoever. Nor would they be held accountable for any dastardly deeds they might commit against Indians, not excluding cold-blooded murders.

Carleton would write General Henry W. Halleck: "Among all my endeavors since my arrival here has been an effort to brush back the Indians, so that the people could get out of the valley of the Rio Grande, and not only possess themselves of the arable lands in other parts of the territory, but, if the country contained veins and deposits of precious metals, they might be found." In another letter to Halleck he said: "There is every evidence that a country as rich if not richer in mineral wealth than California, extends from the Rio Grande, north-westwardly, all the way across to Washoe [Nevada]." And in a letter to Walker in Arizona Carleton would say: "If I can help others to a fortune, it will afford me not quite as much happiness as finding one myself, it is true—but nearly as much. My luck has always been not to be at the right place at the right time for fortunes."

Governor Connelley may have been a party to the agreement between Carleton and Walker. At least he shared unequivocally the general's sentiments. He would tell the New Mexico legislative assembly that Indians "occupy the finest grazing districts within our limits . . . infest a mining region extending two hundred miles . . ." and therefore "an immense [white] pastoral and mining population is excluded from its occupations and the treasures of mineral wealth that are known to exist . . . public interest demands that this condition of things should cease to exist."

* * *

1863

JANUARY

Walker and his men were encamped near the old copper mines of Pinos Altos. This was Mimbreno Country, the high ranges ruled by the great Mangas Coloradas. Ahead along the trail to the west were the sites of numerous fights with Apaches in which scores of soldiers and civilian travelers had been killed. Realizing the perils which might well confront them, Walker devised a scheme which he believed would guarantee them a safe passage. It was to capture by a ruse an Apache leader, and hold him hostage until the dangerous area had been left behind. This, it was believed, would insure them against an Apache attack.

John W. Swilling, a former Confederate soldier, volunteered to attempt to execute the plan, and was given the assignment. At this juncture, a company of Union soldiers en route east from California arrived and made camp with Walker's group. Swilling informed the company commander, Captain E. D. Shirland, of the plan, a plan, as Wellman said, "that would make a Judas blush. Shirland, however, was no Judas. He agreed promptly and without blushing."

Conner accompanied a number of soldiers and prospectors to Pinos Altos to set the trap. He declared it was their intention to capture Mangas Coloradas. This may have been their intention, but it seems improbable that they entertained any real hope of taking the wily old chief. At Pinos Altos they waved white flags until they succeeded in attracting the attention of several Apache and received an answering signal. After an exchange of messages at long distance, the Apaches approached within talking distance and were informed that *nan-tan*, commander of the soldiers, wished to hold a peace parley with Red Sleeves. The Indians vanished. Several hours passed.

At last a large group of Apache were seen stationing themselves behind boulders on a nearby hillside. Then out in the open, riding toward the old Santa Rita mine building in which the soldiers and prospectors were waiting, came the famous Mangas Coloradas and fifteen of his warriors. His bodyguard stopped, but Mangas Coloradas unhesitantly rode up to the white men and dismounted. He knew instantly that he was trapped, that he had trusted the white man one time too many, but he showed no emotion, least of all a sign of fear, as he stared into the muzzles of their rifles. He had come, he said calmly, under a white flag to talk to their chief. In broken Spanish he was told that the white chief awaited him in the camp, and that if he would tell his escort to leave, he would be taken there. If he did not obey he would be shot where he stood.

Mangas Coloradas told his warriors to leave. One of them was a young leader named Geronimo. They voiced objections, but he again commanded them to depart, and they turned on their horses and trotted away, disappearing into the surrounding forest.

Although he was about seventy years old, Mangas Coloradas was still straight, and he towered head and shoulders above his captors. Conner wrote that he looked careworn. He wore a hat with a wide brim and a small crown, of Mexican manufacture, that sat on the top of his great head, as if it were much too small for him, and was secured by a thong tied beneath his chin. From under the brim fell a cascade of thick black hair that reached to his waist. His enormous chest was covered by a checked cotton shirt. Blue overalls were cut off just below the knees, meeting the top of moccasin boots.

Shortly after the gold hunters and soldiers reached the Walker camp with their prize, a contingent of cavalry arrived and bivouacked nearby.

They had been sent by General Carleton to establish a post for the protection of miners in the area. When their commander, Brigadier-General J. R. West, was informed that Mangas Coloradas was a captive, he went at once to look at him. Conner thought the general looked like a pygmy beside the old chief.

West ordered that besides the regular sentries two additional troopers be assigned to guard Mangas Coloradas during the night. The men selected for the duty were Privates James Collyer and George Mead. West personally gave them instructions. According to another soldier, Clark B. Stocking, who was present, the general told the guards:

"Men, that old murderer has got away from every soldier command and has left a trail of blood five hundred miles on the old stage line. I want him dead tomorrow morning. Do you understand? I want him dead."

It was a cold night, and Mangas Coloradas was rolled in a blanket beside a large fire. Conner, also on sentry duty, was walking a beat nearby, and he noticed that a number of times the old chief would jerk and draw up his legs, as if he were suffering spasms of pain. And, indeed, he was. His guards were heating their bayonets in the fire and touching them to his feet. At last Mangas Coloradas sat up and growled at them in Spanish that he was not a toy to be played with.

Both Privates Collyer and Mead, almost simultaneously, shot him with their muskets, then fired several shots with their revolvers into his crumpled body.

The shots brought soldiers and civilians out of their blankets with guns at the ready, but within a few minutes the camp was again quiet. Mangas Coloradas remained lying where he had died through the night. In the morning, Conner took some "curious trinkets" from the body. A soldier, Private John T. Wright, borrowed a butcher knife from a cook and took the chief's scalp, and, after wrapping the long hair around the skin, stuffed it into his pocket.

A surgeon, Captain D. B. Sturgeon, cut off Mangas Coloradas's great head, and boiled it. Sturgeon then boxed the clean skull, stating that he would send it to a New York friend who was a phrenologist.

The decapitated corpse of Mangas Coloradas was thrown into a gully.*

---

*The phrenologist to whom the skull was sent was Professor O. S. Fowler. He announced that it was larger than that of Daniel Webster. In a totally dishonest report on the death of Mangas Coloradas, General West would state that the chief had been captured in a fight with a band of Apache, that six privates and a noncommissioned officer had been assigned to guard him through the night, and that Mangas Coloradas had been killed in an attempt to escape.

FEBRUARY

On the twenty-fourth President Lincoln signed a bill, passed by Congress a few days earlier, which created Arizona Territory.

MARCH

The betrayal and murder of Mangas Coloradas brought constant warfare in the country of the Mimbreno. Soldiers and miners were seldom out of sight of Apache smoke signals. Running clashes occurred almost daily. Troops scoured the region seeking Indian camps. Most of the inhabitants successfully escaped, but their villages were destroyed, their horses, mules, and cattle were either slaughtered or driven away, and perhaps twoscore warriors and a number of Apache women were killed.

MAY–DECEMBER

The Walker Company reached western Arizona in the spring. Gold was discovered first on Lynx Creek, and then in other places. Pauline Weaver, the veteran trapper and guide, led prospectors to rich finds along the Hassayampa River. Weaver, who was part Cherokee, was a native of Tennessee. He had first gone to Arizona in 1830 as a fur trapper for the Hudson's Bay Company. In 1846 he served as a guide for General Phillip St. George Cooke and the Mormon Battalion. He discovered the rich placer mines at La Paz, Arizona. A strange, restless man, he never became wealthy, but seemed to prefer roaming the country to the hard work of developing a claim. Mining districts and diggings were named for both Walker and Weaver.

The strikes in west-central Arizona brought a stampede of several thousand miners into the region. They were quickly followed by farmers, cattlemen, hopeful merchants, and a horde of gamblers and outlaws. Fights with Apaches were almost a daily occurrence.

Fort Whipple was established in the Chino Valley to protect the burgeoning white population. The commander, Major Edward Willis, soon was able to negotiate a treaty of peace with a large band living to the northeast, and there were indications that other groups would come to terms.

As the year neared its end the first governor of Arizona Territory, John N. Goodwin, and other territorial officials were en route westward from Albuquerque with a military escort. Before he had succeeded in negotiating a treaty with the Apache near Fort Whipple, Major Willis had sent word to them to be on their guard against Indians. When the peaceable band was encountered, the troops of the escort immediately launched an attack and killed twenty of the bewildered Apache.

No more treaties would be signed. There would be no peace. Every Apache band in central, western, and southern Arizona took to the warpath.

* * *

In 1864, J. Ross Browne, a special observer for the Department of the Interior, made a tour of Arizona with Indian Superintendent Charles D. Poston. He wrote:

"The most desperate class of renegades from Texas and California found Arizona a safe asylum from arrest under the laws. The Vigilance Committee of San Francisco did more to populate the new Territory than the silver mines. Tucson became the headquarters of vice, dissipation, and crime. It was probably the nearest approach to Pandemonium on the North American Continent. Murderers, thieves, cutthroats, and gamblers formed the mass of the population. Every man went armed to the teeth, and scenes of bloodshed were of everyday occurrence in the public streets. There was neither government, law, nor military protection. The garrison at Tucson confined itself to its legitimate business of getting drunk or doing nothing. Arizona was perhaps the only part of the world under the protecting aegis of a civilized government in which every man administered justice to suit himself, and where all assumed the right to gratify the basest passions of their nature without restraint. It was literally a paradise of devils."

* * *

1864

Arizona was washed in blood.

Raiding Apache swept down on ranches, killed their occupants, burned the buildings and hay fields, and made off with horses, mules, cattle, and sheep. Miners were killed at their work. "Indians were so numerous," states Ogle, "that the region was destitute of transportation. Workmen erecting buildings in Prescott [the territorial capital founded in April] went armed and no one could go beyond the town limits in safety. . . . Conditions were equally bad in the southern part of the territory."

Superintendent of Indian Affairs Poston appealed for more troops, as did Governor Goodwin. General Carleton sent all he could—a full-scale war against the Navajo also was under way—and advised the territorial officials to make use of friendly Maricopa, Pima, and Papago, all deadly enemies of the Apache. "You will be able to secure the efforts of the miners without trouble," Carleton wrote Goodwin. "Let us work earnestly and hard, and before next Christmas your Apaches are whipped." The general expressed the belief that unless troops, citizens, and friendly Indian mercenaries combined forces against the Apache, "you will have a twenty years' war."

The first Territorial Legislature gave full support to Carleton's extermination policy, declaring that relentless warfare was the only means of removing the red menace. Indeed, virtually the entire white population hailed Carleton's orders to military commanders to kill every male encountered and take women and children prisoners. Some strong opposition to Carleton's ruthlessness developed, but it came mostly from the East, from religious societies, organizations advocating the establishment of adequate reservations on which Indians could be protected and taught to become self-supporting, and various other types of humanitarians. Their pleas fell on deaf ears in Arizona. Arizonans did not want Apache reservations—the Apache would occupy good land that belonged to them by right of conquest—nor did they want peace. They wanted Apache annihilation. Women and children as well as men.

And many of them did their best to achieve that desirable goal.

Two Indian boys who wandered into Weaver's diggings to see the sights were shot to death. King S. Woolsey, a rancher and aide to Governor Goodwin, while on a trip in the Bradshaw Mountains, left some pinole where he knew Apache would find it. They did, and a dozen or more of them died in horrible agony. The pinole contained strychnine. Conner wrote that when men in the settlements or the diggings "had nothing else to do" they would go Indian hunting. If an Indian was found he was unceremoniously shot to death, stripped of his clothing, scalped, and left to rot.

Sugarfoot Jack was an escaped convict from Tasmania who by some means had reached San Diego and enlisted in the army. After he had been dishonorably discharged for thievery and striking an officer in Arizona, he had joined the Walker Company. His real name is not known to history.

A group of civilians had been organized to hunt Apache on the Verde River. Sugarfoot Jack, always ready for an adventure and an opportunity to kill Indians, volunteered his services.

An Apache village was found, but the occupants had escaped only moments before the whites attacked. The wickiups were fired. In the course of the destruction Sugarfoot Jack came upon an abandoned papoose. He threw it into a fire, sat down, and watched it burn to death.

Other miners in the group, said Conner, "discovered the little, black, crisped body of the murdered child, lying upon its side with its little hands and knees drawn nearly to its chin. . . . They undertook to take the body out of the ashes, but the skin peeling off every time it was touched made the boys sick, and they left it. . . ."

Sugarfoot Jack, wandering among the burning jacals (huts) of the Apache, came upon another small child who had been left behind in the villagers' mad rush to escape. He sat on a stone and jiggled it on his knee and tickled it under the chin. At last he apparently tired of playing with the infant, and, according to Conner, he drew "a heavy dragoon six-shooter, placed the muzzle to the child's head as it sat upon his knee, turned his own face away, and fired. He thus bespattered his clothes and face with infant brains to the disgust and indignation of everyone who happened to be looking in his direction."

Some of the men threatened to kill Sugarfoot Jack, and he, fully aware that they were not given to making idle threats, fled into the brush. "This matter," wrote Conner, "threw the apple of discord into our ranks. Some thought that it was no harm to kill an Indian of any age, size, or sex. Others declared that they could not nor would not support such brutality nor countenance any war party that did." The group divided, and each party was obliged to fight its way through infuriated Apache back to the safety of settlements.

Woolsey led several volunteer groups on expeditions against the Apache. No count was kept of the number killed. His most successful fight—if it can be called that—took place in Fish Creek Canyon, some dozen miles from Salt River Canyon.* He had with him between forty and fifty whites and fourteen or fifteen Maricopa. Passing through a wash, the company suddenly was faced with an unusually large band of Pinal and Coyotero Apache. Conner, a member of the party, placed the number of Indians at two hundred and fifty, a formidable force, but others state there were between three and four hundred warriors, "all done up in paint and feathers . . . ominously silent."

The two groups came within a hundred paces of each other, but no shots were fired. At last Woolsey called out in a friendly tone: *"Buenos días."* He was answered in broken Spanish with a taunt to "come on and fight." An employee of Woolsey, called Tonto Jack, relayed his message that the white men had not come to fight, but to hold a peace talk. The parley was arranged, and six Apache, including a chief named Par-a-muck-a, came forward to talk with Woolsey and four other white men. The others of the two groups remained a few yards away from the conference.

Woolsey soon learned that the Apache counselors had no interpreter, and could not understand him. Thereupon, he spoke freely in English, telling his men to select a target, and begin shooting when he touched the brim of his hat.

The signal was given a few moments later. The six Apache leaders

---

*Some historians say it occurred in Bloody Tanks Wash, near Miami, but this is probably erroneous.

were slain. A devastating fire was directed against the other Indians. They fought courageously as they retreated up a hillside, pursued by Woolsey and his men.

Twenty-four Apache are known to have been killed. Many more were wounded. The white casualties totaled one killed and several wounded. Actually, said Conner, we "never knew how many Indians were killed on this occasion and never waited to count them."

Records, of course, are far from complete, but as near as can be determined approximately two hundred and sixteen Apache were killed in central Arizona during the year. In the same region only sixteen white persons were slain by raiders during this period. Figures for other parts of the territory are not available. However, a list of fights and skirmishes that occurred would require many pages of type. The fact remains that they contributed nothing in the way of a solution to the problem. There was no peace, and blood continued to flow in almost all sections.

* * *

Captain John C. Cremony, in Apache Country, sometime in the 1860's:

"Apache signal smokes are of various kinds, each one significant of a particular object. A sudden puff, rising from the mountain heights, and almost as suddenly losing its identity by dissolving into the rarified atmosphere, indicated the presence of a strange party upon the plain below. If these puffs are rapidly repeated they are a warning that strangers are well armed and numerous. If a steady smoke is maintained for some time, the object is to collect the scattered bands of savages at some designated point, with hostile intention, should it be practicable. These signals are made at night in the same order by the use of fires which are either alternately exposed and shrouded from view, or allowed to burn steadily."

* * *

1865

An army officer would remark that in Arizona the white people lived on reservations, and the Indians occupied the country.

General Carleton's extermination policy had been no more successful for Americans than a similar policy had been for the Mexicans a hundred years earlier. The murdering of a few Indians only resulted in driving all other Indians to increase the fury and number of their attacks on soldiers and settlers.

One of the greatest difficulties with which military or civilian expeditions had to contend was the elusiveness of the Apache. When they could be trapped—which was not often—they were exterminated to the last man, woman, and child.

A direct confrontation was rarely possible. The Apache seldom attacked unless they believed they held an advantage. Often they would trail a party for days, waiting for an opportunity to catch their victims off guard or in a position where defense would be difficult. In almost every fight the Apache would strike and scatter, making pursuit all but impossible. The long campaigns of the military were for the most part exercises in futility.

The defensive strength of the entire Southwest suffered a severe setback by the transfer of Arizona Territory in January to the Department of California from the Department of New Mexico. Thus, Apacheria was divided between two commands, neither one of which could cooperate voluntarily with the other without specific orders from headquarters. Sometimes as long as three months would elapse before dispatches could be exchanged, and plans for an offensive could be coordinated and executed. The territorial government and the citizens were infuriated, but there was little they could do about the situation, except take matters into their own hands and defend themselves as best they could. Moreover, with the end of the Civil War several companies of California Volunteers, whose members had enlisted in the first place to fight Confederates, not Apache, had to be mustered out. Every garrison in Apacheria was undermanned. At Tucson, for example, an officer reported that he did not have enough men to protect their horses from Apache raiders, and a similar condition existed in other posts. Truly the Apache occupied the country, meeting with few serious restraints.

General Carleton was no longer the ruler of Arizona, but his extermination policy remained popular and in force. The territorial government had authority to raise a force of volunteers, but there was no money in its treasury with which to pay them. Governor Goodwin and the most successful of all Indian killers, King S. Woolsey, were sent to attempt to borrow the necessary funds in San Francisco. Bankers were not interested in investing in Indian fighting, and rejected their proposals. General Irvin McDowell, commander of the Department of California, however, promised to send reinforcements. Within a few weeks a thousand troops, commanded by General John S. Mason, were in Arizona.

Mason at once set out on a tour of inspection. He reported: "At the time of my arrival in the district, I believe every ranch had been deserted south of the Gila. The town of Tubac was entirely deserted, and the town of Tucson had about two hundred souls. North of the Gila, the roads were completely blockaded; the ranches, with one or two exceptions, abandoned, and most of the settlements were threatened with abandonment or annihilation."

Mason created nineteen subdistricts in Arizona, and gave the commander of each one complete freedom to operate against the Apache. Action followed, but the results were negligible, for there were not sufficient troops to wage successful sustained campaigns against the enemy. The Apache easily kept out of their way, and continued their marauding.

General Mason sought to induce Apache leaders to meet with him for the purpose of negotiating a peace program. Not one responded. Five times during the past year Apache had been murdered by white men under a flag of truce. They had had all they wanted of peace parleys.

Frustrated in this effort, Mason then resorted to the tactics Carleton had employed. He organized an offensive of "incessant attacks." The Apache were to be wiped out. He qualified this stern measure, however, with the announcement that any who voluntarily surrendered would be placed on reserves, which he designated at various places in the territory, and would be fed and protected.

Few surrendered. The day when any white man could be trusted had passed. Apache attacks continued, almost on an hourly basis in the Prescott region. So greatly menaced were settlements in this area that the territorial court could not function, for prospective jurors were all busy guarding their homes and families. One military post fell to Apache, the garrison being wiped out. Pinals and Tontos raged through the Salt River Valley, devastating it to such an extent that General McDowell ordered the establishment of a five-company post near the junction of the Salt and Verde Rivers.

Indian Superintendent G. W. Leihy strongly supported a reservation program, but he realized that there was little hope of its being fulfilled. He understood that permanent peace was a chimera, not only because of the lethargy and dishonesty of officials in Washington but because of the contempt and hatred of Indians held by the residents of Arizona.

Mason's vigorous assaults were not completely unrewarding. His troops were victorious in a fight with Cochise's warriors in the Chiricahua Mountains. Other troops won a battle on the Verde against two hundred Apache. But most of the campaigns were failures, the Apache eluding their pursuers.

Since the death of Mangas Coloradas, the Mimbreno frequently suffered setbacks. They were no longer the dangerous antagonists they had been under the great Red Sleeves. Much of their spirit and their determination appeared to have been dissipated. As their homeland was in the Department of New Mexico, General Carleton believed the time had come to force them to move to Bosque Redondo, where the

Navajo and Mescalero were confined. He assigned Captain N. H. Davis to the task.

Davis succeeded in persuading Victorio and other Mimbreno leaders to talk with him at Pinos Altos. They admitted to being destitute and weary of war. Victorio agreed to Davis's suggestion that a committee of Mimbreno go to Bosque Redondo to examine the situation there and to assure themselves that their people would receive rations and protection. A point of rendezvous at which the journey was to begin was named. Davis was there on schedule and waited several days. The Mimbreno delegation did not appear. Davis at last issued orders that every male Indian encountered was to be shot without mercy, and he reported to General Carleton his conviction that the only plan that could be successful in dealing with the "Mimbreno rattlesnakes" was to annihilate them. Carleton didn't disagree with him. The general had believed that for some time.

In the beginning the Apache had not mutilated or scalped the bodies of Americans they killed. American soldiers and civilians scalped, cut off ears and the genital organs of their red victims. Thrapp remarks that the whites' ". . . cruel methods led to a brutalization of Indian warfare." To which Dunn adds: "Both sides were becoming more and more exasperated, and vented their spleen in ways that only served to make matters worse. The Indians were adopting the practice of mutilating the dead, which was formerly contrary to their customs."

The extermination policy was far from dead. Indeed, it had become the policy of both sides.

* * *

Sylvester Mowry, Arizona pioneer booster, mine promoter, newspaper owner, and writer, in 1864:

"There is only one way to wage war against the Apaches. They must be surrounded, starved into coming in, surprised or inveigled—by white flags, or any other method, human or divine—and then put to death. If these ideas shock any weak-minded individual who thinks himself a philanthropist, I can only say that I pity without respecting his mistaken sympathy."

* * *

1866

Although enlistment of new troops had been halted, the desperate situation in Arizona caused Secretary of War Edwin M. Stanton to authorize the recruitment of six companies of cavalry to be known as Arizona Volunteers. One company was composed almost entirely of Pima, traditional enemies of the Apache. Most of the other men enrolled were Mexicans. With one exception, the commanders were Americans. One company was commanded by a halfbreed Wyandotte who had lived among the Pima for years.

Having authorized the force, the War Department virtually ignored it. Equipment, clothing, rations, and weapons remained in short supply. However, there was no lack of fighting. Countless skirmishes and several major clashes occurred. During the summer nearly a hundred Apache were killed. A few women and children were taken prisoner. Several troopers were wounded, but only one died in battle.

A surgeon with one of the companies, according to the Prescott *Miner*, offered to give a volunteer a dollar's worth of tobacco for every Apache he killed, "that they may smoke the pipe of peace over the peaceable and harmless condition of those who fall under their guns."

The Pima smashed the heads of dead Apache with rocks. The practice met with the approval of most of the Americans and Mexicans, but some registered disgust. The veteran Indian fighter and miner Conner would write that "savage civilized men are the most monstrous of all monsters."

The short campaign of the Arizona Volunteers achieved no beneficial results. Most Apache bands in central Arizona either successfully avoided the troops or shifted to remote areas in the southern part of the territory. Cochise was reported to have led some four hundred warriors into Mexico. Below the Gila River Apache raiders continued to operate almost with impunity.

The War Department and the Indian Bureau, both entangled in red tape and suffering from the machinations of grafting officials, were at each other's throats. In the fall of the year the few troops in Arizona were largely inactive. While most army officers and Indian agents favored a reservation system, Washington officials continued to wrangle over who was to pay for it. Major-General H. W. Halleck, commander of the Military Division of the Pacific, favored a continuation of the extermination policy, stating: "It is useless to negotiate with these Apache Indians. They will observe no treaties, agreements, or truces. With them there is no alternative but active and vigorous war, till they are completely destroyed, or forced to surrender as prisoners of war." More troops should be sent to Arizona, he thought, and the Apache should be swept into a military dust bin by vigorous offensives.

Indian Superintendent Leihy declared that with one tenth of the money spent on past fruitless campaigns comfortable homes and adequate reservations could have been provided for all Apache. Many of them, he argued, were destitute and driven to raiding because of their inability to obtain sufficient food in any other way. Settlers had destroyed the game on which they formerly had depended, and they could not remain long enough in one place to grow crops or build herds of their own.

Leihy stated that the operations of the army "tended to embarrass and complicate the Indian difficulties." He charged that many, if not most, of the Apache would have halted their violence if ranchers, miners, freighters, and other civilians had ceased attacking and killing them at every opportunity. The Apache could not be expected to trust any white man.

Governor Goodwin demanded "fair, open, and persistent war" until the Apache were annihilated or driven onto reservations "and made to labor or starve." He wanted them to become self-supporting, to eliminate a "patched-up treaty to benefit speculators in beef."

A prominent merchant, J. D. Cusenbury, appealed to President Andrew Johnson to formulate a definitive Indian policy so that Apache who wished to surrender could do so and be guaranteed protection. It was Cusenbury's belief that the extermination policy was favored simply because the people of Arizona and the military had no other program to guide them. If it were allowed to continue, he predicted, more than ten thousand troops and several years would be needed to kill all Apache in Arizona, and meanwhile hundreds more white persons would lose their property and their lives. But, as Ogle states, "ideas rather than policies were being advanced."

With Apache onslaughts increasing in frequency and intensity, the residents of the Prescott region assembled in a public meeting and organized the Yavapai County Rangers. "Thomas Hodges was requested to raise a company of thirty men to serve for ninety days," reported the Prescott *Miner*. "A liberal sum was subscribed for the outfit, and also for Indian scalps." An amateur theatrical company raised $125 in a benefit performance for the Rangers, and each lady member of the group was promised an Apache scalp for a "fashionable water fall."

In the one battle they are known to have fought, the Rangers fell upon a peaceful group of Indians living in a canyon north of Prescott. These Apache were not marauders and were attempting to support themselves on small farms. Twenty-three men, women, and children were murdered in their huts, and only one young woman was known to have escaped.

"Hurrah for the Yavapai County Rangers," shouted the Prescott *Miner*. "We are glad to know that our Yavapai Rangers do not think it worth the trouble to make prisoners of the murderous red skins. The custom heretofore adopted, even by our regular army, of making prisoners of women and children . . . seems to be dying out."

Regular army troops under Captain George B. Stanford attacked an Apache rancheria in Meadow Valley and killed fifteen warriors. Supplies which these Indians had stored for the winter were burned, leaving the surviving women, children, and aged facing starvation. On another campaign a short time later, Stanford and his troopers came upon a Tonto village and killed six men. Most of the Apache of this band were able to escape.

Not all officers in the field favored the extermination policy. Colonels Guido Ilges and Charles S. Lovell negotiated a treaty with leaders of the Arivaipa, Tonto, and Pinal Apache. Under its terms these people were to settle on a reservation, but were to be permitted to hunt game and gather wild foods to supplement the rations which the War Department would furnish them.

The two colonels were severely reprimanded for their efforts. Their superior, General McDowell, called the treaty "irregular, injudicious, and embarrassing," declared that the authority of the officers was limited to granting armistices, and that they had made promises the army could not fulfill. General Halleck sustained McDowell. The colonels were warned not to exceed their authority a second time.

The Indian Bureau, which did not want the army intruding in what it considered its exclusive field by making treaties, disapproved the peace pact, but stated that it believed the Apache problem could best be solved by a reservation system. However, if such a system were inaugurated, the Bureau and no one else should have control of it. Thus, there was no firm peace with the Arivaipa, Tonto, and Pinal Apache.

Indian Superintendent Leihy was notified that he was to be replaced by G. W. Dent, General Grant's brother-in-law. Before Dent had arrived, Leihy and his clerk, H. C. Evarts, were murdered by a hostile band near La Paz on the Colorado River. The identity of these Indians is not certain, but they were not Apache.

Dent had no qualifications whatsoever for the post of superintendent of Indian Affairs in the Arizona Territory, and he quickly demonstrated the fact. Angered by the refusal of army commanders to bend to his demands, he severely criticized military operations as "purposeless." It was his view that the Apache could be conquered only by "active, offensive, persistent, combined, and simultaneous war." After this had been accomplished by the army, the Apache could be placed under the control of civil authorities. He repudiated an opinion expressed by General McDowell that Indians could not be placed on reservations until some system for providing for them had been established, and that the hostility of the Apache was based on a desperate need for subsistence. Poppycock, said Dent, but he would soon discover that he had a great deal to learn about the situation.

In New Mexico, at Bosque Redondo on the Pecos, an unprecedented and significant event had taken place. Unable to endure the horrors and hunger of their imprisonment, the Mescalero had secretly formulated plans to escape. They were aware of the dangers involved, but

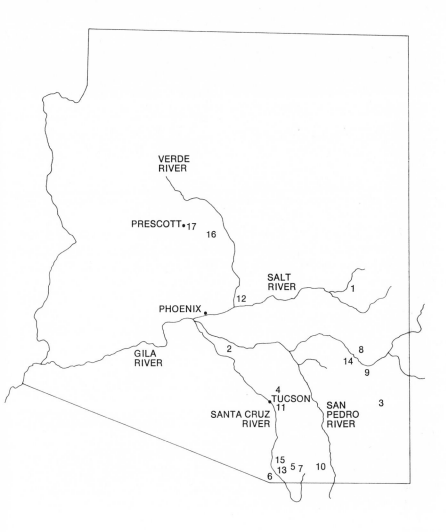

ARIZONA
American military establishments
active in warfare with Apaches

1	Fort Apache	est. 1870	9	Camp Grant No. 2	1872
2	Fort Barrett	1862	10	Fort Huachuca	1877
3	Fort Bowie	1862	11	Fort Lowell	1862
4	Fort Breckinridge	1860	12	Fort McDowell	1865
	(called Camp Grant	1865)	13	Camp Mason	1865
5	Fort Buchanan	1856	14	Fort Thomas	1876
6	Camp Calabasas	1856	15	Fort Tubac	1862
7	Fort Crittenden	1868	16	Fort Verde	1864
8	Fort Goodwin	1864	17	Fort Whipple	1863

American Military Posts in Apacheria

Fort Apache, Arizona: Established 1870. On East Fork of White River. Since 1924 an Indian school.

Fort Barrett, Arizona: Established 1862. Near Sacaton. Closed in same year.

Fort Bayard, New Mexico: Established 1866. Near Silver City. Closed in 1900.

Fort Bliss, Texas: Established 1849. Occupied several locations in El Paso vicinity. Still operative.

Fort Bowie, Arizona: Established 1862. At Apache Pass near Bowie. Closed 1894.

Fort Breckenridge, Arizona (Camp Grant No. 1): Established 1860. At junction of San Pedro River and Arivaipa Creek. Renamed Camp Grant 1865. Closed 1873.

Fort Buchanan, Arizona: Established 1856. Near Patagonia. Abandoned 1861.

Camp Calabasas, Arizona: Mexican presidio occupied by American troops 1856–1858. Near Nogales.

Camp Clark, Texas: Established 1852. Near Brackettville. Abandoned 1946.

Fort Concho, Texas: Established 1867. Near San Angelo. Closed 1889.

Fort Conrad, New Mexico: Established 1851. South of Socorro at Val Verde Mesa. Closed 1854.

Fort Craig, New Mexico: Established 1854. Near San Marcial. Closed 1885.

Fort Crittenden, Arizona: Established 1868. Near Fort Buchanan. Closed 1873.

Fort Cummings, New Mexico: Established 1863. Near Deming. Closed 1886.

Fort Davis, Texas: Established 1854. Near town of same name. Closed 1891.

Fort Duncan, Texas: Established 1849. At Eagle Pass. Closed 1916.

Fort Fillmore, New Mexico: Established 1851. Near Mesilla. Abandoned 1861.

Fort Goodwin, Arizona: Established 1864. Near Fort Thomas. Closed 1871.

Camp Grant (No. 2), Arizona: Established 1872. Southwest of Safford. Closed 1905.

Fort Hancock, Texas: Established 1882. Near town of same name. Closed 1895.

Fort Huachuca, Arizona: Established 1877. Near Huachuca Mountains and San Pedro River. Still a military post.

Camp Hudson, Texas: Established 1857. On Devil's River north of Del Rio. Closed 1868.

Fort Inge, Texas: Established 1849. Near Uvalde. Closed 1869.

Fort Lancaster, Texas: Established 1855. On Pecos River east of Fort Stockton. Abandoned 1861.

Fort Lowell, Arizona: Established 1862. At Tucson. Closed 1891.

Fort McDowell, Arizona: Established 1865. Near junction of Verde and Salt Rivers. Transferred to Interior Department 1890.

Fort McIntosh, Texas: Established 1849. At Laredo. Closed 1946.

Fort McLane, New Mexico: Established 1860. Near Santa Rita. Abandoned 1861.

Fort McRae, New Mexico: Established 1863. North of Hatch, near Rio Grande. Abandoned 1876.

Camp Mason, Arizona: Established 1865. South of Tubac, on Santa Cruz River. Closed 1866.

Camp Ojo Caliente, New Mexico: Established 1859. West of Fort Craig. Abandoned 1882.

Fort Quitman, Texas: Established 1858. On Rio Grande below Fort Hancock. Closed 1877.

Fort Seldon, New Mexico: Established 1865. North of Doña Ana. Closed 1889.

Fort Stanton, New Mexico: Established 1855. On Rio Bonito, Lincoln County. Closed 1896.

Fort Stockton, Texas: Established 1859. At town of same name. Closed 1886.

Fort Sumner, New Mexico: Established 1862. Near town of same name, on Pecos River. Sold in 1868.

Fort Thomas, Arizona: Established 1876. At town of same name. Closed 1891.

Fort Thorn, New Mexico: Established 1853. Near Hatch. Abandoned 1859.

Fort Tubac, Arizona: Established 1862. At town of same name. Closed 1868.

Fort Tularosa, New Mexico: Established 1872. Near town of Reserve. Closed 1874.

Fort Verde, Arizona: Established 1864. On Verde River east of Prescott. Closed 1890.

Fort Webster, New Mexico: Established 1851. At Santa Rita. (Relocated two more times in same region.) Last occupied in 1867.

Fort West, New Mexico: Established 1863. On Gila River north of Silver City. Closed 1864.

Fort Whipple, Arizona: Established 1863. In Chino Valley. Moved to Prescott in 1864. Closed 1913.[21]

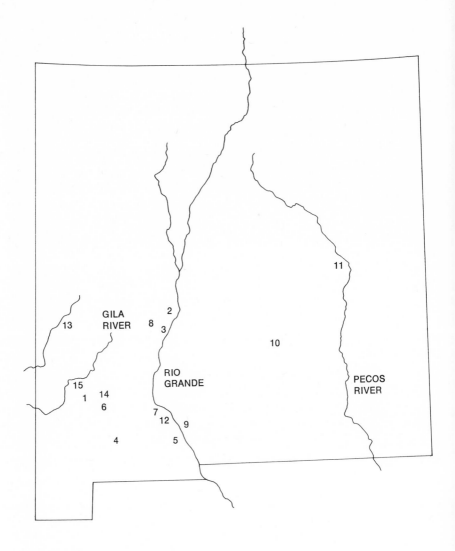

NEW MEXICO
American military establishments
active in warfare with Apaches

1 Fort Bayard	est. 1866	6 Fort McLane	1860	11 Fort Sumner	1862
2 Fort Conrad	1851	7 Fort McRae	1863	12 Fort Thorn	1853
3 Fort Craig	1854	8 Camp Ojo Caliente	1859	13 Fort Tularosa	1872
4 Fort Cummings	1863	9 Fort Seldon	1865	14 Fort Webster	1851
5 Fort Fillmore	1851	10 Fort Stanton	1855	15 Fort West	1863

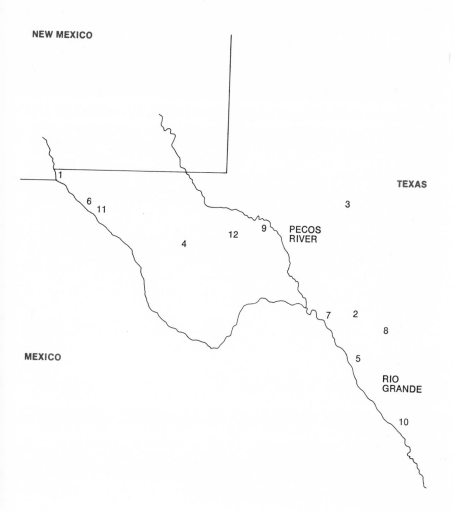

NEW MEXICO

TEXAS

PECOS
RIVER

MEXICO

RIO
GRANDE

TEXAS
*American military establishments
active in warfare with Apaches*

1 Fort Bliss est. 1849   7 Camp Hudson 1857
2 Camp Clark   1852   8 Fort Inge   1849
3 Fort Concho   1867   9 Fort Lancaster 1855
4 Fort Davis   1854   10 Fort McIntosh   1849
5 Fort Duncan   1849   11 Fort Quitman   1858
6 Fort Hancock   1882   12 Fort Stockton   1859

to them death was preferable to their suffering. They reasoned that if they left in small groups, many of them would be pursued and returned to the concentration camp, but if they all slipped away at the same time and spread out they would have a chance. They did not believe the military at the post was strong enough to recapture the entire tribe. Moreover, if the troops left Fort Sumner, thousands of Navajo would escape. They were right.

Nearly five hundred Mescalero men, women, and children vanished into the plains. Only nine who were too sick or badly crippled to travel were left behind.

They scattered to the four winds, some returning to their homeland in the Sierra Blanca, some moving into the plains of the Llano Estacado and joining their ancient enemies, the Comanche, some traveling far into southwest Texas, some moving west of the Rio Grande to find havens with other Apache bands.

The Mescalero were gone.

* * *

1867

The military in Arizona, charged with subduing the Apache, operated in a state of confusion. Orders from California often were rescinded without knowledge of men in the field who were executing them. Orders issued by field commanders to meet emergencies were disapproved at headquarters weeks after they had been carried out. Orders conflicted to the extent that unified operations were impossible.

Post commanders had no authority to make treaties. Not a few of them understood, however, that the extermination policy could not be successful short of years of bloody warfare, and in some areas they began to adopt the only measures available to them with which they could halt the fighting and achieve at least a welcome, if precarious, peace. Apache who agreed to forgo violence in return for rations and protection were permitted to establish camps adjacent to military reservations. A large number, destitute and hungry, accepted the offers, notably in the vicinity of Camp Grant and Fort Goodwin. Others were told that they might gather in the wilderness of the White Mountains, where they would be unmolested as long as they behaved themselves.

The system was practicable and might have brought beneficial results, if it had been officially supported and given a chance to work. There were numerous reasons why it was only partially successful. The civilians of Arizona were unalterably opposed to giving any quarter to

Apache—they favored genocide. Some high-ranking military officers held the conviction that war to the death was the only possible solution to the problem. Others, while subscribing to this view, qualified it with the assertion that only by agreeing to confinement on reservations could the Apache escape death. What reservations? The Indian Bureau had advocated the establishment of adequate reservations, but Congress had neither defined them nor appropriated money for them.

Superior officers not only wrangled with civilian agents of the Indian Bureau, but among themselves. General McDowell demanded that vigorous campaigns be waged. General J. I. Gregg, in command at Prescott with several companies of newly arrived troops, sought to obey, and announced that all Indians not found on reserves would be considered hostiles. Even Indians known to be peaceful and given passes by civilian agents would not be immune from attack. General McDowell thought Gregg's orders too drastic, and declared that it would be inhuman to conduct unrelenting warfare against Indians who faced starvation because of congressional negligence. He criticized Gregg as a publicity-seeker. Gregg retaliated by issuing new orders to the effect that Indians would not be considered hostile unless they acted in concert in committing assaults, that is, as a tribal entity. Depredations committed by individuals would be viewed "as offenses against the common law, the same as if committed by white citizens." The inane, bitter squabbling continued for months, while the Apache continued to scourge the country.

Twenty-seven contingents of troops were widely scattered throughout Arizona Territory. Morale was at a low ebb. There were numerous desertions. Forty percent of the soldiers of one regiment were "over the hill" during the year. Sixteen men deserted from a single company in one month. Although replacements were brought in, it was often difficult to keep some companies up to fighting strength—all the remaining men could do was guard their horses and stores.

Not infrequently badly needed supplies failed to arrive as a result of red tape and thefts. Indian agents sold rations and equipment instead of delivering them to their peaceful charges. Army officers diverted supplies to civilian merchants and pocketed the money. The same equipment and supplies sometimes were resold to the Indian Bureau or army quartermasters.

Contractors took advantage of the opportunity to reap excessive profits. The costs of maintaining a post were enormous. Fort Whipple was a typical example. The army was forced to pay $60 a ton for hay, $12 a bushel for grain, $75 a thousand feet for lumber. The freight rate between California and central Arizona was $250 a ton. The small headquarters building cost $100,000, the post flagpole cost $10,000. General Halleck expressed the belief that expenses might be reduced and the campaigning conducted more effectively if troops could be concentrated in a few large garrisons. But that could not be done without withdrawing protection from many small settlements.

The warfare continued. There were many courageous and loyal men on the fronts. They had a dirty, tedious, unrewarding, and perilous job, but they did the best they could. Captain J. M. Williams, with eighty men, killed fifty-five Apache. The commands of Colonel Guido Ilges and Captain J. H. Vanderslice, operating out of Fort McDowell, kept the Apache on the run in the Tonto, lower Verde River, and Mazatzal regions. Yet aggressive tactics such as these did little to relieve the situation. The Apache continued to terrorize the length and breadth of central and southern Arizona.

In the face of these conditions, McDowell maintained that the Apache really wanted peace, and accused General Gregg of starting more wars than he could handle. General Halleck sent Major Roger Jones to investigate and to make recommendations. Jones had been in Arizona previously for two years, 1857–1859. He was appalled by what he saw in 1867. In eight years very little had been accomplished. The troops were almost powerless against the Apache. He recommended several drastic changes, but General McDowell found them unsound and defended his administration.

General Halleck complained to the War Department that the number of troops assigned to Arizona could not combat the Apache menace. At least three more regiments were necessary if the hostile warriors were to be destroyed or made prisoners of war. Once the Apache had been conquered, some means of holding them in an area remote from white settlement must be devised. Acting Secretary of War U. S. Grant agreed with him, and advised President Johnson of his conviction that attempts to make peace with the Apache by treaty would be futile.

The wheels in Washington moved with painful slowness, and the war in Arizona went on with growing intensity.

* * *

"With the influx of a mining population, the Indians, unable to encroach upon the territory of neighboring tribes, are gradually driven to the most barren part of the mountains, and with the disappearance of game are reduced to the verge of starvation. Whether they oppose bravely at first the inroads of the whites, or submit peacefully to every outrage until forced by famine to seek the means of life among the herds of the intruder, the result is the same.

"Sometimes hunted from place to place in open war; sometimes their warriors enticed away under peaceful promises by one [white] party, while a confederate [white] band descends on the native settlements, massacring women and children, old and young; they are always fading away before the hand of violence.

"No treaty or flag of truce is too sacred to be disregarded, no weapon too cruel or cowardly to be used or recommended by Americans.

"If it is said that the Indians are treacherous and cruel, scalping and torturing their prisoners, it may be answered that there is no treachery and no cruelty left unemployed by the whites. Poisoning with strychnine, the wilful dissemination of smallpox, and the possession of bridles braided with the hair of scalped victims and decorated with teeth knocked from the jaws of living women—these are heroic facts among many of our frontiersmen."

> RAPHAEL PUMPELLY, *a famous mining engineer who went to Arizona in 1860 and was driven out by Apache, many of his companions being killed.*

* * *

1868

Religious, fraternal, civic, service, and even some strong political organizations in the East and Middle West vociferously opposed warfare against the Apache and other southwestern Indians. The residents of Arizona and New Mexico were excoriated for their wantonness, greed, and brutality. The army was condemned for failing to protect the helpless Indians from thieves and murderous civilians. The Indian Bureau, indeed, the entire Department of the Interior, was shown to be a veritable cesspool of corruption. Hardly a day passed without some prominent person or some group demanding that the Federal Government establish reservations on which Indians could be taught to farm and become self-supporting.

The popularity of these views steadily increased, and the politicians began to listen.

The army was not oblivious to the criticism fired at it. General T. C. Devin, commanding the Prescott district, was able to arrange a meeting with the Tonto leader, Delshay. They talked some twenty or thirty miles east of Fort McDowell, an extremely wild and rugged region. The general had no authority to negotiate a treaty in the name of the government, but he offered the Tonto sanctuary in an area bounded by the Verde River, Black Mesa, and the Salt River. It is not known whether Delchay agreed to the proposal, but he and many of the Tonto camped at Fort Reno a few months later, and the military issued them rations and employed some as couriers and hay cutters.

General T. L. Crittenden also induced several bands to establish villages at Camp Grant, and issued them stores.

For obvious reasons neither of these armistices long endured. The Indians were on military reservations, not lands awarded to them. They were not living under a bona fide treaty with the government. They had only the word of some officers that they would be fed and protected from white civilians and Pima and Maricopa, and officers came and went like the moons. The treachery of the white man had been amply demonstrated.

Appeals for reinforcements from both the territorial government and field commanders went unheeded. General Halleck recommended that Arizona be made a separate military department, but no immediate action followed. The number of companies in the Department of California had been decreased, and General E. O. C. Ord, newly in command there, could do no more than urge the existing Arizona forces to greater action. That was easier said than accomplished.

Probably unable to do anything else, the San Francisco Presidio sent Captain Charles A. Whittier to Arizona as an observer. Apparently Whittier was deeply moved by what he saw. Nor was he hesitant about speaking out. The feeding program of the army was inadequate, he declared, and the holding of Indians as prisoners was in direct violation of the law. He advocated that Apache be subsisted through regular annual appropriations. Bands which wanted peace were totally unprotected from "unreasoning civilians" who supported extermination and practiced it. In short, the Federal Government was doing virtually nothing constructive in the struggle to resolve the Apache problem.

Whittier's report vanished into some Washington pigeonhole, but it was not entirely forgotten, and some of his findings would be cited at a later date. Meanwhile, the governor and the Territorial Legislature, giving up hope of getting more federal troops into Arizona, advised the citizens to defend themselves by the simple method of killing every Indian they could.

The result was nothing more than might have been expected. Once again bands of civilians left trails of murder across Arizona. Even peaceably inclined Apache groups were forced to take to the warpath to save themselves, and those who were irreconcilably hostile launched vicious attacks on both civilians and soldiers. Blood ran at every settlement and post in the land.

* * *

J. P. Dunn, Jr.: "The military operations of the '60's were not devoid of results. New Mexico had a season of comparative quiet, in the better settled parts, and Arizona was yielding to the progress of civilization. . . . Yet, in fact, there was merely a change in the seat of war. The Apaches held the mountain fastnesses, as yet unknown, from which they sallied forth to raid into the very heart of the settlements. . . . No Apache tribe was subdued. . . . On the whole the policy of extermination in Arizona . . . proved a dismal failure, after a full and fair trial."

* * *

1869

Investigations of scandals involving officials of the Indian Bureau, the Interior Department, Indian agents, army officers, and civilian contractors for supplies had made it abundantly clear to the entire nation that the Federal Government had been woefully negligent in handling Indian affairs. The protests, registered in meeting halls throughout the country, in newspapers, and in pulpits, at last moved Congress to take action.

In June, President Grant was authorized to appoint a board of Indian commissioners, composed of prominent men willing to serve without remuneration, and who were "eminent for their intelligence and philanthropy." Money was appropriated to pay for all expenses the commissioners might incur.

Both under the act and presidential prerogatives, the board Mr. Grant appointed held extensive powers. It might negotiate treaties, establish reservations, supervise the purchase and transportation of all goods to be furnished Indians, and, not the least important, audit the books of the Office of Indian Affairs.

The commissioners were soon at work throughout the West, and they, as Ogle recounts, ". . . visited the different tribes and counseled with the chiefs and agents; frequently escorted parties of Indians to the cities of the North and East; investigated, reported, and publicized the cruelties committed by white persons against the tribesmen; recommended needed changes and improvements in the service; and championed Indian rights throughout the Nation. . . . The commission became at once a dominant force in determining Indian policy of the government."

Organizations campaigning to halt the warfare against Indians and advocating the establishment of a reservation system had President Grant's ear. He had not long been in office before he held meetings with leading churchmen, executives of missionary societies, and various groups dedicated to the welfare of Indians. Out of these councils evolved what would come to be known as Grant's Peace Policy, sometimes labeled Grant's Quaker Policy.

Most of the proposals proffered by the conferees President Grant found acceptable. He had good reasons for endorsing them. They provided him with an opportunity to shift responsibility for the growing and embarrassing troubles with Indians to other shoulders. Perhaps they would solve some, if not all, of the problems—he fervently hoped so. If the programs failed, he could not be blamed. In any case, he had nothing to lose and everything to gain.

The announced objective of the Peace Policy was to civilize and Christianize the degraded, backward, red infidels, instead of exterminating them by the simpler means of starvation and warfare. This humane goal was to be achieved not by civil justice, not by large appropriations of federal funds, not by the rigid enforcement of existing statutes prohibiting theft and exploitation of Indian resources, but by "the assignment of religious and education work (among the Indians) to the various religious denominations on a regional basis." Collaterally, religious men would be appointed as Indian agents, missionaries would be sent out as teachers, and reservations would be established on which Indians would be taught agrarian pursuits.

Immediately the Peace Policy was hailed throughout most of the country as a panacea. Residents of the West were less enthusiastic. Unfortunately for the Apache, in Arizona it was condemned and blasphemed from the governor's office down to the filthiest bistro.

In one respect, the military was of one mind: they were being soundly beaten and any plan that afforded them relief was welcome. That was not to come, however, by wishful thinking in Washington. The Apache played for keeps. General Ord, faced with the realities of the situation, sent orders to General George Stoneman, in command in Arizona, to hunt down Apache as wild animals. Officers who killed the greatest number would be the first to receive promotion. Shortly afterward Ord changed his mind, and expressed the opinion that perhaps a reservation system was preferable to wholesale murder. The people of Arizona didn't agree with him, and let him know it.

Captain John Barry, scouting in the White Mountains with sixty men, came upon a large number of Apache who displayed no sign of hostility. Around their villages were extensive fields of growing corn. Barry carried orders to kill any Apache he encountered and destroy their resources. He disobeyed his orders and left in peace. His commander, Colonel John Green, charged him with disobedience, but higher officers exonerated him.

If the thinking of most commanders, both in headquarters and in the field, was tending toward favoring establishment of a great reservation on which all Apache could be concentrated, the Apache themselves believed only what they saw, and took nothing for granted. In the latter half of the year they demonstrated that they were still very much in command of the situation.

Mail could be transported only with a strong military escort. Stages and freight caravans were attacked and destroyed, with a heavy loss of life. Although many of them were killed by troops, Tonto and other bands ravaged central Arizona. Coyoteros held mountain passes. Strong bands under Cochise were so successful in the southeast that there was talk of abandoning the region to them. The troops stationed at Fort Bowie were repeatedly thwarted in their attempts to overtake them. During the year seventy-five white persons were killed in Pima County, and scores of Mexicans—no one bothered to count them— were murdered by Apache raiders in the southern part of the territory. Almost all ranches in the San Pedro Valley were abandoned, more than a hundred settlers having been slain in two years.

G. W. Dent, President Grant's brother-in-law, appointed Arizona superintendent of Indian Affairs in 1866, was more interested in graft than Indian problems. Exposed and severely criticized, he resigned under fire.

* * *

General William Tecumseh Sherman writing to Secretary of War William W. Belknap, January 7, 1870:

"The best advice I can offer is to notify the settlers [of the Southwest] to withdraw and then to withdraw the troops and leave the country to the aboriginal inhabitants."

* * *

1870

In Arizona parlance, the slaying of a white person by an Apache was almost invariably a "murder," and the slaying of an Apache—man, woman, or child—was described as a "justified killing." Not only newspapers but official documents adhered to this idiom.

In the hope of stirring the War Department and the Congress to greater action to combat the "Apache menace," the Territorial Legislature appointed a committee to take sworn testimony from the victims of Indian depredations, enumerate "murders" of white persons, and list the value of property captured or destroyed by raiders in 1869 and 1870.

The deaths of some two hundred settlers and soldiers and the loss of several hundred thousand dollars' worth of property were recorded. In the committee's report, sent to Congress, the trend of the thinking in Arizona was graphically revealed:

"It is customary and generally considered to be to the interest of new countries, to conceal as far as possible the hardships and dangers necessarily incident to their first settlement, with a view of inviting immigration and capital as rapidly as possible, and thereby overcoming these obstructions.

"Probably but few countries on the face of the globe present greater natural resources inviting to immigration and capital than the Territory of Arizona. Nearly every mountain is threaded with veins of gold, silver, copper, and lead. Large deposits of coal and salt of an excellent quality are found. Nearly every foot of the Territory is covered with nutritious grasses, and stock thrives the year round without shelter or prepared forage. Nearly every product that grows in the temperate or torrid zone can be grown here to perfection and in abundance. There are vast forests of excellent timber; the mountains and valleys are amply supplied with pure water; the climate is warm, genial, and healthful, equal to any on the American continent."

Doubtless, if an Arizona chamber of commerce had existed at the time, it could not have done a better job of extolling the virtues of the territory. The legislature committee's report continued:

"With all these natural advantages, the subtle Apaches have been so constant in their depredations and destructive of life, that nearly all of the early pioneers have already fallen by their hands, and every industry and enterprise has been paralyzed.

"The recent order withdrawing from the Territory a considerable portion of the Federal troops [not a fact] has excited general alarm among its citizens. The Territory is covered with the ruins of cities and towns that were once undoubtedly inhabited by a people of industry and enterprise, and who cultivated vast fields, as is shown by the remains of large irrigating canals. [These people, however, were prehistoric Indians.] That people have passed away, and no one knows who they were. The cause of their destruction was undoubtedly the ravages of the implacable Apache [this is untrue], and our people now begin to realize, that unless assistance is given them, that they only await a similar fate.

". . . it has been considered by justice and humanity to our people to place upon the record the truth regarding the condition of affairs in this Territory . . . confidently believing that, when these facts are known, the press, the people of the United States, and the Government will demand and aid in subduing our hostile foe, and thereby reclaim from the savage one of the most valuable portions of our public domain."

The committee found that "some of the most fertile portions of our Territory are being abandoned by the settlers, on account of the repeated and destructive raids" of the Apache Indians.

Summing up, the committee stated: ". . . it is our opinion that during the year 1870 the Apache Indians have been and are *now* in more active hostility than at any time since the Territory has been under the American flag."

The committee report was notable for its omissions:

1. Hundreds of Apache men, women, and children had been murdered without provocation in their villages by white men.

2. The Apache were making a desperate last stand to protect themselves, and preserve their rapidly dwindling resources.

3. No recommendation was made that the Apache be awarded lands on which they could be protected, develop an economy of their own, and live in peace.

It was inconceivable, of course, to the great majority of Arizonans that the Apache were entitled to any degree of justice, to any form of civil rights, or to occupy any part of their ancestral homeland.

In 1870 there were slightly fewer than ten thousand white persons in Arizona, and nearly half of them were only partly white, being Mexican. Also, this population total included some eighteen companies of troops. If the complement of these companies averaged thirty men—which is doubtful, as desertions and transfers frequently depleted a company's strength by half or more—there were perhaps six hundred regular army personnel on active duty in the territory.

No one could say accurately how many Apache there were, for there was no means of counting them. A great many of them were rarely, if ever, seen by either soldiers or settlers, as they remained concealed in inaccessible mountain areas. An estimate made by a veteran Indian hunter that the Apache could muster between two thousand and twenty-five hundred able-bodied warriors may be somewhere near the truth. This estimate, however, included Apache fighting men in New Mexico.

The Apache did not conduct raids in large numbers. Seldom did troops campaigning against them encounter bands of greater size than fifty, not including women and children. A report of one engagement which took place in the Pinal Mountains stated that troops commanded by First Lieutenant Howard B. Cushing killed ninety-six "Indians." Whether this figure included women and children is not known. Later accounts of this fight reported that thirty Apache, presumably men, had been killed and a number of women and children captured.

Arizona Territory was made a separate military department in April. General Stoneman remained in command, but made his headquarters in California. He was openly pessimistic about his chances of inflicting sufficient punishment on the Apache to force them to abandon their fight. To his superiors he wrote that the Apache "will never be entirely harmless until they suffer the fate of all aboriginals that come in contact with the whites . . . they must either starve, steal, or be fed; and as they are unwilling to do the former, it becomes simply a question as to which is the best policy, feed them or continue to endeavor to prevent them from stealing."

For several months he kept his troops occupied with road building. Some roads were constructed into areas previously almost impassable, where pursuit of raiders was virtually impossible. One road was built into the White Mountains, the area favored for an immense Apache reservation by army officers and Indian agents. It culminated at a new post, called Fort Apache.

Cochise suffered a severe defeat in the Chiricahua region, sixty-one of his warriors being killed. He elected to refrain from further activity while he and his people licked their wounds. The place he chose for his temporary retirement was Fort Apache, where the commander, Colonel Green, granted him haven. Cochise wanted a just and lasting peace, and offered to bring the Chiricahua band into a reservation. If Colonel Green had possessed the authority to negotiate a treaty, war with the dynamic leader and the Chiricahua might well have come to an end. But Green's hands were tied. The best he could do was offer Cochise the hospitality of a military reservation, offer to provide rations when and if available, and try to keep white persons from attacking the Chiricahua. It was not enough.

Cochise led his strong band back to the region of the Chiricahua Mountains; and in southeastern Arizona during the latter half of the year, raiding, property destruction, and the killing of whites reached unprecedented proportions. Troops were unable to halt the depredations, and on several occasions pursuing cavalry were soundly defeated with a heavy loss of life.

Despite Cochise's refusal to remain at Fort Apache, Colonel Green was able to induce some two thousand other Apache to camp in the area. He issued them beef and other rations, and put many of them to work cutting hay and wood for the military, paying them in foodstuffs, blankets, and clothing. Green pleaded for tools, equipment, garments, and "proper subsistence" for his charges, who had shown "every interest in living in peace and building homes and farms." His appeals were taken under advisement, which meant that they were soon forgotten.[22]

FALL

Colonel George Crook, commander of the Department of the Columbia, with headquarters in Portland, was transferred to San Francisco to serve on a military board handling personnel matters. Sharp decreases in appropriations to the War Department had made it necessary to reduce the size of the regular army, and boards had been established in the various departments to select the men who were to be released or retained. Because of their tendency to clean up troublesome conditions and weed out irresponsible and incompetent officers they were dubbed Benzine Boards. After several years of fighting

Indians, Colonel Crook had looked forward to his new assignment.

He had brought peace to the Northwest. His campaigns had demonstrated a remarkable ability, both as a strategist and a field commander. He had beaten the Indians in conflict, but he had never held the belief that winning battles was all that was required of him. He had been able to convince the Indians he had defeated that he wanted justice for them and would do everything in his power to see that they received it. They had shown their faith in him, and he had negotiated treaties with them which had brought an end to warfare in the vast wilderness of Oregon and Washington.

Crook's accomplishments had won him national acclaim, both as an Indian fighter and an ambassador who could influence wild tribes to abandon the warpath. Quite naturally this reputation resulted in proposals—unofficial in the beginning—that he be sent to Arizona to bring an end to the terrible warfare with the Apache. Even before Crook had gone to San Francisco, on two occasions officers had sounded him out regarding the matter. Bluntly Crook had told them that he "was tired of Indian work, that it only entailed hard work without corresponding benefits." Moreover, he had declared, "the climate of Arizona was so bad" that he feared his health would be harmed if he went there.

Crook: "The Governor of Arizona, A. P. K. Safford, interviewed me on the same subject in San Francisco. After my telling the substance of what I had said to the others, he assured me he would not urge the matter in Washington, whither he was going."

Safford had not kept his word. In Washington he had arranged with California's senators to urge President Grant to send Crook to Arizona. Mr. Grant had promised to give the proposal his consideration.

Secretary of War Belknap and General Sherman protested to the President that appointing Crook to command the Department of Arizona would be unfair to many competent officers who outranked him. Although Crook had been brevetted general for his distinguished service, he received pay as a lieutenant-colonel, his actual rank in the regular army.

There was reason for optimism in some quarters. Apache groups asking for peace were camped at Fort Apache, Camp Grant, Camp Verde, and in Grant County, New Mexico. General Stoneman took the position that the Apache, instead of being annihilated by warfare, could be controlled "through the medium of their bellies." He requested adequate supplies, and seemed convinced that he could persuade them to remain at peace on the unofficial reservations.

Stoneman was sincere, but somewhat naïve. He had not reckoned with the powers or the sentiments of the people of Arizona. The leading merchants, as Ogle states, "were in no frame of mind to allow any entering wedge to their chief means of livelihood—that of supplying the troops. Almost at once the territorial press, the governor, the legislature, and almost all interested groups set up a terrific tirade against the reservation or feeding system, or any other plan that promised to bring a cessation of hostilities."

Stoneman attempted to counter the avalanche of criticism by amending his feeding and reservation plans. He proclaimed two policies, one of peace and one of war. That is, Apache who surrendered were to be fed and protected. Those who did not would be hunted and killed as hostiles.

Tucson was headquarters for a group of merchants who made huge profits out of army supply contracts. As Faulk states: "For them Indian wars were good business. At such times, more troops were sent to Arizona, which meant that rations were purchased locally, along with grain and hay for horses. Beyond this, they connived with Indian agents to furnish substandard rations at standard prices . . . splitting the profits. Sometimes, with the connivance of such agents, they furnished no rations at all and pocketed the money."

Called the Tucson Ring, or the Indian Ring, this band of human vultures contained some of the so-called leading citizens of Arizona. They controlled the commercial enterprises of the territory, and were politically powerful. Newspapers, bending willingly to their demands, printed false stories of Indian atrocities, and conspired with them to malign anyone who sought to pacify and settle the Apache and other tribes.

General Stoneman, "damned if he did and damned if he didn't," would be unjustly blamed for the deteriorating conditions in Arizona. The Tucson Ring feared his program would result in an economic loss to them by decreasing the number of soldiers stationed in the territory. The citizens complained that his Indian policy was too lenient. Eastern opponents of military campaigns against Indians charged that he had not taken the measures which would have brought peace. The press yowled for his removal. Governor A. P. K. Safford and the territory's congressional delegate, Richard C. McCormick, appealed to the War Department to relieve him of his command, indicating their opinion that he was incapable of meeting the demands of the duty. Only one thing appeared certain: if General Stoneman had made mistakes, if he had shown wisdom in some respects, if he had not been forceful enough on certain occasions, he could not please everyone, unscrupulous merchants, corrupt agents, grafting politicians, and white savages. Said Lockwood: "There were staunch and honest citizens in Arizona at the time, but their number was all too few. On the other hand, there were numerous cruel and depraved men." Stoneman had not failed.

"Under the most adverse circumstances," states Ogle, "he had worked out a policy, a combination of peace and war, which was later to solve the problem of Apache control." But nothing could save Stoneman. He was caught in an ambush created by adverse public opinion.

NOVEMBER

First Lieutenant Royal E. Whitman had served with distinction in the Civil War. A native of Maine, he was thirty-seven years of age when he arrived in Arizona with the Third U. S. Cavalry. A man of unquestionable integrity, highly intelligent, conscientious, humane, and dedicated to his career, he was considered one of the most promising officers in the western service. He made no complaint when he was assigned to command the small garrison at Camp Grant, a bleak military post ten square miles in extent, at the confluence of Arivaipa Creek and the San Pedro River, some fifty miles northeast of Tucson.

* * *

"In dealing with the Indian, you must first of all be honest."

"The Indian is a peculiar institution. And still, he is a human being. A good many persons seem anxious to forget that fact."

GENERAL GEORGE CROOK,
In the Apache Country, 1871.

* * *

1871

APRIL

Some eighty "prominent men" composed the organization euphemistically called the Tucson Committee of Public Safety. A more appropriate name would have been Allied Murderers of the Santa Cruz Valley. On the roster were merchants, freighters, saloon and hotel keepers, newspaper editors, lawyers, ranchers, supply contractors, and men of various other occupations. Whatever their respective callings, a common grievance burned in them. It was that the Federal Government was failing to defend Arizona from Apache ravages, and that by protecting and feeding Apaches under the pretense of civilizing them the army was harboring bloodthirsty savages who left their havens at will to raid settlements and ranches and murder white civilians.

Of particular interest to the Committee of Public Safety was the situation at nearby Camp Grant. Although they had no evidence to support it, they charged that Camp Grant Indians were slipping away from the post, killing travelers, robbing the mails, attacking stages and freight caravans, and returning with their spoils to the safety of the military reservation. In their meetings fiery demands were made that drastic measures be taken to halt the depredations, if not by the proper authorities, then by the "doughty knights" of Tucson . . . as one of their number called them.

Secret plans were made, but at the last moment most of the eighty-odd members seemed to find that they were afflicted with a strange weakness of the stomach, and that it was much easier to spout off behind closed doors than to join in the proposed action. However, they were not opposed to hiring men with less sensitive organs to perform in their places.

In Arizona, and especially in Tucson, were to be found any number of cold-blooded outlaws always available for hire for any purpose whatsoever. Moreover, there were indigent Mexicans, and the friendly if destitute Papago, who themselves and their ancestors had suffered from Apache raids for generations, indeed since the days of Cortez, and who were always eager to give vent to their inherent hatred of these "bloodthirsty people." So reasoned the leading citizens of Tucson in the spring of 1871.

Not all members of the committee, however, were reticent about taking action themselves, and they determined to carry out a revised plan. It was this:

A surprise attack would be made on the Camp Grant Indians.

The chief organizer would be William Sanders Oury, lawyer, cattleman, former Tucson mayor, and an Indian-killer of wide renown.

Juan Elias, city councilor and rancher, and his brother, Jesús, also a rancher, would be responsible for recruiting a contingent of Mexicans.

Cooperating with these men would be Sidney De Long, merchant, trader, freighter, newspaper owner, and one-time member of the Territorial Legislature; D. A. Bennett, hotel proprietor and saloon keeper; James Lee, mill operator; Charles Etchells, a blacksmith, ironworker, and interpreter; and David Foley, an employee in Lee's mill.

Although he could not be a participant in the attack, Samuel Hughes, adjutant-general of Arizona, a butcher and government beef contractor, would perform two important functions. He would recruit a strong group of Papago, whose chief, Francisco Galerita, he knew well. And he would furnish all the arms and ammunition the expedition required.

(Twenty-eighth)

In the afternoon the company, traveling in small groups that would not attract attention, assembled at an appointed rendezvous on Rillito Creek, a short distance from Tucson. Oury expressed disappointment that so many of the brave members of the Committee of Public Safety were absent. However, the little clique of conspirators were present to a man, and with them, much to his satisfaction, were forty-two Mexicans and ninety-two Papago warriors.

A heavily laden wagon soon arrived, and the driver informed Oury with a grin that Samuel Hughes sent his greetings, adding that the adjutant-general had given strict instructions that none of the arms were to be distributed to the Papago. "He says it's against the law to let any Indians have firearms, and by God, Sammy ain't going to break any laws," the teamster said.

In the wagon were several crates of rifles—Sharps carbines and Spencers—boxes of ammunition, two barrels of fresh spring water, and "enough food to keep the entire crew going for a few days." On the stocks of the guns were the letters A. T.—Arizona Territory.

The wagon was quickly unloaded, and as the teamster prepared to leave, Oury scribbled a note and gave it to him. It said: "Send a party to the Cañón del Oro on the main road from Tucson to Camp Grant with orders to stop any and all persons going towards Camp Grant until 7 A.M. of April thirtieth." He told the teamster: "Put this in Hiram Stevens's hands. . . . Tell him it's from me. He'll know what to do." Stevens was chairman of the Committee of Public Safety.

As the afternoon shadows grew long behind the cactus and mesquite the long column twisted its way up Rillito Creek. The one hundred forty men advanced until the night was nearly gone. Through the daytime of the twenty-ninth they remained concealed in a thicket along the San Pedro River. As the sun set they moved on up the San Pedro. In the dawn of April thirtieth, a Sunday, they struck.

I shall allow official Federal Government documents to tell the story of the terrible carnage that took place in the Apache village, some five miles from the headquarters of Camp Grant, on that last morning of April.

DOCUMENT NUMBER ONE—Report of First Lieutenant Royal E. Whitman to his superior at Tucson, Colonel J. G. C. Lee:

> . . . Sometime in February a party of five old women came in under a flag of truce, with a letter from Colonel Green, saying they were in search of a boy, the son of one of the number, taken prisoner near Salt River some months before. This boy had been well cared for, and had become attached to his new mode of life, and did not wish to return. The party were kindly treated, rationed while here, and after two days went away, asking permission to return again. They came in about eight days, I think, with a still larger number, with some articles for sale to purchase manta [a cheap coarse cloth], as they were nearly naked. Before going away they said a young chief would like to come in with a party to have a talk. This I encouraged, and in a few days he came with about twenty-five of his band.

In the band were three well-known and dangerous Apache leaders, Eskiminzin (called Skimmy by soldiers), Chiquito, and Santo.

Whitman continued:

> He [Skimmy] stated in brief that he was a chief of a band of about one hundred fifty of what was originally the Arivaipa Apaches; that he wanted peace; that he and his people had no home, and could make none, as they were at all times apprehensive of the approach of cavalry. I told him that he should go to the White Mountains. He said: "That is not our country, neither are they our people. We are at peace with them, but never have mixed with them. Our fathers and their fathers before them have lived in these mountains [near Camp Grant] and have raised corn in this valley. We are taught to make mescal our principal article of food. . . . At the White Mountains there is none, and without it now we get sick. Some of our people have been in at [Fort] Goodwin, and for a short time at the White Mountains, but they are not contented, and they all say, "Let us go to the Arivaipa and make a final peace and never break it."
>
> I told him that I had no authority to make any treaty with him or to promise him that he could be allowed a permanent home here, but that he could bring in his band and I would feed them, and report his wishes to the department commander.

Whitman kept his word, and wrote to General Stoneman. For six weeks he waited for a reply. Then his own letter was returned to him with a note from a clerk that it had not been prepared in proper form. It is not known whether General Stoneman ever saw it.

Whitman continued:

> He [Skimmy] went out and returned about the first of March with his whole band. In the meantime rumors had been in from two other small bands, asking the same privileges, and giving the same reasons. I made the same reply to all, and by about the fifth of March I had over three hundred here. I wrote a detailed account of the whole matter . . . to department headquarters, asking for instructions. . . .
>
> At first I put them in camp about half a mile from the post, and counted them, and issued them rations every second day. The number steadily increased until it reached the number of five hundred and ten. Knowing as I did that the responsibility of the whole movement rested with me, and that in case of any loss to the Government coming of it I should be the sufferer, I kept them continually under observation, and I not only came to know the faces of all the men, but also the women and children. They were nearly naked and needed everything in the way of clothing. I stopped the Indians from bringing in hay [without pay] that I might buy from them. I arranged a

system of tickets with which to pay them and to encourage them; and to be sure they were properly treated, I personally attended to all the weighing. I also made inquiries as to the kind of goods sold them [by the post trader and others] and prices. This proved a perfect success; not only the women and children engaged in the work, but many of the men. The amount [of hay] furnished by them in about two months was nearly three hundred thousand pounds.

During this time many small parties had been out with passes for a certain number of days to burn mescal. . . . I made myself sure by noting the size of the party, and from the amount of mescal brought in, that no treachery was intended. . . . I spent hours each day with them in explaining to them the relations they should sustain to the Government, and their prospects for the future in case of either obedience or disobedience. . . . I made it a point to tell them all they wished to know. They were readily obedient and remarkably quick of comprehension. They were happy and contented and took every opportunity to show it. They had sent out runners to two other bands which were connected with them by inter-marriages, and had received promises from them that they would come in. . . . I am confident . . . we would have had one thousand persons, and at least two hundred and fifty able-bodied men. As their number increased, and the weather grew warmer, they asked and obtained permission to move farther up the Arivaipa to higher ground and plenty of water . . . they were proposing to plant. . . .

Captain Stanwood arrived about the first of April and took command of the post. He had received while en route verbal instructions from General Stoneman to recognize and feed any Indians he might find at the post as "prisoners of war." After he had carefully inspected all things pertaining to their conduct and treatment, he concluded to make no changes, but had become so well satisfied of the integrity of their intentions that he left on the twenty-fourth with his whole troop for a long scout in the lower part of the Territory. The ranchmen in this vicinity were friendly and kind to them and felt perfectly secure, and had agreed with me to employ them at a fair rate of pay to harvest their barley. The Indians seem to have lost their characteristic anxiety to purchase ammuni-tion, and had, in many instances, sold their best bows and arrows. I made frequent visits to their camp, and if any were absent from count made it my business to know why.

Such was the condition of things up to the morning of the thirtieth of April. They had so won on me, that from my first idea of treating them justly and honestly as an officer of the Army, I had come to feel a strong personal interest in helping

to show them the way to a higher civilization. I had come to
feel respect for men who, ignorant and naked, were still
ashamed to lie or steal, and for women who would work
cheerfully like slaves to clothe themselves and children, but,
untaught, held their virtue above price. Aware of the lies and
hints industriously circulated by the puerile press of the Territory, I was content to *know* I had positive proof they were
so.

I had ceased to have any fears of their leaving here, and
only dreaded for them that they might at any time be ordered
to do so. They frequently expressed anxiety to hear from the
general, that they might have confidence to build for themselves better houses, but would always say, "You know what
we want, and if you can't see him you can write and do for us
what you can."

It is possible that during this time individuals from here had
visited other bands, but that any number had ever been out
to assist in any marauding expedition I know is false.

On the morning of April [thirtieth], I was at breakfast at
7:30 o'clock, when a dispatch was brought to me by a sergeant
of Company P, Twenty-first Infantry, from Captain Penn,
commanding Fort Lowell, informing me that a large party had
left Tucson on the twenty-eighth, with the avowed purpose of
killing all the Indians at this post. I immediately sent the two
interpreters, mounted, to the Indian camp, with orders to tell
the chiefs the exact state of things, and for them to bring their
entire party inside the post. As I had no cavalry, and but about
fifty infantry (all recruits), and no other officer,* I could not
leave the post to go to their defense.

My messengers returned in about an hour, with intelligence
that they could find no living Indians.

The camp was burning and the ground strewed with their
dead and mutilated women and children. I immediately
mounted a party of about twenty soldiers and citizens, and
sent them with the post surgeon, with a wagon to bring in the
wounded, if any could be found. The party returned late in
the P.M., having found no wounded and without having been
able to communicate with any of the survivors. Early the next
morning I took a similar party, with spades and shovels, and
went out and buried all the dead in and immediately about the
camp . . . while at the work many of them came to the spot
and indulged in their expressions of grief, too wild and terrible to be described.

Many of the men, whose families had all been killed, when
I spoke to them and expressed sympathy for them, were

---

*Second in command, Second Lieutenant W. W. Robinson, Jr., was on furlough.

obliged to turn away, unable to speak and too proud to show their grief. The women whose children had been killed or stolen were convulsed with grief, and looked at me appealingly, as though I was their last hope on earth. Children who two days before had been full of fun and frolic kept at a distance, expressing wondering horror. I did what I could. . . .

Lieutenant Whitman thought that more than a hundred and twenty-five Apache men had been in the camp when the attack came. A hundred and twenty-eight men had been counted two days earlier. A number of others were away gathering mescal. It seems that in this respect he was mistaken or had been misinformed. If more than a hundred men were in the camp on Sunday morning, in all probability more would have been slain. Whatever the case, the Apache were helpless to defend themselves, for they had no weapons. A man would have had no means of saving his family—his fists against guns and bows and arrows. Undoubtedly a number of men and a few women were able to escape into the surrounding desert.

One fact remains indisputable: the attack was concentrated on women and children. "Nits make lice," was a popular slogan of Tucson's leading citizens.

Whitman reported that a hundred and twenty-five Apache were slain in the Camp Grant massacre. Oury openly boasted that "about one hundred forty-four of the most bloodthirsty devils that ever disgraced mother earth" had been slaughtered. He did not trouble to mention that of the total murdered only eight were men, but others, including Whitman, would make a point of this fact.

Twenty-seven children were taken alive, and turned over as booty to the Papago, who would sell them into slavery in Sonora.

DOCUMENT NUMBER TWO—Sworn report of Dr. C. B. Briesly, acting assistant surgeon, U. S. Army, stationed at Camp Grant:

On my arrival [at the Apache camp] I found that I should have but little use for wagon or medicine; the work had been too thoroughly done . . . those who had been wounded in the first instance had their brains beaten out with stones. Two of the best-looking of the squaws were lying in such a position, and from the appearance of the genital organs and of their wounds, there can be no doubt that they were first ravished and then shot dead. Nearly all of the dead were mutilated. One infant of some ten months was shot twice and one leg hacked nearly off.

I know from my own personal observation that during the time the Indians were in after my arrival, they were rationed every three days, and Indians absent had to be accounted for;

their faces soon became familiar to me, and I could at once tell when any strange Indians came in. And I furthermore state that I have been among nearly all the various tribes on the Pacific Coast, and that I have never seen any Indians who showed the intelligence, honesty, and desire to learn manifested by these Indians. I came among them greatly prejudiced against them, but, after being with them, I was compelled to admit that they were honest in their intentions, and really desired peace.

DOCUMENT NUMBER THREE—Sworn statement of Oscar Hutton, post guide and Spanish interpreter at Camp Grant for three years:
. . . I have never seen Indians on a reservation, or at peace about a military post, under so good subjection, so well satisfied and happy, or more teachable or obedient . . . no raiding party was ever made up from the Indians fed at this post.

DOCUMENT NUMBER FOUR—Sworn statement of F. L. Austin, post trader at Camp Grant:
The Indians while here seemed to be under perfect control, and in all my business with them . . . never had any trouble or difficulty of any kind. They very readily learn . . . they would have remained and increased in numbers had they not been attacked.

DOCUMENT NUMBER FIVE—Sworn statement of Miles L. Wood, beef contractor at Camp Grant:
While the Indians were at this post, I was not absent one day, and personally issued to them every pound of beef drawn by them. They brought tickets to me, on which I issued. . . . I verified [the tickets] by the official count of that day. I never had any trouble . . . have seen a great deal of Indians. Have heard a good deal of the Apaches, and was much surprised at the general intelligence and good behavior of those I saw at this post.

DOCUMENT NUMBER SIX—Sworn statement of William Kness, mail carrier and interpreter at Camp Grant:
I have been on the frontiers for twenty-six years. . . . I had not much faith in Apaches; till I came to Camp Grant I was prejudiced against them. I made it a point to study the character and habits of the Apache Indians at Camp Grant before the massacre. . . . I was convinced they were acting in good faith and earnestly desired peace; they were industrious, the women particularly so. . . . I never met with as great regard for virtue and chastity as I have found among these Apache women.

In regard to the charge [often made by Tucson newspapers and the vaunted knights of the Committee of Public Safety] that after they were fed they went out on raiding parties, I have to say that I do not believe it.

MAY

As they wildly cheered the "heroic deeds" of Oury and the others who took part in the massacre, Arizona newspapers began a campaign of vilification against Lieutenant Whitman. He was made out to be a drunkard and a moral degenerate with an uncontrolled passion for "dusky Apache maidens." Whitman largely ignored the attacks on his character, saying merely that "parties who would engage in murder like this . . . would make statements . . . without end in their justification."

Lieutenant Robinson, who had served under Whitman, came to his defense in a statement to the Board of Indian Commissioners which said in part:

"Attempts have been made, principally through the columns of the Arizona *Citizen*, a journal published in Tucson* . . . to make it appear that this officer was a debauched scoundrel and a slave to vice. Among other things, he has been accused of associating with Indian women, and of being a confirmed drunkard. I know little of this officer's history previous to his assuming command of this post, December last, but from the time the Indians came in . . . to the best of my knowledge he touched not a drop of liquor. The other statement given in the Arizona *Citizen* had not the slightest foundation in truth. Of his official acts, if I had a right to speak, I could speak only in his praise; but the records of this post are his sufficient vouchers."

* * *

To the voters of Tucson, the men who staged the Camp Grant massacre were heroes and deserving of reward. On May 17, Sidney R. De Long was elected mayor. Samuel Hughes and William S. Oury were elected aldermen. Hiram Stevens, chairman of the Committee of Public Safety, was elected city treasurer. Juan Elias was elected dog catcher.

* * *

News of the Camp Grant killings sent a wave of revulsion through the eastern states and Washington. President Grant, terming the tragedy an "outrage" and "purely murder," notified Governor Safford that if the perpetrators were not brought to trial he would place the entire territory under martial law.

---

*Still published there.

Mr. Grant made it clear that he meant what he said by ordering United States District Attorney C. W. C. Rowell to proceed to Tucson from Arizona City at his earliest convenience and seek indictments against all participants in the "indiscriminate slaughter."

Eskiminzin, the leader of the Arivaipa Apache, who had brought his people to Camp Grant and had been influential in getting other groups to move there under a flag of peace, was gone. He had led his followers back to the wilderness warpath. But his trail was plainly marked—with the bodies of freighters and miners and settlers, some of whom he had called friends. There could be no friendship now.

The editor of the Tucson *Citizen* thought in print that "Lt. Royal E. Whitman can now see the fruits of his peace farce."

The Tucson correspondent of the Prescott *Miner* was happy to make a correction in one of his dispatches. He had reported that only sixty Indians had been killed in the attack at Camp Grant, but was "very much pleased" to state that later information "compels me to make a better showing. One hundred and twenty-five defunct redskins were found scattered over the scene."

Numerous other western newspapers accepted without question the *Citizen*'s claim that the Camp Grant "friendlies" had been raiding and murdering throughout southern Arizona, that their "slaughter was justified on the grounds of self-defense," that the "San Pedro, Sonoita, and Santa Cruz valleys were being depopulated" by their depredations, and that "it was either this course, or death to the remainder of the farmers, teamsters, and mail riders. . . ."

Under a headline VICTORY FOR PEACE, the Denver *News*: "We give this act of the citizens of Arizona most hearty and unqualified endorsement. We congratulate them on the fact that permanent peace arrangements have been made with so many, and we only regret that the number was not double. Camp Grant is the last of those victories for civilization and progress which have made Sand Creek, Washita, the Piegan fight, and other similar occurrences famous in western history.* It is just and right and was fully demanded by circumstances of the times."

Reported the Tucson *Citizen*: ". . . the California papers quite generally approve of the Camp Grant massacre. . . . The San Francisco *Bulletin* recites at considerable length good reasons why such massacres are made necessary in self-defense among the Apaches. . . . The Sacramento *Record* heartily endorses the slaughter . . . the San Diego papers speak of it as 'the joyful news.' "

After giving the matter several weeks of consideration, President Grant overruled the objections of Secretary of War Belknap and Gen-

---

*These were other instances in which scores of helpless Indians were mercilessly slaughtered.

eral Sherman, and ordered that Lieutenant-Colonel George Crook be assigned on his brevet rank to relieve Stoneman as commander in Arizona. For all intents and purposes, Crook was now a full-fledged general.

*   *   *

Schellie, of General Crook: "He was the very picture of a military officer. Tall, straight, broad-shouldered, he was sinewy of limb, powerful of muscle. His face was stern; narrow eyes, a sharp nose, bushy burnsides. He was an outdoorsman—a man most at home in the field. Crook wasn't a desk general of the Stoneman stripe. Yet, he was a quiet man, humble, gentle, retiring from the least bit of notoriety. . . . Not one to burden and bedevil his officers with orders and instructions and memoranda, he chose, rather, to merely give them an insight into what was desired of them. . . . He held the respect of virtually every man in his command."

Lockwood: "No soldier ever surpassed Crook in energy, endurance, and indifference to exposure. He used neither liquor nor tobacco, and no soldier ever heard a profane or obscene word from his lips. . . . He rarely wore a uniform when it was not absolutely obligatory. . . . On one of his marches he is described as wearing Government boots, corduroy trousers, a heavy woolen shirt, an old style army blouse, a brown felt hat, and an old army overcoat with red lining and a wolf-skin collar. He was a shade over six feet in stature. . . . His head was clean-cut, and his features sternly chiseled; his blueish-gray eyes were deep set; his nose prominent; his mouth large and firm, but not hard. . . . Decision, sagacity, tenacity of purpose were written in every feature . . . there was no man—soldier or savage—so poor or ignorant that he could not gain access to him."

Thrapp: "Virile, tireless, and intrepid, Crook loved backwoods life. . . . Yet, Crook was never coarsened by his liking for wilderness life. Literate, courteous, abstemious to an unusual degree, never profane or vulgar, considerate of his junior officers while ready to disagree with his superiors, Crook was supremely duty conscious while so averse to ostentation that he rarely ever wore the uniform he so thoroughly graced. The *Miner* once told how he was persuaded to have his picture taken and appeared at the studio with a brigadier-general's dress coat rolled up in a bundle. Once the operation was concluded, he hastily slipped it off and folded it away out of sight again."

Captain John G. Bourke (who long served under Crook): "There never was an officer in our military service so completely in accord with all the ideas, views, and opinions of the savages whom he had to fight or control as was General Crook."

And Bourke thought that during campaigns this knowledge and understanding placed Crook ". . . in the secret councils of the enemy;

in time of peace it enabled him all the more completely to appreciate the doubts and misgivings of the Indians at the outset of a new life, and to devise plans by which they could all the more readily be brought to see that civilization was something which all could embrace without fear of extinction."

General Sherman would call Crook the greatest Indian-fighter and manager ever known.

* * *

JUNE

Without ostentation, and in baggy civilian clothes, General Crook rode into Tucson in an army ambulance one hot morning near the end of the month, and accepted an invitation to make his headquarters in the home of Governor Safford.

Before the day had ended he had sent orders to all commanding officers in Arizona to report to him in person at once. Campaigns could be delayed while he "found out what he had to do before he tried to do it."

Company and post commanders soon began to arrive, and in long conferences with them that often lasted far into the night he questioned them closely about the topography of the country, the trails, the whereabouts of hostile bands of Apache, equipment, supplies, rations, ammunition, guns, horses, mules, wagons, listening attentively to their statements and saying nothing of any plans he might have in mind.

But he soon revealed that he did have plans, and they were not what most of his subordinates expected.

JULY

Two weeks after his arrival in Tucson, Crook was riding with five companies of cavalry on his first inspection trip of the vast domain of deserts and mountains in which he was supreme commander.

Now his intentions were becoming apparent. There would be no Indian fighting until he felt his troops were ready. There would be exhausting marches to train and discipline them, until they understood very well his strategy, much of which was unorthodox, and his ideas of combat, many of which were unique.

Not many days had passed before he disclosed his conviction that the Apache could be beaten only by fighting them with their own methods. Lieutenant Howard B. Cushing, a daring young officer killed by Apache in a bloody fight during the spring, had employed Apache scouts. Crook organized a complete company of Apache scouts, re-cruiting them as he would any men and paying them regular wages. In command of them he placed trustworthy and experienced white scouts. He reorganized the pack train service, weeding out cruel or inefficient packers and establishing small units that could move swiftly to meet any emergency.

Governor Safford had advised him that "Mexicans were the solution of the 'Apache Problem,' that they knew the country, the habits and mode of Indian warfare, that with a little pinole and dried beef they could travel all over the country without pack mules to carry their provisions, that with ten days' rations on their backs they could march over the roughest country at the rate of thirty to fifty miles per day, that they could go inside an Apache and turn him wrong side out in no time at all. . . ."

Crook engaged fifty Mexicans, and soon found out Governor Safford didn't know what he was talking about. The Mexicans were incompetent, disobedient, lazy, and, most important of all, they were utterly terrified at the very mention of the word Apache. Crook fired them all. He would realize that the citizens of Arizona, including the governor, were violently opposed to giving any employment whatsoever to Indians, and especially Apache.

But Crook remained adamant in his contention that only an Apache can find an Apache, and time would prove him right. Most of his Apache scouts would be unqualifiedly loyal, and Crook's successes would be attributed in a large part to their work, their bravery, and their deadly efficiency in tracking down hostile bands.

Trouble not unlike that which had ended in the massacre at Camp Grant was brewing in southwestern New Mexico. The Indian Bureau, in accord with the "peace policy," had been striving to settle peacefully inclined Apache on lands set aside for the purpose at Cañada Alamosa. A number had accepted the offers of protection and rations made to them. This was not a plan which met with the approval of the white inhabitants of the region, and complaints were being made that the Cañada Alamosa Apache were stealing stock. What the white residents wanted, of course, was the removal of all Apache from the area.

Threats that "white men would take matters into their own hands" were heard. One of these was made in a letter from Probate Judge Richard Hudson to O. F. Piper, Indian agent at Cañada Alamosa. Said Judge Hudson:

"What we want to know is, whether our stock can be recovered from Indians on your reservation . . . or are we to be forever at the mercy of these thieving, murderous Apaches, who have a house of refuge at Alamosa? . . . the citizens of this country are determined to put a stop to it, and, if they carry out their program, the Camp Grant massacre will be thrown entirely in the shade. . . . I can assure you that unless something is done soon, our indignant citizens will turn out *en masse* and settle the Alamosa reservation question fully."

Agent Piper reported to Nathaniel Pope, superintendent of Indian Affairs at Santa Fe, that some animals had been stolen by two or three wild young men, but that the Apache leaders at Cañada Alamosa had cooperated with him, and that all the stolen stock, except one horse, had been recovered and returned to the owners. "I am confident," said Piper, "that the leading men are doing all in their power to prevent any of their people from committing depredations. . . ." Pope promptly instructed Piper to drive the thieves from the reservation and keep Apache scouts on the lookout for any white attackers "in time to call for troops . . . and prevent a repetition of the Camp Grant affair."

The Board of Indian Commissioners, occupied with Indian matters in other parts of the West, had not yet got around to "the Apache problem." The menacing situation at Cañada Alamosa prompted President Grant to order that an emissary "with all necessary powers" be sent there to restore peace, and he instructed the War Department to cooperate fully with the Indian Bureau in the mission. The man selected was Vincent Colyer, a member of the Indian Commission, and a staunch supporter of the administration's peace program.

Colyer's powers were soon expanded. Instead of dealing only with the Indians at Cañada Alamosa, he was authorized to sign peace treaties with all segments and groups of the Apache tribe, any place in the Southwest, and to select suitable sites for permanent reservations.

AUGUST

Vincent Colyer's character was complex, and in some respects unusual. His manner was mild and reserved, yet he was capable of being persuasive and forceful. A Quaker, born in New York City in 1824, he had been well educated. He was a talented and highly paid artist. An antislavery crusader before the Civil War, at the outbreak of hostilities he had organized a Negro regiment and served as its colonel during the conflict. Thereafter he had devoted himself to social causes, particularly in the field of oppressed groups, and had achieved distinction in the work. He held an indestructible conviction that only through the establishment of adequate reservations and just treatment could the Indian problems of the West be resolved. He was an idealist, but not a fanatic, and he demonstrated on numerous occasions that he could be coldly practical.

General Crook was ready to begin his offensive, his troops trained and organized to the peak of efficiency, when he received word that Colyer was en route to Arizona with powers that superseded his own. Crook was not in sympathy with the procedures of what he termed the "Indian Ring" in Washington, by which he meant "Peace Ring," for two reasons. He did not believe they could be successful in dealing with hostile Apache, and he did believe that the people of the Southwest would do all in their power to prevent them from being successful.

"I had no faith in the success of his [Colyer's] enterprise," he would write, "but I was afraid if I continued my operations and he was to fail, I would be charged with interference. So I at once countermanded all my orders looking to active operations against the hostiles, and directed all persons under my control to furnish Mr. Colyer all assistance . . . in carrying out his peace policy."*

It is improbable that any man in the history of Arizona Territory was more maligned, insulted, vilified, and discredited than Vincent Colyer. Even before he had reached the territory the newspapers began an attack on his character. It had become so violent by the time he began his journey through Apacheria that Governor Safford thought it necessary to issue a proclamation calling upon the people to treat him and his colleagues "kindly." Said the governor to his constituents: "If they come among you entertaining erroneous opinions upon the Indian question and the condition of affairs in this Territory, then, by kindly treatment and fair, truthful representation, you will be enabled to convince them of their errors."

The governor's appeal had no effect on either the crude and gauche citizens of Arizona or the vicious press of the Southwest. Said one newspaper: "The people of Arizona, in justice to our murdered dead, ought to dump the old devil Colyer into the shaft of some mine, and pile rocks on him until he is dead. A rascal who comes here to thwart the efforts of military and civilians to conquer a peace from our savage foe deserves to be stoned to death, like the treacherous, black-hearted dog that he is." Said another: "Colyer's home in Washington was struck by lightning last week. Unfortunately Vincent was not hit."

In his letters to the Board of Indian Commissioners and the President, Colyer made only brief mention "of the threats so freely made to 'mob me,' 'lynch me,' 'hang me in effigy,' 'stone me to death,' as a 'thief,' 'robber,' 'murderer,' 'red-handed assassin,' &c., and the abuse generally of the press of Arizona and elsewhere." In a calm understate-

---

*Unaccountably, Crook had taken a dislike to Lieutenant Whitman even before he met him. It may have been that he believed Whitman's unqualified support of the Grant peace policy reflected unfavorably on his ability to serve as an officer in combat against the Apache. Without any irrefutable evidence, in an action quite uncharacteristic of him, he accused Whitman of having "gone over to the Indian Ring." Nevertheless, when the Tucson *Citizen* charged Whitman with being drunk on duty, gambling, consorting with Indian women, and other crimes, Crook demanded of the editor that the charges be substantiated or retracted. The newspaper responded with the declaration that the charges could be substantiated by responsible witnesses, and refused to retract them. Crook then decided that the best way to resolve the issue was to try Whitman by court-martial. Whitman was acquitted.

ment he remarked that "the President's peace policy does not meet with much approval out here . . . and anyone who comes here to execute it must expect to meet with disapprobation."

Colyer not only held extraordinary administrative and legal powers. Congress had appropriated $70,000—considered very generous at the time—"to collect the Apache Indians . . . upon reservations, furnish them with subsistence and other necessary articles, and to promote peace and civilization among them." Armed with the authority to expend these funds as he deemed necessary, Colyer was able to demonstrate to the Apache with material evidence the good faith of the government. This was a position no military officer or Indian agent previously had enjoyed.

Accompanied by Indian Bureau officials and a strong military escort —the army, in view of the threats against him, was taking no chances —Colyer reached Cañada Alamosa late in the month.

OCTOBER

For more than two months Colyer had traveled through the heart of Apacheria. His hope to meet the notorious Cochise had not materialized, but he had held councils with scores of other Apache leaders, and conferred at length with numerous army officers, including Crook, "who courteously received me."

He had established four major Apache reservations. They were located in the Tularosa Valley of southwestern New Mexico, at Fort Apache, at Camp Verde, and at Camp Grant, in Arizona. Within a few weeks, more than four thousand Apache, pledging themselves to remain peaceful, to labor, develop farms, and adopt the ways of the white man's world, had flocked into these sanctuaries.

Colyer's narrowest escape from injury, or possible death, had come at Camp Grant. There he was in council with Apache leaders—one of them the dangerous Eskiminzin, who agreed once more to remain peaceful—when word was received that some two hundred armed white men from Tucson were approaching with the intention of repeating the Camp Grant massacre and "taking care" of any "peace lovers" who stood in their way.

Colyer ordered the Camp Grant commandant, Captain William Nelson, to halt the mob, by force if necessary. Nelson sent a noncom and several troopers to warn the "Tucson delegation" to turn back. The message was delivered, but the invaders replied that they were determined to carry out "their mission, soldiers, or no soldiers." When he received the noncom's report, Nelson then directed Lieutenant Whitman "to ride out and meet the party and inform them that he was prepared to enforce his order, and had his guns in position, and would open fire upon them on their appearance at the mouth of the canyon opposite the post."

Said Colyer: "Captain Nelson loaded up the water wagon belonging to the post and sent it out to them, that they would not suffer in case they should conclude to go back . . . which they very reluctantly concluded to do. They left with the declaration that they could use the white flag as well as we, and if that would bring in the Indians they would bring them in and put them on a reservation where it would not cost much to feed them."

The incident provided new fuel for the newspapers in their campaign against the peace policy. They printed totally dishonest stories that Lieutenant Whitman, long their target, and his superior, Captain Nelson, had turned their guns on an innocent group of prospectors en route to the mountains who were suffering excruciatingly from thirst.

Crook either believed the stories or saw in them an opportunity to strike at Nelson, whom he felt was disposed to favor the policies of the "good Vincent Colyer" to the detriment of the army's best interests. Crook could not openly criticize Colyer, at the moment the ranking federal official in Arizona, but there was nothing to keep him from delivering a stinging rebuke to Nelson, and he did so, notifying him that his threat to fire at citizens was "unwarranted, as you transcended the limits of your authority." Shortly afterward Crook had Nelson transferred out of the Department of Arizona.

In this matter, it was Crook's, not Nelson's, actions that were unwarranted. Nelson had received orders to cooperate in every respect with Commissioner Colyer, and to comply with his wishes and instructions, and he had done no more than that.

When Colyer left Prescott for Washington, by way of rail from San Francisco, he believed that he had succeeded in completing the groundwork for an enduring peace with the Apache in Arizona.

General Crook knew better, but he bided his time, awaiting orders to launch the plans which he believed were the only means by which the Apache could be defeated and controlled.

Events would indicate that he was right. Colyer had no more than departed before hostile Apache who had not subscribed to the peace program attacked freight caravans, stages, and ranches in several parts of the territory. One of the chief offenders was Cochise, who had spurned an invitation to visit the Great White Father in Washington with the blunt statement that the time for trusting any white man had passed. In the raids a number of white persons were slain, and property damage and livestock losses were heavy.

U.S. District Attorney Rowell was having trouble with the grand jury appointed to consider the Camp Grant massacre. After listening to the evidence he presented for a week, the jurors continued to reject his request that indictments be returned against the massacre participants.

On the verge of defeat, Rowell had a private conversation with a close friend, Andrew H. Cargill, a member of the jury. The Attorney General in Washington, he told Cargill, had notified him that President Grant was again threatening to place Arizona Territory under martial law. If that happened, everyone involved in the massacre would be arrested and tried before a military court.

According to Schellie, Rowell "conveniently made himself absent from the next meeting of the grand jury. Cargill dutifully relayed the information to that body. He explained to his fellow jurors that trial by court-martial would mean certain conviction; feeling against the raid ran high among most army men. . . . Then too, there was plenty of evidence against the participants. But—Cargill argued—if the grand jury would indict the men they would be tried in district court and the jurors would be their fellow Arizona citizens. And what Arizona jury would convict their friends for killing Apaches?"

Reluctantly the grand jury agreed, but made clear their feelings by condemning in their report the "beastly drunkenness among army officers," charging that officers at Camps Grant, Goodwin, and Apache were "getting rich by cheating the Government," and were "in the habit of using their official position to break the chastity of Indian women."

One hundred and eight murder indictments were voted.

NOVEMBER

Early in the month near Wickenberg a stagecoach was attacked and seven of its eight passengers were killed. Three of them were members of the Wheeler Surveying Expedition, a War Department project.

The identity of the raiders was not immediately established. Some dispatches indicated the slayings were committed by white outlaws. Peace policy advocates, seizing on these reports, issued press statements accusing the War Department of falsely attributing every atrocity to Indians. Captain Charles Meinhold was sent to make a thorough investigation. His report presented evidence conclusively showing that the attackers had come from a reservation at Date Creek, where more than a thousand Apache–Mohave and other Indians were being regularly supplied with rations. The report, widely circulated in the East, was a serious setback for the Peace Party.

Colyer had been back in Washington only a few days when he understood that the tides of both public and official opinion had turned against himself and the Board of Indian Commissioners. Obviously news of the Wickenberg killings and dispatches from General Crook had prompted the President to harbor doubts that Colyer had succeeded to the extent he claimed.

Crook had charged, as Ogle notes, "that the peace policy 'managers' were merely using Colyer as an 'instrument' to make it appear that a lasting peace could be made with the 'much abused and injured Apache' were it not for the opposition of the military. . . ." Furthermore, terming Colyer's peace a humbug, Crook had maintained that in reality the peace policy advocates were eager to have him wage unrelenting war on the Apache so that he "would be abused as the great North American Butcher." Secretary Belknap accused Colyer of interfering in War Department business, and declared that he was waiting for authority from the President to increase Crook's forces in Arizona.

Mr. Grant summoned Belknap, Interior Secretary Delano, and Colyer to confer with him at the White House for the purpose of formulating "a general line of policy" for handling the Apache problem.

In spite of the existing acrimonious atmosphere, they succeeded in hammering out a fundamental program which they believed—or at least hoped—would resolve the issue to the satisfaction of all concerned. It was this:

1. The President would order that the tracts selected by Colyer in Apacheria "would be regarded as reservations."

2. The various bands of roving Apache would be notified that they "are required to locate upon the reservations immediately, and that, upon so doing, they will be fully protected and provided for by the Government so long as they remain on said reservations and preserve peaceable relations with the Government, each other, and the white people; and that unless they comply with this request they will not thus be provided for and protected."

3. The Apache will not be permitted "to send their old men, women, and children upon such reservations, and permit their young men and braves to go on the war-path."

4. The white people of New Mexico and Arizona will be notified of the government's determination "to preserve, if possible, peace between the whites and Indians, and that neither will be allowed to depredate or trespass upon the other, with impunity."

5. The Superintendent of Indian Affairs for Arizona will move his office to the headquarters of General Crook, and cooperate fully with him "in the execution of the purpose of the Government."

6. "Suitable and discreet" army officers would be appointed as Indian agents on the reservations to serve until, at the discretion of the President, they were supplanted by civilian agents.

DECEMBER

Crook had his orders. Endorsed by Secretary Belknap and Generals Sherman, Schofield, and Sheridan, they left no doubt that the "war party" was in control, and the "peace party" had been relegated to a back seat. In Washington, said Crook, "Colyer had his head chopped off."

To supplement and support the Apache program announced in November, reinforcements would be sent to Crook, a military telegraph would be constructed to Arizona, and greater appropriations would be made to pay for the offensive against the Apache which Crook would conduct. General Sherman sarcastically informed the War Department that since the Office of Indian Affairs was rarely able to supply any food for Indians, the army also would have to furnish funds to be sure that Apache held on reservations would not starve to death.

President Grant, Sherman, and Secretaries Belknap and Delano sent assurances to Crook that he would be "warmly supported in rigorous aggressive operations." He was given full authority to proceed with any measures he deemed necessary in order "to give full effect to the policy of the government."

That policy virtually placed the army—in the person of Crook—in supreme control of Apacheria, that is, southern and central Arizona and southwestern New Mexico. Fundamentally it provided that all roving bands of Apache must go upon reservations at once, and those who did not obey were to be punished as outlaws. Families of renegade warriors were to be held as prisoners. A tribe or band, unless found guilty of giving aid to hostiles, was not to be punished for the depredations of individuals over which they held no control. No white persons, except officials, were to be permitted on reservations without permission from the army officer in command. Vigorous operations were to be carried out against hostiles until they submitted. Each Apache on a reservation was to receive a specified amount of rations, the distribution to be supervised by army personnel.

Crook was completely unfettered, free to proceed as he wished. He elected to give the Apache time to comply with the stringent orders, and sent Indian emissaries throughout the vast wintry wilderness of Apacheria with a message: All Apache will surrender at a reservation before the middle of February. Those who did not appear would be hunted down and punished. It was peace or war to the finish. The

Apache had less than two months to decide which they wanted.

The trial of the Camp Grant murderers began in Tucson on the fifth before a jury in the court of U.S. District Judge John Titus. It was one of the greatest farces in the history of American jurisprudence.

During five days of taking testimony Judge Titus discredited prosecution witnesses. He virtually ordered the jury to return a verdict of not guilty. He gave credence to the testimony of defendants that Camp Grant Indians had left the reservation on raids, had killed white persons, destroyed property, and stolen livestock. In his instructions to the jurors he reminded them that most of the male Apache had been absent from the village on the morning of the attack. "Where they were," he said, "and what they were doing are not proved. The absence is, however, an emphatic comment regarding those who are claimed to have been kept with any of the strictness of prisoners of war. All but two of the victims were women and children."

Thus, he was suggesting, as the defendants had claimed, that the Apache men were engaged in depredations when their families were slaughtered. And he continued:

"To kill one engaged in actual unlawful hostilities or in undoubted preparation with others for active hostilities would not be murder. In a country like this, the resident is not bound to wait until the assassin, savage or civilized, is by his hearth, or at his bedside, or at his door, or until the knife of the assassin is at his throat. If he had undoubted evidence that others are preparing, alone or in combination, to destroy him and his property, he may anticipate his foe and quell or destroy him to secure his own personal safety.

"In a country like this, with few people, with none or very little police, filled with murderous savages far more numerous than the orderly and peaceful, that, I charge you, is the law.

"Here, amid innumerable perils, the citizen must take care of himself . . . the defendants have been schooled to agonizing apprehension, where the blood red line of a troubled frontier is expanded into a vast domain of blood, where the very roads are traced by the gore and the graves of fallen wayfarers. . . .

"If the Apache nation continues to depredate against the others, then it forfeits the right of protection from the United States."

Judge Titus told the jurors he would await their decision. He didn't leave the court, for he knew he wouldn't have to wait long. And he didn't. The jury was out only nineteen minutes.

The verdict: Not guilty for all one hundred eight defendants, white men, Mexicans, and Papago.[23]

* * *

1872

JANUARY

There was not only one war in Arizona. There were three. And it would be difficult to determine which was the most injurious, vindictive, and vicious, or which one was the greater threat to the territory and its people, both red and white.

The conflict with the Apache, of course, had been raging for more than two and a half centuries.

Correlatively now were two other conflicts:

1. The clash of philosophies, theories, methods, and convictions as propounded and proclaimed respectively by the so-called Peace Party and War Party.

2. The bitter struggle for control between the War Department and the Department of the Interior.

While the war with the Apache would be increasingly contained, the other two wars would increase steadily in intensity.

Reaction of the Apache to Crook's stringent warning of the previous December had been gratifying. Several thousand had made camps on the reservations. However, the situation was deceptive. It was winter. Much of Apacheria was covered with snow, and the higher elevations were bitterly cold. Whether they were sincere in proclaiming a desire for peace or not, the Apache welcomed the chance to enjoy protection and regular issues of rations during the period of the year when obtaining adequate food was always difficult.

Crook was not fooled. Still unheard from were several strong and dangerous bands. Killings and thefts were occurring in various parts of the territory and in Mexico. He had as counselors experienced white scouts—such men as Al Sieber, Jack Townsend, Gus Spear, Willard Rice, Mason McCoy, and trustworthy Apache who served as spies—and the intelligence they brought him was not promising. "In my judgment," he wrote headquarters, "if these Indians don't soon break out in open hostilities, they will do what is much worse, that is, while their old and decrepit women and children (who are their only encumbrances in the shape of baggage) are living protected and supplied on the reservations, the warriors will, with impunity, keep up their bloody work. . . ."

He was not advocating the abolishment of the reservation and feeding program—far from it. Indeed, he wanted to give it every chance to work, but he was not blinded to realities. A great many Apache would never surrender until they were soundly beaten on the field of battle. There was no other road to success.

He combined a boast with a slap at civilian authorities and Indian rights organizations by telling his superiors that if the entire Apache problem were left to him alone, "I have not the slightest doubt of my ability to conquer a lasting peace with this Apache race in a comparatively short space of time, and a peace that will not only save the Treasury millions of dollars, but will save the lives of a good many innocent whites and Indians."

Military leaders believed him, and provided him with all the support they could in men, munitions, and money, but the antiwar groups were not in any sense conceding defeat and continued to pound on Washington doors, claiming that there was no reason to use brutal and bloody measures, as most of the Apache were already living peacefully on reservations. The Interior Department, of which the Indian Bureau was a part, realizing that the prosecution of Crook's war plans would mean greater entrenchment of military control, called for judicious forbearance and less volatile measures. This view was supported by the Board of Indian Commissioners.

President Grant didn't help matters by expressing inconsistent views. He approved the orders sent to Crook to wage a vigorous campaign against hostile Apache. Then he gave the Peace Party grist for its mill with the statement: "I do not believe our creator ever placed different races of men on this earth with the view of having the stronger exert all their energies on exterminating the weaker. If any change takes place in the Indian policy of the government while I hold my present office it will be on the humanitarian side of the question."

FEBRUARY

Crook's command was ready to take to the field. He sent word to all Apache that any of them not on a reservation by the sixteenth of the month would be considered hostile, and when captured would be held as prisoners of war, that is, confined to a concentration camp.

The deadline came, and as Crook prepared to start his offensive he was once more frustrated and obliged to announce that all operations would be postponed indefinitely. The peace advocates once again had demonstrated the extent of their influence in Washington. President Grant and Secretaries Delano and Belknap had decided that, after all, war might not be the most feasible method for resolving the Apache problem, and that a new effort should be made to induce all the Apache by persuasive means to settle on the reservations. An even better solution, to their way of thinking, might be to create a new reservation for them in the wilderness of New Mexico.

Crook was informed that a representative of the Department of the Interior was en route to Arizona to cooperate with the military in preserving peace and to expedite the execution of the new policy of the government. It wasn't a new policy. It was an old policy revived, the same policy under which Colyer had gone west, and which had emerged from the coma into which it had fallen.

The man chosen for the mission was General Oliver Otis Howard, popularly known in army circles as "Bible-Quoting Howard," a veteran officer with a distinguished combat record, a champion of the underprivileged, and a religious fanatic.

MARCH

Crook and his powerful, excellently trained and equipped troops were forced to remain idle, while Cochise and other hostile leaders plundered wagon trains, killed settlers, and sacked ranches.

APRIL

Howard arrived at Fort McDowell. He had been given plenary powers to deal with the Apache situation as he deemed necessary. Crook —under the circumstances Howard's subordinate—met him. Their conferences were reported to be "harmonious." They may have been on the surface, but beneath them was a brooding dislike in each man for the other. Crook would accuse Howard of "prostituting my command" by attempting to induce officers with whom he conferred to "espouse Howard's views as contrary to mine." To some officers, in an effort to turn them against Crook, Howard offered inducements of duty in the East.

Wrote Crook: "General Howard was fond of public speaking. His themes generally were 'How He Was Converted' and 'The Battle of Gettysburg.'

"I was very much amused at the General's opinion of himself. He told me that he thought the Creator had placed him on earth to be the Moses to the Negro. Having accomplished that mission, he felt satisfied that his next mission was with the Indians."

After visiting several posts, Howard ordered Apache chiefs to confer with him at Camp Grant. Messengers were sent out to the various bands with his request.

MAY

The most important Apache leader to attend the Camp Grant council was Eskiminzin. Since the massacre, in which members of his large family were slain—he had several wives—he and his warriors had been on the warpath. In one fight with troops, thirteen of his men had been killed, and he had been wounded. He had no fear, however, of appearing at Camp Grant, under a flag of truce, for two officers whom he knew he could trust would be present—General Crook and Lieutenant Whitman.

NINETEENTH CENTURY: PART II [295

The Apache counselors were assembled under cottonwood trees on the bank of the San Pedro River. Howard arrived in an army ambulance. When he had walked to within a few yards of them, he dropped to his knees, folded his hands, turned his face toward heaven, and began to pray out loud. The Apache scattered as if a bomb had been thrown in their midst.

Skimmy hid behind a building. At last he peered around a corner and beckoned to his friend Whitman. When the lieutenant had joined him, he asked, his eyes blazing with anger:

"Have you gone over to the enemy, too? What do you mean bringing that man [Howard] here to make bad medicine against us?"

Whitman laughed: "That doesn't mean anything. He always does that when he begins any undertaking—just as you spit on your hands when you go to draw your bow."

After further explanations, the Apache were reassembled.

Howard opened the council by "informing the Indians that he had commanded thirty thousand men during the Civil War, and if they did not behave themselves and do what he told them, he would come sweeping through their country and exterminate them all." The threat was hardly in accord with the purpose of his mission, to make peace by persuasion, but in the short time he had been in Arizona Howard had learned much more about conditions there than he had previously known. His presence had not prevented raids in the Tonto Basin, along the Verde River, and in the mountainous country of the Chiricahua along the Mexican border.

"Now," Howard told the stony-faced Apache before him, "I think you know that I want to do well by you and am your friend." Then he asked a question which indicated his supreme egotism: "Could I not come into your lodges at any time?"

"Not unless you want to get killed," Eskiminzin told him.

Taken aback by the reply, Howard demanded: "Could any white man do it?"

"Yes," said Eskiminzin. "Lieutenant Whitman."

Some of the Apache complained that barren, hot Camp Grant was not a suitable location for the large permanent reservation. Howard agreed with them, and designated as a new reservation an immense tract north of the Gila River and adjoining the White Mountain Reservation.* The name San Carlos was given to it. Old Camp Grant would be abandoned as soon as feasible.

Ten Apache leaders accepted his invitation to accompany him back to Washington. Eskiminzin was not one of them.

---

*Later renamed Fort Apache Reservation.

Although his mission was to promote the peace policy, Howard admitted to Crook that "amongst the incorrigible hostiles there is no course left but to deal with vigor, according to your discretion."

JUNE

Howard had not accomplished a great deal, but statements ascribed to the members of the Apache delegation he brought east made it appear that his mission had been highly successful. They were having a fine time seeing the sights in Washington and New York. Whether they were talking with forked tongues, as they so often accused white men of doing, was hardly a debatable question. Perhaps they did hope that hostilities in Apacheria could be halted. Perhaps words to this effect had been put in their mouths, and they had seen no reason not to utter them. Nothing was to be gained by antagonizing gracious hosts. In any case, eastern sentiment for peace was strengthened, and the Peace Party happily proclaimed that warfare in Apacheria would soon be a thing of the past.

This optimistic attitude was considerably dampened by news dispatches from Arizona and New Mexico. It sometimes took weeks for reports from isolated military posts to pass through headquarters and reach newspapers. The stories now being printed in the East revealed that even while Howard was holding his meetings with Apache leaders, some of their brethren were scourging settlements and military reserves. Ranches had been raided in the Williamson Valley. A beef contractor's herd had been stolen from Camp Verde. Tonto had got away with some two thousand sheep from a range within a mile of Fort Whipple. At least a dozen troopers had been slain and many others wounded in battles with the raiders. In Davidson Canyon a corporal was tied to a burning tree and tortured to death while his comrades made a desperate attempt to fight their way to his rescue. In an attack on ranches in the Sonoita Valley thirteen Mexicans were slain.

An estimated thirty white persons—settlers, travelers, and freighters —were murdered during the spring and early summer. All raiders were reported to be armed with good rifles and well supplied with cartridges. The weapons were being sold to them by white traders, although some had been stolen from military supplies, captured in battle with troops, or obtained from freight caravans. They could also be obtained in Mexico.

Of all the hostile bands, it appeared that the Chiricahua were the most active. Led by Cochise, they were leaving trails marked by the bodies of their victims, destroyed ranches, and burned wagon trains across southwestern New Mexico, southern Arizona, and northern Mexico. Property losses in the region were exceeding those of the bloodiest years of the past. Mails were being robbed, and carriers slain.

JULY

After consultations with his advisers on Indian Affairs, President Grant concluded that the Apache Peace Policy could not succeed unless the Chiricahua agreed to accept it. He ordered General Howard to return to Arizona and negotiate a treaty with Cochise.

Crook still waited for permission to start a major campaign.

AUGUST

Howard reached Fort Apache about the middle of the month. There he was delayed eight days by an explosive situation caused by a dispute between military and Indian Bureau officials. Unaccountably the War Department had ordered officers to halt issues of rations to the Apache living on the reservation. Red tape—or most likely graft—had caused a delay in the necessary approval of a beef contract by the Department of the Interior. The Apache were angry and were threatening to take to the warpath. The army then imprisoned six of their leaders. Howard induced the contractor to issue beef on vouchers he certified, freed the Apache prisoners, removed the officer acting as Indian agent and replaced him with a civilian, and arranged to have nonmilitary employees resume the issuance of rations.

He then hurried on to the Tularosa Reservation, where he hoped that he would find a means of meeting Cochise. There he encountered more trouble. The Apache didn't like the Tularosa Valley, which Colyer had selected for them, and demanded to be allowed to return to their former homes in the vicinity of Cañada Alamosa. They also complained that blankets issued to them were too shoddy to be of any use, and fell apart when damp. After several meetings with them, Howard was able to placate them by liberally increasing their rations and promising to take the matter up with the President.

SEPTEMBER

After several futile attempts to arrange through Apache on the Tularosa Reservation for a meeting with Cochise, Howard learned of a white man who purportedly was a close friend of the Chiricahua leader. He went to see him. The man was Thomas J. Jeffords, whom Howard described as tall, spare, "with reddish hair and whiskers of considerable length."

After serving as a dispatch bearer and scout for the Union in the Civil War, Jeffords had wandered out to the Southwest. He established a stage line in the Chiricahua Country. Oddly enough, his vehicles were not attacked, although Cochise's warriors were ravaging the area. A popular report was that he "worked his way into the confidence of Cochise, they liked each other, made a pact, and remained fast friends." There was more to the story. Jeffords's pact with Cochise was, in fact, an agreement under which Jeffords would furnish Cochise ammunition in exchange for stolen livestock.

Jeffords agreed to take Howard to Cochise only if the general would go alone with him and two Apache friends. Howard agreed. The four men rode away into the mountains.

* * *

Captain Bourke, who served long as chief aide-de-camp to General Crook, would write of Cochise:

"He is a fine-looking Indian . . . straight as a rush—six feet in stature, deep-chested, roman-nosed, black eyes, firm mouth, a kindly and even somewhat melancholy expression tempering the determined look of his countenance. He seemed much more neat than other wild Indians . . . and his manners were very gentle. There was neither in speech nor action any of the bluster characteristic of his race."

Lockwood would write of Cochise:

"Though born and bred a savage, Cochise was a man of distinction. His only home was a wickiup that could be constructed in half an hour and vacated with all its belongings in half a minute, yet he had the same qualities of person, intellect, and moral force that mark our leaders among the civilized nations of men. All men of prominence who met him and had dealings with him . . . testify to a certain poise and dignity of character that marked his behavior. . . . He bore himself with stateliness and assurance. It is sufficient evidence of his superior intelligence and great force of character that for ten years he coped successfully with the best brains and the strongest wills that the United States Government could array against him. He . . . had his native schooling whetted to its keenest by contact with the cruelty and perfidy of white men whom he trusted, but who betrayed and outraged him.

"Cochise was a man of like passions with other men. . . . He was subject to pride, cruelty, pity, and honor. His nature was not simple and shallow, but very complex and passionate. . . .

"Cochise had supreme respect for his word. There was apparently no quality he admired so much as straight speaking. He preferred either to speak the truth with others or to remain silent, and desired that men should do likewise with him. This virtue is repeatedly alluded to in the accounts we have of him from those who knew him."

* * *

We have only General Howard's word for what Cochise said to him when they met in the famous leader's Dragoon Mountain stronghold.

Jeffords served as interpreter. Purportedly the conversation between the two men took this form:

COCHISE: *Buenos días, señor.* Why do you come?

HOWARD: The President sent me to make peace between you and the white people.

COCHISE: No one wants peace more than I do.

HOWARD: Then, as I have full power, we can make it.

COCHISE: How long will you stay in my camp? I must call in my chief warriors. I cannot make peace without their advice. Will you stay until I send out messengers to bring them in?

HOWARD: Yes. I have come from Washington to make peace. How long will it take?

COCHISE: Ten days. But will not the soldiers fire on my men as they come in?

HOWARD: I will send word to Camp Bowie so that this cannot happen.

A treaty was negotiated and signed, but apparently no copies were made. Howard stated that under its terms the Chiricahua were to be given a reservation in the region they most preferred, their ancient homeland in the Dragoon and Huachuca Mountains. Jeffords would serve as their agent, and would be given absolute authority in handling the affairs of the band without political interference of any type. Soldiers would be allowed to pass along the roads of the reservation, but could not be stationed on it. White civilians would not be permitted to settle on the reservation or to exploit its resources in any manner.

Try as he did, General Crook could not obtain a copy of the treaty. Said Crook: "I never could get to see the treaty stipulations, although I made official applications for them. . . . The treaty stopped all operations against them [Cochise and the Chiricahua] by me. It had a bad effect on my Indians, as they thought I was afraid of Cochise."

But Crook's Apache scouts and other Indians who were well informed about the Howard treaty told him of the serious flaw it contained. Cochise had told Howard, said these informants, that he could not prevent his warriors from raiding across the border into Mexico, for that was being done by Apache from all areas. Howard had elected to allow the matter to remain unresolved. Thus, the Chiricahua and other southern bands construed his negligence as meaning that the United States did not propose to chastise them so long as they confined their raiding to Mexico.

Indian scouts Crook had sent to the Date Creek area firmly identified the tribesmen who had killed the passengers on the stage near Wickenberg. Crook went after them. In a wild but short hand-to-hand fight he narrowly escaped being killed. Lieutenant William J. Ross was able to deflect the rifle of an Apache who was taking aim at the general. Seven Indians were killed and several troopers wounded, but most of the wanted warriors escaped. Crook sent a cavalry column commanded by Captain Julius W. Mason, and some eighty Hualapai scouts led by Al Sieber, in pursuit of them. The scouts tracked them into the wild country of the Santa Maria Mountains, where they were overtaken. In the ensuing fight the troops killed forty of the renegades and took a number of prisoners. More important than the success of the operation was the fact that it marked the end of Indian resistance in western Apacheria.

OCTOBER

The reservation-feeding program could not be termed a complete failure. Several thousand Apache were at peace. Yet, neither could it be termed a complete success. For offsetting its achievements were two irrefutable factors: (1) Depredations and killings by Apache were continuing throughout most of Apacheria, and (2) several thousand Apache, among them the most hostile leaders, remained in their wilderness retreats, having rejected all offers of peace and refusing to submit to confinement.

Crook reminded the War Department that for a year he had strenuously sought to avoid taking any steps that might interfere "with the success of the peace policy or cause an affront to public opinion." Now he submitted a long list of atrocities proved by investigations to have been committed by Apache living on the Colyer and Howard reservations. Once again he reiterated his conviction that the Apache hostiles would have to be reduced in combat before the Southwest would know a genuine peace.

He had a great deal of strong support both outside and within the Administration. General Schofield declared that "no course is open except a vigorous and unremitting prosecution of the war, until they are completely subdued, and the Department Commander [Crook] should have ample power of restriction over reservation Indians." If there were any high-ranking officers and officials who disagreed with this view, they either remained silent or their voices could not be heard in the Washington clamor for action.

Certainly President Grant did not disagree. The administration turned once more to a policy of war. Crook's hands were untied. Adroitly he requested the full cooperation of Indian Bureau employees and other civil officials of the government stationed in Arizona. Assurances that he would receive it were sent to him.

The burden of the Apache conflict, and all problems correlative to it, now rested entirely on his shoulders.

NOVEMBER

The long-delayed offensive which Crook launched against the avowedly hostile bands was probably the most carefully planned military operation in the history of warfare against American Indians. His troops were disciplined, experienced, thoroughly trained, and equipped to meet all conceivable contingencies. Each company of cavalry was supplemented by thirty to forty Apache scouts. Although these deadly fighters—actually no less primitive and savage than the hostile warriors they would hunt—were commanded by officers and white scouts, no attempt was made to transform their habits and their methods of warfare or to force them to comply with customary army regulations, either in or out of bivouacs. They were allowed to march as they desired—usually they scattered out, seemingly without pattern or order.

From the beginning the campaign proceeded with the prescribed precision, brilliantly executed.

Crook's strategy:

Highly mobile contingents would strike out in several directions, all supported by an efficient and dependable pack train system.* Strike the hostiles wherever they could be found. Keep them on the move. Drive them toward the Tonto Basin, a high, cold country where in winter they would have difficulty obtaining food. Bottle them up, and then send in strong forces to crush them.

Crook's orders to his men:

Accept any offers of surrender. Attack any Apache who refused to capitulate. Make every effort to avoid killing women and children. Prisoners must not be abused. Give every hostile band all the fighting they ask for. If a trail is discovered, never abandon it. If horses play out, follow the enemy on foot until he is captured or killed. Scouts will precede all columns. It takes an Apache to track and trap an Apache. There will be no rest. No hardships or sacrifices will be too great. The campaign must be short and decisive.

DECEMBER

Gratifying reports were sent to headquarters:

Captain Emil Adams's troops killed eleven warriors on the east side of the Chino Valley.

Lieutenant William F. Rice's command killed thirteen, and took several prisoners in the Verde Country.

The contingent led by Captain George F. Price captured nine

---

*Crook's mule pack-train system would serve as a model for army jungle operations as late as World War II.

women and an old man belonging to a band that had been committing depredations along the Gila River, but the warrior raiders escaped.

Captain George M. Randall's expedition trailed a strong band led by the notorious Delshay—one of Crook's prime targets. The hostiles were surprised near Bad Rock Mountain. In the fighting twenty-five Indians were killed and a number of squaws and children were captured. But Delshay got away.

Numerous camps were found and destroyed. Numerous warriors were slain in brief skirmishes and running fights. The hostiles, as Crook had demanded, were being kept on the move, although a number of daring troopers were being killed, many were wounded, and all were suffering from lack of water, weariness, and bitter cold. Snows increased the hardships, but relieved the thirst of both horses and men.

Two columns commanded by Major William H. Brown and Captain James Burns, and containing nearly three hundred troopers and scouts, united on Christmas Day in high country along the Salt River. Two days later, scouts found a large Apache camp. The leader of these hostiles was Nanni-Chaddi, listed high on the roster of most wanted rebel chiefs. According to Captain Bourke, Nanni-Chaddi had visited Fort McDowell the previous year and had talked "with that spawn of hell, Vincent Colyer, from whom he received presents of blankets and other necessaries, promising in return to comply with the demand of the lawful government and obey its orders." He had also appeared at Fort Grant, and had boasted to the commandant that "no troops ever had found his retreat and none ever would."

The walls of Salt River Canyon stood more than a thousand feet above the stream. Nanni-Chaddi's rancheria—his retreat—was located in an elliptical nook, before a cave. Across the mouth of the cave was a natural sandstone rampart ten feet in height.

In the first sudden attack six warriors were slain. The other Apache, men, women, and children, dashed for the protection of the cave. Bourke recorded that twice the besieged were called upon to surrender their families, "promises being given that no harm should befall them but, confident in their ability to repel us, their only answers were yells of defiance."

From below and above, the troops began firing into the mouth of the cave, and for three minutes "every man in the command opened and closed the breech-block of his carbine as rapidly as his hands could move."

Shots from the cave steadily decreased and finally stopped. Cautiously the soldiers moved forward. Even veteran troopers were sickened by the sight which met their eyes as they looked into the cave. Seventy-six men and women were lying dead in bloody masses, piled one upon the other. Twenty women and children had been able to shield themselves to some extent, and were alive, although nearly all were wounded "more or less severely, but by good fortune we succeeded in bringing them off in safety."

Nanni-Chaddi and his hostile band had been wiped out.

1873

Captain Burns wrote that without Apache scouts "soldiers were worth nothing."

Captain Bourke declared: "The longer we knew the Apache scouts, the better we liked them. They were wilder and more suspicious than the Pimas and Maricopas, but far more reliable, and endowed with a greater amount of courage and daring. I have never known an officer whose experience entitled his opinion to the slightest consideration, who did not believe as I do on this subject."

Thus was Crook's conviction sustained by men who did the fighting.

Sickness more than Apache threatened to defeat Crook's offensive as it was verging on success. A disease, termed "epizootic," for want of a more precise medical term, swept through Arizona killing thousands of horses. Many cavalry companies were without mounts, but shouldering packs they carried on the campaign on foot.

Crook had nine columns in the field. At the beginning of the year it was estimated that in excess of five hundred hostiles, not excluding a large number of women unavoidably slain, had been killed. Another hundred met death from troopers' guns during the first weeks of the year. Military losses were surprisingly small. In most major engagements no more than one or two troopers died. A relatively small number succumbed to wounds and sickness. Only a handful of scouts lost their lives. For example, in the fierce Salt River Cave fight there was only one fatal casualty, a Pima scout.

Crook's circle of death steadily tightened with results that clearly demonstrated its terrible effectiveness. The fight that seemed to break the spirit of the Apache took place on Turret Mountain, a few miles west of the junction of the Verde and East Verde Rivers. A column commanded by Captain George M. Randall killed more than sixty warriors and took prisoner one hundred and thirty-seven men, women, and children.

By early spring hundreds of Apache in small groups were straggling along the trails to the various posts and reservations. They were, in Crook's words, "emaciated, clothes torn in tatters, some of their legs were not thicker than my arm."

Cha-lipun, leader of one of the largest surrendering bands, told

Crook: "You see, we are nearly dead from want of food and exposure. My people cannot sleep at night because they fear a dawn attack. We cannot hunt with guns because every rifle crack brings troops down upon us. We cannot cook because flame and smoke draws the enemy. We cannot stay in the valleys because we would be found, but if we go to the snowy mountains the troops follow us there. I do not surrender to you because I like you, but because I am afraid of you."

Crook shook hands with him, and said: "If you promise to live in peace, I will be your best friend."

He issued orders regarding the surrendering Indians: "They should not be judged harshly for acts which in the civil codes would constitute minor offenses, but care should be taken that they do not succeed in deceiving their agents and the officers in matters of greater import, being careful to treat them as children in ignorance, not in innocence."

The Apache of central and western Arizona had been broken, but there was one important task left to be accomplished. Delshay had not surrendered—the last dangerous and important leader still at large in the region. He was reported to be in the Mazatzal Mountains, and Captain Randall, with a strong contingent of troopers and scouts, was sent after him.

After an intensive hunt they caught up with him on Canyon Creek, near the Mogollon Rim, and surrounded his camp. Only a few shots had been fired before Delshay raised a white flag and came forward to surrender. Randall demurred. "You have broken your word too often," he told the notorious Apache. "We have no confidence in you."

Then, as Crook would write: "Delshay commenced crying and said he would do anything he was ordered to do. He wanted to save his people, as they were starving. Every rock had turned into a soldier. . . . He would accept any terms. . . ."

Delshay and the remnants of his once powerful band were taken to the White Mountain Reservation.

In his reports Crook was unstinting in praising his men for their courage, tenacity, dedication, and sacrifices. They had, he said, ". . . outwitted and beaten the wiliest foes with slight loss, comparatively, to themselves," and they had finally "closed an Indian war that has been waged since the days of Cortez."

Crook himself was the national hero of the hour. Congratulations poured in on him from Washington and other military headquarters. Newspapers called him the Napoleon of Indian fighters.

The Arizona command deserved all the adulation poured upon it, but Crook's statement that the age-old warfare had ended was, to say the least, somewhat premature.

In the eastern end of Apacheria the Mescalero were fighting to survive under the pressures of settlers who coveted the land which had been tentatively assigned to them for a reservation. The rations and other goods promised them "so that they may progress in the ways of civilization and peace" were being regularly stolen. They existed on the verge of starvation. Not a few of them had gone to Mexico, and others had joined wild bands west of the Rio Grande and were preying on ranchers and travelers.

In the Dragoon Mountains Cochise and the Chiricahua were living under the protection of their unratified treaty with Howard. Safe from Crook, they continued to terrorize northern Mexico. Other depredations committed in Arizona and New Mexico were attributed to them, but could not be proved.

Crook soon found himself faced with serious problems in the area over which he had jurisdiction. Taking him at his word that the Apache war was "virtually at an end," the administration dusted off the old Grant Peace Plan. This program, it will be recalled, recommended that various religious denominations appoint Indian agents. The Apache drew the Dutch Reformed Church, a sect that had few if any members in Arizona. Wrote Ogle: "The church was handicapped from the start, due to the few frontiersmen among its converts . . . church officials fully agreed . . . that an agent's religious views had little to do with his ability to manage savage and erratic Indians, but the officials also knew that their organization would be held accountable for their appointees' moral conduct. They were therefore compelled to appoint eastern men. . . ."

That comprised only half the picture. Congress decided, much to the delight of the Indian Ring members in Washington and Arizona, that full civilian control of reservations should be reestablished as rapidly as possible. The gates were thrown open to the wolves. Under the guise of simplifying Indian management, it was decreed that each agency would purchase what supplies were needed, and report directly to the Indian Bureau. The President was empowered to appoint five Indian inspectors who were to audit each agency at least twice a year. These regulations in effect directed each thief operating in the field to inform the fountainhead of corruption how much he had been able to steal. The corrupters of the Interior Department, including Secretary Delano, were not taking chances on being cheated out of their shares.

"As soon as the Indians became settled on the different reservations," wrote Crook, "the Indian agents who had sought cover before, now came out as brave as sheep, and took charge of the agencies, and commenced their game of plundering." Conspiring with them were the contractors and suppliers holding contracts with the Indian Bureau.

Crook charged that Dr. Herman Bendell, for only a short time superintendent of Indian Affairs in Arizona, "carried off some $50,000 for his share of the spoils."

Bendell, a medical doctor from Albany, New York, according to Crook's report, sent a cohort to serve as agent at Beale's Spring. The Indians on the reservation there were soon "complaining of not getting sufficient to eat." He directed a Captain Byrne to make an investigation, and Byrne "stationed himself with witnesses where they could see the issues made . . . and had the Indians bring to him what had been issued to them. He had these articles weighed; and, for instance, an Indian family that was entitled to ninety-five pounds of beef only received fifteen."

Captain Byrne took charge of the rationing, and only in time to prevent a serious Indian outbreak. The Indian superintendent promptly filed a complaint charging "usurpation of the prerogatives of the Interior Department, and high-handed acts on the part of the military." A court of inquiry was ordered, and it was found that the Indian agent "had sent wagon loads of Indian food to the mines, and sold them, and among the many other little dodges practiced . . . was to change the pea on the scales, so that a beef that would weigh three hundred pounds was made to weigh thirteen hundred pounds."

George H. Stevens had been appointed agent at Camp Grant by General Howard. He was competent, honest, and sincere. There were few complaints from the Indians under his management. He effectively thwarted the machinations of the local Indian Ring thieves. And that was his undoing. A letter scurrilously attacking Howard, bearing Stevens's signature, was received in the Indian Bureau. Before it was discovered that the letter was a forgery, Stevens was dismissed. Howard was instrumental in having Charles F. Larrabee, a Maine Quaker recently mustered out of the army, assigned to replace him.

Living in Maine, Larrabee would need several weeks to place his affairs in order and travel to San Carlos by a roundabout route to San Francisco, Los Angeles, and Tucson. The Indian Ring was quick to seize on the opportunity to have one of their members named as interim agent. Oddly enough the man they chose was also a medical doctor, R. A. Wilbur of Tucson. For several years Dr. Wilbur had been supplementing his income as a physician by working with unscrupulous contractors to defraud the government. His capabilities as a crook far surpassed his surgical talents.

Orders came from Washington to remove all Indians from Camp Grant to the San Carlos Reservation. Crook sent troops to assist Wilbur, and some fifteen hundred Apache were transferred without incident. There serious troubles arose. The most turbulent spirits of all the Apache who had survived Crook's campaign were now thrown together. Conflicts for leadership began. Two major factions soon evolved, one led by Eskiminzin and Chiquito, the other by Chunz, Cochinay, and Ba-coon—all desperados, and all die-hards who had never accepted in their hearts the peace that had been forced upon them. Violence frequently occurred. Chiquito's favorite wife was sexually attacked by a Chunz partisan. Heads were smashed. One of Chunz's followers shot and killed a warrior of Eskiminzin's band. Moreover, although they were fighting each other, all the leaders threatened to break out if two companies of cavalry stationed on the reservation were not removed.

Larrabee arrived to face this explosive situation. Angered at being relieved, and thus being deprived of the authority to purchase reservation supplies to the advantage of himself and the contractors with whom he had been conspiring to cheat the Indians, Dr. Wilbur fomented opposition against Larrabee in the hope he would be killed or forced to leave. In either case, Dr. Wilbur felt that he would be reappointed, at least for another interim term, to the lucrative post.

Larrabee was not easily intimidated, but he did not deceive himself as to the perilousness of his position. Nevertheless, he attempted to carry on. He held conferences with the warring leaders with their rifles pointed at him. He increased rations. He persuaded them to begin work on an irrigation canal which would permit the development of new farmlands. He refused to accept beef "on the hoof," demanding that it be delivered to the agency in dressed form that could be easily weighed. This halted the overcharging so profitable to Dr. Wilbur and his gang of swindlers.

Dr. Wilbur persisted in his nefarious activities behind the scenes. Realizing that an uprising was in the making, Larrabee requested that a company of cavalry be stationed at the agency. The arrival of these troops undoubtedly prevented a general stampede from the reservation, but they in no way curtailed the vicious scheming of Dr. Wilbur.

While rations were being issued on an early summer day, Larrabee narrowly escaped being assassinated by an outlaw of Cochinay's band. In the melee which followed, Lieutenant Jacob Almy, commanding the cavalry at the agency, was brutally murdered. Larrabee at once placed the reservation under full military control. A few days later he concluded that his influence had been completely destroyed by the plotting of the Indian Ring. He submitted his resignation with a recommendation that an experienced frontier officer be appointed agent.

An employee of the beef contractor, Elijah S. Junior,* would confess that Dr. Wilbur had "used his influence with the Indians by false

---

*His surname was Junior.

representations . . . to have all the white people at San Carlos massacred after his departure" from the agency.

The San Carlos Reservation, Captain W. H. Brown informed Crook, long "has been rotten to the core. The Indians have been tampered with, the agents have been rascals and knaves, the interpreters have been liars and thieves."

Crook ordered Brown to inaugurate a "firm and decided policy . . . impartial justice to all who do well, the olive branch to all who desire to be at peace, but certain punishment to the wrongdoers. . . . Let no Indian profit by his own misdeed, but let it be unprofitable to the last degree to the willfully persistent lawbreaker."

Brown soon convinced the San Carlos Apache that he would deal justly with them, that they would receive the rations promised, and that he would tolerate no disorders. Many Indians demonstrated a willingness to work, build homes for themselves, and develop farms. Breeding cattle were brought in, and they showed a sincere desire to build up profitable herds. Their industry, he declared, only needed proper direction to make it permanently beneficial to them. The great majority were eager to cooperate to improve their economy.

Progress and peace might well have continued at San Carlos had the Indian Bureau been content to allow the reservation to remain under military authorities. With army personnel in charge of supplies and rationing, the nefarious activities of the Indian Ring had been all but halted at one of the most lucrative sites in the Southwest. Before Brown had taken charge the swindlers had been paid for rationing more than three hundred Indians than there were on the reservation.

In its first step toward regaining control, the Indian Bureau transferred James E. Roberts, a Dutch Reformed Church appointee, from Fort Apache to San Carlos. Roberts, a man of unquestionable integrity, was to serve only until the Bureau found a way to replace him with a man who would be more amenable to cooperating with the organized thieves. But Crook refused to be taken in by this scheme, and retained full command of the agency.

Brown was replaced by Major George M. Randall, who had been highly successful in the campaign against the hostile bands. Randall inflicted disciplinary measures far more stringent than those maintained by Brown, and he soon had serious trouble on his hands.

Meanwhile, dangerous developments were taking place at other reservations. Reports came in that renegades from Camp Verde, Tularosa, and the Mescalero Country were joining the Chiricahua in the southern part of the territory and placing themselves under the leadership of Cochise. Conditions at Verde were especially bad. There Delshay was living on a rancheria several miles from the post, and malcontents were rallying about him. Lieutenant Walter S. Schuyler notified Crook that he feared an outbreak was imminent. "By all means arrest Delche [*sic*] and send him with a strong guard to Camp Verde," Crook replied. It was too late. Delshay and a strong band of warriors had vanished into the wilderness.[24]

1874

On the first day of the New Year, Major Randall arrested Eskiminzin on charges his followers felt were unfair, and they threatened reprisals. Randall refused to yield. Eskiminzin was in the guardhouse only three days before he escaped. He fled into the mountains with a number of the most desperate warriors. Seven other strong bands soon vanished. Several of them were led by men who had contested Eskiminzin's bid for leadership at Camp Grant and San Carlos. They broke out not so much to show their sympathy for him as to demonstrate their resentment of Randall's stern discipline.

Crook now faced the situation of having five of the most powerful and dangerous Apache leaders once more loose in the mountain wilderness—Eskiminzin, Delshay, Chunz, Cochinay, and Chan-deisi. With them were several hundred renegade warriors.

Crook prepared to renew the war which he so optimistically nearly a year earlier had declared was virtually ended. Reports of Apache raids soon began to come in. Teamsters were killed, their goods stolen. Herders and farmers were shot down in their fields. Several settlers were murdered in their San Pedro Valley homes. Thefts of livestock occurred over a large area.

Crook organized columns to track down the hostiles and "take no prisoners." Fortunately for the Apache renegades the weather turned against him. The bitter cold and snow forced one large group to return to San Carlos while Crook was there and plead to be forgiven.

"I refused to accept their surrender," wrote Crook, "but told them I could not harm them, as they had thrown themselves on my mercy, but I would drive them all back into the mountains, where I could kill them all, that they had lied to me once, and I didn't know but what they were lying to me now. They begged to be allowed to remain, making all kinds of promises for the future. I finally compromised by letting them stay, provided they would bring in the heads of certain of their ringleaders, which they agreed to."

Two days later several of the Indians appeared before Crook's headquarters with a heavy grain sack. When they raised it, seven bloody heads rolled out. Crook could not be certain just whom the heads had belonged to, but as they were without question the heads of Indians, he indicated he was satisfied that the agreement had been fulfilled.

Believing the system might prove to be effective, Crook made a similar offer to some Tonto who also were suing for peace. To escape punishment for breaking out, they were to bring in Delshay's head. He was startled to discover that Delshay apparently had two heads, for "when I visited the Verde reservation they would convince me they had brought in his head; and when I went to San Carlos they would convince me they had brought in his head. Being satisfied that both parties were earnest in their beliefs, and the bringing in of an extra head was not amiss, I paid both parties."

The head brought into San Carlos was Delshay's. It was identified by scouts who knew him well. He had been killed by warriors sent to hunt him under the leadership of a prominent Apache named Des-a-lin.

Extraordinary snows and then rains delayed Crook's second offensive. The weather prevailing after the outbreak and continuing for weeks he described as "the most inclement and rigorous ever experienced in Arizona since the American occupation. The whole country was flooded and streams ordinarily attenuated brooks, changed into swollen torrents impassable by troops . . . our pack trains could not advance one step."

When the rampaging elements subsided, fast-moving columns of cavalry, Apache scouts, and mule pack trains moved into the Tonto Basin, the Superstition Mountains, the Pinal Range, and other wilderness areas. The efficiency and deadliness of the operation was soon made apparent.

Major Randall's command killed twelve renegade Apache in the Pinal Creek area, and took twenty-five prisoners. Troopers and scouts led by Lieutenant Alfred B. Bache, operating in the same area, had even greater luck, killing thirty-one and capturing fifty of the enemy.

Lieutenant Ben Reilly's cavalry, after a severe fight, captured an Apache rancheria, killing seventeen warriors and taking a large number of women and children prisoners.

Eighty-three hostiles fell before the guns of soldiers and scouts commanded respectively by Lieutenant Schuyler and Al Sieber in the region of the Arivaipa Mountains. They delivered twenty-six captives to Fort Verde.

Yet, in all the skirmishes and battles that took place, not one of the leaders Crook wanted the most—Chunz, Cochinay, Eskiminzin, and Chan-deisi—had been killed or captured.

"These Indians," he would report to the War Department, "were so encamped with their followers that in almost every case of attack by the troops and allies who were constantly in pursuit, the blow fell upon the followers and the leaders got away, until these followers began to see that they were the great sufferers, after which desertions to our side became more numerous, and it was through these desertions that we were finally enabled to get the ringleaders."

Cochinay made the mistake of attempting to attack ranches within a few miles of Tucson. Apache scouts were waiting for him. They brought his head into San Carlos.

Chunz had only six loyal warriors left when Apache scouts led by Des-a-lin, whose men had killed Delshay, trapped him in the Santa Catalina Mountains, only fifteen miles from Tucson. The heads of the seven desperate fugitives were taken to San Carlos and displayed on the parade ground.

Lieutenant John B. Babcock notified headquarters that troops had succeeded at last in running down Chan-deisi. His head adorned a post at Fort Apache.

Eskiminzin in despair brought the remnants of his hungry, terrorized band into San Carlos.

Crook's second major campaign was no less a victory than his first one. Indeed, in one respect, the western press, undoubtedly catering to views prevailing among readers, considered it an even greater success, for many of the most dangerous renegade Apache had been slain. Once more Crook—whom the Apache called Gray Fox—was hailed as a hero and a brilliant soldier from coast to coast.

Within a few weeks after the hostilities had ended, the Interior Department and the Bureau of Indian Affairs, with the enthusiastic support of the swindlers of the Indian Ring, reopened with renewed vigor the conflict with the military for civilian control of the agencies. A new scheme, urged by Tucson contractors who envisioned in it new opportunities to defraud the government, was approved by Indian Bureau officials. It was to concentrate all Apache at San Carlos.

* * *

For two years only persons in his confidence had known that Cochise was suffering from a mysterious organic affliction. Often he had been in great pain, and had found it difficult to find food he could assimilate.

Now the famous leader was stricken, and he summoned his old and trusted friend, Agent Thomas Jeffords, to his bedside. For some time they talked, reminiscing of their days together in the rugged Chiricahua Country which Cochise had struggled fiercely to hold for his people. At last Jeffords announced that he would go to Fort Bowie for an army doctor.

"Do you think you will see me alive again?" Cochise said.

"No, I don't think so," said Jeffords.

Cochise's eyes were glazed by his illness as he said: "I think I will die about ten o'clock tomorrow morning. Do you think we will meet again?"

Jeffords stared at him, somewhat taken aback by the question.

Then he said: "I don't know. What do you think about it?"

"I don't know, either," Cochise said. "It is not clear in my mind
. . . but I think we will . . . somewhere up there."

Jeffords left on horseback for Fort Bowie.

Cochise died at ten o'clock the next morning.

* * *

August

Nothing but the campaigns of General Crook had brought greater
changes in Apache affairs than the arrival at San Carlos of a young man
named John Philip Clum.

Twenty-three years of age, he had been a meteorologist with the
Signal Corps in New Mexico. Appointed Indian agent on the recommendation of the Dutch Reformed Church—of which he was a member
—he quickly became embroiled in a bitter, and often ludicrous, conflict
with the military.

Ogle wrote of him that in addition "to superior education and frontier experience, he possessed extraordinary energy and tenacity of
purpose." Thrapp pulls out more stops in describing him as ". . . physically short though agile and strong, he was presumptuous, belligerent, cocky, and cantankerous and apparently had an ingrained contempt for officers and the military in general. . . . But Clum also was
intelligent, thoroughly honest, able, willing to assume authority and
responsibility alike, and utterly fearless."

Clum thought his orders entitled him to assume absolute control of
the agency. The officer in command, Major John B. Babcock, refused
to give way to him, and asked Crook for instructions. Crook ordered
Babcock to disregard Clum's "wishes if they became an impediment
to the safety of the reservation." Clum appealed to Washington with
the result that the military was instructed to work in harmony with him.
Clum interpreted the word "harmony" to mean that he had been
accorded control of all affairs, and he proceeded on that basis.

His success in dealing with the Apache was nothing short of remarkable. His approach to the vexatious problems was unique. His first step
was to demonstrate to his charges, among whom were some of the
wildest and most dangerous men in captivity, that he trusted them, was
sympathetic to their needs, that he was not there to punish or discipline them but to help them. He formed a civil government, allowing
them to select their leaders. He organized a police force, not only for
the purpose of maintaining order on the reservation but to pursue and
capture any renegades who might attempt to interfere with the smooth
functioning of reservation affairs or to foment dissatisfaction among
peaceful Indians.

Clum created a court in which lawbreakers were tried by Apache judges. The faith and trust which the Apache had in him was never better demonstrated than by their agreement to surrender all their arms and halt the making of *tiswin,* the liquor that had brought so much tragedy in the past. If a reliable warrior wanted to go hunting, he was permitted to draw a rifle which he could use only for a specified time. If a man succumbed to temptation, or to his thirst, and made a bit of *tiswin,* his crude still was promptly smashed by the police, on occasion by Clum himself, and the miscreant was sentenced to serve a term in the agency hoosegow.

Clum launched a building program from which, to their fury, all civilian contractors were excluded. He requested an appropriation of five thousand dollars for the work, and received twelve thousand dollars. Only Apache workers were employed. They were happy to receive as wages the munificent sum of fifty cents a day. He launched an extensive farm program, and found the Apache eager to labor unstintingly and long hours to make it a success. He maintained rigid supervision of the rationing system, keeping careful accounts. No one was cheated. He checked the vouchers of contractors, made certain that goods and foodstuffs charged to the agency were delivered.

Much to the displeasure of the military, the San Carlos Apache leaders let it be known that they were willing to fight for Clum. One of them was Eskiminzin, who was held in chains when Clum arrived. Clum freed him. The two became fast friends, and the notorious outlaw chief was one of his most trustworthy aides.

Clum was unwavering in his conviction that most Apache problems emanated from "a deadly mixture of civil and military control." He maintained that the Apache were an intelligent, energetic people, eager to better themselves, and fully able to achieve self-government under just and sensible procedures. They would, he declared, never respond nor progress satisfactorily wherever the administration of their affairs and the handling of their problems was divided between officers and civilian agents. Under such circumstances only chaos could result.

Conditions at the Fort Apache Reservation provided strong support for his theory. There, as Thrapp succinctly summarizes the situation, ". . . a typical dispute between the military, represented by Major Frederick D. Ogilby, and the Indian service, represented by Agent James E. Roberts, had resulted in the military's forcibly occupying the agency buildings and taking over management of the place. The trouble apparently was no one's fault. Several severe epidemics had ravaged tribesmen, and the survivors turned to *tiswin* drunks to relieve their distress and fears. Disorders resulted, including slayings and even depredations upon whites. Ogilby felt that Roberts could not control the situation; Roberts believed the military was usurping his authority. . . . Bickerings between the factions reached a new high, or low, as each sought to gain some advantage."

Agent Roberts telegraphed Washington for instructions, and then went to San Carlos to consult Clum. Orders came to Clum from the Indian Bureau to take charge of Fort Apache. With Roberts he went there. Ogilby had placed an army doctor in charge of the agency. According to Thrapp, "Clum arrested him for opening Roberts's mail. Clum ordered a count of the Indians. . . . Ogilby threatened to attack those who responded to Clum's demand. Clum rode his horse over to confer with the beef contractor at the fort, and the officer of the day tried to arrest him for riding too fast on the parade ground. Clum insisted that all Indians should be under his control, so Ogilby released all guardhouse prisoners, including two murderers Clum wanted held."

Caught in the middle of this puerile wrangling were the Apaches of the reservation. Clum concluded that nothing could be gained by continuing it, and set out for Washington. He returned with orders which the military could not ignore. They were to move the Indians at Fort Apache—White Mountain and Coyotero bands—to San Carlos. Some of the Fort Apache Indians refused to move, but most of them agreed to leave, and they were escorted to San Carlos, and assigned to locations Clum had reserved for them.

Clum now had some 4,300 Apache under his charge. An Indian Bureau inspector visiting San Carlos was highly impressed "with the happiness and satisfaction noticeable among all the bands." Their general health was good. They had been vaccinated against smallpox. Clum had won them to programs in personal hygiene and to improved sanitary conditions, supplying them with ample quantities of strong soap. The birthrate, he reported, was steadily increasing.

1875

General Crook was transferred to command the Department of the Platte, and fight the Sioux on the northern Great Plains.

He departed from Arizona with a strong protest against the "unwise policy of concentrating all Apache at San Carlos." The Apache, he said, were not a united people. The many independent bands had only one thing in common, and that was an inherent hatred of the white man. Moreover, each group was deeply attached to the homeland it had known for centuries, and should be permitted to reside in it to the greatest extent possible. Of course, exceptions had to be made, for there were Apache who were thoroughly bad people, who would never fully capitulate and take the white man's road. These should be singled out and dealt with as the situation demanded. Even if that were done successfully, the concentration program would throw together bands which were distrustful of each other, and there would arise internal conflicts that would lead to fights and outbreaks. Herding all Apache together would dangerously disrupt the progress and peace that had been achieved. The concentration policy would lay the foundation for a renewal of warfare that might endure for years before it could be halted.

The year would not be ended before the wisdom of Crook's words would be made tragically apparent.

But the chances of his advice being accepted were virtually nil. The Indian Ring politicians and grafters dominated the Washington scene. Concentration meant money and greater opportunities to steal on a large scale. The Tucson contractors were especially anxious to have the Apache crowded into San Carlos, for they would gain the advantage of having large numbers of New Mexico Indians, and others from various remote regions of Arizona Territory, brought within the boundaries of their own realm of operations.

Crook's successor was General August V. Kautz, a man of little imagination, perhaps less ingenuity, and a deadly opponent of the Indian Bureau. He raised innumerable roadblocks to disrupt the progress of Clum's programs of agrarian and civil reform. He maintained that Clum's plans could never succeed without military assistance, and that a large new military post would have to be built and supported at great expense at San Carlos to assure control of the various bands. It was his pronounced belief—and in this he naturally received support from his superiors—that the Indian Bureau should be transferred to the War Department "so the purer service of the military could eliminate the graft of the civil officers."

Clum had no ulterior motives in fighting for civilian control. He sincerely believed that he, and he alone, could guarantee peace and hold the Apaches in line. He wanted all of them under his jurisdiction. His Indian policy, he maintained, was the only force needed to keep order.

Clum might well have been successful, but the Indian Bureau politicians and the military took steps to bring about his failure.

An example of their machinations will suffice, but numerous similar situations were created. Several hundred Indians remained at Fort Apache, and Clum was ordered to move them to San Carlos. When he went to Fort Apache he discovered a new agent stationed there in the person of a phony colonel named W. E. Morford, a political appointee from New York. Morford refused to permit the Indians to be transferred. Rufus Ingalls, quartermaster-general of the army, interceded on Morford's behalf in Washington and apparently received White House support. "Turn over the Camp Apache Indians to Agent Morford," Indian Commissioner E. P. Smith wired Clum. "There is no other way for the present."

Morford charged Clum with deceit and falsity, and the military seized the opportunity to aid him in the fracas, hoping, as Ogle points out, "thereby to undo Clum's work by preventing the completion of the removal plans. They advanced arguments to show that Clum's success was merely the fruition of their own early efforts. . . ." Morford, pretending to agree to transfer the Apache to San Carlos, asked for help from the military with the false contention that they would leave in peace. He knew before making the request that Kautz would refuse to furnish the troops.

It was soon revealed that Morford was resisting removal so that he might conspire with dishonest contractors, that his son would have a job as chief clerk at Fort Apache, and his daughter would be appointed head reservation schoolteacher. Morford was quietly transferred to the Colorado River Reservation among the Yuma and other tribes. By order of the President the Fort Apache agency was abolished. However, not all the Indians in the Fort Apache region were removed.

The confusion created by the designs and the pigheadedness of the unholy triangle—the Indian Bureau, the military, and the crooks— continued without abatement.

But "peace and good-fellowship" prevailed at San Carlos. The Indians were industrious, and many of them were clamoring to be awarded farmlands they could "truly call their own." There were few arrests. Clum came in for some reprimands for expending funds without proper authorization, but the discrepancies were satisfactorily adjusted without serious reflection on him. Even the swindler's best friend, the Arizona *Citizen,* was obliged to admit that "nearly all visitors and travellers to San Carlos report the law and order of the reservation fully equal to that found in any civilized community on the frontier." Undoubtedly this was especially true of Tucson.

But as the year ended ominous clouds were gathering on the southern horizon.

1876

FEBRUARY

Angered by the unfounded accusations brought against him and the continuing attacks on his character, Clum submitted his resignation. Commissioner Smith accepted it, but changed his mind when an outbreak of the Chiricahua occurred, and he persuaded Clum to remain at least until the serious developments in southern Arizona had been settled.

If his methods were unorthodox and some of his activities were questionable, Agent Thomas Jeffords had done a remarkable job among the Chiricahua. No one knew them better, and no white man was more trusted by them. However, since the death of Cochise his task had grown steadily more difficult. Cochise had not broken the promise he had made to General Howard to live "in peace in Arizona," but the great chief's son, Taza, who had succeeded him, was neither as influential nor as trustworthy as his father. Taza was not a strong nor a capable leader.

Jeffords operated his agency at Pinnery Creek in a haphazard manner. He made no attempt to disarm the Chiricahua, and they were permitted to roam on their horses as they wished. It was his contention that "too large doses of civilization and unnecessary discipline" would make them suspicious and restless and cause them to leave, with the result that the border frontier would be bathed in blood. His counts were irregular, and often widely separated. He issued rations with little system, for he claimed that he and his clerk knew every face and the number in each family. An Indian Bureau inspector, E. C. Kemble, reported that Jeffords dealt out rations "with a rapidity and a power of ready reckoning that surpassed the lightning calculator," but he did not recommend that Jeffords be required to abolish his loose methods. Jeffords, the inspector felt, knew what he was doing, and, indeed, Jeffords did.

Reports began to come in that depredations on a large scale were being committed along the international border and south of it in Sonora. Stolen horses, mules, and cattle were tracked to the Chiricahua Reservation and the vast wilderness surrounding it. Jeffords was extraordinarily successful in recovering a large number of the animals. Investigations carried out by himself and others showed that in the great majority of cases the raids had not been made by Chiricahua in his charge, but by other bands and by Indians who made their homes in Mexico. He did not deny, however, that there were a few Chiricahua on the reservation whom he could not control.

Jeffords's chief troubles stemmed from two sources: Indian visitors and unscrupulous white men.

The Chiricahua Reservation was becoming a refuge for outlaw Apache from both south and north of the border. Renegades from the Mescalero Country east of the Rio Grande, from the White Mountains, from San Carlos, from the Warm Springs reserve, and from other places, visited among the Chiricahua to recover from the strains of their rampages. As many as two hundred of these untamed and untamable spirits might be present at one time, causing dissension and making trouble. Jeffords tried to feed them and induce them to abandon their wild life, but sufficient supplies were not always available. When some desk bureaucrat in Washington, who most likely had never been out of sight of the Potomac, decided that Jeffords's beef allotment should be halved, the agent not only could not feed visitors but he was forced to tell the Chiricahua that they would have to supplement their meager rations by hunting. Thus the Chiricahua were obliged to travel far beyond the confines of their reservation to obtain the necessary game. Many of them were, therefore, absent for long periods, their whereabouts unknown to Jeffords. Complaints began to come in indicating that the hunters were not always particular as to their prey. Cattle and sheep disappeared, presumably ending up over Chiricahua cooking fires.

MARCH

With their freedom almost totally unrestricted, and Jeffords's control reduced virtually to the point of ineffectiveness, the inherent independence and individualism that characterized all Apache began increasingly to assert itself among the wandering Chiricahua. Taza's authority, never very great, decreased even more, and bands began to overrule the decisions of other leaders they had obeyed on the reservation. Dissension developed into violence, and in one fight three warriors were killed. Some Chiricahua, fearing reprisals from troops, returned to the agency. Taza was among them. A group led by a chief named Skinya disappeared into the Dragoon Mountains. One or two other bands set out on raids into Mexico. In addition to livestock and various goods, they brought back a considerable amount of gold dust and silver pesos.

APRIL

There were two main outlets in the reservation area through which the Chiricahua raiders could dispose of their plunder. One was an isolated stage station in which two white men, remembered only as Rogers and Spence, were employed. They operated a still, and bartered rotgut whiskey at ten dollars a bottle to the Apache for stolen goods. Travelers along the main east-west road were seldom molested —most of the Chiricahua still keeping Cochise's promise—but raiders soon discovered that travelers willingly exchanged whiskey, weapons, and ammunition for stolen horses and mules.

One of the most dangerous and unruly Chiricahua was Pionsenay, a brother of the rebellious Skinya. In a drunken fight he killed two of his sisters. He and several of his followers next killed Rogers and Spence at the stage station, stole their store of liquor, guns, and ammunition, then made a series of raids in the San Pedro Valley, murdering two prominent ranchers. Troops guided by Jeffords pursued the outlaws into the Dragoon Mountains, engaged in a running fight with them, but were unable to capture or kill any of them.

Jeffords was correct in maintaining that only a relatively few Chiricahua were committing the outrages, and that the great majority of them were frightened by the disorders and were living in peace. The explanation was not acceptable to either Governor Safford or the Arizona press.

"The kind of war needed for the Chiricahua Apaches," trumpeted the Arizona *Citizen*, "is steady, unrelenting, hopeless, and undiscriminating war, slaying men, women, and children . . . until every valley . . . shall send to high heaven the grateful incense of festering and rotting Chiricahuas."

The governor telegraphed a demand to Washington that the Chiricahua Reservation be abandoned and that they be moved to San Carlos. He expressed the belief that only one man, Agent Clum, "has the nerve, ability, and confidence" to accomplish the task.

Jeffords reported that he could stop the illicit traffic on the transcontinental road if he were permitted to move his agency to Apache Pass. After some delay his request was granted. His Indian police succeeded in halting the raiders from obtaining whiskey from travelers for stolen animals.

Jeffords continued to maintain that the great majority of Chiricahua were happy, contented, and loved their reservation homeland, where they had resided for centuries. To punish all of them for the irrational acts of a few would be a gross miscarriage of justice. Eventually, he declared, the renegades would be either killed or imprisoned, and it would be inhuman to disrupt the progress that had been achieved toward permanent peace. Send adequate rations, tools, supplies, and other goods, and the Chiricahua would move forward steadily toward civilization with a stable economy.

He was pleading in vain. The politicians, sensitive to the shouts for blood of the southwestern newspapers, and the cries of the greedy territorial government and Arizona citizenry that the Chiricahua were occupying valuable land that should be given to white settlers, closed their ears to the advice of the man who knew more about the Chiricahua and the entire problem than anyone else.

MAY

Early in this month the Bureau of Indian Affairs—no doubt with the sanction of the administration—made one of the greatest mistakes in its history.

Clum was instructed by telegraph to suspend Jeffords from duty, and "if practicable" move the Chiricahua to San Carlos, where they would be under his control.

* * *

It was this telegraphed order that would launch a war in which the inhabitants of Arizona would get blood they demanded, but not all of that shed would be Indian blood. Far from it. The larger part would be the blood of soldiers, ranchers, freighters, herders, travelers, emigrants, and residents of settlements in Arizona, New Mexico, and Mexico.

Out of the terrible conflict would come great new Apache leaders—Juh, Nolgee, Pionsenay, Geronimo, Victorio, and others—daring, dangerous, desperate, cruel, unyielding, powerful, influential men whose command was law.

They were the outstanding patriots of their ancient people, far superior as military strategists to their counterparts of past centuries. With only a few hundred loyal warriors they would outwit, outmaneuver, and for the most part outfight thousands of troops for nearly ten years. They would be beaten, but rarely on the field of battle. They would be victims at last of promises broken, of the deceit and trickery and criminal frauds perpetrated by immoral, unconscionable, corrupt officials of the United States Government.

* * *

JUNE

Clum had refused to undertake to remove the Chiricahua until he was assured that troops would come to his assistance in case of trouble. The War Department balked, but the White House ordered the Secretary of War to assign troops to the duty. General Kautz then moved into the Chiricahua Country with twelve companies of cavalry and two companies of Indian scouts.

With this strong military force in the vicinity, Clum went to the Chiricahua Agency, accompanied by fifty-four of his San Carlos policemen, and talked with several leaders. At their request he granted them time to hold a council to deliberate on the matter. In the meeting, which was attended by several hundred Indians, Skinya and Pionsenay urged that they refuse to move and take to the warpath. Taza and his brother, Nachee, advocated that they capitulate and go to San Carlos in peace.

The meeting itself was anything but peaceful. With the factions deadlocked, a fight broke out. Skinya and six of his supporters were killed. Pionsenay was badly wounded.

Now Geronimo, Juh, and Nolgee informed Clum that they also would take their bands to San Carlos with those of Taza, Nachee, and the others. Clum gave them three days to assemble their people. All Geronimo, Juh, and Nolgee wanted was sufficient time to escape. When last heard of, they and all their followers had vanished into the fastnesses of the Sierra Madre in Mexico, safely avoiding a strong force of cavalry which had attempted to stop them from crossing the border.

Of the three hundred and twenty-five Chiricahua Clum succeeded in moving to San Carlos, two hundred and sixty-five were women and children, and only sixty were men, many of them in advanced years. A man who could not easily admit failure, he would write that the "terrible shade of the Chiricahua's dreaded name had passed away. . . ." This, of course, was sheer poppycock.

The truth was that less than a third of the tribe had been transferred to San Carlos, and two thirds had been driven into hiding in the immense wilderness on both sides of the international border. Taza and Nolgee were the only prominent leaders under confinement. The home of the Chiricahua, which the government had assured them would be permanently theirs, had been destroyed. They had no home.

General Kautz was ordered to maintain strong patrols in the region of the former Chiricahua Reservation and to kill or capture "as hostile Indians" any Chiricahua found on it.

JULY

No depredations had occurred in southern Arizona for a month. Now the refugee bands began to strike. Two miners were slain near Bowie. Twenty other white persons were killed in raids on ranches north of the border. Kautz's twelve companies of cavalry failed to apprehend a single murderer. Troops in the Department of New Mexico, commanded by General Edward Hatch, were more successful. They trailed marauders into the Florida Mountains and killed twenty of them.

The Arizona newspapers railed against Kautz, accusing him of negligence and inactivity. The governor called upon the Secretary of War for five hundred guns, and threatened to call out the Arizona militia. Stung by the criticism, Kautz dispatched a strong patrol under Captain T. C. Tupper to track down the renegades. Tupper found numerous trails but no quarry. After a lengthy ride through much of southern Arizona he reported that it was "the safest country against Indians that he had ever scouted through."

Kautz promptly attributed the depredations and killings which had occurred to white outlaws, and charged that "prominent Arizonians exaggerated the disorders so more soldiers would be sent to the region to bolster its economy." This attitude, needless to say, did nothing to improve his image in the eyes of territorial officials or the press.

Lieutenant J. A. Rucker, with a contingent of fifty cavalry and thirty

Indian scouts, pursued a renegade band for more than two hundred miles, and at last succeeded in making a surprise attack on their camp. Ten warriors were slain, and forty-six horses and a large quantity of supplies which had been taken from the Chiricahua Agency were recovered. Rucker reported that the country through which he had passed was "overrun with hostiles."

On the basis of this information, Kautz expressed the belief that the rampaging Chiricahua were being joined by renegades from the Hot Springs Reservation of New Mexico. Although true, this was hardly a relevant factor at the moment. Wherever they came from, the raiders were growing bolder, and their devastations were increasing as the year drew to a close.

* * *

The removal—rather, the partial removal—of the Chiricahua was not only a complete breach of faith on the part of the government, but destroyed the last bit of hope in those who had sincerely tried to live in peace and made outlaws out of the other members of the tribe.

An Arizona historian, Lockwood, would write:

"The removal of the Chiricahua Apaches from their reservation was the crowning folly of the Indian Bureau. Not only did the Chiricahua dislike the region of San Carlos; not only was it already overpopulous with tribes averse, or even hostile to each other, held there against their will; but the Chiricahua were keenly aware of the fact that their own reservation had been taken away from them, not because of the disloyalty of the Chiricahua as a people, but as a result of the misdeeds of a small, violent faction arising directly from the wicked greed of a white man placed in their midst."

Jeffords could hardly be described as the soul of honor, but the charges of malfeasance brought against him were undeserved. He was bonded for fifty thousand dollars, and if he had been a notorious swindler—as he was accused of being—his sponsors hardly would have imperiled their own fortunes to such an extent. When his agency accounts were audited, after his suspension, only minor discrepancies were revealed, and his bondsmen were released without penalty.

* * *

1877

FEBRUARY

Fifteen white persons were killed and more than a hundred horses were stolen by Indians near the little settlement of Sonoita. Troops pursued the raiders, but some of them disappeared into Mexico, while others escaped in the vicinity of the Warm Springs Reservation.

MARCH

Governor Safford took pen in hand to write a scathing indictment of Kautz for the readers of the Arizona *Citizen*, charging that if the general were permitted to continue his inept methods, twenty years and the entire United States Army would be needed to halt the depredations. The general now disclosed his conviction that the governor was in league with Tucson contractors who wanted more troops to feed and more posts to supply.

The Territorial Legislature supported the governor by appropriating ten thousand dollars to be spent in organizing and equipping a company of friendly Indian scouts to pursue and kill hostiles. White men who would join such a perilous undertaking were extremely difficult to find. The scouts were recruited and placed in command of Clay Beauford, chief of the Indian police at San Carlos. They were in the field for several weeks, but accomplished nothing. The ten thousand dollars was wasted.

Large numbers of the Mescalero had fled to Mexico, others had gone to the Warm Springs Reservation, and some were wandering in the country of the Gila Apache. These flights had been caused not so much by rebellious spirit as by persecution by white men. Those who remained in the Mescalero Country were hungry and hopeless. Frequently they were driven from their homes and little farms by white ruffians. White cattlemen moved their herds onto the good grass ranges of the Mescalero Reservation. Mescalero crops and livestock were stolen by white raiders. Mexican and American settlers established farms on Mescalero lands. L. G. Murphy, leader of a powerful band of thieves, murderers, and outlaws, controlled the Mescalero Country—the trading, the courts, and the politics. One of his cohorts, J. C. Dolan, held contracts for supplying the Mescalero. The two men were growing rich selling government beef and other commodities on the open market. White bootleggers traded whiskey with impunity for almost anything an Indian had to offer—blankets, grain, horses, cattle, hides, and stolen goods. Occasionally there had been thoroughly honest agents assigned to the Mescalero, but the Murphy faction had successfully blocked their attempts to improve conditions and usually drove them out of the country. Things had run smoothly only when a dishonest agent was in office—which was most of the time. Even the military was thwarted in its efforts to halt white lawlessness. All depredations were attributed to Indians, and Washington chose to believe the swindlers and thugs.

General John Pope was moved to write in a report:

"It is in painful reluctance that the military forces take the field against Indians who only leave their reservations because they are starved there, and who must hunt food for themselves and their families, or see them perish with hunger.

"It is revolting to any humane man to see such things done, and far more so to be required to be the active party to commit violence upon forlorn Indians, who, under the pressure of such necessity, only do what any man would do under like circumstances."

* * *

The Warm Springs Reservation was located at the junction of the Rio Grande and Alamosa Rivers. Established for the Southern Apache in 1874, it had quickly developed into the New Mexico branch of the main Indian Bureau cesspool in Washington.

It had become a haven for many of the wild bands and rebellious individuals—Mimbreno, Gila, Chiricahua, Mescalero, and others. Raiders returned to rest there, and trade their plunder, get drunk on the whiskey always made available to them by agents, contractors, and traders, and enjoy protection while planning their next bloody exploits. Prominent among the renegade leaders who sojourned at Warm Springs were Pionsenay, Gordo, Poncé, Francisco, Victorio, and Geronimo.

Not one to injure the Warm Spring Agency's scandalous reputation, Agent J. M. Shaw reported that he was without sufficient rations to feed both permanent residents and visitors. He had, he informed the Indian Bureau, a surplus of sugar, and he asked permission to exchange it for excess flour and beef in the possession of adjacent military contingents. Suspicious that Shaw was scheming to make a few dollars for himself without sharing them, officials of the Indian Bureau rejected his request on the ground that it was irregular. Shaw was warned that he might be replaced unless he practiced greater economy, and he did not mistake the meaning of the threat.

Indian Commissioner Smith instructed an inspector, E. C. Kemble, to visit Warm Springs and investigate conditions there. As far as the Bureau corrupters were concerned, this was a stupid mistake. Kemble reported:

1. Agent Shaw and suppliers were guilty of outright graft.

2. Rations were being drawn for a thousand more Indians than were receiving them.

3. No ration tickets were issued.

4. No counts were being made of Indians on the reservation.

5. Three times as much hay was being purchased as was needed to feed agency livestock.

6. Government blankets were sold in white settlements along the Rio Grande.

7. Government supplies were traded to merchants for whiskey.

8. No attempts were being made to develop farms.

9. Shaw should be immediately removed.

Three months after Kemble's report had been received, Shaw had been replaced by James Davis. This was a blow to the grafters, for Davis bought only dressed beef, halting the theft of live animals, inaugurated agricultural and irrigation projects, at least attempted to keep an accurate count of Indians, and drew no more rations than were actually required.

However, if the nefarious operations of the Indian Ring had been temporarily disrupted, the depredations of the rebellious elements continued. Davis was no more able to control the renegades than his predecessor, although he made more of an effort.

* * *

Lieutenant Austin Henely, scouting with a contingent of cavalry, telegraphed intelligence that thoroughly alarmed Washington. The Warm Springs region was infested with Apache outlaws. He had located Geronimo and his band near Las Palomas. Geronimo had just returned from a raid with more than a hundred stolen horses "and was very indignant because he could not draw rations for the time he was out."

On the twentieth of this month, J. Q. Smith, who had a short time earlier replaced E. P. Smith as Indian Commissioner, wired Agent Clum at San Carlos: "If practicable, take Indian police and arrest renegade Indians at Southern Apache Agency. Seize stolen horses in their possession. Restore property to rightful owners. Remove renegades to San Carlos and hold them in confinement for murder and robbery."

Clum's first reaction was that he didn't want the duty, which would involve a round-trip horseback ride of eight hundred miles and present extremely dangerous conditions. He sent in his resignation, then without citing his reasons he suddenly changed his mind and announced that he was eager to go "on one of the most important and exciting campaigns I have ever undertaken." General Kautz refused to cooperate with him, giving the excuse that the Indians to be arrested were in the military district of New Mexico.

APRIL

Clum went over Kautz's head in requesting military assistance. From the Department of the Missouri orders were sent to General Edward Hatch, commander in New Mexico, to give all support necessary to Clum. Hatch ordered nine companies of cavalry to unite in the Warm Springs region, and rendezvous with Clum on the twenty-first.

With the veteran frontiersman Beauford as his chief aide, and one hundred and two Indian police, Clum reached a remote part of the reservation on the twentieth. Taking only twenty men of this force with him, he rode to the agency. There he learned that Geronimo was encamped only three miles away with "eighty to a hundred" warriors, and that "from two hundred and fifty to four hundred well-armed, desperate Indians" were in the vicinity. The troops, however, had been delayed and were not expected to arrive for two or three days. Fearing that Geronimo and other wanted leaders might escape if he waited for the cavalry, Clum decided to take immediate action.

Under cover of darkness the remainder of the police were brought into the agency and secreted in a large commissary building. Early in the morning Clum sent a message to Geronimo, requesting him and his important men to come into the agency for a talk. Clum would write:

"They came quickly—a motley clan, painted and equipped for a fight. Supported by a half dozen of my police I took my position on the porch of the main agency building." It was apparent by their sneers and looks of contempt that Geronimo and his men, who had sat down on the ground, thought they could easily defy the agent and overcome the small force visible to them. They were unaware, of course, of the presence of the eighty police concealed in the commissary. The reserves had been "instructed that at a signal from Captain Beauford their sergeant would swing wide the great commissary doors and then race eastward along the south line of the parade ground, and they were to follow hot on his trail at intervals of about two paces—every man with his thumb on his gun."

CLUM: If you listen to my words with good ears no serious harm will be done to you.

GERONIMO: If you speak wisely no serious harm will be done to you.

Clum concluded that in view of this defiant attitude nothing would be accomplished by continuing the conference. He told Beauford to give the signal to the men in hiding. Instantly they burst out of the commissary. The Indians were surrounded.

"I ordered Geronimo to the guardhouse. He did not move. Then I added, 'You must go now.' Like a flash he leaped to his feet. There was a picture I shall never forget. He stood erect as a mountain pine, while every outline of his symmetrical form indicated strength and endurance. His abundant ebony locks draped his ample shoulders, his stern features, his keen, piercing eye, and his proud and graceful posture combined to create in him the model of an Apache war-chief. . . . His eyes blazed fiercely under the excitement of the moment and his form quivered with suppressed rage. From his demeanor it was evident to all that he was hesitating between two purposes, whether to draw his knife . . . and die fighting—or to surrender. . . . Sergeant Rip sprang forward and snatched the knife from Geronimo's belt . . . the muzzles of a half dozen needle guns pointed at him. . . . With flashing eyes he permitted himself to indulge in a single swift, defiant glance at his captors. Then his features relaxed. . . ."

In his own tongue he said that he would surrender.

When the cavalry finally arrived, Clum had shackled in irons Geronimo, Gordo, Poncé, Francisco, and thirteen other prominent and hostile Apache leaders. Pionsenay and Nolgee, it was learned, had left a few days earlier on raids into southern Arizona and Mexico. Clum sent Beauford and seventy-five Indian police to scour the area of the Dos Cabezas Mountains in the hope of intercepting them. They failed.

Meanwhile, the continuance of depredations over a wide area from western Texas to southern Arizona had convinced the Indian Bureau that the concentration policy should be pursued to all possible limits. Clum was preparing to leave Warm Springs when he received new and more drastic orders. Besides the hostile leaders he was to remove all Apache from Warm Springs to San Carlos. The military was instructed to aid him to whatever extent was necessary.

Clum arranged a conference with Victorio and reported that the chief was agreeable to the transfer. The truth was that Victorio understood that resistance on his part would be useless, and undoubtedly result in his own death and the slaying of many of his best fighting men. Better to go quietly to San Carlos, and wait for an opportunity to break out, an opportunity he felt certain would come.

Nearly five hundred Apache were assembled at the Warm Springs Agency. Then a controversy over the military escort began.

General Hatch asked General Kautz to relieve him of the task at the Arizona–New Mexico line. Kautz agreed. Clum, whose contempt for General Kautz was unrestricted, wired him that as he had not requested an escort of Arizona troops, none was wanted and none would be accepted. Kautz informed the War Department of Clum's attitude. General Sherman agreed that it was a "breach of personal and official courtesy," and declared that Clum had no business to refuse the Kautz escort. Clum retorted that General Sherman had no business interfering in his business. This my-father-can-lick-your-father type of childish wrangle was ended when, "more out of compliment than necessity," Clum agreed to accept a small escort of General Hatch's troopers.

M A Y

The long and tiresome trek began on the first day of the month. The shackled leaders were carried in wagons. Most of the others trudged over the desert and mountain trail on foot.

Three weeks later, four hundred and fifty-three ragged, hungry, and hopeless Apache men, women, and children reached the forlorn San Carlos Agency. A number of elderly persons had died on the grueling march. Many were ill. Some were suffering from smallpox and were placed in isolation.

Word was received that more than two hundred Apache were still scattered throughout the Warm Springs Reservation, having escaped Clum's net. Troops were sent to round them up and treat them as hostile, but few were taken, for most of them fled to join wild bands.

* * *

Terming the removal of the Warm Springs Apache a breach of faith on the part of the government and "contrary to the best judgment of Army officers," Lockwood condemned the concentration policy as unwise and ineffectual.

Captain Bourke: "The Warm Springs Apaches were peremptorily deprived of their little fields and driven away from their crops, half-ripened, and ordered to tramp to San Carlos; when the band reached there the fighting men had disappeared, and only decrepit warriors, little boys and girls, and old women remained."

General Orlando B. Willcox (who would succeed Kautz): "It is believed by many that Victorio was unjustly dealt with in the first instance, by the abrupt removal of his people from Ojo Caliente [Warm Springs], New Mexico, to San Carlos; and that such a removal, if not a breach of faith, was a harsh and cruel measure, from which the people of New Mexico have reaped bitter consequences."

General Pope, never an admirer of the Apache: "Victorio and his band have always bitterly objected to be placed at San Carlos, one of the reasons given by him being the hostility of many of the Indians of that agency. He always asserted his willingness to live peaceably with his people at the Warm Springs Agency, and, so far as I am informed, gave no trouble to anyone while there. I do not know the reasons of the Interior Department for insisting upon the removal to San Carlos agency, but certainly they should be cogent to justify the great trouble and severe losses occasioned by the attempts to coerce the removal."

Dunn: "The original source of the trouble was the removal of the Chiricahuas. Two drunken Indians killed two whiskey smugglers, and forthwith the Indians who happened to live on the same reservation, who had no connection with the killings, were ordered to be removed from their homes; fugitives from this reservation took refuge at Ojo Caliente, and forthwith the Indians there, guilty and innocent alike, were ordered to be removed. . . .

"If concentration were beneficial, why were not some of its good effects shown on the tribes that had been concentrated at the cost of life, treasure, and broken faith? It is a perversion of the English language to call such a system a peace policy."

The national concentration policy was beneficial—to the swindlers of the Interior Department and the Indian Bureau. It opened opportunities to steal vast amounts of every type of food and goods paid for by the taxpayers of the nation. It provided a system of concentration camps in which Indians could be neglected until thousands of them had perished of malnutrition, exposure, and disease.

* * *

Clum had no sooner returned from Warm Springs than he and General Kautz were at each other's throats in their reports and in the newspapers. Clum charged that the military was keeping the few Indians still living at Fort Apache peaceable by giving them liquor, guns, and ammunition. He demanded that a major be court-martialed for buying a young Apache squaw and forcing her to live with him in his quarters. It was true that many officers maintained Indian mistresses under the pretense that they were maids and housekeepers. Kautz claimed that as a result of Clum's arbitrary actions, a very dangerous situation prevailed at San Carlos. Many renegades, said Kautz, had strayed away because of a lack of food, and "the resultant saving of rations probably accrued to those who issue them." A newspaper quoted Kautz as saying that most of the troops' labor was caused "by the inability or inefficiency, to say nothing of the reputed criminality of the agents." Clum also turned to the press, in letters to editors denouncing Kautz's administration of military affairs in Arizona, and boasting that his Indian police had demonstrated that they were more active and efficient than troops. Give him enough money to pay for two more companies of Indian police, he said, and the military would not be needed. The Indian Bureau refused his request.

July

When military officers, with the sanction of the Indian Bureau, were stationed at Arizona agencies as "inspectors," Clum once again resigned, declaring he would not be a party to political maneuvering. This time he did not change his mind.

August

Agent J. L. Hart was assigned to San Carlos.

Meanwhile, Kautz had established Fort Huachuca to intercept raiders along the border. Things had not been going well for his troops. Although contingents almost continually scouted through large areas, few renegades were captured or killed. On the other hand, the toll of white persons and the losses of livestock continued.

Agent Hart worked hard and efficiently to resolve the countless problems at San Carlos. The irrigation system was enlarged, and farm products were greatly increased. Yet Indian Bureau Inspector William Vandever found that the Apache were bewildered and discouraged largely, he thought, because of the constant conflict between the military and the agents. The Indians didn't know whom to believe, trust, or obey, and he predicted that serious trouble was in the making.

SEPTEMBER

Vandever was right.

Pionsenay, the renegade Chiricahua, returned from Mexico, slipped into the San Carlos Reservation, and held secret talks. He boasted of his triumphs in Mexico, and the southern parts of New Mexico and Arizona. When he slipped out again he took with him a number of women and young people of his band.

This was the encouragement that Victorio and the rebel leader Loco needed. With more than three hundred men, women, and children they struck out into the mountains. At Fort Apache they stole a number of horses.

Indian police were soon on their trail, and overtook them near Nantanes Mountain. The stolen animals were recovered, but the fugitives escaped into the great canyons. In a second encounter near Ash Creek, several Apache were killed, and thirty women and children were taken prisoners, but once more the leaders escaped.

Victorio had planned to go to Mexico, but with large numbers of troops and Indian police pursuing him, he was forced to turn northward. He led his harried and dwindling band into the rough region south of Fort Wingate. This was Navajo Country. They killed six or seven white men on isolated ranches, and stole the livestock they needed to keep from perishing of hunger. Determinedly, troops from several posts kept after them.

At last, with cavalry closing a ring about them, and suffering from hunger, Victorio led nearly two hundred of his followers into Fort Wingate and surrendered. Some fifty others soon followed. Fifty-six of his warriors had been killed in clashes with soldiers. He realized that any further struggle would mean the death of many others, and he pleaded for another chance to live in peace with his people.

The situation presented a perplexing problem. The military held the view that if Victorio were returned to San Carlos another outbreak would soon occur. He could not be permitted to remain on the Navajo Reservation. Some officers thought he should be sent either to the Mescalero Reservation in New Mexico or to the Indian Territory [Oklahoma]. Secretary of War George W. McCrary temporarily solved the problem by ordering that Victorio and all those with him be sent back to their old home at Warm Springs. There they were to be closely guarded until the Department of the Interior found a suitable permanent reserve for them.

DECEMBER

Although Kautz kept patrols constantly on the move throughout Arizona, strong bands under Juh and Nolgee captured a large and heavily laden wagon train near Stein's Peak, killed the teamsters, and then raided ranches in the area, murdering several white persons, and stealing large numbers of cattle and horses. The marauders headed for the Sierra Madre in Mexico. Eighty troopers commanded by Lieutenant John A. Rucker discovered their camp in the Animas Mountains, killed fifteen of them, captured one warrior, and recovered many of the animals.

Numerous depredations occurred and several ranchers were slain in the region west of San Carlos. These were attributed to reservation Indians given passes at the San Carlos Agency which allowed them to roam the country. Whether this was correct or not was not established, although it was probable that some San Carlos Indians were guilty. Renegades, however, were known to be in the area on occasion. In any case, troops were kept riding hard on winter campaigns.[25]

1878

MARCH

The apparent inability of General Kautz to deal efficiently with the dire problems at last convinced the War Department that he should be relieved. General Sherman's recommendation that General O. B. Willcox replace him as commander of the Department of Arizona was accepted.

Willcox soon transferred the center of his offensive operations to southeastern Arizona, where, as Sherman had reported, more murders of white persons had been committed during the previous year than along the entire wild frontier of Texas. A temporary supply station was established near the international border. Willcox's orders to his field officers were simple—clear the region of renegades. Within a short time strong contingents of troops were combing the mountains and deserts of southern Arizona and southern New Mexico. The intensive action forced the bands of Apache raiders to remain in their retreats in Mexico, and depredations on the American side of the border all but halted.

April–August

But while the effectiveness of the military operations continued, affairs at the immense San Carlos Reservation steadily deteriorated until they reached an almost chaotic state.

Geronimo, Poncé, Francisco, and several other notorious renegades being held prisoner decided they had had enough. With a small group of warriors they slipped away. Riding hard they soon had crossed the Mexican border and had joined Juh and Nolgee in the Sierra Madre.

Strangely no official report of their escape was made.

Agent Hart had been able to keep some Indians busy at farming, but they were obliged to cultivate with worn-out hoes and shovels and pointed sticks. Tools that had been purchased mysteriously disappeared en route to the agency. Some seeds were received, but too late to be planted. Other supplies for which contracts had been issued failed to arrive.

Hart was suspected of deliberately issuing short rations, but documentary proof that he was in league with the Tucson Indian Ring was not brought to light. If that were not true, however, he issued what Ogle terms "an extravagant number of passes," allowing hundreds of Indians to roam at will through the country in search of natural foods.

The Commissioner of Indian Affairs ordered Hart to conduct more frequent counts. Had this been done, the number of Indians absent from the reservation might have been determined. Hart ignored the instructions. General Willcox demanded that Hart stop issuing passes which permitted Indians to leave the reservation. The commissioner ruled that "off-limits" passes be granted only with his permission. Hart refused to obey, maintaining that "his Indians" were well behaved.

The weekly quota of flour issued to an Indian family was sufficient only for three days. Coffee, sugar, and other rations were reduced fifty percent. Such small quantities of beans—a main staple—were distributed that they were of no benefit.

White miners, cattlemen, farmers, and lumbermen were violating reservation boundaries to exploit its resources. According to Ogle, who obtained his information from official government files, mining operations were "taking hold on the western boundary of the reservation to an alarming degree . . . numerous camps and sawmills subsidiary to them were operating well within the reserve limits. . . . Other intruders appropriated all available agricultural, grazing, and wooded areas . . . as far as six miles within the reservation." Hart brazenly obtained an interest in one of the mines.

Willcox demanded that the white invaders be driven from the reservation. The War Department supported him, but the Indian Bureau was able to prevent any action in this respect. It could be accomplished, said the Bureau, only by maintaining a solid line of soldiers along the borders, an enormous expense that was neither justified nor necessary.

Apache leaders decided, understandably, that reservation lines should be no more binding on them than on whites. They began to move with their bands into the mountains and valleys not yet invaded by the exploiters. Others gathered around settlements, mines, and mills, seeking employment by which they could sustain themselves. Willcox, fearing that bloody clashes were sure to occur, proposed that all Indians at San Carlos be considered prisoners of war. Under these circumstances his commissary could lawfully feed them, and they would be subject to his control. The War Department was not prepared to take such a drastic step. Willcox then "lent" Hart seventeen thousand pounds of flour. This only served to relieve the situation a few days, but it had the effect of putting the Indian Bureau in an unfavorable light. Ten thousand dollars were telegraphed to Hart "to meet any emergency." This was merely a face-saving gesture. The money was soon spent. The ration deficiency continued. The morale of the Indians sank to an unprecedented low level. Hungry, ragged, prevented from benefiting from the natural resources that belonged to them, they threatened a mass outbreak. It was prevented only when strong pressures by high administration officials forced the Indian Bureau to resume regular issues of adequate rations and other supplies.

OCTOBER

For nearly a year the army had been obliged to guard Victorio and his large band at Warm Springs, whither they had been taken after their surrender at Fort Wingate, and the War Department was tired of bearing the expense and the responsibility while Indian Bureau officials remained undecided as to their final disposition. At last General Sherman warned that the entire band would be turned loose unless the Indian Bureau quickly made a decision. The threat brought action. The Bureau requested that the War Department escort them back to San Carlos.

No more irrational, unintelligent, and cruel solution of the problem could have been proposed. Since their return to Warm Springs Victorio and his people had developed farms, built homes, behaved themselves, and had given every indication of being contented. Now they were to be thrown back once more among the suffering people on the barren and overcrowded San Carlos Reservation. There they would be prey to the grafting civilian agents and contractors, and that, of course, was most agreeable to the Tucson Indian Ring, although the newspapers and residents of Arizona were somewhat less enthusiastic about having more Apache brought into their midst from New Mexico.

Captain F. T. Bennett was ordered to conduct the transfer. He summoned Victorio to a meeting and explained that Warm Springs was no longer an Indian reservation, but was being restored to the public domain, that is, it would be thrown open to white settlers.

Victorio's broad, dark red marble face with its large nose and wide, straight mouth remained impassive. He stared at Captain Bennett for several moments, as if in disbelief, then he spoke.

VICTORIO: This is our home, our country. We were born here, and we love it. We will not go to San Carlos again.

BENNETT: I have to obey my orders, and I must take you.

VICTORIO: You can take our squaws and our children in your wagons. I cannot stop you. But I will not go. My men will not go.

Some stories recount that with a yell Victorio leaped up and disappeared. Others indicate that Bennett, desirous of avoiding a fight in which both Indians and soldiers would be killed, granted the chief time to consult with his people. It does not matter which is true. Long before morning Victorio and a hundred of his most capable fighting men had vanished into the mountains. Their trail was obliterated by a fierce rainstorm.

DECEMBER

All efforts to track down Victorio and his warriors had been unsuccessful. Deep snow covered the mountains of southwestern New Mexico. Abandoning the search, troops loaded one hundred and sixty-nine elderly Mimbreno, and women and children, into wagons and set out on the bitterly cold journey of four hundred miles over almost impassable rut roads to San Carlos.

1879

FEBRUARY

Some troops had been left at Warm Springs, and their commander, Lieutenant Charles W. Merritt, was startled one morning to see Victorio and twenty-two warriors ride into the post. They had spent the winter in high mountain country, and were badly in need of food and clothing.

VICTORIO: We are willing to surrender, if you will let us stay here. That is all we ask. We would rather die than go to San Carlos.

MERRITT: You can stay here until I receive orders telling me what to do with you. I will do whatever I can for you. You have my sympathy, for I know this is your home country, and I would like to see you permitted to remain in it as long as you make no trouble. I will supply you with food.

VICTORIO: We will make no trouble.

Merritt telegraphed General Hatch. Hatch sent the message to Washington. No answer came, as the Indian Bureau and the War Department once again began a bitter wrangle over what should be done with the controversial Victorio.

* * *

Agent Hart at San Carlos at last would be exposed as one of the cleverest grafters in the Indian service. He had previously been protected by a corrupt inspector, J. H. Hammond, with whom he had conspired to defraud the government, and who had submitted false reports covering their thefts.

Hart was buying herds of beef cattle, then turning many of them back to the contractors, ostensibly to be grazed until they were needed. The animals were sold elsewhere, and Hart and the contractor pocketed the money. It was estimated that only half the rations and supplies purchased reached the Indians. Frequently entire shipments disappeared. Hart and Hammond conspired with one supplier to submit samples of first-rate New England flour and then after a contract had been approved to substitute flour of much poorer grade made in Arizona. Hart and Hammond sold "vast amounts" of goods and supplies sent to the agency to mining camps and to merchants in Tucson, Globe, and other settlements.

By an inaccurate survey, Hammond excluded from the reservation a mine which had been sold by Hart to one Edward Knapp. Edward Knapp, it turned out, was Edward Knapp Hayt, the son of Commissioner of Indian Affairs E. A. Hayt. Secretary of the Interior Carl Schurz promptly discharged Commissioner Hayt and allowed him only an hour to clear out his desk. Further investigation revealed that Hayt had been protecting Hammond and Hart by concealing reports of their nefarious practices, and had been given a share of their graft.

General C. B. Fisk, president of the Board of Indian Commissioners, would make a personal investigation, and would state that San Carlos "made a stench in the nostrils of honest men," and had "suffered through the administration of a mining speculator, conducting his mining through means derived from the sale of agency supplies. Sugar, coffee, meat, blankets were taken by the wagon load from our warehouse to his mining camps."

Hart and Hammond quietly left the country with "genial social relations," their pockets bulging with money.

But the situation at San Carlos had not been unique. The same thing was happening all over the western United States—wherever the Indian Bureau could get its sticky fingers in the economic pie.

A reputable military officer, Captain Adna R. Chaffey, was named temporary agent at San Carlos. He quickly abolished the corruption, issued adequate rations regularly, organized a strong contingent of Indian police, and moved several of the bands to locations in the vicinity of Fort Apache where they could live under beneficial conditions. But he had his share of difficulties. Annuity goods failed to arrive on time, and sometimes not at all. Some of the Indians were "virtually naked, shoeless, shirtless and blanketless." Moreover, as a military man and a temporary appointee he received little support in his efforts from the Indian Bureau, which was anxious to have him replaced by a civilian.

The replacement agreed upon was J. C. Tiffany of New York, who was recommended by the Dutch Reformed Church.

Tiffany, who promptly organized Sunday schools and Bible classes on the reservation, was an accomplished crook. Some of his criminal acts, but by no means all of them, were soon discovered. On various occasions he had signed for 15,251 pounds of sugar when only 2,168 pounds were received; 3,349 pounds of coffee when none was received; and 5,000 pounds of tobacco when 4,000 pounds were received. According to Ogle, ". . . rations had been issued short to make up for wastage and shrinkage. Short issues in other instances had been manipulated to the profit of the agent."

But Tiffany was not ousted. He was permitted to establish a profitable ranch of his own. His evil practices increased. Payrolls were padded, materials for buildings were stolen. He became securely entrenched with the Tucson Ring, and the political connections of the ring, extending clear back to Washington, were too powerful to be broken. Tiffany was safe.

* * *

APRIL

Word reached Warm Springs that Victorio was to be sent to the Mescalero Reservation. He and his people once more disappeared.

JUNE

Victorio changed his mind, and brought his band into the Mescalero Reservation. The agent there said he would make an effort to have their wives and children brought to them from San Carlos, if they promised to farm and remain peaceful. They promised.

JULY

The citizens of southern New Mexico angrily denounced both the army and the Indian Bureau for granting Victorio's "band of cutthroats" sanctuary on the Mescalero Reservation. When it appeared evident that Victorio would be permitted to remain, they schemed to destroy him. Law-enforcement officials and members of the judiciary willingly joined in the "worthy cause." In Silver City a grand jury was assembled and quickly indicted Victorio and all his followers for murder and stealing livestock.

Meanwhile, intelligence from Mexico stated that Geronimo, Nolgee, Juh, and Francisco were engaging in a "heavy traffic in stolen goods with the citizens of Janos." Some officers proposed a plan for returning them to Arizona, but it was not approved by headquarters.

AUGUST

Law officers had intended to say nothing about the indictment until Victorio had been taken into custody, but apparently someone talked too much. By some unknown means Victorio was warned of it, and he and his warriors thereafter moved about cautiously, heavily armed and prepared to fight for their freedom.

No law officers were seen, but as the month was ending a hunting party passed through the reservation. They came from Silver City, and among them were a judge and the prosecuting attorney of Grant County. Victorio concluded that they were looking for him, and successfully avoided them.

SEPTEMBER

In an almost uncontrollable rage, on the first day of the month Victorio confronted Agent S. A. Russell and accused him of making promises out of both sides of his mouth without intending to keep any of them. In a furious argument he pulled the agent's beard, and threatened to raid the agency and steal its stores and livestock. Russell sought to convince him that the group from Silver City were not looking for him, but the effort failed. He then sought to calm Victorio by issuing ration tickets to him and his men.

"There are other things besides rations," Victorio snarled. "I will live. My men will live. In three days we will leave this reservation."

He tore the ration tickets to shreds, threw them in the agent's face, and stamped out. Badly frightened, Russell sent a courier to Fort Stanton requesting troops to protect him.

A contingent of cavalry rode to the agency in record time.

Victorio was gone.

It did not take long to discover that besides his own warriors a number of Mescalero had gone with him—perhaps a hundred and fifty able fighting men in all.

* * *

Before Victorio fled he had taken time to talk with Dr. J. H. Blazer, who operated a ranch and sawmill near the agency, and whom he considered a trustworthy friend. As he shook hands with the doctor, he said in a tone of regret that he would never again try to make a home on a reservation.

"From now on it will be war," he said. "War to the death. There is no other way."

Dr. Blazer's hand was the last white man's hand he would shake.

* * *

Telegraphic orders sent troops from almost every post in Apacheria racing out to intercept Victorio. Strong forces attempted to block every trail crossing the international border.

The way he had gone from the Mescalero Reservation soon became tragically apparent. His band left two dead sheepherders in Temporal Canyon, butchered a number of sheep, and took the meat and the herders' horses with them. Going on westward into the Gila Country, they crept up on a grazing horse herd of a company of the Ninth Cavalry, killed five soldiers and three civilian herders, and got away with nearly fifty fresh mounts. Their trail across the Black Mountains and the San Andreas Range was marked with dead settlers, burned ranch houses, and stolen stock.

Near the headwaters of Animas Creek, they caught Captain Bryan Dawson and forty-six troopers in a cleverly laid ambush. Fifty more soldiers and civilians from Hillboro, responding to a message for help from the trapped men, were unable to do more than aid them in extricating themselves. So strongly were Victorio and his band entrenched that after fighting a day and a night, the soldiers retreated. Eight troopers, two civilians, and two Indian scouts had lost their lives. Fifty-three cavalry horses and mules were abandoned to the renegades. Thirty-two horses had been killed, and most of the military baggage and supplies had been discarded during the desperate fight to escape from the trap.

The debacle brought additional troops into the region. Several running fights occurred, and thirty-five more soldiers and civilian volunteers were slain before Victorio disappeared into Mexico.

D E C E M B E R

The plan to bring Geronimo and the other Apache leaders back from Mexico had been revived, and veteran agent Jeffords was able to get in communication with them. He was informed that the profitable trade in stolen goods had been disrupted, they were being hard-pressed by Mexican soldiers, and were suffering privations. Jeffords, with General Crook's old scout, Archie McIntosh, and Captain A. S.

Haskell, aide to General Willcox, offered to meet them at the border if they were willing to go to San Carlos. The offer was accepted. With one hundred and eight men, women, and children, Geronimo and Juh surrendered at Camp Rucker, the temporary supply station Willcox had established in Cochise County.

If this was good news, other military dispatches were alarming and discouraging to soldiers and citizens alike. Wild bands of Mescalero from their New Mexico reservation and from the Davis Mountains of Texas, Chiricahua who had been hiding in the Mescalero Country and in Mexico, and Comanche renegades were joining Victorio. It was estimated that he now had with him more than three hundred and fifty fighting men.

1880

JANUARY

More than a thousand American cavalry, operating in numerous contingents, were hunting Victorio. They were reinforced on occasion by groups of irregulars, townsmen and ranchers, and by several companies of Indian scouts.

Raiding along the Rio Puerco and in the San Mateo Mountains, he was overtaken twice by Major A. P. Morrow's troopers. Two sharp fights took place, without decisive results. Several soldiers were killed and half a dozen wounded.

FEBRUARY

Captain L. H. Rucker's company was ambushed in the San Andreas Mountains, and narrowly escaped annihilation. In this engagement Victorio's warriors acquired considerable equipment which the troopers were forced to abandon.

MARCH

Victorio disappeared. Presumably he circled into Mexico. In certain areas south of the border, ranchers willingly supplied him with ammunition, and allowed him to take what sheep he needed for food, to save their own lives.

APRIL

A company of cavalry which had picked up Victorio's trail came upon a flowing spring and paused to rest and refresh themselves. The water contained gypsum. Men and animals were stricken and were unable to continue the pursuit.

General Hatch with seven companies narrowly missed trapping Victorio's entire band. The general passed on, completely unaware of their presence in a high mountain hideout. Victorio watched the troops ride through a canyon, but made no attack. The great chase might well have ended there had Victorio been spotted, for the renegades could easily have been surrounded, and they were almost out of ammunition.

Although most Mescalero on the Sierra Blanca Reservation remained peaceful, a few were running meat, guns, and horses to Victorio's hideouts. Hatch ordered the entire Mescalero tribe disarmed, and sent troops to the agency for the purpose. They killed twoscore or more innocent men and women. One helpless group was slaughtered when camped near the agency to draw rations. Most of the Mescalero were disarmed, but a large number escaped into remote country with their weapons.

MAY

Victorio swept through the Black and Mogollon Ranges, burning ranches, stealing livestock and horses. Thirteen Mexican sheepherders were murdered.

Cooney's Camp on Mineral Creek was attacked. Two Americans were killed, and a number of horses were stolen.

A wagon train was captured and destroyed, and several teamsters were slain, on the Gila. This raid was led by Victorio's son, Washington.

Seventy-eight persons, civilians and soldiers, were killed by Victorio's renegades during the month.

The troops were exhausted by the long, grueling campaigns. Their horses were spent. Supplies were depleted. They were forced to halt the pursuit to rest and replenish their stores and ammunition.

Newspapers were excoriating the military for its failure to run down Victorio. Commanders in the Department of the Pacific, the Department of the Missouri, and army headquarters in Washington were aggravated by the situation and agitated by the criticisms. There was very little they could do, however, but defend Hatch and Willcox, and order more troops sent to the devastated area.

H. K. Parker, chief of Indian scouts at Fort Bayard, long recognized as one of the most competent, deadly, and astute Indian fighters in the Southwest, informed Major Morrow that he had some seventy scouts capable of taking the field, and he asked permission to undertake a campaign with them.

"You see the condition we're in," Morrow said. "I have no orders to give you. Go do the best you can."

Parker set out. A few days later he reached Hatch's command recuperating near Ojo Caliente.

"Go out and kill one or two Indians," Hatch told him. "We have got to keep things stirred up until I can get the troops in shape to continue."

Two days later Parker and his men picked up Victorio's trail on the Palomas River. They pressed forward without rest. When their mules became exhausted, they transferred packs to their own backs, and continued on foot. When they located Victorio's camp they were undetected.

In the dawn they launched an attack from two sides. Taken completely by surprise, a number of warriors and several women were killed by the first withering volley. Believing themselves surrounded, the renegades hastily threw up defensive works. Parker sent a courier to Hatch with word that he had Victorio trapped and asking for reinforcements.

The fighting continued throughout the day. Parker's scouts had only five cartridges each left. He pulled them back a short distance to a safer position. For two more days and nights he waited, but no reinforcements appeared. The scouts' food was gone, and they slaughtered two horses. At last Parker concluded that the courier had not got through. With the small quantity of ammunition available he could do nothing but give up, and he took his men back to Ojo Caliente. Hatch's soldiers were there, but Hatch had gone.

It did not take Parker long to learn what had happened. His courier had reached Hatch, but instead of sending troops to help Parker the general had hurried by horseback to Fort Craig. There he had telegraphed headquarters in Santa Fe that his command, with Indian scouts as an advance guard, had struck Victorio's band and would wipe them out. Hatch's officers were furious at the situation, but could not respond to Parker's request without orders. Some of them openly denounced their commander as an imbecile.

For months Hatch's large command had failed to halt Victorio. He feared that a few scouts would succeed where he had failed, and he did not propose to let that happen. He was willing to send a false report so that he would receive the nation's plaudits. But the newspapers soon learned the truth, and their condemnation of Hatch rose to new heights.

According to official reports, before they had been forced to withdraw, Parker and his men had killed fifty members of Victorio's band, and Victorio himself had been wounded in the leg. Parker was more modest, stating that probably no more than thirty of Victorio's warriors were slain, but a large number were wounded. Whatever was the correct number of casualties, Victorio had suffered a stunning blow.

When a few days later Major Morrow was permitted to resume the pursuit, Victorio was tracked to Cook's Canyon. In a running fight ten more warriors were killed, one of them Washington, Victorio's son.

But before the month was half gone, Victorio was once more safe in a Chihuahua hideout.

JULY

It took Victorio only a few weeks to secure new horses, new supplies, and new renegades—Mescalero, Chiricahua, and Comanche—to take the places of those who had fallen in the fights with Parker and Morrow. Fully recovered from his leg wound, he swept with a powerful band into Texas below Eagle Pass. Close on their heels were three hundred Mexican troops whose commander, Colonel A. I. Valle, had been given permission to carry his pursuit across the Rio Grande into the United States, if necessary. Companies of Texas Rangers and U.S. cavalry joined in the hunt.

Half a dozen fights occurred in the next fortnight, with several casualties on both sides, but the amalgamated Mexican and American commands were proving to be too much for Victorio, and, scattering his forces, he fled back to Mexico.

AUGUST

The Mexican Government offered a reward of three thousand dollars for Victorio's head. When a report was received that he was hiding in the Candelaria Mountains, U.S. cavalry was granted permission to cross the border to join in the hunt for him with a thousand troops under General Joaquin Terrazas.

SEPTEMBER

Victorio was traced to a remote area about a hundred miles north of Chihuahua City. As a ring began to close about him, the Mexican Government suddenly revoked its policy of international cooperation. The American troops were ordered to leave Mexican soil at once. Almost on the eve of victory they were obliged to turn back to the Rio Grande.

OCTOBER

After a furious chase, General Terrazas and his troops surrounded Victorio's band in a small valley between two peaks. The fighting began late in the afternoon, and ended by morning. It was more of a massacre than a battle, for the renegades had little ammunition.

A Tarahumari Indian scout was given the credit for killing Victorio.

He received the reward, and the state of Chihuahua presented him with a nickeled rifle.

Victorio and sixty warriors and more than a score of women and children were slain. Sixty-eight women and children were captured. Only three Mexican soldiers were lost.

But thirty of Victorio's men had fought their way out of the trap and escaped. One of them was an aged leader named Nana.

Victorio was dead, but the war he had begun was far from being ended.

NOVEMBER

Nana was seventy years of age, a Gileno Apache of the Warm Springs band. He was participating in raids on Mexican settlements and ranches when Victorio was a child. For several decades he had been a leader of marauding groups, but in middle life he had suffered from prolonged periods of sickness. He had sustained several serious wounds, one of which had given him a permanent limp. His limbs had become afflicted with rheumatism, and he was often in great pain. Younger men had superseded him as a chief.

Yet Nana seemed to be indestructible. There were times when he had difficulty getting on a horse, but once mounted he could endure as well as young men all the hardships and ordeals of a long flight from pursuers. On more than one occasion when troops were pressing Victorio's band he was known to have ridden three horses to death, traveling with others as much as seventy or eighty miles without stopping. Despite his advanced years and poor health, he had not mellowed. He had lost none of the courage, none of the spirit, none of the shrewdness and cunning which had for so long made him a dangerous and capable fighter. And, perhaps most important of all, the fire of his hatred for the invaders of his homeland still burned in him with undiminished fury.

It was the aged, bent, crippled, grizzled Nana who rallied the remnants of Victorio's shattered renegades. He inspired them with his refusal to admit defeat, with his unqualified zeal and determination. He took command and he set out with them on a series of swift raids by which they obtained new supplies of weapons and ammunition, food and equipment, and fresh horses.

Before he raided north of the border there was one thing Nana wanted to do, and that was to avenge the death of his great friend and commander, Victorio. For sheer daring, if not madness, his plan had few equals in the annals of Apache warfare.

Nana and his warriors—there could not have been more than forty of them, and probably fewer than that—lay in ambush near Carrizal, where the main road between Chihuahua City and El Paso passed through a defile between bluffs. His scouts had reported that General Terrazas, the conqueror of Victorio, was to pass that way, and the intelligence proved to be accurate.

Preceded by a company of cavalry, and surrounded by an escort of ten aides, General Terrazas appeared. In the first volley, nine soldiers died and as many were wounded. The Apache concentrated their fire the next moment on the general's escort. Nine of them were killed, and the general was saved only by the quick action of troopers who rushed to protect him. The general and his rattled men fled along the road at a wild gallop.

Nana and his warriors swept down and finished off the fallen wounded. One of them was a Mexican sergeant who was adorned with trinkets taken from Victorio's body. He was quickly cut into small pieces.

Nana and his band, with more horses and Mexican guns and cartridges, vanished toward the mountains.

* * *

The situation of the Apache people:

On several occasions reservation lines had been relocated to favor mining, timber, and irrigation developments of white men.

Politicians in Washington agreeably permitted them to be defrauded of resources that would have more than met the costs of sustaining them.

Groups that had toiled to develop community farms were summarily ordered to move, sometimes in the midst of the growing season, thus their labors were in vain. Their crops were harvested by agents and sold to merchants.

Seldom was there a sufficiency of rations, clothing, tools, or other essential goods.

They were hungry.

The political influence, the grafting, and the boldness of the Indian Ring reached unprecedented heights. Example: Agent Tiffany wrote the Tucson firm of Lord and Williams, with which he conspired to commit enormous thefts of Indian goods, to send a clerk to the agency to make their books agree. Colonel Richard I. Dodge had stated that in his belief only five to twenty percent of congressional appropriations for Indians ever reached them.

Large numbers of emigrants—a majority of them Mormons—settled on good agricultural lands both east and west of the San Carlos and Fort Apache Reservations. They soon were diverting so much water that irrigation projects—which Apache farmers had constructed—largely with their bare hands—were destroyed, and crops could not be grown in areas below the diversions. Nothing was done to protect the

Apache farms, for Indians were not legally entitled to hold water rights.

When large deposits of coal were discovered on the southern part of the San Carlos Reservation, white men rushed in to open mines, driving Indian residents from the lands at gunpoint. The military forced the intruders to leave. But they were soon back. Agent Tiffany induced fifty-three Apache leaders to sign a contract with them under which the tribe would receive small royalties purportedly on all minerals taken from the reservation deposits. The tribe got very little. Most of the royalties paid by mine operators went into the pockets of Tiffany and his Indian Ring cohorts. The contract eventually was canceled by the Secretary of the Interior.

The government of Arizona, from the office of Governor R. C. McCormick down to the lowest clerk, reeked of corruption.

Indians given passes to leave the reservation to hunt for food and employment were murdered by white men. The murderers, although they openly boasted of their wanton deeds, were not arrested. Indeed, a grand jury recommended that all dissident Apache be hanged as outlaws. The proposal met with the enthusiastic approval of some newspapers, but not of the contractors of the Indian Ring and the crooked agents. The more Indians held in the filthy concentration camps, the more they could steal. But rapacious settlers wanted the lands that had been set aside for the Apache. In all probability only the presence of strong military forces prevented white mobs from staging mass slaughters.

Living in constant fear, suffering from malnutrition and disease, defeated in every effort to improve their terrible conditions, thoroughly discouraged and hopeless, many Apache saw nothing before them but slow and agonizing death. But not all of them were willing to accept such a fate without fighting to the end of their endurance. Courage was not a completely destroyed characteristic of the Apache—far from it.

* * *

1881

JUNE

Old Nana and his warriors were reported to have crossed the Rio Grande below El Paso and to be hiding out on the Mescalero Reservation, or in rugged mountains adjacent to it. Telegraph keys chattered out this electrifying news throughout Arizona and New Mexico. Indian scouts were sent out to locate their camp. They failed, or at least they said they couldn't find it. Knowing Nana's record and his intentions, they couldn't be blamed if they didn't make much of a search. But they did return to the Mescalero Agency with alarming intelligence. Forty of the most notorious warriors of the Mescalero tribe had disappeared with guns and horses and had joined Nana's renegades. He now had at least seventy fighting men with him.

July–August

Nana's greatest raid lasted approximately six weeks.

It began with the murder of several ranchers in the Sacramento Mountains of southern New Mexico. It ended near the southern end of the Black Range with the ambushing of a small contingent of cavalry. Of the twenty men in the patrol six were killed and three were wounded before Nana decided to end the fight and start back to Mexico.

In this short period Nana and his band:

Rode more than a thousand miles, sometimes traveling as much as seventy miles in a day.

Doggedly pursued by more than a thousand cavalry and two hundred civilian volunteers, they fought a dozen skirmishes, won them all, and suffered very few casualties.

Killed an estimated fifty soldiers, ranchers, and miners, and wounded at least a hundred others.

Stole more than two hundred horses.

Kidnapped two New Mexican women.

Sustained themselves by eating stolen livestock, worn-out horses, and indigenous foods such as the mescal, the mesquite bean, and the prickly pear.

Burned the buildings and killed the stock of a score of ranches.

Military summations of the brief, bloody, devastating raid of the old man were in many respects inaccurate. While the troops, some of which were Negro companies, fought with extraordinary persistence and outstanding bravery, the claims that they were victorious in many of the engagements and had succeeded in driving Nana back to Mexico were without foundation. Said one army report:

"The difficulties of the country, among the most inaccessible mountains of that region, were very great, and the Indians scattered themselves so much when closely pressed that it was necessary to hunt them down almost individually . . . but it can be truthfully said that the troops did everything that was possible, and pressed the Indians so closely and persistently from so many directions that they had no time to rest, and finally were driven across the Mexican line . . . the Indians remounted themselves with stolen horses . . . and scattered through the mountains by twos and threes . . . to unite again at points well known to them, and as it was therefore necessary to scatter the troops considerably to follow up the trails, it happened that whenever the troops met the Indians the forces were not unequal generally, and the fights were correspondingly severe and the loss on both sides unusually large. ... There was no great difficulty in dealing with them when found. The difficulty is to find them."

In fairness to the troopers who did find Nana and his men, the report might have stated that often with exhausted horses and men, worn-out equipment, and insufficient supplies of ammunition and food, they were sent against some of the finest guerrilla fighters the world has ever known.

History is replete with instances in which people long destitute and disheartened have turned to some form of religious worship in a desperate hope of escaping the manacles of suffering and fear. And so it was with the abused, defrauded, and malnourished Apache confined on the San Carlos and Fort Apache Reservations. Now came into prominence a strange and mystical personality. It was embodied in the slight spare figure of Noch-ay-del-klinne, a White Mountain medicine man thirty-six years of age, and popularly called The Dreamer because of his custom of periodically going alone into the wilderness to pray and fast and meditate and, or so it was said about Apache campfires, have marvelous dreams in which the spirits communicated with him.

The Dreamer had been sent by missionaries to an Indian school in Santa Fe. He had not remained long, but long enough to demonstrate a superior intellectual capacity and to display unusual interest in the Christian religion. Lieutenant Thomas Cruse, who knew The Dreamer as well as any officer, wrote that in school he had been "particularly impressed by the story of the Resurrection and when he went back to his own people it was to think about the withdrawal of Christ for meditation."

A scout informed Cruse at Fort Apache that The Dreamer was attracting a large following and addressing gatherings in a mountain valley some eighteen miles from the post. Wild dances were being staged, and, said the scout, they were the kind of dances "that always mean trouble." The Dreamer had served for a time as a scout for General Crook, and was known as a man of peace. Nevertheless, Cruse thought the situation warranted an investigation. He personally observed one of the dances, and he would write: "As I looked at the swaying, engrossed figures, moving like automations to the thump of drums, I was amazed at the fraternizing between tribes and elements which had always held for each other the most deadly aversion."

The Dreamer was telling the people that he had been given the power to restore to life two Coyotero leaders, Diablo and Eskiole, and crowds of Apache men and women were following his instructions to pray and dance about their graves. Agent Tiffany ordered his Indian police to put a stop to the ceremonies, but they too came under The Dreamer's spell and refused to obey. Ordinarily the Apache at San Carlos were required to obtain authorization to move about the reservation. When Tiffany refused to issue passes, hundreds went to The Dreamer's meetings without permission. Indian police informed Tiffany they were powerless to stop them, and the agent advised the military of his inability to control his excited Indians.

When, after the passage of several weeks, the resurrections did not occur, The Dreamer was threatened with violence by suspicious and disappointed Apache. He saved himself by convincing them that his failure was due to the presence of soldiers and other disbelievers in the area. The miracle could be successful only after all white persons had been killed, and their extermination must be completed before the corn was ripe.

General E. A. Carr, commander at Fort Apache, telegraphed this intelligence to General Willcox and asked for instructions. After a delay of several days, Carr received orders to take the medicine man into custody. Carr sent two messages to The Dreamer to appear at the post for a conference. He got no replies. By telegraph Tiffany advised Carr that The Dreamer should be "arrested or killed or both." Carr thoughtfully considered the situation. As a precaution he had disarmed his scouts, whom he believed had become untrustworthy, having fallen under The Dreamer's influence. He sent a third request to The Dreamer to come to the post. When it, too, was ignored he decided to arrest The Dreamer at his camp on Cibicu Creek.

Carr set out from Fort Apache with a force of eighty-five officers and troopers, guides, interpreters, several civilians, and about twenty Indian scouts whom he considered loyal. On the second day after leaving the post, The Dreamer was taken prisoner before a crowd of several hundred Apache, among them at least a hundred heavily armed warriors.

Lieutenant Cruse would recount that when the purpose of Carr's mission had been explained and "was understood by the Apaches, I could actually feel the stiffening in that crowd, Indian by Indian. I thought that the clash was coming then. The soldiers tensed in their saddles. They felt the strain too."

It being late in the day, Carr established camp on a stream a few miles from the scene of the arrest. The Dreamer and his guards were confined in a circle of pack saddles and supplies. Arms were stacked, cooking fires were built, horses were fed, sentries were assigned, and the soldiers prepared to eat and relax.

Carr remarked that he was "somewhat ashamed to come out with all this force to arrest one poor little Indian."

Cruse pointed out to him that a strong group of warriors had gathered nearby, and Carr ordered Captain E. C. Hentig to tell them to go away. Hentig walked toward the Apache waving and yelling at them to clear out. He was answered by blood-curdling yells. Out of the trees poured three hundred Apache, firing as they charged the camp.

Captain Hentig and eight cavalrymen were instantly killed. The Dreamer tried to crawl out of the pack-saddle corral, and was shot to death by his guards. Grabbing madly for their weapons, the troopers scrambled for cover behind rocks and trees. A score of them were wounded. The firing continued until darkness fell. Then the attackers vanished.

Cruse estimated that as many as eight hundred Apache were in the immediate area, and thought that if they "had owned one leader of consequence they would have annihilated us." Nearly sixty horses were lost, either shot or captured by the Indians. Not enough pack mules were left to transport the reserve ammunition of the troops, and between three and five thousands rounds were left behind and quickly recovered by the Apache.

The badly beaten and crippled force of General Carr crawled into Fort Apache the next afternoon.

SEPTEMBER

Murderous bands of Apache swept out of the valley of Cibicu Creek in several directions, all well supplied with cartridges. One band boldly attacked Fort Apache, set fire to two buildings, killed three soldiers, and wounded several. Four Mormon ranch workers were shot and then burned to death almost within sight of the post. A band raced through Pleasant Valley, firing ranch buildings, stealing horses and cattle, and killing several members of ranch families.

General Willcox rushed strong reinforcements to both the Fort Apache and San Carlos areas. Scouts brought in word that a general uprising had been planned, but evidently the large number of troops scouring the reservations and the surrounding territory convinced the ringleaders that it could not be successful. Nevertheless the flames which had been ignited could not be completely extinguished.

The entire War Department, as Ogle notes, "became electrified with apprehension as soon as news of the Cibicu fight reached Washington." Press dispatches from Arizona, as usual, were exaggerated, if not dishonest, and gave the impression that another Custer massacre had occurred. After consulting with Secretary of War Robert T. Lincoln, General Sherman ordered General R. S. Mackenzie to move from New Mexico to Fort Apache and take charge of all field operations. Thus,

General Willcox was deposed. "I want to hear results, not intentions," said Sherman. He got results, but they were not what he expected.

OCTOBER

More reinforcements were sent to Arizona from both the Department of the Pacific and the Department of the Missouri. The San Carlos–Fort Apache region was virtually an armed camp. Some two hundred Indians identified as hostiles were taken into custody and imprisoned at Forts Thomas, Grant, and Lowell. Several were sent as military prisoners to Alcatraz Island in San Francisco Bay. Three Indian scouts convicted of treason were sentenced to be hanged.

Colonel James Biddle was dispatched from Fort Apache with a company of cavalry to rearrest two leaders, George and Bonito, who had previously been in custody but had been released. Biddle bungled the job. He found George and Bonito at the San Carlos sub-agency with their bands. It was ration day, and the chiefs persuaded Biddle to delay arresting them until the issuing had been completed.

When that time came, George and Bonito informed Biddle that they would voluntarily come to Fort Apache the next day, and that he need not wait for them. Biddle insisted that they go with him at once.

George and Bonito suddenly mounted their horses and disappeared before the troops could take them. They raced through the immediate area, where large numbers of Apache were camped awaiting to receive rations, shouting that Biddle intended to kill all Indians at the post.

Not all the Apache present took alarm and fled. But four bands did. They were led by Geronimo, Juh, Chatto, and Nachee.

Within a few hours they were well on their way to Mexico. Four troops of cavalry from Fort Thomas sought to head them off. Their trail was not difficult to follow, for they killed any traveler or rancher unfortunate enough to get in their way. Near Cedar Springs they attacked a wagon train, and killed seven men. While looting the wagons they were surprised by the appearance of five companies of cavalry under the command of General Willcox.

In the fighting Willcox narrowly escaped being captured. Under the leadership of Geronimo, the Chiricahua warriors took positions behind rocks. For twelve hours they held the soldiers at bay while their women and children, with a large herd of stolen horses and cattle, moved with all possible speed out of danger.

When the Chiricahua withdrew they rode hard through Arivaipa Valley, burning ranches and killing several white persons. Troops did not catch up with them again before they crossed into Mexico.

They had with them some six hundred head of beef cattle and a large herd of horses with an estimated value of twenty thousand dollars.[26]

* * *

Hundreds of Chinese laborers had been imported to construct the Southern Pacific Railroad in Arizona.

All the workmen required could have been obtained among the Indians. A sufficient number of Indian men, rotting in idleness, underfed, and defeated in their efforts to make themselves self-sustaining, eagerly would have gone to work at low wages.

Corrupt Indian Bureau officials and politicians in league with crooked contractors prevented their employment. They protested that giving savages freedom was providing them with the opportunity to break out of control, raid settlements and ranches, and slaughter white men, women, and children. What these thieves feared, of course, was that if Indians were permitted to support themselves—even on a temporary basis—federal appropriations might be lowered, and both the size of their contracts and their own opportunities to steal would be decreased.

* * *

1882

JANUARY

Loco was getting old. A Mimbreno, he had been a lieutenant of Mangas Coloradas, and he had been an adept pupil of the great chief. After Mangas Coloradas had been murdered by American soldiers, Loco had avenged his death by leading his warriors on devastating death-dealing raids through large parts of Arizona and New Mexico. No man knew better the terrors and tragedies of warfare. He had been wounded several times, but the greatest damage to his body had been done not by white antagonists but by a bear. In a fight with a grizzly he had lost an eye and his face had been badly disfigured. Those who knew him best, however, both army officers and Apache leaders, maintained that he was a man of amiable disposition and that his sinister appearance belied his true character.

In spite of the almost unsupportable indignities and hardships he had suffered, he had remained peacefully for several years on the San Carlos Reservation. " . . . in his wisdom," states Thrapp, "he saw no future in war with the white man. One might wonder what he saw in peace at San Carlos for his people. . . ." But Loco counseled peace. He had refused to bolt with Geronimo, Juh, Chatto, and Nachee* the previous fall, and thereby had incurred their anger. Loco had been influential enough to prevent several hundred Apache from joining them in their flight to Mexico, and they had let him know that one day they would return and take it upon themselves to free his

---

*Sometimes spelled Nachez.

people from their bondage—over his dead body if necessary.

In the first month of this year they kept their promise.

One night several warriors slipped into Loco's camp. They had, they said, been sent by Juh and Nachee to warn him that in forty days the renegade bands would start north from Mexico on a raid, and that he and his people would be forced to return with them. He had better be prepared to leave.

Loco kept his silence, but someone in his camp let the secret out. Perhaps it was disclosed when several Mimbreno families, anxious to avoid the trouble that surely would come, fled northward, hoping to find safety in the Navajo Country. Any movement of this type would soon have been known to Indian scouts or reservation police.

FEBRUARY

Chief of Scouts Al Sieber told Agent Tiffany and General Willcox he had heard a rumor that Juh and others were coming north. Neither placed much credence in the intelligence. Tiffany was sure that he could control the reservation Indians, but Willcox decided it might be prudent to send out some troops on patrol along the border and to notify all posts to watch for a sign of the hostiles.

MARCH

Columns of cavalry, supplemented by Indian scouts, continued to crisscross Arizona and New Mexico in a grid pattern, but no evidence that raiders had come north from Mexico was discovered.

APRIL

General Sherman, on a tour of inspection, stopped for a short time at San Carlos. It was his opinion that with several thousand troops in Apacheria prepared for war and constantly on the alert, residents need not be apprehensive.

He had been gone on his way less than a fortnight before Geronimo, Juh, Chatto, and Nachee, with perhaps sixty warriors, swept down upon the San Carlos Agency. They had successfully avoided several thousand Mexican and American troops who were watching for them.

Ten men died in the fighting near the agency. One of them was Chief of Police Albert D. Sterling. The raiders cut off Sterling's head and tossed it back and forth as they headed for Loco's camp.

While some exhorted Mimbreno to gather their meager possessions and flee with them back to Mexico, Chatto and Nachee confronted Loco. Wildly excited Indians were gathering about the old chief's lodge, shouting to him to leave with them. Loco was looking into the muzzles of several rifles. He stared with one blazing eye at the dark faces of the desperate men before him. Then he nodded and said: "We will go."

Within a few hours more than seven hundred men, women, and children, and the sixty raiders from Mexico, were traveling with all possible speed toward the rough desert country of the Gila River Valley. They looted several wagons, but miraculously the drivers escaped. A man died heroically defending his family whom he was driving to Globe. For some unknown reason his wife and children were spared.

The immense band crossed the Gila not far from Fort Thomas. With two companies of cavalry, Colonel George W. Schofield set out in pursuit. They soon came upon the bodies of three prospectors, "still warm." The Apache, aware that the troops were approaching, began to scatter. Strangely, Schofield ordered a rapid retreat, reporting that a shortage of rations compelled him to return to his post.

Commanders expected the Apache to hold to a direct course toward Mexico, and sent troops in east and west movements to intercept them. However, instead of pressing on toward the border, the renegades turned up the Gila to the Clifton region. Obtaining sufficient food each day for nearly eight hundred persons was a difficult problem. It was temporarily solved at one ranch where they murdered seven men, a woman, and two children—one of whom they threw alive into a fire— and butchered a large herd of sheep.

Striking southeast they were unaware that General Sherman and a small escort passed almost within their sight. Continuing his tour of inspection, Sherman was en route to New Camp Grant. By this narrow margin did the ranking general of the United States Army escape capture and almost certain death, most probably by torture.

Several groups of warriors left the main group to forage for cattle and fresh mounts. One band raided along the Southern Pacific Railroad, while another was attacking ranches on the Gila, and still a third ravaged the Lordsburg area. On these forays ten white men were killed, and a large number of livestock were stolen.

A small patrol of nine men under Lieutenant David N. McDonald, an experienced and courageous campaigner, encountered a hundred and fifty of the hostiles in the Stein's Peak Range. McDonald immediately sent a courier to Colonel G. A. Forsyth whose column of six companies of cavalry was searching the high country on the eastern side of the mountains.

Pinned down by the superior force, McDonald and seven men held off the Apache for nearly an entire day in Horse Shoe Canyon. Upon reaching the scene, Forsyth divided his troops into two strong flanking groups. The Apache were driven into the higher peaks of the range. They offered stiff resistance as they retreated. At last, after they were out of range of the cavalry guns, they vanished. It was realized afterward that they had delayed their withdrawal only long enough to allow the main band to cross the San Simon Valley to the Chiricahua Mountains.

By the time troops again got close on their trail they had crossed the border into Mexico. Behind them were the graves of at least fifty white persons, a score of soldiers, two or three dozen destroyed ranches, and a number of burned wagon trains.

A column commanded by Captain T. C. Tupper, and consisting of two companies of cavalry and one of Indian scouts, picked up the Apache's trail in the Chiricahua Mountains and followed it south. Tupper ignored the international border as if it had not existed. In his opinion this was not a time to delay until permission to cross was obtained through diplomatic channels, although he realized that he might well face a court-martial for his unauthorized actions.

The trail was clear, for the Apache, believing they were safe from American troops, traveled at a relatively leisurely pace. After a day and night of hard riding, Tupper's scouts located their camp and got close enough to determine that they were celebrating their escape.

At dawn Tupper attacked from two sides. The Apache quickly took cover behind large rocks on a ridge, leaving a dozen dead by their campfires. One of the casualties was a son of Loco. Nearly a hundred Indian horses were captured or killed, but the Apache could not be dislodged from their strong defensive position.

After six hours of fighting, the troops had left only three rounds of ammunition per man. Faced with this perilous situation, Tupper ordered a withdrawal from the field. Only one soldier had been killed, and one had been badly wounded. The troops moved back nine miles. They were verging on complete exhaustion, for they had had no rest and little food in thirty-six hours.

While eating supper they were astonished to see a long column of American troops approaching. It consisted of seven cavalry companies and three companies of Indian scouts commanded by Colonel Forsyth. After resting on the Gila, following the Horse Shoe Canyon fight, Forsyth also had followed the Apache's trail southward from the Chiricahua Mountains. If Tupper had been advised of his pursuit he might have done no more than merely attempt to hold the Apache at bay until the arrival of the stronger force.

Forsyth took his command on to the scene of the battle. As expected, the Apache had vanished, moving into high mountains to the south. Seventeen warriors and seven squaws lay dead on the field. Forsyth followed the trail, but he had gone only ten or twelve miles when he met three hundred Mexican soldiers under the command of Colonel Lorenzo García.

Now it was disclosed that the retreating Apache had made a disastrous mistake. Believing that the American troops would soon be in pursuit of them, most of the warriors had remained in the rear to protect the women and children and elderly. They had left their front unguarded, unaware of the approach of García.

The Mexicans had caught them in an ambush and had killed seventy-eight—the majority women and children—before the others were able to extricate themselves and escape. Twenty-one Mexican troopers had died in the fight.

García, although amicable and polite, handed Forsyth a letter in which he formally protested the "invasion of Mexican territory" by the Americans. Also in writing, Forsyth defended the action on the ground that it had been effective and had demonstrated the willingness of the United States to cooperate with Mexico in destroying Indians hostile to both nations.

After courteously wishing each other good luck and long life, the commanders parted, Forsyth turning back to Arizona and García to continue his pursuit of the renegades. Forsyth's report was returned to him by his superior officer. If García informed his government of their meeting, Mexico chose to let the matter drop and made no protest to the Department of State.

* * *

Whiskey, an inherent hatred of all Indians, and newspaper editorials vitriolic in their criticisms of the military, led irrational, unthinking, and dense citizens of Arizona—of which there were a good many—to believe that by their own devices they could succeed where the army had failed in ending the Indian menace, once and for all. These persons decided to sponsor a series of campaigns that would emulate in general the structure of a cheap and badly staged comic opera.

The Tucson Rangers were furnished with horses and arms by the government of Pima County. Their captain was William Ross, a former army officer. He was made a deputy sheriff and the others were designated as his posse. Described as fifty "hard-riding, rough-and-tumble frontiersmen," they were sent off to eliminate the hostile Apache in Mexico.

Below the border they killed thirty-seven Indian women and children whom they "hoped" belonged to a hostile band, although no one could be certain of the tribal affiliation of their helpless victims.

Their next action came when they espied at a distance a band of men. Assuming they were Indians, they gave chase, and were on the verge of opening fire when they discovered that the riders were a contingent of Mexican cavalry commanded by a Captain Ramírez.

Ramírez arrested them, and they had difficulty in persuading him not to execute them. They were held prisoners for several days while

Ramírez waited for orders. At last General Bernardo Reyes, with more than six hundred troops, arrived. He furiously scolded Captain Ross for having entered Mexico illegally, ordered all the arms of the Tucson Rangers confiscated, and sent them back across the border. Fortunately, as they were without weapons of any kind, they did not encounter any Apache on their ride back to Tucson.

Fifteen stalwart citizens of Globe, led by "Captain" D. B. Lacy, set out to fight hostiles. An army officer wrote that they departed with great enthusiasm, "well primed with the best brand of whiskey and carrying an ample supply with them." While they were taking a siesta at the home of a friend one warm noontime, Indians stole their horses. They returned to Globe on foot.

The Tombstone Rangers were organized for the express purpose of "solving the San Carlos problem." The "solution" proposed by prominent citizens, among them two judges and a lawyer who would become attorney-general of Arizona, was a mass slaughter that would make the Camp Grant massacre "look like a Sunday school picnic."

With great fanfare and much cheering and gun-firing the Tombstone Rangers, a motley company of "bar-room Indian fighters," set off to wipe out the Indian population of San Carlos. How they were to accomplish this while several hundred troops were stationed there with orders to arrest them on sight was a strategic secret which, if they knew it themselves, was never disclosed.

Lieutenant Davis wrote that near the southern line of the reservation the Tombstone Rangers "met with an old Indian who was gathering mescal. . . . They fired at him, but fortunately missed. He fled north and they fled south. That ended the massacre." Captain Bourke sarcastically reported that "the whiskey taken along was exhausted, when the organization expired of thirst."

* * *

JUNE

Apparently fearing that the hounds of justice would soon have him treed, Agent Tiffany resigned. He gave "poor health" as his reason for departing. If he was not well, there was nothing wrong with his bank account. He departed from San Carlos a very wealthy man.

JULY

After returning to Washington from his inspection trip, which took him through the larger part of Apacheria, General Sherman had advocated a drastic military reorganization in the area. He submitted three recommendations:

1. The creation of a new Department of the Border, embracing Arizona and New Mexico.

2. The transfer of General Willcox to the Department of the Platte.

3. The reassignment of General Crook as commander-in-chief in the Apache Country.

The first proposal had been put aside for further consideration, and was abandoned when the latter two were approved.

CROOK COMING BACK announced the newspapers in their largest type, and most of the people in Arizona enthusiastically welcomed the news. There were, however, some who were disappointed. They were the merchants, politicians, and contractors of the Indian Ring. With Crook once more in command they could envision harder times ahead.

The fight which took place in Big Dry Wash was brief but of great historical importance.

Na-ti-o-tish had never been a leader of prominence, yet his small band of followers were no less imbued than he with an indestructible hatred of all white men, and they comprised one of the most vicious factions on the San Carlos Reservation. Although an irreconcilable, he had refused to join Geronimo, Juh, Loco, and other insurgents on their flights to Mexico, electing to remain in remote areas and attempt to create dissent and foment violence with fiery oratory. He had been an ardent supporter of The Dreamer, and he preached that the killing of the mystic in the battle of Cibicu Creek was premeditated murder by the military. He pleaded for a general uprising to avenge The Dreamer's death. Most of the Apache, thoroughly disheartened and knowing the futility of attempting to defy the thousands of troops surrounding them, took his diatribes for what they were, invitations to commit suicide.

Thwarted in his main purpose, Na-ti-o-tish was able to inspire sixty warriors to join him in a harebrained outbreak. They struck first at the San Carlos Agency, killed Chief of Police J. L. Colvig and three of his Indian deputies, forced several squaws to go with them, and disappeared toward the west. Their next target was McMillenville, ten miles northeast of Globe. They fired into the town but succeeded in wounding only one white man.

By this time, army posts, alerted by telegraph and couriers, had sent strong contingents riding hard from several directions to intercept the raiders. It was from the beginning a superbly coordinated action.

Na-ti-o-tish and his bloodthirsty renegades moved pell-mell northward, descended Salt River for a short distance, then turned up Tonto Creek to the wild, rugged, beautiful country of the Tonto Basin. The incomparable Apache scouts, leading the troops, easily followed their trail.

The chase came to an end in Big Dry Wash, a forbidding canyon that cuts deeply into the Mogollon Rim. There the hard-pressed belligerents were surrounded by fourteen companies of cavalry. The ring of steel was steadily tightened about them.

The culminating fight was vicious but short. When the firing stopped, Na-ti-o-tish and twenty-five warriors lay dead among the boulders. Perhaps almost as many had suffered wounds. Only a handful had managed to slip away unscathed, and they would return to the reservation much wiser men than they had been when they left it on the inane escapade. Military casualties: two troopers killed, several wounded.

The battle of Big Dry Wash was historically important for the reason that it marked the end of an era. It was the last major engagement between soldiers and Apache to take place in Arizona.

Except for the Chiricahua still hiding in the Sierra Madre of Mexico —the small bands of Geronimo, Chatto, Bonito, Loco, Nachee, Chihuahua, and a few others—the Apache were a beaten people.[27]

FALL

Arriving at San Carlos early in September, Crook talked first with Apache leaders in a series of meetings at various places on the reservation, then summoned each commissioned officer to his headquarters for a private interview.

He found the Apache in "deplorable" condition, due almost entirely to the "rascality of the Indian Ring and the agents, the greed and covetousness of white commercial interests, and the failure of Arizona authorities to act against white criminals."

His aide, Captain Bourke, recorded that Crook established, among other things, these facts:

Supplies and clothing intended for the Indians were being sold by the Indian Ring to merchants and traders in Tucson, Globe, and other places. White men destroyed fields and crops of Apache farmers who were able to support themselves and families, compelling all "who could be forced to do so to depend upon the agent for meagre supplies." Punishment was inflicted upon Indians without investigation, "without trial, or without testimony of any kind." The size of the reservation had been cut without any negotiations with the Apache, and "five times had this been done, and much of the most valuable portion had been sequestered." For years insufficient rations had been distributed, and the "rottenness" of the Indian Ring and the San Carlos Agency "extended all the way to Washington, and included in its meshes officials of high rank," among them the Commissioner of Indian Affairs and the Inspector-General of the Indian Bureau.

"Bad as Indians often are," said Crook, "I have never yet seen one so demoralized that he was not an example in honor and nobility to the wretches who enrich themselves by plundering him of the little our Government appropriates for him."

It is doubtful that any other military man could have prevented a general uprising of the desperate people under the circumstances. Crook held their trust and reestablished the confidence they had placed in him before he had been transferred nearly a decade earlier. He was able to convince them that warfare was just what their white enemies wanted, and "that peace was their only salvation." He influenced them to accept his policy of strict discipline under military supervision. Indian policemen would be appointed to keep order. Lawbreakers would be tried before Indian juries. Mountain bands would be permitted to move from the arid valley of the Gila to homelands in higher altitudes. White depredations on the reservation would be halted. Adequate rations would be justly distributed—at least he would make every effort to see that this was accomplished. He was not deluding himself as to the power of the politicians.

In the beginning, a new agent, P. P. Wilcox, indicated a willingness to cooperate, and supported Crook's proposals. Improvements resulted, and for a time operations on the reservation functioned smoothly. Wilcox, however, found himself faced with serious difficulties. Contracts made by the Indian Bureau with crooked contractors were still in force, and he had no authority to revoke them. Substandard foods and supplies continued to arrive at the agency. According to Ogle, he "found it almost impossible to get competent employees to replace the unscrupulous henchmen of his predecessor. In an effort to stamp out the graft and illicit liquor traffic which seemed to emanate from the agency store, he discharged the Tiffany holdovers and appointed his son-in-law to the lucrative post. This action, he felt, would insure honesty in all Indian trading."

Behind the scenes, the Indian Ring vigorously opposed many of Crook's policies, and put pressure on their collaborators in the Indian Bureau to disapprove them. Crook was accused of unwarranted interference in administrative matters. A great fear of the thieves was that the reservation might be placed under the complete control of the military. Caught in the middle of the old jurisdictional struggle between the War and Interior Departments, Crook and Wilcox themselves were soon at odds. In several disputes Crook came off second best. One of the most important in which he was overruled involved counting the reservation population. Crook maintained that only by frequent counts was it possible to determine with any accuracy whether Indians were slipping away. Each Indian was required to wear a metal tag identifying him. This system also would specify with relative exactness how many mouths must be fed and the quantities of rations required, figures that the Indian Ring, for obvious reasons, had always padded. Over the strong opposition of Crook and General Sherman, the Indian Bureau succeeded in stopping the counts. Thereafter, they were haphazardly conducted at widely separated intervals—after all, an annual accounting did have to be made to the appropriations committees of the Congress—and without exception the totals reported were excessively on the high side.

Crook reissued his general orders of 1873 in which he had decreed that no mercy was to be shown to renegades who committed depredations or chose the warpath instead of peaceful capitulation, but he supplemented them with additional instructions which left no doubt that humanitarian policies would prevail to an even greater extent than before. "Officers and men serving this department," he declared, "are reminded that one of the fundamental principles of the military character is justice to all—Indians as well as white men—and that a disregard of this principle is likely to bring about hostilities. . . . In all their dealings with the Indians, officers must be careful not only to observe the strictest fidelity, but to make no promises not in their power to carry out. . . . Grievances, however petty, if permitted to accumulate, will be embers that smoulder and eventually break into flame. . . . Each officer will be held to a strict accountability that his actions have been fully authorized by law and justice, and that Indians evincing a desire to enter upon a career of peace shall have no cause for complaint through hasty or injudicious acts of the military."

Crook made plain his conviction that there could be no complete and final peace with the Apache Nation until all the wild bands below the border had been destroyed or had surrendered. Even before he had returned to Arizona, negotiators between Mexico and the United States had signed an agreement under which troops of each nation were granted the right to pursue hostiles across the boundary. Some of the provisions were equivocal and open to different interpretations.

Crook was dissatisfied and uncertain as to the extent of his authority under the ambiguous international understanding. He interpreted it as meaning that he would have to await a raid into the United States from Mexico before he could act. But as he sought clarification of the terms, he prepared for war. He established border patrols, and moved his own headquarters to the little town of Willcox on the Southern Pacific Railroad in southeastern Arizona. Trainloads of supplies and equipment were assembled, and a strong expeditionary force was organized.

He was severely criticized by Arizona officials, private citizens, and the press for reactivating and arming several companies of Apache scouts. He told a Los Angeles *Times* correspondent, Charles F. Lummis

—not one of his critics: "To polish a diamond there is nothing like its own dust. It is the same with these fellows [hostile Apache]. Nothing breaks them up like turning their own people against them. They don't fear the white soldiers, whom they easily surpass in the peculiar style of warfare which they force upon us, but put upon their trail an enemy of their own blood, an enemy as tireless, as foxy, and as stealthy and familiar with the country as they themselves, and it breaks them all up. It is not merely a question of catching them better with Indians, but of a broader and more enduring aim—their disintegration.

"The invention of the breech-loading gun and the metallic cartridge has entirely transformed the methods and the nature of Indian warfare. . . . They are no longer our inferiors in equipment . . . they now have the best makes of breech-loading guns and revolvers. For white soldiers to whip the Chiricahuas in their own haunts would be impossible. The enormous country which they range is the roughest in America. . . . It is almost utterly bare of anything upon which a white man could exist, but it supplies everything the Chiricahuas need to prolong life indefinitely. There is no end of the mescal plant everywhere in their territory, and if there was nothing else whatever, the Apache could live very comfortably on the varied products of that wonderful plant. He has no property which he cannot carry along in his swiftest marches. . . . He roves about like the coyote, as unencumbered and more elusive. He knows every foot of his territory, and can live through fatigue, lack of food and of water which would kill the hardiest white mountaineer . . . unless we can surprise them the odds are all in their favor.

"When it comes to a fight . . . we can't see anything of our foe . . . nothing but the puffs of their rifles. Nothing is exposed but here and there an eye, peering from behind some rock. *You* can't see that eye, but those fellows, with their marvelous vision, will see your eye at a hundred yards. No white man can take advantage of the ground as they do. Our soldiers have to expose themselves, since they are the attacking party.

"No, to operate against the Apache we must use Apache methods and Apache soldiers, under, of course, the leadership of the white soldier. The first great difficulty is to discover the whereabouts of the hostiles, and this can be done well only by Indian scouts. Their stronghold once located, the next thing is to reach it secretly. The marches must be made with the utmost stealth and by night. Fires and noise are absolutely prohibited. The Indian scouts must be kept far enough in front and on the flanks to discover the enemy without being seen themselves, leaving no trail whatever, but slinking along from cover to cover. As soon as they locate the hostile camp, they noiselessly surround it . . . meantime sending runners back to us. We make forced marches . . . come up and attack . . . if they have not already flown. It is impossible to pursue them, for every rock may hide an Apache at bay, and with his breechloader he can kill as many pursuers as he pleases, himself secure. There is nothing for us to do but return to our base of supplies . . . and then repeat the same tedious operation."

The fall and winter passed without incident. Crook had wired headquarters at the San Francisco Presidio: "There is not a hostile Apache in Arizona." Nothing had been heard from the Chiricahua in Mexico. However, Indian scouts serving under Captain Emmett Crawford along the border had ascertained that the hostile bands were hiding in the Sierra Madre, but their attempts to communicate with them had failed. Yet Crook made no prediction that trouble would not come . . . that was inevitable. The only question: When and where would they come north the next time?

He was ready.

1883

Late in March the raid Crook had expected took place. Chatto, Bonito, and Chihuahua, with twenty-three warriors, selected for their daring and ability as fighters, crossed the border from Mexico and entered Arizona over little-used trails through the Mule Mountains. Separating into small parties, they attacked ranches and camps south of Tombstone, near Charleston, Total Wreck, Sulphur Springs Valley, San Simon Valley, and in New Mexico near Ash Springs, Silver City, and Lordsburg.

In six days the twenty-six Chiricahua killed twenty-five white men, one white woman, kidnapped a six-year-old white boy, obtained a sizable supply of weapons and ammunition, and stole several hundred cattle and horses.

In this short period they rode an estimated four hundred miles—sometimes traveling seventy-five to a hundred miles in twenty-four hours—in Arizona and New Mexico. At least ten companies of cavalry were out hunting for them, but they slipped back into Mexico without being sighted by any of the troops. Their losses were one killed (by a miner), and one deserter, Tse-ay, who decided to abandon the life of a renegade.

Tse-ay made his way alone to San Carlos and surrendered to the commander, Lieutenant Britton Davis. He had, he informed Davis, come to the realization that continued defiance by the Chiricahua in Mexico was unwise and futile. Eventually all of them would be killed in senseless fighting. He believed he could do more for his people by taking the road to peace and working to improve their welfare. Informed of Tse-ay's capitulation Crook wired Davis to ask him if he were willing to enlist as a scout. Tse-ay agreed, and was taken to Crook at his Willcox headquarters. Captain Bourke described Tse-ay—who was soon nicknamed Peaches—as highly intelligent, courageous, and "the handsomest man the world ever saw." Peaches supplied Crook with invaluable intelligence regarding locations of the strongholds of the various bands in Mexico. He offered to serve as a guide. Placed on the payroll at a wage of thirteen dollars a month, he soon demonstrated his ability and sincerity. He would become one of Crook's most trusted and loyal scouts. The white residents of the Southwest would owe him a great debt for his service in helping to bring about the end of Apache warfare, a debt that would be repaid by the basest ingratitude.

Crook bluntly informed the War Department that troops could not hope to halt the raids from Mexico with defensive tactics. They must be captured or destroyed in their hideouts of the Sierra Madre. The ambiguities of the convention regarding border-crossing privileges had not been removed. As it stood, Crook regarded the agreement as too confusing to be of much use to him. General Sherman replied to his inquiries with instructions to pursue raiders "without regard to department or national boundaries." Crook was not satisfied. The terms of the agreement stated that an American force could enter Mexico "only in close pursuit of a band of savage Indians," that the *entrada* must be made only in unpopulated areas, at least several miles from any town in either country, and that after engaging in a fight with the pursued Indians or losing their trail, the Americans must immediately return to their own country. No prolonged hunt or campaign would be permitted. Moreover, the commander of the troops crossing "was to give notice of the time of the crossing, or before if possible, to the nearest military commander or civil authority of the country entered."

"Crook now found himself face to face," wrote Captain Bourke, "with the following intricate problem: The Chiricahuas occupied a confessedly impregnable position in the precipitous range known as the Sierra Madre. This position was within the territory of another nation so jealous of its privileges as not always to be able to see clearly in what direction its best interests lay. The territory harassed by the Chiricahuas not only stretched across the boundary separating Mexico from the United States, but was divided into four military departments —two in each country; hence an interminable amount of jealousy, suspicion, fault-finding, and antagonism would surely dog the steps of him who should endeavor to bring the problem to a solution." Obviously each commander of a military district could interpret the convention as he chose.

Crook had an understanding with General R. S. Mackenzie, commander of the Department of New Mexico. None of the conditions Bourke had feared would arise on the American side of the border. He sent telegrams and letters to various commanders in Mexico, requesting a definitive agreement with them. When it became apparent that he would receive no replies, he got on a train and visited Mexican military headquarters in Guaymas, Hermosillo, and Chihuahua. In each place he was graciously received, and was advised that any force he led into Mexico to destroy Apache would be welcomed and assisted in every possible way.

When he returned to his Willcox headquarters in mid-April he advised the War Department of his success in negotiating with the Mexican commanders of the states of Sonora and Chihuahua, and expressed the belief that a literal construction of the terms of the Mexican-American convention would bring "failure in the settlement of pending Indian hostilities. It is all important that we on the ground be permitted to vary these stipulations to the extent required by the best interests of the two Governments. . . ."

The answer he received, signed by General Sherman, advised him that the government—presumably the State Department's position—"instructed him that no military movement must be made into, or within the territory of Mexico, which was not authorized by the agreement." Sherman also stated that negotiations for modifying the agreement were "now going on with the Mexican Government, but it cannot be inferred that the Mexican Government will assent to any modification."

Not a little aggravated by the situation, Crook decided to take matters into his own hands, and he informed his superiors that he would be "outside normal communications for an extended period."

Late in April he moved from Willcox to San Bernardino Ranch, on the border in extreme southeastern Arizona, where he established a base camp. On May 1 he crossed into Mexico, disappearing on one of the most daring and dangerous campaigns in the long history of warfare with the Apache.

Reserve companies were left at the San Bernardino Ranch. In the relatively small force Crook took with him were eight commissioned officers, a surgeon, forty-two troopers, three white scouts, two interpreters, nearly two hundred Indian scouts and five pack trains. Every man had been selected personally by Crook, and every man had been "tested under fire." They represented the most competent, experienced, and trustworthy soldiers and scouts that Crook, a shrewd judge of men, could assemble.

Now came silence. No couriers returned with dispatches recounting the progress of the expedition. No one knew where Crook was, what he had accomplished, or where he was going. Concern mounted in Washington. Fables began to appear in newspapers: he had been captured; he had been wiped out; his scouts had massacred the white troops and joined the hostiles; he had engaged the renegades and had destroyed them; Apache warfare was forever ended.

The War Department, under heavy pressure from the national press, felt constrained to state that it did not "credit the rumors of disaster to Crook's column," and it was "disposed to credit the report that General Crook engaged the Apaches and defeated them." But the army had no more factual information than any of the correspondents in the Southwest—no one could be certain of anything.

With Indian scouts scattered out ahead, Crook pushed steadily southward, up the Bavispe River, through the old town of the same name, on through Bacerac, Huachinera, Teserababi, Cumbre. Directly ahead were the massive uplifts of the Sierra Madre. Peaches and other scouts led him through a series of immense canyons and over ridges that seemed to break into the bright blue sky. Wrote Captain Bourke: ". . . the hills and ridges became steeper as we struck the trail lately made by the Chiricahuas driving off cattle from Sahuaripa and Oposura." Soon a trail was found that was fresh and well-beaten—by hundreds of stolen ponies and cattle. "Climb! Climb! Climb! Gaining the summit of one ridge only to learn that above it towered another." Ten pack mules were crushed into pulp when they slipped from the narrow paths and plunged into chasms. Innumerable trails made by the hostiles were crossed, "and upon them were picked up all sorts of odds and ends plundered from the Mexicans—dresses, saddles, bridles, letters, flour, onions . . . the Apache scouts trudged without complaint . . . their tread as untiring and as stealthy as the panther's, their vision as keen as a hawk's, and ears so sensitive that nothing escapes them." They were not big men, but their "chests were broad, deep, and full, shoulders perfectly straight; limbs well-proportioned, strong, and muscular . . . hands and feet small but taper and wiry; heads well-shaped, and countenances often lit up with a pleasant, good-natured expression . . . disheveled gypsy locks of raven black, held away from the face by a broad, flat band of scarlet cloth . . . each wore a loosely fitting shirt of red, white, or gray stuff, generally of calico. . . . This came down outside a pair of loose cotton drawers, reaching to the moccasins."

After ten days of struggling slowly forward in a country "grand to look at but infernal to travel through," the column passed into a narrow, gloomy, and rocky gorge, which gradually widened into a small amphitheater. It was the stronghold, Peaches informed Crook, that had been occupied by the Chiricahua raiders when he was with them. It was admirably situated "for all purposes of defense. Water

flowed in a cool sparkling stream. . . . Pine, oak, and cedar in abundance . . . clung to the steep flanks of the ridges, in whose crevices grew
much grass. The country, for a considerable distance, could be
watched from pinnacles . . . their huts had been so scattered and
concealed in the different brakes that the capture or destruction of the
entire band could never have been effected. . . . The heads and bones
of cows and ponies were scattered about on all sides. . . . At one point
the scouts indicated where a mother had been cutting a child's hair;
at another, where a band of youngsters had been enjoying themselves
sliding down rocks . . . bows and arrows, and a Winchester rifle had
likewise been left behind. . . .

"Being now in the very center of the hostile country, unusual
precautions were taken to guard against discovery. . . ." After climbing
laboriously out of the deserted amphitheater they descended a "fearful
chute" into another "gloomy chasm. . . . There was no longer any
excitement about Chiricahua signs; rather, wonder where none were
to be seen." They passed the frameworks of scores of huts, ashes of
campfires, "play-grounds and dance-grounds, mescal pits and acorn-
meal mills."

Now the great value of Peaches was fully appreciated. They could
not be a great distance from their quarry, he said, and the slow progress of the pack trains was holding the scouts back. He was supported
by other scouts in a proposal that the pack trains and white soldiers
"remain in camp at this point, and in future move so as to be a day's
march or less behind the Apache scouts," who, with three officers and
several white scouts, "would move out well in advance to examine the
country thoroughly in front.

"If they came upon scattered parties of the hostiles they would attack
boldly, kill as many as they could, and take prisoners. . . . Should the
Chiricahua be entrenched in a strong position, they would engage
them . . . until reinforced by the rest of the command."

General Crook agreed to the strategy, cautioned them not to kill
women and children, and appointed Captain Crawford to command
the advance force. Supplies were distributed, and the scouts vanished
into the primeval wilderness.

Four days later, at dawn, an Apache courier handed Crook a small
piece of paper. It was a message from Crawford, advising the general
that shots had been exchanged between the scouts and the renegades.
Crawford was pursuing them, and "I think you had better come after
us as rapidly as possible. . . . The bearer will bring you after us."

Crook and the cavalry were on their way in a few minutes. Until
almost midafternoon they maintained a forced march. Then they
heard the sound of firing ahead. Soon Crawford and a number of
scouts appeared. The first blood had been taken. They had come upon

a band of Bonito, and in a running fight had killed nine warriors and captured a young squaw, two boys, and two little girls. The entire village might have been killed or captured had not several impetuous young Apache scouts opened fire too soon, giving Bonito and many of his people time to escape.

The captured squaw seemed to have no fear in the presence of Crook after being assured that she would not be harmed. She had much to say, and she talked freely. The rancheria attacked belonged to both Chatto and Bonito. The Chiricahua were totally unaware that Crook's force was in the country. She "was positive that the Chiricahuas would give up without further fighting," for they were anxious to make peace, and often had talked of sending emissaries to San Carlos for permission to go there in safety and surrender.

Crook told her that his scouts had informed him that five miles ahead was an excellent campsite. He would go there, and he would wait three days for the renegade leaders to appear before him and surrender. If in that time they had not appeared, he would resume his campaign and hunt them down. Then he gave the squaw and the eldest of the two captured boys a quantity of meat and hardtack, and sent them back "to tell your people what I have said."

Two days later the notorious Chihuahua stood before Crook. He had come to give up. All he asked was that he be allowed a day to gather his people and bring them in. Permission granted, Chihuahua rode away. He kept his word.

The next day Geronimo and forty of his warriors arrived to talk with Crook. The general was fully aware that if he was to be victorious he must come to terms with this dangerous and influential leader. Bourke thought that in physical appearance Geronimo and his men were "the finest body of human beings I had ever looked upon. . . . There wasn't a weak face . . . not a soft feature. Each countenance was indicative of boldness, cunning, and cruelty."

Geronimo stated that he wished to have a talk with Gray Fox, the Chiricahua name for Crook.

"I am not here to talk with you, but to listen to you talk," Crook told him in a cold voice. "You can see what has happened. Your own people have come down with me to capture or kill you. Large forces of Mexican troops can soon be expected to arrive here. You make your choice, peace or war."

Geronimo wanted peace. If General Crook would take him and his people back to San Carlos, and guarantee them protection, they would work and "follow the path of peace." But he wanted a just peace, and if that could not be guaranteed to him he would go on fighting until he and his people were in their graves.

"Make up your mind," said Crook.

Geronimo asked for permission to talk overnight with his counselors. He would inform Crook of his decision the next morning.

The general told him to go. "I am not taking your arms from you because I am not afraid of you," he said. "You have been allowed to go about camp freely, merely to let you see that we have strength enough to exterminate you if we want to."

Geronimo left. At dawn he returned. He would surrender. His people were widely separated, but he and Nachee would assemble them as soon as possible. "I do not know how long that will take," he said. "If you are gone, I will follow you to San Carlos as soon as I can without danger. But I will not leave here until I have gathered up the last man, woman, and child of the Chiricahua."

"That is your promise?" Crook asked.

"I promise," answered Geronimo.

"Then I accept the terms of your surrender," Crook told him.

Crook made similar agreements with Chatto and Ka-ya-ten-nae, a young leader rapidly rising to power, and allowed a mixed band to start at once for San Carlos. When he rode out of the Sierra Madre he had with him the bands of Nana, Loco, and Bonito, numbering three hundred and twenty-five men, women, and children. Ka-ya-ten-nae and thirty-two warriors joined the procession. From the border Captain Crawford's command took the renegades on to San Carlos, arriving there late in June. Of all the prominent leaders in Mexico, Crook had failed to locate only Juh. Chatto and others had said that all of Juh's followers had been killed in fighting with Mexicans, and that his efforts to recruit a new band of raiders had failed. He had then disappeared with several squaws, and his whereabouts was unknown. That may not have been a true story. In any case, scouts eventually would learn that Juh had died of a heart attack after getting drunk near Casa Grande, Chihuahua.

As months passed and the hostiles left in Mexico did not surrender as they had promised, Crook was severely criticized for having trusted the villainous Geronimo and other Apache. A rabble-rousing state senator from Texas, Barnett Gibbs, without any supporting evidence, was the source of a report that Crook had been captured by Geronimo and had been forced to accept the chief's terms in order to save himself. Crook, inwardly seething with rage, remained outwardly calm. He wrote Secretary of War Lincoln that ". . . while I can overlook the design and intent to injure me . . . I cannot ignore the great damage likely to ensue from disingenuousness and misrepresentation to the end sought by me . . . in the solution of this intricate Indian problem."

But Captain Bourke showed temper, and while on leave he told an eastern newswriter that Gibbs was a liar. Banging a table he declared that Crook had not been defeated, and "I say this positively, without regard to the assertion of so-called state senators or of military dudes in Washington."

Steadfastly Crook maintained that Geronimo would keep his word. He kept troops on patrol along the border to watch for the hostiles and escort them to San Carlos. A few days before Christmas thirteen Chiricahua suddenly arrived to surrender. But the year ended without any word from Geronimo and Chatto.

1884

January passed. Then early in February Chatto and nineteen warriors rode into the camp of a border patrol, gave themselves up, and reported that Geronimo was "on his way north" but was obliged to travel slowly because he was bringing with him a large herd of cattle and a pack train. He was telling the truth.

When Geronimo crossed the border shortly after the beginning of March he had with him eight men, women, and children, three hundred and fifty head of stolen cattle, and a number of pack mules loaded with plunder.

Calmly he explained the reason for his late arrival. After Crook had left the Sierra Madre, he and Nachee, as promised, had assembled their people. Then he had decided that it would be improper for a leader of his greatness to return to San Carlos without gifts for all his friends and relatives there. He had postponed his departure for the United States until he had acquired goods in what he considered suitable amounts for such an important occasion. There was only one way, of course, to obtain them, and that was by raiding. With his warriors he had plundered a number of Mexican settlements and ranchos. Besides stealing horses and cattle, they had looted stores of merchandise and had taken attractive articles—perhaps gold chains, watches, pins, rings, earrings, silver ornaments and dishes, and clothing—anywhere they were available. Unfortunately, a number of persons were foolish enough to fight him. However, he had spared many of his victims. He also had secured a number of good rifles and hundreds of cartridges from Mexican soldiers who had been stupid enough to pursue him. With a laugh, he declared that the soldiers had been such poor fighters that he and his men had been able to kill most of them with rocks.

Geronimo demanded a military escort to San Carlos, and Crook gladly provided it.

Small parties of renegades continued to arrive from Mexico. In a midsummer report to the War Department Crook stated that "for the first time in the history of that fierce people, every member of the Apache tribe is at peace." There was not, he said, a small town in the East more peaceable and law-abiding than the five thousand Apache on the San Carlos Reservation.

Fearing that Crook's success might persuade the administration to give the War Department full administrative control of Apache affairs, the Interior Department, the Indian Bureau, and their henchmen in the Indian Ring opened fire on the fundamental policies of the military. The old jurisdictional dispute was soon raging once more with all its former vindictiveness.

The sniping of the civil officials came from several directions. They publicly criticized Crook's progress in the press, and accused him of being unrealistic, idealistic, and visionary. San Carlos Agent Wilcox charged that granting the hostile Chiricahua from Mexico all freedom and privileges enjoyed by others on the reservation was breaking down the morale of Apache who had remained peaceful and had worked hard to improve their economy. The fallacy of this contention, however, was apparent to anyone willing to recognize it. Most of the hostile Chiricahua at once and enthusiastically engaged in agricultural projects which gave every indication of becoming highly profitable. Moreover, all Apache demonstrated that their faith was in Crook and unequivocally endorsed the programs he proposed. Chatto became a sergeant of Indian scouts. Geronimo, Bonito, Loco, and other leaders pronounced themselves fully satisfied with conditions, and were hard at work cultivating land.

Indian Bureau officials played up the case of Ka-ya-ten-nae to support their argument that the Chiricahua would cause serious trouble, but Crook soon deprived them of this ammunition. The young chief was, indeed, an irreconcilable. He moved about the reservation sowing seeds of discontent, advocating uprising, and urging the people to return to Mexico and fight to the end for their freedom. At last he allowed his rebelliousness to get out of control, and made an attempt to take the life of an army officer. He was tried by an Apache jury, found guilty, and sentenced to three years' imprisonment. Crook ordered him confined at Alcatraz, but recommended that after a short period of imprisonment he be allowed to go about the city of San Francisco "so that he may become acquainted with civilization and thus learn something that may be of benefit to his people when he is returned to the reservation."

The Secretaries of War and the Interior evolved a plan which, while not fully satisfactory to either of them, they hoped would have a salutary effect on the bitter dispute between their departments. Under it the military would be responsible for keeping the peace, administering justice, and punishing lawbreakers, and the Indian Bureau's representative at San Carlos would direct administrative affairs, including the negotiating of contracts for supplies and the development of farming and livestock-raising projects.

Agent Wilcox at once predicted that a policy of dual control was infeasible and would create new difficulties. In this contention he was supported by his superiors. He soon accused Captain Crawford, commander at the agency, with usurping his authority and attempting to place barriers before "the progressive programs of the Indian Bureau."

Crook insisted that if he, aided by such honorable and capable men as Captain Crawford and Lieutenant Davis, were allowed full freedom to execute his policies the Apache would steadily advance toward the desired goal of permanent peace. He advised: just treatment under all conditions; a paternal attitude; ownership of lands in severalty; trial of offenders by Indian juries; the right of Apache to bear arms; the rejection of all proposals to remove them from their traditional homeland; and the granting of full citizenship and enfranchisement.

As Ogle succinctly and correctly states, he defended his system "with vigor and intelligence. To disarm the Indians, he said, would not only be an injudicious expression of whites' fears but also a folly, especially on a frontier infested with white criminals. Besides, the Indians' habit of caching arms would make their disarmament almost an impossibility. Equally foolish to him would be their removal. It would start them toward ultimate extinction, and completely destroy their confidence, which factor, Crook knew, was absolutely necessary to retain if they were to be adjusted to white civilization. Worse yet, he predicted that such a step would start one of the bloodiest wars in Indian history."

Crook also opposed trial of Apache lawbreakers in white civil courts, where obtaining a fair trial for them would be impossible. He pointed out that under the Apache social system every man was individually responsible for his own acts, and chiefs were mere figureheads and could not be held accountable for misdeeds of members of their bands. The Apache, he declared, had no comprehension of the whites' code of justice.

Crook would write: "The Indian is a human being. One question today on whose settlement depends the honor of the United States is, 'How can we preserve him?' My answer is, 'First take the government of the Indians out of politics; second, let the laws of the Indians be the same as those of the whites; third, give the Indian the ballot.' But we must not try to drive the Indians too fast in effecting these changes. We must not try to force him to take civilization immediately in its complete form, but under just laws, guaranteeing him equal civil rights. If this is done, the Indian question, a source of such dishonor to our country and of shame to true patriots, will soon be a thing of the past."

1884

Some of the bands virtually had become self-sustaining, an achievement that greatly displeased suppliers holding contracts with the Indian Bureau. They, and military contractors as well, were angered by Crook's prediction that if the present rate of progress were maintained the economy of the Apache would soon be stabilized on a level that would bring a sharp curtailment of government expenditures for their support. Moreover, many Apache were being employed by ranchers as cowboys and field workers. Apache hay and grain were being purchased by the military. Sizable herds of cattle were being developed.

Altogether it was an intolerable situation to the Indian Ring, and they took measures to enact changes favorable to them. The method that seemed certain to bring results in the fastest way was disruption of the progress by demonstrating to the Indians that Crook, the man in whom they had the greatest faith, had failed to keep his promises to them and had been deprived of his authority.

Agent Wilcox conveniently took a three months' leave. The Indians complained to Captain Crawford that diseased and worthless cattle, some without teeth, were being supplied to them for beef and as breeding stock. The animals were so bony that they were worthless as food, and incapable of being bred. Seeds did not arrive and fields cleared for cultivation remained unused. Large quantities of food distributed were either spoiled or of such poor grade that they were worthless. Projects had to be abandoned because of a shortage of tools.

Crook registered strong complaints, advised cancellation of Indian Bureau contracts and the authorizing of new ones through the War Department, or preferably through his own office. This, he believed, would bring an end to the corruption of "that thieving bureau of the Interior Department." Crawford issued passes to six hundred Apache which allowed them to hunt and gather wild foods outside the reservation. This action brought howls of protest from Arizona residents and officials, and an Indian Bureau inspector reported that Crawford's only reason for allowing his charges to roam was "to gratify his hatred of white citizens."

Agent Wilcox returned to his post in the fall, and strongly reiterated his belief that all the difficulties were the result of the policy permitting dual control. He urged its immediate abolishment, and that full control, except police work, be restored to the Indian Bureau. When he became convinced that no such revision was forthcoming, he resigned.

His successor, C. D. Ford, arrived in November, and soon left no doubts that he was an implacable foe of the military. The outlook was grim as the year ended.

1885

Crawford, seeing storm clouds gathering, attempted to take charge of all farming on the reservation. Agent Ford in a vehement protest warned the Indian Bureau that he would resign unless Crawford were ordered to desist. Crook stood behind Crawford. Secretary of War Lincoln thought it advisable that Crook leave all farming operations to the agency authorities.

Captain Crawford, weary of the bitter wrangling and lack of support from Washington, requested a transfer. He was ordered to rejoin his regiment in Texas.

Agent Ford recommended that the fight over dual control be resolved by a compromise. Let the military have complete authority over all affairs of the Indians—among them the Chiricahua bands of Chatto, Nachee, Chihuahua, and Geronimo—living in the Fort Apache region, and he be given complete authority over the three thousand in the San Carlos area. The idea was unacceptable to Crook. "I thought we were to put the Apache to work raising corn instead of scalps," he said, and insisted that he be given "full control of the entire reserve or none."

While a new administration was still mulling and wrangling over the question in Washington, Geronimo settled it.

As dusk fell on the evening of May 18, forty-two warriors and ninety-two squaws and children abandoned their farm homes near Fort Apache and vanished into the surrounding mountains. With Geronimo were Nachee, Mangus (a son of the famous Mangas Coloradas), the aging Nana, Chihuahua, and some of the most dangerous and desperate fighters among the Chiricahua who had previously been renegades in Mexico. Loco, Bonito, and Chatto had refused to join Geronimo in the outbreak.

Within a few hours cavalry units were in pursuit from Fort Apache, San Carlos, and other stations. Contingents also were dispatched to attempt to head off the renegades along the border. They were never overtaken.

Early in June they were back in Mexico, well on their way to the old strongholds in the Sierra Madre. So well had their flight been executed that they had easily eluded hundreds of troopers scouring the country for them. They had crossed from Arizona into the mountainous area of western New Mexico and swept southward. So swiftly did they travel that on one occasion they rode a hundred and twenty miles over a zigzagging route without stopping for food or rest. Raiding ranches for fresh mounts, they killed at least a score of white persons, wiping out one family of a man, woman, and two small children within three miles of Silver City, a large cavalry post. One of the children, aged three, was left hanging alive on a meat hook. Just before escaping over the international border they demonstrated their contempt for the American military by raiding a supply camp in Guadalupe Canyon, near Fort Huachuca. At the time, troops from the depot, commanded by Captain H. W. Lawton, were out scouting, and only a sergeant and seven troopers had been left on guard. Five of the soldiers were slain, the other three wounded. The raiders, reportedly numbering between thirty and forty and led by Chihuahua, stole two mules, three horses, several thousand rounds of ammunition, a quantity of stores, and fired the buildings. The scouting troops returned to the disastrous scene without having come upon their trail.

President Cleveland suspended Agent Ford and placed the Apache Reservation completely under the control of the War Department. Crook ascribed the outbreak to these causes:

1. The Chiricahua, and especially Geronimo and Chihuahua, believed that he had been stripped of authority to the extent that he could no longer help or protect them, and that they were, therefore, facing injury from civil authorities.

2. His inability to provide farming implements, mills, clothing, blankets, and other things which had been promised to them had caused them to lose faith in him.

3. They were deeply grieved by the failure of the government to restore to them members of their families who were being held captive at Fort Union, New Mexico, and others who had been distributed as slaves among prominent families in old Mexico.

4. Geronimo had become convinced that he and other leaders would be turned over to Arizona authorities and hanged.

5. Chihuahua and others contested Crook's authority to forbid wife-beating and the making of liquor on the reservation. Chihuahua had become an alcoholic.

6. Undoubtedly some of them had grown tired of the confining reservation life, yearned for the freedom they once had known, and had succumbed to the urgings of the eloquent Geronimo to break out.

Two cavalry columns commanded by Captains Wirt Davis and Crawford, who had been returned to Arizona, pushed rapidly into Mexico. They forced the hostiles out of the Sierra Madre, but succeeded in killing only three and capturing thirty, most of them women and children and aged noncombatants. The exhausted troopers returned to Arizona in September, their campaign largely a failure.

Their rest was short. A number of Chiricahua reentered the United States through Guadalupe Canyon. Davis and Crawford were soon on their trail with strong forces of soldiers and scouts. All ranches had been warned to corral their horses and keep them under guard to prevent the raiders from obtaining fresh mounts. In the Chiricahua Mountains the troops began to find horses which had been ridden to death, and it soon was apparent that most of the renegades were on foot.

Lockwood records that "by a circumstance maddening to the soldiers" the hostiles were able to steal thirty of the best horses in Arizona. At White Tail Canyon "the cattlemen of the San Simon Valley had met for their fall roundup. Only the night before they had been warned that these dismounted Indians were in the vicinity; yet they went to sleep at a ranch house around which were lariated thirty crack cow ponies. The next morning the horses were gone; and, better mounted than ever, the Apaches were beyond pursuit."

The band vanished back into Mexico. In this short-lived foray they had killed three white men, but had obtained very little plunder.

The next invasion from Mexico, besides being disastrous for troops, white civilians, and a number of peaceful reservation Indians, was comparable in its viciousness, daring, and duration to any Apache raids occurring on American soil since the occupation of the Southwest by the United States. It was led by a Chiricahua about whom almost nothing was known. He was Josanie, a younger brother of Chihuahua, and he demonstrated tragically that he was the equal, if not the superior, of the boldest desperados of his people.

Crossing the border with only ten men early in November, Josanie soon met a band of sixteen hostiles who had preceded him north by a few days. With troops after them they killed two civilians and an Indian scout and wounded a soldier in the Florida Mountains. The two groups were together only a short time, the band of sixteen, for some undetermined reason, electing to return to Mexico.

Josanie and his ten warriors vanished, and for nearly three weeks nothing was heard of them. Suddenly they appeared near Fort Apache, sneaking into camps with word that Geronimo wanted all Apache to break out and join him. They met with cold refusals, and furious at their failure, they fiendishly killed eleven women, five men, and four children. Several young squaws were forced to leave with them. However, before they again disappeared they killed two wranglers with the reservation beef herd and stole a number of horses belonging to Bonito. From the Fort Apache region they traveled south and southeast, soon reaching the wilderness of western New Mexico.

Crook admitted that the failure to overtake the raiders "clearly demonstrated that when Indians get through the line into rough country north of the railroad it is practically impossible to do anything with them. The country is so indescribably rough that any pursuit is almost a farce."

Yet Crook kept his command in a relentless pursuit—to no avail. Late in December, with a blizzard raging in the mountains along the border, Josanie and his little band disappeared into Mexico. In less than two months they had ridden twelve hundred miles, killed thirty-eight persons, among them six troopers, stolen several hundred horses, and had lost only one man, a warrior identified by the impossible name of Azariquelch. Crook's statement regarding the impossibility of tracking down and capturing fast-moving raiders had been sadly illustrated. Josanie and his men had committed their ravages in a region dotted with eighty-three companies of cavalry.

Meanwhile, General Philip Sheridan had arrived at Fort Bowie, and he and Crook had made plans for a new campaign in Mexico. Sheridan had reservations about Crook's theory that only Indian scouts could destroy the hostiles in their Mexican strongholds, but he did not oppose their use in the forthcoming operation. Therefore, in the force sent south from the border under Captain Wirt Davis were several companies of Indian scouts but only one troop of cavalry. Another contingent under Captain Crawford, except for a few white officers, was composed entirely of a hundred Apache scouts.

As the new year began, the two columns were deep in the mountains of Mexico, and closing in on the renegades.

1886

Davis and Crawford took different routes, but their paths crossed several times. Toward the middle of January, Crawford's scouts located the main hideout of the Chiricahua in a remote canyon south of the Haros River. Lieutenant M. P. Maus would report: "Captain Crawford now decided to continue our march and attack the hostile camp at daylight the next morning. A hard day's march already had been made, but there was a chance we might be discovered and our present opportunity lost. The scouts requested the officers to take off their shoes and put on moccasins—this to avoid all noise if possible. All night the command toiled over the mountains and down into cañons so dark on this moonless night that they seemed bottomless. However, an hour before daylight, after an eighteen-hour march, within a mile and a half of the hostile camp, tired and foot-sore, many bruised from falling during the night . . . the four companies were disposed . . . so as to attack the camp on all sides at the same time."

Only moments before the assault began, a Chiricahua sentinel sighted some of the scouts and sounded the alarm. The renegades fled on foot in wild disorder, but so swiftly did the scouts descend upon the camp that their entire horse herd was captured and a number of women and children were taken prisoner. All the possessions and stores were destroyed.

The outlaw bands were without mounts, food, or reserve ammunition, and the stronghold in which they believed they were secure had been penetrated. Although most of them were alive, they realized that under such conditions they could not hope to survive. Within a few hours a squaw waving a white rag appeared in Crawford's camp and informed him that Geronimo and other leaders had sent her to ask for a conference under a flag of truce the following day. Crawford agreed, but he was never to meet them.

Mexican authorities more than once had charged that Crook's Apache scouts had committed depredations in Mexico and had robbed and abused Mexican citizens. This, of course, was not true, but Mexicans, both the military and civilians, hated all Apache, no matter what their guise. If this emotion were understandable, under the present circumstances it was totally unjustified. For it was the Apache scouts who were on the verge of freeing Mexico of the Apache menace.

At dawn a detachment of Mexican irregulars, also pursuing the Chiricahua hostiles, attacked Crawford's camp. Four men were wounded in the first volley. Scouts scattering for cover returned the fire, killing four and wounding five Mexicans.

"Although we tried in every way by waving handkerchiefs and calling out in Spanish who we were," said Lieutenant Maus, "they continued a sharp fire for about fifteen minutes, then it seemed we had made them understand we were American soldiers and friends. A party of them then approached and Captain Crawford and I went out about fifty yards from our position in the open and talked to them." Maus again told the Mexicans in Spanish "we were American soldiers, called attention to our dress, and said we would not fire." Crawford instructed Maus to return and make sure that no more firing was done by the Apache scouts. The lieutenant had taken only a few steps when several shots came from the Mexican line. Whirling around, Maus "saw the Captain lying on the rocks with a wound in his head, and some of his brains upon the rocks. . . . There can be no mistake; these men knew they were firing at American soldiers at this time." Crawford was mortally wounded, and Maus took command.

The Mexicans threatened to resume hostilities unless Maus supplied them with several mules on which to remove their wounded. Maus sent the animals to their camp, and the Mexicans departed. The lieutenant then moved back along the trail several miles. On the following day Geronimo and several other leaders, followed by a group of women and children, appeared for a meeting with him.

The superannuated Nana immediately surrendered. Geronimo and Nachee placed their personal families in Maus's care, but declared they needed time to gather other members of their bands and arrange with Chihuahua and Josanie to capitulate. They agreed to bring all their followers north "in two moons" for a peace conference with Crook.

They would surrender to no one else, and Crook must come to the parley "without soldiers." Geronimo named the Cañón de los Embudos, a short distance below the border, as the site of the meeting.

Observing the renegades before him, Maus shrewdly concluded that they were thoroughly discouraged and convinced that they would soon be destroyed by Crook's unlimited forces. Moreover, both his ammunition and rations were insufficient to permit him to conduct the extended campaign he knew would be necessary if he were to attempt the reduction of the hostiles with his small force. He accepted Geronimo's proposal and started north with the captives.

Late in March Crook sent a pack train to Cañón de los Embudos to establish a camp. When he received a message at Fort Bowie that the Chiricahua had arrived, he set out with a small escort of officers and scouts. He was endangering his life, but, as he said, Maus had made an agreement "and I was bound to abide by it." He left five companies of troops at the border prepared to dash into Mexico if trouble occurred, but if the Chiricahua had been plotting to ambush him he would have been killed long before the cavalry could have reached the site.

Always fearful of treachery, the Chiricahua held a strong defensive position. "We found them in camp," Crook reported, "on a rocky hill about eight hundred yards from Lieutenant Maus in such a position that a thousand men could not have surrounded them with any possibility of capturing them. They were able on the approach of an enemy . . . to scatter and escape through dozens of ravines and canyons. . . . They were armed to the teeth, having the most improved guns and all the ammunition they could carry . . . obtained in Mexico. Even if I had been disposed to betray the confidence placed in me, it would have been simply an impossibility to get white troops to that point either by day or by night without their knowledge, and had I attempted to do this the whole band would have stampeded back to the mountains. So suspicious were they that never more than from five to eight of the men came into our camp at one time, and to have attempted the arrest of these would have stampeded the others to the mountains."

The leaders—Geronimo, Chihuahua, Josanie, Nana, Nachee—came individually to confer with Crook. He bluntly told them in turn that he would accept nothing but their unconditional surrender, that he had orders to send them and their people to Florida as prisoners of war. "Decide at once on unconditional surrender or fight it out," he said. If they chose the latter "hostilities would commence at once and the last one of them would be killed, if it took fifty years."

Washington headquarters had instructed Crook to make no promises "unless necessary to secure the surrender" of the Chiricahua. The leaders agreed to surrender and go to Florida with the stipulation that after being held there for two years they would be returned to the Apache Reservation. Crook thought that a reasonable bargain, agreed to it, and shook hands with them.

After ordering Lieutenant Maus and a number of scouts to escort the prisoners to the border, he left for Fort Bowie. He had not requested that the hostiles surrender their guns, knowing that there was danger of their being attacked by Mexican troops or by a mob of white citizens before reaching the post. In such event soldiers, scouts, and captives would have been slain, and he held the fervent hope that the shedding of blood was forever ended in the Apache Country.

Crook immediately advised Washington of the surrender agreement. A message came back from General Sheridan that both disheartened and angered him. President Cleveland, said Sheridan, refused to "assent to the surrender of the hostiles on the terms of their imprisonment [in the] East for two years with the understanding of their return to the reservation. He instructs you to enter again into negotiations on the terms of their unconditional surrender, only sparing their lives."

Crook refused to obey. The hostiles were still in Mexico, accompanied by only Maus and a few scouts. To tell them that the terms on which they had surrendered to him were not to be honored would not only be a reflection on his own integrity, and utterly destroy their faith in him, but it would result in their bolting and scattering once more into the formidable mountains of Mexico.

Now the Indian and army contractors, to whom warfare meant money, made a desperate attempt to prevent the capitulation of the renegades from Mexico. They could see only one result if Crook were successful, and that was the removal from the Southwest of large numbers of troops.

A rascal of Swiss descent, Charles Tribolet, who had for some years maintained a small ranch and trading post near San Bernardino Springs, was instructed by the Indian Ring, of which he was a member in good standing, to make an effort to sabotage Crook's operations and prevent the surrender. Tribolet was a fence for goods stolen by Indians. He was a bootlegger who sold vile whiskey to Indians on both sides of the border, and he held contracts to furnish beef to several army installations.

After traveling slowly for two days Maus and the Chiricahua were only a short distance below the border. The next day they would have crossed into the United States. As a precaution the Indians had spread their camps over a wide area. Tribolet camped not far away at a spring appropriately called Contrabandista. He had brought with him a mule loaded with gifts and several kegs of liquor. An assistant had no difficulty slipping through the darkness to adjacent cooking fires and making his presence known. As no restrictions were placed on the renegades, Tribolet was soon surrounded by an enthusiastic group eager to have a few free drinks. Tribolet passed whiskey out in generous quantities. He usually charged ten dollars silver a quart.

His guests were soon drunk, and among them were Geronimo, Chihuahua, and Nachee. Tribolet well understood that no one, even when cold sober, was more suspicious than an Apache, and no one "spooked" as quickly as a drunken Apache. Calling the inebriated leaders aside, he warned them—and he was a convincing man—that they and their people were riding into a death trap. As soon as they crossed the border they would be ambushed by a wild mob of white citizens and slaughtered to the last man, woman, and child.

Perhaps Chihuahua, a heavy drinker, was too drunk to take him seriously or to comprehend the meaning of his words, but that was not the case with the other two leaders. They obviously believed him—at least they were not willing to take a chance that he was not telling the truth—and before morning Geronimo, Nachee, twenty warriors, and nineteen women and children were gone.

Lieutenant Maus and several Indian scouts followed their trail southward for several miles and then turned back, realizing the futility of attempting to overtake them.

A few days after they arrived at Fort Bowie, the bands of Chihuahua, Nana, and Josanie—seventy-seven men, women, and children in all— were put on a train for Fort Marion, Florida.

Regarding Tribolet, Crook told news correspondent Lummis:

"That man is the cause of this whole trouble. If it had not been for his whiskey, Geronimo and the others never would have decamped, the whole thing would now be settled . . . there's no way of dealing with Tribolet. He has been tried before, but bought his way out. If we had shot him down like a coyote, as he deserved, it would have raised a terrible row. Why, that man has a beef contract for our army! The government is obliged to advertise and let the contracts to the lowest bidder. Tribolet got one. It doesn't make any difference how big a scoundrel a man may be. That doesn't disqualify him. Punish him by law? We have no laws here . . . and such fellows can undo the work of a great government, while we have no recourse."

General Sheridan chose to blame the outbreak on the negligence of the Indian scouts, furiously wiring Crook that "it seems strange that Geronimo and party could have escaped without knowledge of the scouts." Crook had wearied of trying to make the "bullion and lace" generals ensconced behind desks in Washington understand that without loyal Indian scouts Arizona and New Mexico would still be a "vast domain of blood," and warfare with the Apache would be far from ended. Without Indian scouts no number of troops could have effectively combated the Apache, much less have conquered them. But he had explained all that in numerous long dispatches, and he did not repeat it in replying to Sheridan. He merely said: "There can be no question that the scouts were thoroughly loyal and would have prevented the hostiles from leaving had it been possible."

Sheridan was neither convinced nor satisfied. He telegraphed Crook: "Geronimo will undoubtedly enter upon other raids of murder and robbery, and as the offensive campaign against him with scouts has failed, would it not be best to take up defensive and give protection to the people and business interests of Arizona and New Mexico? The infantry might be stationed by companies on certain points requiring protection, and the cavalry patrol between them. . . . Please send me a statement of what you contemplate for the future."

Crook sent the statement the same day, April 1. It wasn't what Sheridan had expected.

"I believe," Crook told his superior, "that the plan upon which I have conducted operations is the one likely to prove successful in the end. It may be, however, that I am too much wedded to my own views in this matter, and as I have spent nearly eight years of the hardest work of my life in this [Arizona] department, I respectfully request that I may be relieved from its command."

Twelve days later Brigadier General Nelson A. Miles took command at Fort Bowie, and Crook departed for a short leave before returning to the Department of the Platte.

* * *

Thrapp: "General Miles was an experienced Indian campaigner, but he lacked Crook's brilliance, thorough knowledge of the Apache, originality, and perhaps even his integrity. The officer came to Arizona imbued with Sheridan's notion that the proper way to fight the Apache was with white troops, and he labored to put this into practice."

Noted western scholar J. Frank Dobie: ". . . puffed-up Miles, who betrayed good Apaches and Crook both and who lied to the nation . . ."

* * *

Anatomy of an Anticlimax

General Miles had more than five thousand troops with which to capture or destroy approximately a score of Apache warriors, all of whom were "lost somewhere in the mountains of Mexico." In addition, he had the help of several thousand Mexican soldiers who were also after Geronimo.

Two of the hostiles who had bolted at Contrabandista Spring, after sobering up, had voluntarily surrendered at Fort Bowie, and it was believed that no more than nineteen men remained with Geronimo and Nachee.

Adopting the tactics advised by Sheridan, Miles stationed infantry at waterholes, in passes, and at supply depots. The cavalry was kept on constant patrol, accomplishing nothing but wearing out both men and horses in a futile search. Crook's companies of Indian scouts were discharged, and sent to San Carlos and Fort Apache Reservations. "Be good boys when you get home," Miles cautioned them.

A campaign in Mexico was planned, but before Miles could get it organized and under way, the renegades taught him a lesson. Geronimo and Nachee, with no more than ten or twelve warriors, swept up the Santa Cruz Valley. Separating into small parties of three or four men each, they raided over a large area, some going as far north as Fort Apache.

All the cavalry and infantry in Miles's command was sent after them. Almost within sight of pursuing troops, they stole fresh horses and vanished. On one occasion they ambushed a small contingent, killed two soldiers, wounded two others, and got away with half a dozen horses, several rifles, and a quantity of ammunition.

In June Miles sent a force into Mexico to search for the renegades under Captain H. W. Lawton. Next in command was Lieutenant Leonard Wood, an assistant surgeon who had requested combat duty. Miles thought white troops could perform the mission, but he was persuaded by veteran officers who had served under Crook that at least a few Indian scouts should be sent along. Somewhat begrudgingly he reenlisted twenty experienced Apache scouts to supplement the company of infantry and the thirty-five cavalrymen assigned to Lawton.

After a few weeks of fruitless searching for the wild band the horses were worn out and had to be abandoned. The cavalry was on foot with the infantry. So rigorous had been the hunt that the troops were virtually in rags. Wood had nothing to wear but a pair of cotton flannel drawers, an old blue blouse, a pair of moccasins, and a hat without a crown. Captain Lawton was dressed in overalls, an undershirt, and the rim of a felt hat. The others were similarly garbed.

Miles was in line for promotion to major-general, but with all his operations, including the campaign in Mexico, failing to achieve the desired results, he feared that he might be passed over in favor of some other officer. In desperation he admitted that new plans he had devised would involve a return to some extent "of the methods which constituted the distinctive feature of the policy adopted and followed by General Crook." He would not send strong columns of Indian scouts into Mexico, as Crook had done, but he would send a detachment capable of great mobility. It would be commanded by the experienced Indian fighter Captain Charles B. Gatewood and would consist of twenty-five cavalry and twenty-two Indian scouts. Much to Miles's discomfiture, Gatewood wanted two Chiricahua scouts whom he knew to be thoroughly trustworthy, and the privilege of selecting the others. Nor did Gatewood want the cavalry. "Hell," he said, "I couldn't get anywhere near Geronimo with twenty-five soldiers." And he managed to arrange with commandants at several posts to state that they could not spare any troops for the assignment.

Gatewood and his scouts, starting south late in July, encountered a cavalry patrol commanded by Lieutenant James Parker. Parker could spare no men, but he offered to accompany the scouts for some distance as a temporary escort. Gatewood had determined to find Lawton and Wood, and he headed directly where he thought they would be operating. Parker soon left him and went back north.

Early in August Gatewood and his scouts came upon Lawton's camp on the Haros River. The whereabouts of the hostiles was unknown, but scouts picked up the intelligence that they were probably in the vicinity of Fronteras. That town became their destination.

The march was temporarily disrupted when the scouts got gloriously drunk in a small village and began shooting at each other. Officers and a few Indians who had remained sober were able to restore order without any casualties occurring. Fortunately most of the rioters had been so inebriated that they had been unable to take aim.

Gatewood, his scouts, and several soldiers Lawton assigned to him pushed on ahead of the column and made a forced march of eighty miles to Fronteras. There it was learned that two Chiricahua squaws had been in town that day, purchased supplies, and had talked with the prefect about negotiating a treaty with the hostiles. The prefect had assured them that he would be glad to sign a treaty with Geronimo, and they had departed ostensibly to carry this welcome news to the renegades.*

Gatewood found that as soon as the women had left, the prefect had sent for two hundred Mexican soldiers. His plan was to secrete them in buildings and when the Apache appeared to talk about peace he would get them drunk "and then kill all the men and enslave all the women and children."

Gatewood agreed not to upset the prefect's scheme, and announced that he was going south to rejoin Lawton, but as soon as he was outside the town he circled around until his scouts had picked up the trail of the squaws.

---

*It would be learned in time that Geronimo had instructed the women to make an offer of peace so that they could obtain supplies and avoid capture. Geronimo had no intention of making peace with any Mexicans. All he had wanted was some coffee, beans, and flour.

"Slowly and cautiously," Gatewood would write, "with a piece of flour sacking on a stick to the fore as a flag, we followed the squaws the next three days over rough country full of likely places for ambush. By the third day the trail was very fresh." Gatewood sent a courier back to inform Lawton that he was on the trail of the renegades.

Two of Gatewood's scouts located the Chiricahua camp in the Torres Mountains and boldly entered it to deliver a message advising them that General Miles would meet them at the border in a peace parley. One of the scouts was held hostage, while the other was allowed to return with word that Geronimo would talk only with Gatewood and that all troops must remain where they were or there could be no meeting. Gatewood did not know then that all the time he had been trailing the squaws he was being observed through field glasses by Geronimo.

Gatewood, certainly one of the bravest officers ever to grace an army uniform in the West, went on alone. Some Chiricahua men soon appeared, and he obeyed their command to proceed with them.

For two days Gatewood sat with Geronimo and Nachee, whom he had come to know well at Fort Apache, in solemn council. Because of his prominent nose, he was called by them—indeed by all Apache—*Bay-chen-day-sen,* signifying beak. They liked him, but more important they trusted him. Miles had instructed him that if they gave themselves up they would be reunited with all members of their families and all their relatives who still remained on the Fort Apache Reservation. Dutifully Gatewood obeyed. He did not know, of course, that Miles had no intention of keeping the promise; indeed, that Miles intended to do just the opposite, separate them from their families and relatives and throw them into dungeons. Unlike Crook in dealing with Indians, Miles did not consider keeping his word a matter of honor.

After a lengthy talk with the other Apache, Geronimo appeared before Gatewood and said with quiet dignity: "We will go with you to surrender to General Miles. Send word to him to meet us in Skeleton Canyon [near the border]. You will travel with us."

Gatewood agreed. On August 25, Geronimo, Nachee, twenty-two warriors, and fourteen women and children set out with Gatewood on their final march into captivity.

Of all the hostile leaders known to be in Mexico, only Mangus, who had not offered to surrender, was still hiding, reportedly in the Sierra Madre. He was not to be feared, for he had no band of warriors.*

From Skeleton Canyon, Miles took Geronimo and Nachee with him

---

*He would be captured without resistance later in the year near the border. With him were only two men, three women, two half-grown boys and a girl, and four small children.

in an army vehicle to Fort Bowie. Three days later the other prisoners arrived at the post.

Then it was learned that while Gatewood had been in Mexico, Miles had concluded that the Chiricahuas who had been living peacefully on the Fort Apache Reservation were a "disturbing element." Quietly he had moved several companies of troops to the agency. Word was sent to the Chiricahua to come in for a "routine count." When they dutifully appeared—three hundred and eighty-two men, women, and children—they were quickly surrounded and informed they were prisoners of war. Within a few days they were put on a train and started for Fort Marion, Florida. Miles also arrested and sent east a number of the most loyal Indian scouts who had served faithfully for years under Crook.[28]

On September 8, under heavy guard, Geronimo, Nachee, and those who had surrendered with them were marched to Bowie station on the Southern Pacific, where several coaches and an engine were waiting to take them to a steamy Florida concentration camp.

As the train pulled out, the Fourth Cavalry band played "Auld Lang Syne."

NOTES AND BIBLIOGRAPHY

In deference to readers who are not concerned with authorities, I have not burdened the pages of this book with copious footnotes. A responsible historian, however, is required to enumerate his sources, not only for the benefit of persons who may wish to give additional attention to the subjects treated, but also to aid scholars who are interested in assessing the soundness and merit of his work. A third reason might be noted: other authors justly should receive credit for material they provided.

Therefore, in various places in the text I have inserted numbers which refer to skeletal citations.

No good purpose would be served by listing the innumerable books, scientific papers, articles, manuscripts, journals, and other documents which I consulted in my research. A large proportion of them yielded no useful or significant information. In view of this, I have compiled a Selected Bibliography which I believe adequately meets the demands of my obligation. Moreover, most of the sources cited in it also contain bibliographies.

In the Selected Bibliography will be found bibliographical details of the numbered skeletal citations.

NOTES

1. Cabeza de Vaca's *Relación* was first published in Spain in 1542. See Smith; Fanny Bandelier; Winship; Bolton (1911); Hallenbeck (1940); Terrell (1962, 1968-A, 1970); Hodge (1907-B); Bishop.
2. See Hopkins; Laughlin; Muller-Beck; Wormington; Driver; Coon; Hodge (1907-A); Terrell (1971); Martin, Quinby, and Collier (1947).
3. See Hammond (1940); Bancroft (1884); Bolton (1916, 1949); Hammond and Rey (1940); Winship;. Terrell (1962, 1968); Baldwin; Bloom; Sauer; Wagner.
4. The Navajo and the Kiowa–Apache, although they spoke dialects of the Athapascan

language, have always been treated as distinct tribes by ethnologists, mainly for the following reasons:

As early as the seventeenth century the Navajo had adopted many Pueblo customs and beliefs, had established fixed habitations and highly productive irrigated farms, and maintained breeding herds of sheep and cattle. While they bolstered their economy by raiding, and fiercely defended their homeland against white invaders, their way of life otherwise was largely in sharp contrast to that of their more nomadic relatives, the Apache.

The Kiowa–Apache were so designated because since the earliest traditional period they lived with the Kiowa of Tanoan stock and probably connected with the Shoshonean stock as well. The Kiowa–Apache were not affiliated with other Apache groups—although closely related to the Lipan and Jicarilla—but they always spoke their own peculiar dialect of the Athapascan tongue. They were with the Kiowa in the northern Great Plains and mountains, moved south with them under pressure from other tribes, and remained with them during the period of the Kiowa alliance with the Comanche. They participated in Kiowa–Comanche raids against the Spanish, which frequently penetrated deep into Mexico. See Forbes (1960); Hennepin; Nasatir; Moorhead; Hoijer; Swanton (1952); Wedel; Hyde; Goodwin; Young (1961); Sayles (1936); Sonnichsen; Quebbeman; Ogle; Terrell (1971); Hackett (1923); Bancroft (1889).

5. Pedro de Castañeda wrote the most important narrative of the Coronado Expedition, in which he served as a soldier. His original manuscript is not known to exist. Winship translated a copy of it which was made in Seville in 1596, and is now owned by the New York Public Library. The Winship translation was first published in the Fourteenth Annual Report of the Bureau of American Ethnology, Smithsonian Institution, in 1896, and since has appeared in numerous other works. Besides Winship, see Bolton (1949); Hammond and Rey (1940); Terrell (1962, 1968); Horgan; Thomas (1935); Villagra; P. W. Powell; Twitchell (1911, 1914).

6. The quotations of Gallegos are from a translation of his account made by George P. Hammond and Agapito Rey (q.v. 1966). The original Gallegos manuscript is in the Archives of the Indies, Seville, Spain.

Various interpretations of the Espejo and Luxán accounts have appeared in numerous histories. Hammond and Rey made new translations of them in recent years, and the excerpts used here are from their work, which was published by the University of New Mexico (Hammond and Rey, 1966). Espejo's report to King Philip was first printed in Spain in 1586. See Thomas (1935); Goodwin; Forbes (1960); Swanton (1952); Hyde; Bancroft (1889).

7. "Purgatory" was the best American pioneers could do with *El Río de Las Ánimas Perdidas en Purgatorio*. It was corrupted by early American cattlemen to "picketwire," and so it is called by local residents today. On maps it is "Purgatoire."

8. See Twitchell (1911);. Horgan; Hackett (1923); Dale; Henshaw under "Slavery" in Hodge (1907-A); Forbes (1960); Bancroft (1889); Terrell (1970); Benavides.

9. Forbes (1960) is a concise history of the early Spanish period in New Mexico, but is quite adequate as a guide, for very little relevant source material remains unmentioned in it. See Bolton (1916); Hammond and Rey (1953); Thomas (1932); Villagra; Hackett (1942); Powell (1952); Hodge (1907-A); Bancroft (1889).

10. The notes about Apache infants were excerpted from Grenville Goodwin's famous work, *The Social Organization of the Western Apache*, first published by the University of Arizona in 1942, and issued in a new edition in 1969. Goodwin spent years among the Apache when much of their traditional culture still existed. He knew more about them than any ethnographer who ever lived.

11. See Roe; Villagra; Forbes (1960); Denhardt; Wissler (1922); Webb; Worcester (1951); Hammond and Rey (1928); Benavides; Wedel; Terrell (1962, 1968). The histories of the Navajo and Apache in certain years of the seventeenth and eighteenth centuries are closely interwoven. I have drawn heavily on my own works, *The Navajo* (1970) and *An American Indian Almanac* (1971), both of which contain bibliographies.

12. Excerpted and condensed from *The Land of Poco Tiempo*, by Charles F. Lummis, first

published in 1893. The material I used was taken from the 1906 edition. I consider it the best description of an Apache warrior ever written.

13. The translations of official Spanish manuscripts for the years 1696–1727 by Alfred Barnaby Thomas (1935) are valuable and reveal many facts previously unknown. See Wallace and Hoebel; Horgan; Abert; Bancroft (1889); Terrell (1968, 1970); M. E. Opler (1941); Twitchell (1911, 1914); Bolton (1921).

14. See Moorhead; Prescott; Sonnichsen; Thomas (1932); Dale; Terrell (1970); Faulk (1970); Worcester.

15. Josiah Gregg's *Commerce on the Prairies* is a classic of western Americana. I used a 1954 reprint edited by Max L. Moorhead, published by the University of Oklahoma. Moorhead's notes immeasurably increased the value of the work. While the *Personal Narrative of James Ohio Pattie* is a loosely connected narrative of hair-raising adventures, many of them bordering on the incredible, it contains enough factual material to make it of value to historians. Pattie was not the author of the book. He "recalled" it for a magazine editor, Timothy Flint, in Cincinnati. See Corle; Faulk (1970); Cremony; Sonnichsen; Bancroft (1889); Terrell (1968-A, 1970); Thrapp; Wellman.

16. John C. Cremony's *Life Among the Apaches* incomparably enriches the annals of the Southwest and remains today one of the most notable and valuable works of western Americana. It was first published in San Francisco in 1868; a new edition was printed in Tucson in 1954. I used a 1969 reprint. See Gibson; Ogle; Terrell (1970); Bancroft (1889); Bailey (1966); Hodge (1907-A); Thrapp; Dunn; Garber; Sonnichsen; Swanton (1952); Calhoun.

17. See the annual reports for the period of the Secretary of War, the Secretary of the Interior, and the Commissioner of Indian Affairs; Frazer; Wellman; Cremony; Garber; Ogle; Bennett; Sonnichsen; Dunn; Goodwin; Thrapp; Corle.

18. Horgan; Hoopes; Sonnichsen; Ogle; Bennett; Elliott; Farish; McClintock; annual reports of the Secretary of War, the Secretary of the Interior, and the Commissioner of Indian Affaris.

19. Chittenden; Wellman; Ogle; Farish; McClintock; Elliott; Sonnichsen; Terrell (1970); Thrapp; Faulk (1970); annual reports of the Secretary of War, the Secretary of the Interior, and the Commissioner of Indian Affairs.

20. Sabin; Keleher; Faulk (1970); Cremony; Wellman; Thrapp; Sonnichsen; Terrell (1970); Ogle; Conner; Bailey (1966); Young (1968); Dunn; annual reports *(op. cit.)*.

21. Lockwood (1932); McClintock; Terrell (1970); Wellman; Bailey (1964); Conner; Frazer; Brandes; Thrapp; Dunn; Sonnichsen; annual reports *(op. cit.)*.

22. Young (1968); *Arizona. Territorial Legislature Report on Apache Outrages* (1871); Ogle; McClintock; Thrapp; Dunn; Faulk (1970); Terrell (1970); annual reports *(op. cit.)*.

23. Don Schellie's *Vast Domain of Blood*, a history of the Camp Grant massacre and the farcical trial of the participants, is outstanding. It contains a large amount of "'local color" and analysis of the personalities involved that is not found in other works on the subject. Vincent Colyer's *Peace with the Apaches* (1872) is valuable as source material pertaining to the Indian policy of the Grant Administration, the conditions in Arizona and New Mexico, and events which transpired in these territories at the time. See Crook (1960); Faulk (1970); Ogle; Thrapp; Wellman; Lockwood (1932); Lummis (1966); Bourke (1891, 1968); McClintock; annual reports *(op. cit.)*.

24. Howard (1872, 1907); Crook (1886, 1960); Ogle; Sonnichsen; Thrapp; annual reports *(op. cit.)*. Valuable collections of Crookiana and material pertaining to other military officers and frontiersmen of the period are available in the Arizona Pioneers' Historical Society Library, Tucson; Bancroft Library, Berkeley, California; Huntington Library, San Marino, California; Rutherford B. Hayes Memorial Library, Fremont, Ohio; Southwest Museum Library, Los Angeles; and the University of New Mexico Library, Albuquerque.

25. Pope (1876); Dunn; Wellman; Lockwood (1932); Crook (1886); Sonnichsen; Ogle; Thrapp. See also General Crook's Annual Reports for 1871–1875 and 1881–1886 to the War Department, and annual reports *(op. cit.)*.

26. Cruse; Crook (1886); Lummis (1966); R. I. Dodge (1877); Thrapp; Bourke (1886, 1891); annual reports *(op. cit.)*; Crook's annual reports *(op. cit.)*. Newspaper files in Tucson, Prescott, Silver City, Santa Fe, Denver, San Diego, San Francisco, and other

cities for the most part are unreliable as sources. Very few of the accounts printed accurately portray events as they occurred, and many were deliberate fabrications.
27. Forsyth; Bourke (1886, 1891); Davis; Lummis (1966); Thrapp; Ogle; Crook (1886); annual reports *(op. cit.)*.
28. Davis; Crook (1886); Bourke (1886, 1891); Schellie; McClintock; Thrapp; Ogle; Lummis (1966); annual reports *(op. cit.)*.

SELECTED BIBLIOGRAPHY

ABEL, ANNIE HELOISE, *The Official Correspondence of James S. Calhoun While Indian Agent at Santa Fe and Superintendent of Indian Affairs in New Mexico*, Washington, 1915.
ABERT, JAMES W., *The Comanche Indians* (John Galvin, editor), San Francisco, 1970.
AMSDEN, CHARLES AVERY, *Prehistoric Southwesterners from Basketmaker to Pueblo*, Los Angeles, 1949.
Arizona Territorial Legislature Report on Apache Outrages in 1869–1870, San Francisco, 1871.
BAILEY, L. R., *The Long Walk*, Los Angeles, 1964.
——*Indian Slave Trade in the Southwest*, Los Angeles, 1966.
BALDWIN, PERCY M., "Fray Marcos de Niza and His Discovery of the Seven Cities of Cibola," *New Mexico Historical Review*, April, 1926.
BANCROFT, HUBERT HOWE, *History of Mexico*, San Francisco, 1883.
——*History of the North Mexican States and Texas*, San Francisco, 1884.
——*Native Races*, Vols. 1 to 5, San Francisco, 1886–1890.
——*History of Arizona and New Mexico, 1530–1888*, San Francisco, 1889.
BANDELIER, ADOLPH F. A., *The Delight Makers*, New York, 1890.
——*Final Report of Investigations Among the Indians of the Southwestern United States*, Cambridge, 1890.
——*Contributions to the History of the Southwestern United States*, Cambridge, 1890.
BANDELIER, FANNY, *The Journey of Álvar Núñez Cabeza de Vaca and His Companions from Florida to the Pacific, 1528–1536.* Translated from the 1542 edition of Cabeza de Vaca's *Relación*. New York, 1905.
BARNES, WILL C., *Arizona Place Names*, Tucson, 1960.
BARNEY, JAMES M., *Tales of Apache Warfare* (pamphlet), Phoenix, 1933.
BARTLETT, RICHARD A., *Great Surveys of the American West*, Norman, 1962.
BELLAH, ROBERT N., *Apache Kinship Systems*, Cambridge, 1942.
BENAVIDES, ALONSO DE, *Memorial of 1630* (Mrs. Edward E. Ayer, translator), Chicago, 1916. Reprinted Albuquerque, 1965.
BENNETT, JAMES A., *Forts and Forays: A Dragoon in New Mexico*, Albuquerque, 1948.
BILLINGTON, RAY ALLEN, *Westward Expansion*, New York, 1949.
BISHOP, MORRIS, *The Odyssey of Cabeza de Vaca*, New York, 1933.
BLOOM, LANSING B., "Who Discovered New Mexico?" *New Mexico Historical Review*, April, 1940.
——"Was Fray Marcos a Liar?" *New Mexico Historical Review*, April, 1941.
BOAS, FRANZ, *Race, Language and Culture*, New York, 1949.
BOLTON, HERBERT E., "The Jumano Indians of Texas," *Texas State Historical Association Quarterly*, July, 1911.
——*Spanish Exploration in the Southwest*, New York, 1916.
——*The Spanish Borderlands*, New Haven, 1921.
——*Rim of Christendom*, New York, 1936.
——*Coronado*, New York, 1949.
BOURKE, JOHN G., *An Apache Campaign in the Sierra Madre*, New York, 1886.
——*On the Border with Crook*, New York, 1891.
——*With General Crook in the Indian Wars*, Palo Alto, 1968.
BRANCH, E. DOUGLAS, *The Hunting of the Buffalo*, New York, 1929.
BRAND, DONALD, "Prehistoric Trade in the Southwest," *New Mexico Business Review*, Vol. 4, Albuquerque, 1935.

BRANDES, RAY, *Frontier Military Posts of Arizona*, Globe, Arizona, 1960.
BROWNE, J. ROSS, *A Tour Through Arizona: Adventures in the Apache Country*, New York, 1869. Reprinted Tucson, 1951.
CALHOUN, JAMES S. (*see* Abel).
CASTANEDA, PEDRO DE (*see* Winship).
CHARD, C. S., *New World Migration Routes*, College, Alaska, 1958.
CHITTENDEN, HIRAM MARTIN, *History of the American Fur Trade of the Far West*, New York, 1902.
CLUM, JOHN P., *The Truth about the Apaches Told in Annual Reports*, Los Angeles, 1931.
——"Apache Misrule," *New Mexico Historical Review*, April, 1930.
——"Eskiminzin," *New Mexico Historical Review*, October, 1928.
CLUM, WOODWORTH, *Apache Agent: The Story of John P. Clum*, New York, 1936.
COLTON, HAROLD S., "Prehistoric Trade in the Southwest," *Scientific Monthly*, August, 1941.
COLYER, VINCENT, *Peace with the Apaches of Arizona and New Mexico: Report to the Board of Indian Commissioners*, Washington, 1872.
CONNER, DANIEL ELLIS, *Joseph Reddeford Walker and the Arizona Adventure*, Norman, 1956.
COOKE, PHILIP ST. GEORGE, *Conquest of New Mexico and California*, New York, 1878.
COON, CARLTON S., *The Story of Man*, New York, 1962.
CORLE, EDWIN, *The Gila, River of the Southwest*, New York, 1951.
CREMONY, JOHN C., *Life Among the Apaches*, San Francisco, 1868. Reprinted Tucson, 1954.
CROOK, GEORGE, *Résumé of Operations Against Apache Indians from 1882 to 1886*, Washington, 1886.
——*Autobiography*, Norman, 1960.
CRUSE, THOMAS, *Apache Days and After*, Caldwell, Idaho, 1941.
CUTTS, JAMES MADISON, *The Conquest of California and New Mexico, 1846–48*, Albuquerque, 1965.
DALE, EDWARD E., *The Indians of the Southwest*, Norman, 1949.
DAVIS, BRITTON, *The Truth about Geronimo*, New Haven, 1963.
DENHARDT, ROBERT MOORMAN, *The Horse of the Americas*, Norman, 1947.
DIAZ DEL CASTILLO, BERNAL, *True History of the Conquest of New Spain*, New York, 1927.
DOBIE, J. FRANK, *Apache Gold and Yaqui Silver*, New York, 1939.
——*The Mustangs*, Boston, 1952.
DODGE, RICHARD IRVING, *The Plains of the Great West and Their Inhabitants*, New York, 1877.
——*33 Years Among Our Wild Indians*, New York, 1882.
DRIVER, HAROLD E., *Indians of North America*, Chicago, 1961.
DUNN, J. P., JR., *Massacres of the Mountains*, New York, 1965.
EASON, NICHOLA J., *Fort Verde*, Camp Verde, Arizona, 1966.
ELLIOTT, WALLACE W. (Editor), *History of Arizona Territory*, San Francisco, 1884.
EMMETT, CHRIS, *Fort Union and the Winning of the Southwest*, Norman, 1965.
FARISH, THOMAS E., *History of Arizona*, San Francisco, 1914.
FAULK, ODIE B., *Too Far North—Too Far South*, Los Angeles, 1967.
——*Arizona: A Short History*, Norman, 1970.
FORBES, JACK D., *Apache, Navajo and Spaniard*, Norman, 1960.
——*Warriors of the Colorado*, Norman, 1965.
FORSYTH, GEORGE A., *Thrilling Days in Army Life*, New York, 1900.
FRAZER, ROBERT W., *Forts of the West*, Norman, 1965.
FREEMAN, LEWIS R., *The Conquistadores*, New York, 1923.
GARBER, PAUL N., *The Gadsden Treaty*, Philadelphia, 1923.
GATEWOOD, CHARLES B., *The Surrender of Geronimo*, Order of the Indian Wars of the United States, Washington, 1929.
GIBSON, GEORGE R., *Journal of a Soldier under Kearney and Doniphan* (Ralph P. Bieber, editor), Glendale, California, 1935.
GODDARD, PLINY E., *Indians of the Southwest*, New York, 1913.
——*San Carlos Apache Texts*, American Museum of Natural History Anthropological Papers, Vol. 24, Part 3, New York, 1919.
——*White Mountain Apache Texts*, American Museum of Natural History Anthropological Papers, Vol. 24, Part 4, New York, 1920.

GOETZMANN, WILLIAM H., *Exploration and Empire*, New York, 1966.
GOODWIN, GRENVILLE, *The Social Organization of the Western Apache*, Tucson, 1942. Reprinted 1969.
GREGG, JOSIAH, *Commerce on the Prairies*, New York, 1845 (Many reprints.)
GUNNARSON, D. A., *The Southern Athapascans: Their Arrival in the Southwest*, Museum of New Mexico, Santa Fe, 1956.
HACKETT, CHARLES WILSON (Editor and Translator), *Historical Documents Relating to New Mexico, Nueva Vizcaya, and Approaches Thereto, to 1773*, Washington, 1923.
——*The Revolt of the Pueblo Indians of New Mexico and Otermin's Attempted Reconquest, 1680–1682*, Albuquerque, 1942.
HAGAN, WILLIAM T., *American Indians*, Chicago, 1961.
HALL, EDWARD TWITCHELL, JR., "Recent Clues to Athapascan Prehistory in the Southwest, *American Anthropologist*, Vol. XLVI, No. 1, Menasha, Wisconsin, 1944.
HALLENBECK, CLEVE, *Journey and Route of Cabeza de Vaca*, Glendale, California, 1940.
HALSETH, ODD S., *Prehistory of the Southwest*, Phoenix, 1949.
HAMMOND GEORGE P., *Coronado's Seven Cities*, Albuquerque, 1940.
——and AGAPITO REY (Editors and Translators), *Obregon's History of Sixteenth-Century Explorations in Western America*, Los Angeles, 1928.
——and AGAPITO REY, *The Narratives of the Coronado Expedition*, Albuquerque, 1940.
——and AGAPITO REY, *Don Juan de Oñate, Colonizer of New Mexico, 1595–1628*, Albuquerque, 1953.
——and AGAPITO REY, *The Rediscovery of New Mexico*, Albuquerque, 1966.
HENNIPEN, LOUIS, *A New Discovery of a Vast Territory in America*, Minneapolis, 1938.
HENSHAW, H. W., "Slavery" (*see* Hodge).
HODGE, FREDERICK W. (Editor), *Handbook of Indians North of Mexico*, Bureau of American Ethnology, Washington, 1907-A.
——*Spanish Explorers in the Southern United States*, New York, 1907-B. Reprinted 1959.
HOIJER, HARRY, *Chiricahua and Mescalero Texts*, Chicago, 1938.
HOOPES ALBAN W., *Indian Affairs and Their Administration, 1849–1860*, Philadelphia, 1932.
HOPKINS, DAVID M. (Editor), *The Bering Land Bridge*, Stanford, 1967.
HORGAN, PAUL, *Great River: The Rio Grande in North American History*, New York, 1954.
HOWARD, O. O., *Account of General Howard's Mission to the Apaches and Navajos*, Washington, 1872.
——*My Life and Experiences among Our Hostile Indians*, Hartford, 1907.
HYDE, GEORGE E., *Indians of the High Plains*, Norman, 1959.
INMAN, HENRY, *The Old Santa Fe Trail*, New York, 1897.
KAPPLER, C. J., *Indian Affairs, Laws and Treaties*, Washington, 1902.
KELEHER, WILLIAM A., *Turmoil in New Mexico*, Santa Fe, 1952.
KING, CHARLES, *Campaigning with Crook*, Norman, 1964.
KINO, EUSEBIO FRANCISCO, *Historical Memoir of Pimeria Alta*, Cleveland, 1919.
LAUGHLIN, W. S., "Human Migrations and Permanent Occupation in the Bering Sea Area" (*see* Hopkins).
LOCKWOOD, FRANK C., *Pioneer Days in Arizona*, New York, 1932.
——*The Apache Indians*, New York, 1938.
LOOMIS, NEIL M., *The Texan-Santa Fe Pioneers*, Norman, 1958.
LOWERY, WOODBURY, *The Spanish Settlements Within the Present Limits of the United States, 1513–1561*, New York, 1901.
LOWIE, ROBERT H., *Indians of the Plains*, New York, 1954.
LUMMIS, CHARLES F., *The Spanish Pioneers*, Chicago, 1893.
——"Fray Zarate Salmeron's Relation," *Land of Sunshine* magazine, October, 1900, Los Angeles.
——*The Land of Poco Tiempo*, New York, 1906.
——*General Crook and the Apache Wars: A Correspondent's Reports*, Flagstaff, Arizona, 1966.
McCLINTOCK, JAMES H., *Arizona: Prehistoric—Aboriginal—Pioneer—Modern*, Chicago, 1916.
MANJE, JUAN MATEO, *Luz de Tierra Incognita* (Harry J. Karns, translator), Tucson, 1954.
MARION, J. H., *Notes of Travel Through the Territory of Arizona* (Donald M. Powell, editor), Tucson, 1965.

MARTIN, PAUL S., GEORGE I. QUIMBY, and DONALD COLLIER, *Indians Before Columbus*, Chicago, 1947.
MAYHALL MILDRED P., *The Kiowas*, Norman, 1962.
MILES, NELSON A., *Personal Recollections and Observations of General Nelson A. Miles*, New York, 1896.
MILLER, JOSEPH, *Arizona Cavalcade*, New York, 1962.
____*Arizona: The Last Frontier*, New York, 1956.
____*The Arizona Story*, New York, 1952.
MOONEY, JAMES, *The Aboriginal Population of America North of Mexico*, Washington, 1928.
MOORHEAD, MAX L., *The Apache Frontier*, Norman, 1968.
MULLER-BECK, HANSJURGEN, "On Migrations of Hunters Across the Bering Land Bridge in the Upper Pleistocene" (*see* Hopkins).
NASATIR, A. P., *Before Lewis and Clark*, St. Louis, 1952.
NESBIT, PAUL H., *The Ancient Mimbrenos*, Beloit, Wisconsin, 1931.
NEWCOMB, W. W., JR., *The Indians of Texas*, Austin, 1961.
NUNEZ CABEZA DE VACA, ALVAR (*see* Fanny Bandelier, Buckingham Smith).
OGLE, RALPH HEDRICK, *Federal Control of the Western Apache, 1848–1886*, Albuquerque, 1970.
OPLER, MORRIS E., *An Apache Life Way*, Chicago, 1941.
____"A Chiricahua's Account of the Geronimo Campaign of 1886," *New Mexico Historical Review*, October, 1938.
____and CATHERINE H. OPLER, "Mescalero Apache History in the Southwest," *New Mexico Historical Review*, January, 1950.
PATTIE, JAMES OHIO, *Personal Narrative*, Cincinnati, 1831. (Many reprints.)
PAXSON, FREDERICK L., *The Last American Frontier*, New York, 1910.
POPE, GENERAL JOHN, *Report to the Secretary of War*, Washington, 1876.
POSTON, CHARLES D., *Apache Land*, San Francisco, 1878.
POWELL, DONALD M., *An Arizona Gathering*, Tucson, 1960.
POWELL, PHILIP WAYNE, *Soldiers, Indians and Silver*, Berkeley, 1952.
PRESCOTT, WILLIAM H., *History of the Conquest of Mexico*, New York, 1843.
PUMPELLY, RAPHAEL, *Across America and Asia*, New York, 1870.
____*Pumpelly's Arizona* (Andrew Wallace, editor), Tucson, 1965.
QUEBBEMAN, FRANCES E., *Medicine in Territorial Arizona*, Phoenix, 1966.
RISTER, CARL COKE, *The Southwestern Frontier*, Cleveland, 1926.
ROE, FRANK GILBERT, *The Indian and the Horse*, Norman, 1955.
RUSHMORE, ELSIE M., *The Indian Policy During Grant's Administration*, New York, 1914.
SABIN, EDWIN L., *General Crook and the Fighting Apaches*, Philadelphia, 1918.
____*Kit Carson Days*, New York, 1935.
SAUER, CARL O., "The Credibility of the Fray Marcos Account," *New Mexico Historical Review*, Vol. XII, 1937.
SAYLES, E. B., *An Archeological Survey of Chihuahua, Mexico*, Gila Pueblo Medallion Papers, No. 22, Globe, Arizona, 1936.
____and ERNST ANTEVAS, *The Cochise Culture*, Gila Pueblo Medallion Papers, No. 24, Globe, Arizona, 1941.
SCHELLIE, DON, *Vast Domain of Blood*, Los Angeles, 1968.
SMITH, BUCKINGHAM, *Relación of Álvar Núñez Cabeza de Vaca*, translated from the 1555 edition, Washington, 1851.
SONNICHSEN, C. L., *The Mescalero Apaches*, Norman, 1958.
SPRAGUE, MARSHALL, *The Great Gates*, Boston, 1964.
SWANTON, JOHN R., *The Indian Tribes of North America*, Bureau of American Ethnology, Bulletin 145, Washington, 1952.
TERRELL, JOHN UPTON, *Journey into Darkness*, New York, 1962.
____*Traders of the Western Morning: Aboriginal Commerce in Precolumbian America*, Southwest Museum, Los Angeles, 1967.
____*Estevanico the Black*, Los Angeles, 1968-A.
____*Zebulon Pike*, New York, 1968-B.
____*The Navajo*, New York, 1970.
____*An American Indian Almanac*, New York, 1971.

THOMAS, ALFRED BARNABY, *Forgotten Frontiers*, Norman, 1932.
——*After Coronado*, Norman, 1935.
——*Teodoro de Croix and the Northern Frontier of New Spain*, Norman, 1941.
THRAPP, DAN L., *The Conquest of Apacheria*, Norman, 1967.
TWITCHELL, RALPH E., *Leading Facts of New Mexico History*, Cedar Rapids, Iowa, 1911.
——*The Spanish Archives of New Mexico*, Cedar Rapids, Iowa, 1914.
VILLAGRA, GASPAR PEREZ DE, *History of New Mexico* (Gilberto Espinosa, translator), Los
  Angeles, 1933.
WAGNER, HENRY R., "Fr. Marcos de Niza," *New Mexico Historical Review*, Vol. IX, April,
  1934.
——"A Fray Marcos de Niza Note," *New Mexico Historical Review*, Vol. IX, July, 1934.
WALLACE ERNEST, and E. ADAMSON HOEBEL, *The Comanches*, Norman, 1952.
WATERS, FRANK, *The Colorado*, New York, 1946.
WATTS, JOHN S., *Indian Depredations in New Mexico*, Washington, 1858.
WEBB, WALTER PRESCOTT, *The Great Plains*, New York, 1931.
WEDEL, WALDO R., *Prehistoric Man on the Great Plains*, Norman, 1961.
WELLMAN, PAUL, *The Indian Wars of the West*, New York, 1947.
WINSHIP, GEORGE PARKER (Translator), *The Narrative of the Expedition of Coronado by
  Castañeda*, Bureau of American Ethnology, Washington, 1896.
WISSLER, CLARK, *The American Indian*, New York, 1922.
WORCESTER, DONALD E., *Instructions for Governing the Interior Provinces of New Spain, 1786,
  by Bernardo de Gálvez*, Berkeley, 1951.
WORMINGTON, H. M., *Ancient Man in North America*, Denver, 1957.
YOUNG, ROBERT W., *The Navajo Yearbook*, Window Rock, Arizona, 1961.
——*The Role of the Navajo in the Southwestern Drama*, Gallup, New Mexico, 1968.

INDEX

Forsyth, G. A., 353, 354, 355
Fort Apache, 254, 268, 288, 297, 311,
    330, 375, 382
Fort Apache Reservation, 268, 269,
    274, 286, 295n, 297, 313–14,
    315–16, 329, 336, 344–45, 347–
    49, 350, 373, 384, 385
Fort Barrett, 254
Fort Bayard, 254
Fort Bliss, 182, 184, 224, 254
Fort Bowie, 232, 254, 265, 376, 378,
    379, 380, 381, 385
Fort Breckenridge, 221, 254
    see also Camp Grant (No. 1)
Fort Buchanan, 219, 220, 221, 222,
    254
Fort Concho, 254
Fort Conrad, 254
Fort Craig, 226, 227, 254, 341
Fort Crittenden, 254
Fort Cummings, 254
Fort Davis, 225, 254
Fort Defiance, 224
Fort Duncan, 254
Fort Fauntleroy, 224
Fort Fillmore, 221, 225, 254
Fort Goodwin, 254, 258, 274, 288
Fort Hancock, 254
Fort Huachuca, 254, 329, 374
Fort Inge, 254
Fort Lancaster, 255
Fort Lowell, 254, 276, 350
Fort Lyons, 224
Fort McDowell, 255, 260, 294, 302
Fort McIntosh, 255
Fort McLane, 255
Fort McRae, 255
Fort Marion, 380, 385
Fort Quitman, 255
Fort Reno, 261
Fort Seldon, 255
Fort Stanton, 184, 208, 225, 234,
    235, 236, 255, 337
Fort Stockton, 255
Fort Sumner, 236–37, 255, 258
Fort Taylor, 173
Fort Thomas, 255, 350, 353
Fort Thorn, 206, 212
Fort Tubac, 255
Fort Tularosa, 255
    see also Tularosa Reservation
Fort Union, 227, 228, 374

Fort Verde. See Camp Verde
Fort Webster, 196, 197, 200, 212,
    215
Fort West, 255
Fort Whipple, 242, 255, 259, 296
Fort Wingate, 330
Fossil Creek Tonto Band, 25
Fowler, O. S., 241n
France (and the New World)
    fur trappers, 133, 156
    and Indians, 116, 123–24, 129–33
        passim
    Louisiana Territory sold to U.S.,
        149
    missionaries, 24, 109
    in New Mexico, 156, 166
    and Spanish, 113, 116, 122, 123–
        24, 127, 129, 130, 131, 132
    trade, 116, 130, 132–33, 156
    voyageurs, 24, 36n, 109–10, 130
Franciscans, 49, 61, 93, 94, 98, 142
Francisco, 325, 327, 332, 337
Franco-Spanish War, 132
furs, 19, 83, 93
    French trappers, 133, 156
    U.S. trappers, 153–55, 158, 162,
        163, 175, 178, 215

Gadsden, James, 203
Gadsden Purchase, 203, 210, 212,
    213, 218, 223
Galerita, Francisco, 272
Gallatin, Albert, 215
Gallegos, Hernán, 45, 46, 47, 48,
    388n
Galve, Conde de, 111, 112
Galvéz, Bernardo de, 141, 142, 143
    Instructions for the Governing of the In-
        terior Provinces of New Spain,
        141–42
gambling, 136, 159, 242, 243
    by Indians, 61, 142, 169
Garber, Paul N., 202
García, Diego, 95–96
García, Lorenzo, 354, 355
Garland, John, 204, 205, 207, 209,
    211–12
Gatakas Band, 24
Gatewood, Charles B., 382–83, 384,
    385
George, 350
Geronimo, 164, 240, 320, 321, 324,

Ugarte y Loyola, Jacob, 141, 142, 143, 144
Ulibarri, Juan de, 122–23, 124
Unis, Juan, 155, 156
United States
  and Apache, xiii–xvii *passim*, 153–58, 161–62, 163, 165, 166, 168, 174–85 *passim*
  Civil War, 223–34 *passim*
  expansionist policies, 169
  fur trapping, 153–55, 158, 162, 163, 175, 178, 215
  and Indians, 149, 175–76, 181, 186, 202, 263–64; *see also* Board of Indian Comissioners; Department of Interior; Indian Bureau
  Indians as mercenaries and scouts, 249, 250, 282–83, 292, 299, 300, 301, 303, 310, 311, 323, 339, 345, 350, 352, 354, 357, 360–65 *passim*, 370, 376, 377, 380–81, 382, 383, 385
  and Mexico, 169, 173, 176, 177, 213, 342, 344–45, 355–56, 363, 364, 377, 381, 382
  Treaty of Guadalupe Hidalgo and problems of enforcement, 180, 181, 186–87, 189, 192, 198, 201, 202, 203
  war, 173–81 *passim*
  mining and prospecting, 158, 163, 182, 195, 196–97, 215, 222–23, 237–38; *see also* minerals and mining
  and Navajo, 174, 177, 194–95, 200, 201, 208, 210, 223–24, 232, 234, 243, 258
  trade, 149, 168, 175, 178, 189, 190
  see also Arizona (U.S. rule); California; New Mexico (U.S. rule); Texas
Universal Geography, 157
Usher, John P., 237
Utah, 169
Ute, 121, 142, 143, 153
  and Jicarilla, 124, 138, 183, 205
  and Spanish, 142, 143
  and U.S., 183, 201, 204, 205, 207, 224
utensils. *See* household utensils

Valero, 131
Valle, A. I., 342
Valverde, Antonio, 126–32 *passim*
Vanderslice, J. H., 260
Vandever, William, 330
Vaquero, 24, 63, 64, 66, 76, 77, 79, 95
  see also Eastern Apache; Plains Apache
Vargas Zapata Luján Ponce de León, Diego de, 109–16 *passim*, 125
Velasco, Don Luis de, 55, 56
venereal disease, 60, 159, 179
Victorio, 164, 249, 320, 324, 327, 328, 330–31, 333–43 *passim*
Vigil, Juan B., 174
Villanueva, Fernando de, 99, 100
Villasur, Pedro de, 131–32, 133

Walker, Joseph R., 237–42 *passim*
Wallace, 218–22 *passim*
Ward, Felix, 219
warfare (Indians as allies, mercenaries, and scouts)
  for French, 116, 123–24, 129–33 *passim*
  for Mexicans, 153, 173
  for Spanish, 98–99, 103, 116, 125–32 *passim*, 138, 143, 152
  for U.S., 249, 250, 282–83, 292, 299, 300, 301, 303, 310, 311, 323, 339, 345, 350, 352, 354, 357, 360–65 *passim*, 370, 376, 377, 380–81, 382, 383, 385
warfare, intertribal, 60, 70, 82, 84, 101, 102, 107, 133
Warm Springs Band, 25, 343
  see also Gila Apache
Warm Springs Reservation, 317, 322–28 *passim*, 331, 333, 334–35
Washington, 340, 342
weapons arrows and arrowheads, 20, 53, 66, 77, 82, 153, 157
  artillery (used by U.S.), 231
  bows, 20, 62, 66, 77, 82, 153
  flint, 66, 82
  guns (used by Indians), 80–81, 82, 83, 97, 124, 141–42, 153, 175, 231, 296, 329, 361
  guns (used by Spanish), 38, 40, 46
  hatchet, 82
  lance, 18, 82, 157